The Invariance Principle

The Invariance Principle

David Lopez-Paz

The MIT Press
Cambridge, Massachusetts
London, England

The MIT Press
Massachusetts Institute of Technology
77 Massachusetts Avenue
Cambridge, MA 02139
mitpress.mit.edu

The MIT Press would like to thank the anonymous peer reviewers who provided comments on drafts of this book. The generous work of academic experts is essential for establishing the authority and quality of our publications. We acknowledge with gratitude the contributions of these otherwise uncredited readers.

This book was set in Latin Modern Roman by David Lopez-Paz. Printed and bound in the United States of America.

Library of Congress Cataloging-in-Publication Data is available.

ISBN: 978-0-262-05334-1

EU Authorised Representative: Easy Access System Europe, Mustamäe tee 50, 10621 Tallinn, Estonia | Email: gpsr.requests@easproject.com.

To Rocío.

Contents

III   Invariance Setups   **125**

Contents

Preface

The year is 2026, and suddenly we find ourselves surrounded by AI systems once limited to the realm of science fiction. It is now commonplace to chat with machines to enlist their help in drafting essays, summarizing content, forming arguments, and accessing the entirety of human knowledge. However, these systems crumble by leaps and bounds when the distributions of their training and testing examples differ in spurious correlations. As a result, even state-of-the-art large language models struggle with basic string manipulations and arithmetic operations, hallucinate nonfactual information, ignore what they do not know, and fail to extend our knowledge beyond basic pattern matching. This is a far cry from humanlike AI, which demands not only humanlike performance but, more importantly, humanlike strategies.

Seeking a path to progress, this book introduces the Invariance Principle, a new epistemological tool beyond training error minimization, designed to unearth correlations that are invariant across diverse collections of empirical data. This principle, encapsulated in the axiom "Frame your question so its answer matches across circumstances," will not only find its practical incarnation in the family of invariant risk minimization algorithms, but also illuminate our understanding of various philosophical theories of causation, permeating topics such as environment discovery, large-language models, self-supervised learning, data augmentation, uncertainty estimation, and fairness. In the concluding chapter, I wrap up with some personal reflections on how the Invariance Principle has influenced my understanding of my subjective experience and shaped my interpretation of wisdom traditions, both Eastern and Western. It is my hope that *The Invariance Principle* will serve as a first baby step toward AI systems better aligned with human incentives, and inspire its readers to recognize the profound role of statistical invariance in intelligence.

Before we proceed, two disclaimers are in order. Firstly, this book adopts an admittedly unconventional style, blending technical rigor with philosophical exploration. By taking this unorthodox approach, I aim to engage both the mind and spirit, reaching a broader audience that includes computer scientists and computational philosophers alike. Secondly, the tools of invariance presented here are in their infancy and have yet to supplant empirical risk minimization. This renders research in statistical invariance a timely and exciting endeavor, with many opportunities for conversation and collaboration. As the field rapidly evolves, possibly thanks to your individual efforts, an open-source and potentially more up-to-date version of this book will remain available at:

`https://github.com/lopezpaz/TheInvariancePrinciple`

I am deeply thankful to many whose support was essential to completing this work. First and foremost, I owe my heartfelt gratitude to my employer, Meta, for granting me the time and the intellectual environment necessary for this project. I am particularly indebted to Armand Joulin, Antoine Bordes, and Naila Murray—my managers throughout the three-year span it took to write this book. The views expressed here are personal, and not necessarily the same as those of Meta or its affiliates.

Many colleagues at Meta's Fundamental AI Research lab (FAIR) reviewed parts of this manuscript, provided me with invaluable feedback, and helped me correct countless embarrassing mistakes. For their contributions, I bow my head to Kartik Ahuja, Sam Bell, Mark Ibrahim, Julia Kempe, Polina Kirichenko, Mohammad Pezeshki, Natasha Tagasovska, and Mark Tygert. I must also extend my appreciation to my wonderful scientific co-authors, whose research contributions underpin much of this work. In particular, this book would not have been possible without the insights of Martín Arjovsky, Léon Bottou, and Ishaan Gulrajani, which led to our previous work on invariant risk minimization. Thanks are also due to the MIT Press staff, including Francis Bach (the series editor), Susan Hartman, Malerie Lovejoy, and Elizabeth Swayze. Additionally, I commend John Acker, Katherine Dhurandhar, and Roger Wood for their meticulous and graceful copyediting of this manuscript. I am profoundly grateful to my family and friends, who remain an invariant source of joy and support.

Lastly, the views expressed in this book are my own, and do not reflect the views of my employer Meta Platforms, Inc.

David Lopez-Paz
December 20, 2025
Madrid, Spain

Part I

Opening

Chapter 1

Introduction

1.1   Discovering the Laws of Nature

We are immersed in a universe replete with changing patterns. While stable at first glance, these patterns appear only to vanish as our experience unfolds. Yet hiding beneath this kaleidoscopic display are the truly unchanging components that structure the world: the invariant laws of nature. This book introduces the *Invariance Principle* as an epistemological tool to unearth these hidden mechanisms governing the observed swirls of empirical data:

"Frame your question so its answer matches across circumstances."

As I will argue throughout, this Invariance Principle is pivotal to understanding learning, causation, science, conscious experience—and to develop AI systems able to weather storms of change.

Current AI systems learn by minimizing their training error, yet the learning problems themselves are often underspecified. This means there are numerous ways to attain zero training error (humanlike performance), but only a few solutions result in machines that understand the task at hand (humanlike strategy). Unfortunately, AI systems focused on minimizing training error frequently fall prey to a faulty simplify-and-memorize bias. In this scenario, the machine quickly learns a simplistic pattern that addresses the majority of training examples, while merely memorizing the minority of examples that contradict this pattern. These simplistic patterns tend to be spurious or lack invariance; they appear valid within the training dataset but fail to hold up under novel test *environments*. As a result, the out-of-distribution generalization capabilities of these AI systems crumble by leaps and bounds. Because many problems relating to spurious correlations persist even with infinite data, we must reconsider if the scaling hypothesis—training larger systems on larger data—will suffice to obtain robust, humanlike AI systems.

Seeking a path to progress, the present book advocates for a new generation of algorithms capable of learning patterns that remain *invariant* across diverse data environments. Central to this approach is the Invariance Principle, which deepens our understanding of causation and can be implemented through the family of invariant risk minimization algorithms. This principle bears significant relevance to fields such as environment discovery, model selection, large language models (LLMs), self-supervised learning, data augmentation, uncertainty estimation, and AI alignment. If we define intelligence as "an agent's ability to achieve goals in a wide range of environments,"[1] then humanlike performance observed across increasingly diverse data environments should emerge from humanlike strategy—the unobserved invariant mechanism of interest. With these ideas in mind, and as you read the following pages, I invite you to ponder: What does it mean for an AI system to truly understand the learning task at hand?

1.1.1 A Horse Named Clever Hans

In the opening years of the twentieth century, retired mathematics teacher Wilhelm von Osten claimed that his horse, Clever Hans, was able to perform an impressive array of mental operations, such as arithmetic, spelling, and ranking of musical tones. Figure 1.1a depicts both horse and master. As enthusiastically reported by *The New York Times* in September of 1904,[2] von Osten and Clever Hans toured Germany in a show that "stirred up the scientific, military, and sporting world of the Fatherland."[2] During the shows, von Osten would ask questions such as "What is five plus three?" to which Clever Hans would reply by stamping down his foot exactly eight times. The German authorities, led by psychologist Carl Stumpf, could not make sense of the animal wonder:

> Except a few skeptics, the majority of biologists, psychologists, and medical doctors, experts of all kind, and laymen were rather convinced by this example that animals are able to think in a human way and to express human ideas in nonverbal human language. In 1904, the German board of education even set up a commission to determine if the claims made about Hans were genuine. After an extended period—a year and a half of study—they concluded that there was no hoax involved.[3]

Eminent zoologist Karl Möbius, then the director of Berlin's Natural History Museum, added to the confusion by claiming that Clever Hans "possesses

(a) Clever Hans, 1904.

(b) Llama 3, imagined by Meta AI, 2024.

Figure 1.1: This time is different, isn't it?

the ability to see sharply, to distinguish between mental impressions from each other, to retain them in his memory, and to utter them by his hoof language."[2]

The investigation was later transferred to Oskar Pfungst, a volunteer assistant in Carl Stumpf's laboratory. Pfungst carried out experiments to examine Clever Hans's performance in various *environments*, noting that "the observations on the horse under ordinary conditions would have been quite insufficient for arriving at a decision as to the tenability of the several possible explanations." To Pfungst's surprise, Clever Hans could correctly answer questions even without von Osten, interacting with questioners who had never met the horse. However, further tests revealed that Clever Hans failed to answer correctly when the questioner was out of sight, or when questioners did not know the answer to the question themselves.[4] These failures led Pfungst to solve the conundrum: As the horse's taps approached the right answer, questioners would involuntarily tense their facial muscles, then suddenly relax them on the final, correct tap.

In an impressive work of precision, the horse had learned to interpret these minute muscular relaxations as cues to stop tapping his hoof. Clever Hans had found a shortcut[5] to answer questions in the environments that he had been trained on, but his simplistic strategy did not transfer to novel environments without facial cues. In other words, the horse was right for the wrong reason: He minimized training error by absorbing a spurious correlation while learning no mathematics. His humanlike performance did not arise from a humanlike strategy. Just like Clever Hans, today's AI systems might appear to function well, but their simplify-and-memorize strategy quickly breaks down when tested under different environments.

Alas, Clever Hans was drafted at the beginning of World War I in 1914, and he died shortly afterward.

1.1.2   Two Models of the Solar System

In Ancient Greece, philosophers such as Plato and Aristotle believed that the Earth was a stationary sphere at the center of the universe. In this geocentric model, standardized by Claudius Ptolemy (100–170 CE), the apparent motion of most celestial bodies in the night sky was accounted for, except for the five planets in the solar system known at the time. To explain the apparent retrograde motion of these five planets, Ptolemy argued that each planet orbited around a small circle of its own—an epicycle—which in turn orbited around a larger circle around the Earth—the deferent. The left side of figure 1.2 shows the resulting orbit for Mars when combining its epicycle and deferent. Ptolemy's model proposed a *simple circular orbit for the majority* of celestial bodies, while *memorizing a minority of noncircular orbits* to explain the movement of five planets. With such an explanation, Ptolemy secured us a very special place in the universe: right at its center.

It took more than one thousand years to update the Ptolemaic geocentric model. By a radical reframing, Nicolaus Copernicus (1473–1543) realized that all orbits, including those of the planets, would reflect an approximately circular shape if one considered the Sun at the center of the universe. The resulting Copernican model is shown on the right side of figure 1.2. While both solar system models achieved zero training error, only Copernicus's model, by framing the problem around the Sun, allowed describing the orbits of all celestial bodies by means of the same (invariant) mechanism. Understandably, his model generated a fair amount of persecution, as it ensued the painful loss of our place at the center of the universe. (But, have we really accepted that loss? We continue to say *sunrise* and *sunset* to this day.)

1.1.3   Lights and Shadows in AI Models

Centuries after Ptolemy, Copernicus, and Clever Hans, we now coexist with AI systems able to perform a wide variety of tasks at beyond human-level performance.[7] These include classifying and generating images,[8–10] recognizing speech,[11] translating among hundreds of languages,[12,13] playing games such as Go, poker, StarCraft, and Diplomacy,[14–17] driving vehicles,[18,19] providing medical diagnoses,[20–22] winning art competitions,[23] and aiding the exploration of difficult scientific problems, such as protein structure

Ptolemaic system (100AD)   Copernican system (1543AD)

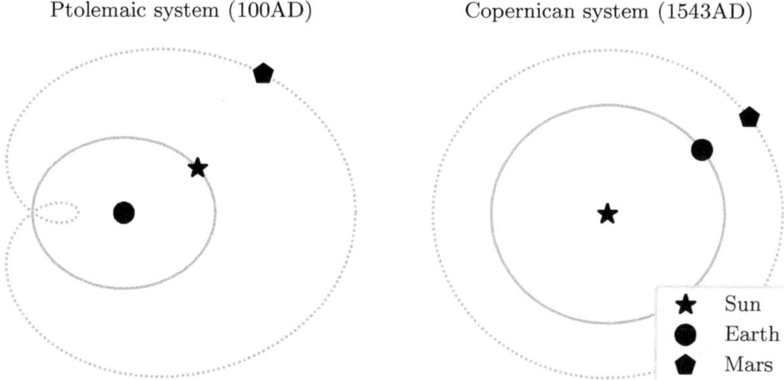

Figure 1.2: Two models of the solar system, a case study courtesy of Mohammad Pezeshki.[6] The geocentric model of Claudius Ptolemy (100–170 CE) placed the Earth at the center of the solar system. The geocentric model explains the apparent circular movement of most celestial bodies around the Earth. However, all other planets in the solar system exhibited apparent retrograde motions and changes in brightness. To explain this phenomenon, Nicolaus Copernicus (1473–1543) argued that planets orbit in a small circle called an epicycle, which in turn orbits around a larger circle called a deferent. This gives raise to non-elliptical orbits, like the one of Mars illustrated on the left side of the figure. Over one millennium later, the heliocentric model by Nicolaus Copernicus (1473–1543) placed the Sun at the center of the solar system. While this required a large change in perspective, the movements of all celestial bodies could now be approximately explained in terms of simple circular orbits.

prediction and climate change.[24,25] As I write, conversational agents like GPT-4,[26] which would trick Alan Turing himself, are stirring a global debate about the dawn of artificial general intelligence (AGI). These achievements, confined to science fiction just a few years ago, are revolutionizing how we live and understand our role in the world.

In spite of these achievements, motivated by the Story of Clever Hans, we might now ask: Is this time different, or just a sophisticated repeat of Clever Hans (see figure 1.1b)? A deeper scrutiny of AI systems reveals numerous failures. For instance, computer vision systems drastically alter their predictions when faced with invisible perturbations,[27] changes in object pose,[28] background,[29] texture,[5] or even modifications of a single pixel.[30] Systems built to answer questions about images ignore all visual content when the question alone provides clues for guessing the answer.[31] Natural language systems similarly rely on superficial patterns, such as the presence of the word *not*, to determine whether complex statements support or contradict each other.[32] Reinforcement learning systems cheat their way to winning at computer games—for example, by hitting *pause* to never lose at Tetris.[33] During the recent pandemic, "deep learning systems to detect COVID-19 from chest radiographs relied on confounding factors rather than medical pathology, creating an alarming situation in which the systems appeared accurate but failed when tested in new hospitals."[34] Their specific failures were disturbing:

> Many unwittingly used a data set that contained chest scans of children who did not have COVID as their examples of what non-COVID cases looked like. As a result, the AIs learned to identify kids, not COVID. ... Because patients scanned while lying down were more likely to be seriously ill, the AI wrongly learned to predict serious COVID risk from a person's position. ... In yet other cases, some AIs were found to be picking up on the text font that certain hospitals used to label the scans. As a result, fonts from hospitals with more serious caseloads became predictors of COVID risk.[35]

Out of sixty-two machine learning systems proposed for detecting COVID, Michael Roberts and colleagues concluded that none were "of potential clinical use due to methodological flaws and/or underlying biases."[36] Meanwhile, state-of-the-art large language models, trained on a large fraction of text produced by humanity, sometimes offer bizarre advice such as eating rocks or adding glue as a pizza topping.[37] (It was later revealed that the rock-eating advice first appeared in the satirical newspaper *The Onion* and likely made its way to the LLM pretraining corpus.) For many more interesting cases of AI failure, please see *AI Snake Oil* by Arvind Narayanan and Sayash Kapoor.[38]

(a) AI imagining "some salmon swimming down the river" (https://x.com/haylafy/status/1584338104994799616).

(b) A cow on the beach, a rare sight captured by Vinsen Cekrani (https://unsplash.com/photos/la6MhvutekA).

Figure 1.3: Chance-like patterns abound in the world.

As a general rule of thumb, AI systems exhibit worse performance on certain subgroups of the data that differ from the majority, raising concerns about whether they can be responsibly deployed in diverse contexts. For instance, commercial face recognition systems have higher error rates on minority groups,[39] algorithms to predict recidivism flag non reoffending Black people two times more likely,[40] image search engines show mostly white males when users search for *CEO*,[41] and sport classification systems assign *ping-pong* to all Asian athletes— and *basketball* to all Black athletes— regardless of the physical activity shown in the image.[42] Self-driving systems have played a role in fatal accidents,[43] have been shown to repeatedly hit strollers and child mannequins,[44] and have confused the Moon with a yellow traffic light on the freeway.[45] When asked to generate an image of "salmon swimming down the river," a generative AI system produced figure 1.3a, depicting a host of cooked salmon fillets floating in the water.[46] Some of these problems are not new, at least. Many decades ago, the legend goes, a tank classification system focused solely on weather conditions because all photos of enemy tanks were taken on cloudy days.[47] These failures, I would like to argue in this book, arise from AI systems absorbing spurious correlations that allow zero training error, but do not generalize to novel environments.[48] The next section offers a sketch on the mechanics of how these failures emerge.

1.1.4 The Cow-on-the-Beach Problem

Consider the idealized *cow-on-the-beach* problem,[29,49] in which the goal is to distinguish images of cows from those of camels. In this problem, the majority of training data portrays cows on green grasslands or camels on beige beaches, while a minority of examples depict cows on beige beaches or camels on green grasslands. After training a machine to zero training error on this data, we proceed to evaluate its performance on a fresh collection of testing examples. While the machine correctly classifies all cows on grasslands and all camels on beaches, the machine bewilderingly errs on all cows in beaches (including the one in figure 1.3b) and all camels in grasslands. (Because cows have been known to attack beach-goers, failing to detect cows on the beach may lead to dangerous circumstances.[50]) Upon closer inspection, we realize that the machine took a shortcut[5] on its path to zero training error. Namely, the machine implemented a prediction rule that (1) classifies mostly green training images as cows, (2) classifies mostly beige training images as camels, and (3) memorizes the label of the minority of training examples contradicting these simplistic patterns.

I call this learning strategy *simplify-and-memorize*. Initially, the classifier latches onto a spurious correlation that addresses the majority of the training examples. Subsequently, the classifier resorts to memorization to achieve zero training error on the minority of examples contradicting the simplistic explanation. This resulting predictor, "If example is prototypical **then** use spurious correlation **else** return memorized label," is a machine that learned nothing whatsoever about mammals.

Classifiers are likely to absorb spurious correlations when they are (1) the only ones admitting the correct classification of all the training examples, or (2) easier to capture than the relevant invariant pattern. In the latter scenario, the learning machine quickly locks onto the spurious correlation, starving the signals necessary to discover the invariant patterns that would lead to an actual understanding of the task at hand. The different choices that we make to learn from data—the architecture of the classifier, the training data that we collect, the error function that we minimize across such examples, and the optimizer we employ to find our solution—all influence the machine's appetite for spurious correlations. Therefore, each of these factors deserves careful scrutiny when learning with out-of-distribution generalization in mind.

Therefore, the main challenge is to guide the learning process toward classification systems following a humanlike strategy, while avoiding machines that achieve zero training error through simplification and memorization. In particular, for the cow-on-the-beach problem, we must teach machines to understand the concept of a cow; but what makes a cow a cow? At the statistical level, we humans must be able to extract certain features that describe cows reliably not only *on average*, but *invariably across a wide array of environments*. Features relating to horns and muzzles, for example, should be stable across environmental changes such as landscape color, time of the day, and photography equipment. These features are valuable because they induce cow-classifiers that are both accurate and invariant across environmental conditions. The Invariance Principle, as proposed in this book, is an alternative to training error minimization that can help us discover such invariant predictors from heterogeneous collections of data.

1.2   Book Outline

The thesis of this book can be simply stated. Large learning machines, when trained to minimize average training error, adopt a *simplify-and-memorize* strategy that absorbs spurious correlations and produces predictors that fail to generalize out-of-distribution. In contrast, humans are able to learn rules that, despite being more imprecise, afford generalization over a wider array of circumstances. While we often describe such rules using causal language, I posit that this is, in reality, just a storytelling tool to identify patterns stable across interventions. This book seeks to reverse the epistemological program and take such stability, or invariance, directly as the chief learning principle. Therefore, we shall not search for causation to discover invariance, but search for invariance to find generalization and, in certain cases, causation. In particular, the Invariance Principle teaches us to *frame the question so its answer matches across circumstances*. While simple learning scenarios provide us with such circumstances or *environments* explicitly, I will also describe algorithms to discover them from large pools of training data. I shall also pay special attention to sequential data, such as that treated by large language models (LLMs), where our environment is described in terms of rich prompts and contexts. In addition, the book explores a host of related techniques useful for pursuing invariance, such as learning from combinations of examples to alleviate reliance on spurious correlations, learning rich feature spaces to surface rare-yet-invariant patterns, and estimating predictive uncertainty to demarcate the environments under which an invariant model is expected to generalize. Using all of these materials as background, I will later discuss the role of invariance in building fair and aligned AI systems. The book concludes by offering some nonscientific reflections on the use of the Invariance Principle to understand the structure of our subjective experience, including links to Eastern philosophical traditions.

I must admit that this book has an unusual style. Passages with philo-sophical character abound, and I have taken the liberty of alternating formal

symbol	description
X	input random variable, taking values in $\mathcal{X}$
Y	target random variable, taking values in $\mathcal{Y}$
E	environment random variable, taking values in $\mathcal{E}$
ϕ	featurizer or representation, mapping from $\mathcal{X}$ to $\mathcal{H}$
w	classifier or regressor, mapping from $\mathcal{H}$ to $\mathcal{Y}$
$f = w \circ \phi$	predictor, the composition of the featurizer and classifier
$\Phi = \phi(X)$	representation random variable, taking values in $\mathcal{H}$
$(x_i, y_i) \sim P$	example (input-target pair), drawn from P
$\mathcal{E}_{\text{tr}}$	set of training environments
$\mathcal{E}$	set of all relevant environments
X^e	input random variable at environment $E = e$
Y^e	target random variable at environment $E = e$
$\Phi^e = \phi(X^e)$	input representation at environment $E = e$
$(x_i^e, y_i^e) \sim P^e$	example at environment $E = e$, drawn from P^e
citation[49]	*Invariant Risk Minimization*

Table 1.1: Main notations.

material with promising speculation. This is an effort not only to widen the book's audience—which I hope includes both machine learning researchers and computational philosophers—but also to embed AI system improvement within the larger program of understanding our own minds and their place in the universe. We are building an amazing and powerful technology, so I believe that thinkers from all fields and backgrounds should collaborate in crafting AI systems that benefit us all. The rest of this introduction briefly summarizes each subsequent chapter, as well as giving table 1.1 to summarize the main notation and citation styles used in this book.

Chapter 2: Minimizing Training Error

We begin with the standing approach to building AI systems, framed by the philosophical problem of induction. Currently, our machines learn about the world by minimizing their prediction error over a set of training examples. This process, known as empirical risk minimization (ERM), is optimal when both the training and testing examples are identically and independently distributed (iid) according to the same probability distribution. However, large learning machines often achieve zero training error by the simplify-and-memorize strategy described in this introduction. Consequently, large machines trained via ERM often fail to generalize to new test environments.

Chapter 3: Theories of Causation

Humans commonly use causal language to discern between spurious and invariant patterns for prediction. This chapter provides the necessary philosophical background to understand the major theories of causation, often considered as when building robust learning systems. Specifically, I review some classic accounts of causation, developments by Hume and Kant, and modern theories such as the interventionist and counterfactual accounts. This background helps show the close relationship between statistical invariance and the interventionist account, whereby a causal relations are those that remain stable throughout manipulations on the system under study. The chapter concludes by discussing the relationship between causation and time, as well as the role of invariance as a cognitive bias to learn about causal structures in the natural world.

Chapter 4: Practice of Causation

We move on to practical implementations of some of the philosophical accounts of causation described in the previous chapter. Topics include variable selection and coarsening, structural equation models, observational distributions, interventional distributions, counterfactual distributions, causal discovery, potential outcomes, and instrumental variables. Throuhgout this chapter, we will anticipate various incarnations of the Invariance Principle in causal algorithms, in terms of technical conditions such as conditional exchangeability and ignorability. However, estimating causal structures from empirical data is beset by problems. Because of this reason, this chapter concludes with a proposal to reverse our epistemological program—rather than searching for causation to find invariance, the sequel proposes to use statistical invariance as the chief learning signal to build robust AI systems.

Chapter 5: The Invariance Principle

This central chapter introduces the Invariance Principle:

frame your question such that the answer matches across circumstances.

In supervised learning, the Invariance Principle translates into invariant risk minimization,[49] which advocates *learning a feature representation ϕ such that the optimal classifier w matches across environments $\mathcal{E}$*, where each environment $e \in \mathcal{E}$ provides us with input-target examples (x_i^e, y_i^e). This statement, sometimes summarized as the conditional independence

$Y \perp E \mid \phi(X)$, can be approximated by the practical IRMv1 learning objective:

$$\min_{\phi:\mathcal{X}\to\mathcal{Y}} \sum_{e\in\mathcal{E}_{\mathrm{tr}}} (1-\lambda)\cdot R_{P^e}(\phi) + \lambda \cdot \left\| \nabla_{w|w=1.0}\left[R_{P^e}(w\cdot\phi)\right] \right\|^2 .$$

The chapter closes by reflecting on the relationship between the Invariance Principle and other fields of knowledge, such as mathematics, physics, cognitive science, and metaphysics.

Chapter 6: Domain Generalization Algorithms

This chapter discusses the problem of domain generalization, which is a classic take on the problem of learning across multiple environments. It includes a presentation of invariant causal prediction (ICP), the predecessor and main inspiration behind IRM. The chapter also reviews distributionally robust optimization, data balancing, and feature matching techniques. It closes with some reflections about the inherent difficulties of model selection in domain generalization, setting the stage for the next chapter.

Chapter 7: Discovering Environments

In many practical applications, data lacks environment annotations. In these cases, the *discovery* of environments hidden in large pools of training examples is a necessary step before applying the machinery described in the previous chapter to learn invariant predictors. This chapter describes the cross-risk minimization (XRM) environment discovery method, its use as a model selection tool in the multiple environment setting, and its relation to the issue of memorization in the presence of spurious correlations.

Chapter 8: Invariance in LLMs

This chapter describes various concepts in large language models under the lens of invariance. These include attention mechanisms, in-context learning, test-time adaptation, continual learning, induction heads as a new form of generalization, environment amortization, chain of thought, and multi-token prediction. The sequential nature of LLM environments allows a finer discussion on the differences between likelihood and verisimilitude. We conclude by discussing some recent philosophical works that compare LLMs to *fiction machines*.

Chapter 9: Learning Diverse Features

This chapter explores algorithms that extract diverse explanations from data as a helpful preprocessing step to avoid simplify-and-memorize biases and promote the learning of invariant predictors. These methods include regularizing the confidence of the network, dropping out random subsets of activations, setting up self-supervised learning objectives, and building model ensembles.

Chapter 10: Learning from Combinations of Examples

This chapter discusses methods to reduce underspecification in learning problems by learning on mixtures of training examples, as pioneered by the *mixup* data augmentation protocol. Machines learning with these methods exhibit improved generalization capabilities, predictive uncertainty, calibration, and resistance to adversarial examples. Although the mixup approach originally suggested learning on *random* pairs of examples, this chapter also discusses methods to combine examples in ways that cancel out spurious correlations. Finally, this chapter reviews extensions of the mixup framework to treat unlabeled data, test-time adaptation, and uncertainty estimation.

Chapter 11: Uncertainty Estimation

The chief concern of this chapter is uncertainty estimation, or how to endow learning machines with a degree of awareness about their operational boundaries. It reviews both aleatoric and epistemic uncertainty estimates, as well as methodologies to combine them into a unified score. The chapter closes with some thoughts on how to estimate uncertainty in LLMs, as well as its relationship to invariance.

Chapter 12: Fairness and Alignment

This chapter investigates the role of the Invariance Principle in learning machines that generalize like humans and *for humans*. More specifically, I argue that certain desirable aspects of AI systems, such as fairness and alignment, are features of the invariance of the mechanisms implemented by our predictor. Because mechanistic invariance is not directly observable, the chapter proposes to measure fairness and alignment as out-of-distribution performance across societally relevant *stress environments*. In conclusion, while scaling ERM may be all you *may* need to learn machines that show humanlike *performance*, this chapter argues that a focus on invariance is necessary to learn systems that follow a humanlike *strategy*.

Chapter 13: Esoterica

The present book concludes with a philosophical investigation on how the Invariance Principle can help us understand the structure of subjective experience. This chapter, nonscientific in nature, attempts to bridge AI with fields such as psychology and wisdom traditions. If we want to build AI systems that inherit our values and increase our happiness, I argue, we must deepen our understanding of the phenomenology of our own conscious experience and its potential implementation in learning machines.

Part II

Background

Chapter 2

Minimizing Training Error

2.1 Introduction

Our starting point is the quintessential principle for learning machines from data: Minimize their training error. During the past two and a half centuries, the principle of minimizing training error has gifted us the first regressions of Euler and Mayer (1750s), the least-squares method of Gauss and Legendre (1800s),[51] the perceptron neural networks of Minsky and Rosenblatt (1950s),[52] and the deep learning revolution[53,54] that pervades our lives in the form of computer vision systems[9] and large language models.[55] Yet, as we shall learn in this chapter, carelessly minimizing training error can mislead machines into insidious pitfalls.

To learn about these issues, the present chapter begins by framing the principle of minimizing training error within the broader philosophical problem of induction. Namely, under what circumstances can we generalize past observations to predict the future? In the company of one of my personal heroes, eighteenth-century philosopher David Hume, I shall argue that all prediction must assume (without a possible rational justification) certain invariant structures piecing together past and future observations. In machine learning, this inductive assumption commonly supposes that all of our data are identically and independently distributed. This *iid* assumption states that all of the training and testing examples are picked at random from an invariant, unknown, and possibly infinite population, described mathematically in terms of a probability distribution.

In cases where our data is iid, the principle of minimizing training error, known as empirical risk minimization, is an optimal recipe to learn machines from data. This result is due to the 1968 learning theory of Vapnik and Chervonenkis, known as VC-theory, which instructs us to minimize training error using the *simplest* possible family of learning machines. VC-theory also turns out to be a mathematical formalization of the falsifiability criteria of Karl Popper, a contemporary of Vapnik and Chervonenkis, who sought to alleviate Hume's concerns about inductive reasoning. It would appear that we have come, rather beautifully, full circle with a recipe to address prediction tasks with artificial intelligence systems.

Unfortunately, modern practice stands in stark contrast with classical VC-theory. As recent experiments show, one should in fact pursue zero training error using the *largest* possible learning machine to achieve the best possible predictor. By making use of generalization *double-descent* theories, we shall see that this is only an apparent contradiction. In what seems to be a gift from over-parameterized nonconvex optimization that we neither understand nor deserve, it turns out that training *larger* machines allows us to find *simpler* zero training error predictors generalizing well on iid data.

While attaining zero training error with smooth predictors sounds desirable, it does not necessarily mean that the machine has understood the learning problem at hand. The difficulty, paraphrasing Bertrand Russell, lies in *underspecification*: "Given any finite set of observations, there are always an infinite number of formulae verified by all of them." How can we distinguish between zero training error solutions that address the problem we intended to solve and illusory Clever Hans tricks?

As I suggested in the introduction, large learning machines often minimize average error by following a strategy called *simplify-and-memorize*.[6] This recipe comprises two steps. First, the machine finds a simplistic (superficial, rudimentary, naïve) explanation that allows the correct classification of the *majority* of the training data. Second, the machine uses its remaining storage to memorize the *minority* of training examples that do not comply with the simplistic explanation. The *cow-on-the-beach* problem, which I briefly mentioned earlier, showcases this issue. We'll return to it later in this chapter, to illustrate how the simplify-and-memorize bias arises from multiple sources—including the irregularity of our training data, use of large learning machines, reliance on stochastic gradients for optimization, and regularization techniques that promote small weights or large margins.

The simplify-and-memorize bias generalizes poorly to regions underrepresented or outside the support of the training distribution. These are the regions yielding minority examples, unlikely to comply with the simplistic feature that the learning machine latched onto too early (and held onto too tightly) in its descent to zero training error. These simplify-and-memory machines are prone to particularly large errors when the minority becomes the majority in test environments. Such out-of-distribution failures motivate the core focus of this book: exploring alternatives to empirical risk minimization to learn predictors with stronger generalization abilities.

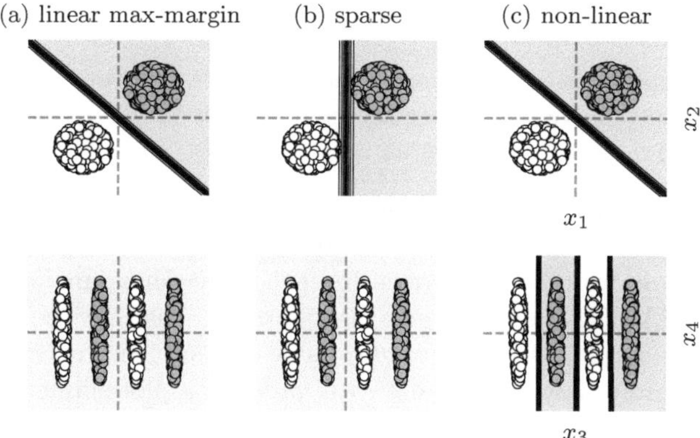

Figure 2.1: Three proposals to address a four-dimensional binary classification problem. The *linear max-margin* solution recruits (x_1, x_2) to promote the margin, measured as the distance between the decision boundary and the nearest training example. The *linear sparse* solution only recruits (x_1) to promote sparsity, the use of a minimal amount of features. The *nonlinear* solution recruits all four features, in order to implement a nonlinear decision boundary. These three zero training error solutions are equally preferable in light of the available training data, absent additional expert knowledge.

2.2 Prediction and the Problem of Induction

To understand how machines learn, we must start by stepping into their tennis shoes. Let's first consider the four-dimensional binary classification problem depicted in figure 2.1. The task at hand is to draw a decision boundary separating the white and gray training examples, by using the four features (x_1, x_2, x_3, x_4). While there is an infinite number of such boundaries, the figure offers three candidates that attain zero training error. Solution (a) is a linear classifier promoting maximum margin, defined as the distance between the decision boundary and the closest training example. Solution (b) is a linear classifier promoting sparsity, that is, using the minimum amount of features—here only x_1—to address the learning problem. Solution (c) is a nonlinear classifier having access to all four features to draw its decision boundary. All three are equally preferable in light of the available training data, absent additional expert knowledge. But which one should we pick to predict about new test examples?

Each of these three solutions can be obtained by minimizing training error within a family of classifiers. The validity of this approach, where we expect the classifier to generalize to new test data, rests upon the *inductive learning hypothesis*:

> Any hypothesis found to approximate the target function well over a
> sufficiently large set of training examples will also approximate the
> target function well over other unobserved examples.[56]

More formally, this condition assumes that all training and test examples
(x_i, y_i) are *identically and independently distributed.* Identically distributed
means that all examples are drawn from the same invariant probability distribution $P(X, Y)$. Independently distributed means that the examples are
drawn at random, where different draws do not influence each other. These
conditions imply that the test data will produce a plot similar to figure 2.1,
and that the three solutions will continue to generalize. But under what
conditions is it appropriate to assume this uniformity in data?

Scientists and philosophers have relied on the *uniformity of nature* since
biblical times ("He set the earth on its foundations, so that it should
never be moved," Psalm 104:5). For example, we expect physical laws to
remain invariant across space and time. Theoretical physicist and Nobel
Prize winner Eugene P. Wigner (1902–1995) argued that these principles of
invariance are a primary epistemological guide in discovering the laws of
physics:

> The statement that absolute time and position are never essential
> initial conditions is the first and perhaps the most important theorem
> of invariance in physics. If it were not for it, it might have been
> impossible for us to discover the laws of nature.[57]

However, patterns do sometimes change. Bertrand Russell vividly illustrates
this with the following vignette:

> The man who has fed the chicken every day throughout its life at last
> wrings its neck instead, showing that more refined views as to the
> uniformity of nature would have been useful to the chicken.[58]

While induction has led to numerous scientific discoveries across disciplines,
philosophers continue to debate its rational justification: When should we
trust rules inferred from particulars? Answering this question engages the
philosophical problem of induction, our next key topic.

2.2.1   The Problem of Induction

It should come as no surprise that the study of reasoning is as old as
philosophy. We must reach back to 350 BC to find the first formalizations
of reasoning, appearing in the syllogisms of Aristotle's *Prior Analytica*. A
syllogism is a form of *deductive* reasoning that translates true premises

into true conclusions, going from laws into particulars. For example, given the two premises "All men are mortal" and "Socrates is a man," we can safely deduce the conclusion that "Socrates is mortal." While deduction is logically valid—if the starting premises are true, then the conclusion is also true—the technique is non-ampliative because it does not extend our knowledge about the world. This makes deduction an insufficient tool for the purposes of prediction and scientific discovery, which focus on reasoning from particulars to laws.

Two millennia later, Francis Bacon (1561–1626) published *Novum Organum* to criticize Aristotle's deductive reasoning—back then the gold standard taught at the University of Cambridge—as a tool unfit to discover the laws of nature. Instead, Bacon put forward induction as the "true but unattempted way" to drive scientific discovery:

> There are and can exist but two ways of investigating and discovering truth. The one hurries on rapidly from the senses and particulars to the most general axioms, and from them, as principles and their supposed indisputable truth, derives and discovers the intermediate axioms. This is the way now in use. The other constructs its axioms from the senses and particulars, by ascending continually and gradually, till it finally arrives at the most general axioms, which is the true but unattempted way.[59]

Bacon's inductive method lists particulars where a phenomenon appears, particulars where a phenomenon does not appear, and particulars where the phenomenon appears in varying degrees. The invariance revealed by these lists allows scientists to hypothesize theories useful for prediction. For example, to inquire about the nature of heat, Bacon painstakingly described various hot bodies, cold bodies, and bodies of varying temperatures (bears and porridge were not involved). By examining his records, Bacon recognized a relationship between rapid particle motion and heat, useful to predict body heat based on the presence of rapid particle motion. Bacon's lifelong interest in heat proved fatal, as he contracted a fatal case of pneumonia while stuffing a chicken with snow during Europe's Little Ice Age, in an attempt to study the use of cold to preserve meat. However, his inductive method sparked a scientific revolution fueled by many of his contemporaries. One notable example is Robert Boyle (1627–1691), founder of the Royal Society. Armed with the inductive method, Boyle transformed chemistry from a semi-mystical field rooted in alchemy into a rigorous scientific discipline.

In contrast to Aristotle's deductive syllogisms, Bacon's inductive method is ampliative: By extrapolating past observations into generalizations, induction *extends* the content of the particular premises into a law-like conclusion. For example, the claim "All pieces of bread are nourishing, therefore this

	premise 1	premise 2	consequence	logically valid?
I	$p \supset q$	p	q	yes
II	$p \supset q$	$\neg p$	$\neg q$	no
III	$p \supset q$	q	p	no
IV	$p \supset q$	$\neg q$	$\neg p$	yes

Table 2.1: The four figures of syllogistic implication, where $p \supset q$ means "p implies q." (I) The constructive *modus ponens*, attributed to Aristotle, allows logically valid deductions from laws to particulars, such as going from "Raining implies the floor will be wet" and "It is raining" to "The floor will be wet." (IV) The destructive *modus tollens*, attributed to Karl Popper, allows for logically valid falsifications of laws from events, such as going from "Newton being right implies light will not bend around the Sun" and "Light bends around the Sun" to "Newton is wrong." (II) and (III) are logically invalid. Importantly, (III) is the main tool of modern science, the inductive method attempts to conclude laws from particulars. As we will see, David Hume heavily critiqued this approach.

piece of bread will be nourishing" uses deductive reasoning, going from a law into particulars. The conclusion is logically valid and true, but it does not extend our knowledge about the premises. On the other hand, "All pieces of bread I have eaten in the past have been nourishing, therefore all pieces of bread will be nourishing" is one example of inductive reasoning, from particulars into a law. Here, the conclusion extends the contents of the premises, but it is not logically valid—the inferred law could prove false if somebody poisons the next piece of bread. Deduction and induction are two of the four figures of syllogistic implication, summarized in table 2.1.

While inductive reasoning set in motion the Age of Enlightenment across seventeenth-century Europe, the harshest of criticisms came swiftly. Specifically, David Hume (1711–1776) formalized the *problem of induction* as a question of epistemological character: On what grounds are we to trust inductive arguments? Ultimately, Hume argues that there is *no logically valid route* to justify the assumption that patterns structuring past observations will obtain the same results in future cases. Hume developed his extensive attack on induction throughout his magnum opus *A Treatise of Human Nature*, written when the philosopher was twenty-three years old and largely ignored by the public at the time. For example, in the chapter "Of the Probability of Causes," we read:

> First we may observe, that the supposition, that the future resembles the past, is not founded on arguments of any kind, but is deriv'd entirely from habit, by which we are determined to expect for the

> future the same train of objects, to which we have been accustom'd.
> ... That there is nothing in any object, consider'd in itself, which
> can afford us a reason for drawing a conclusion beyond it; and, That
> even after the observation of the frequent or constant conjunction
> of objects, we have no reason to draw any inference concerning any
> object beyond those of which we have had experience.[60]

Similar objections arose in Ancient Greece, as it turns out. A millennium
before Hume, Pyrrhonist philosopher Sextus Empiricus noted this in his
second book, *Outlines of Pyrrhonism*:

> It is also easy, I consider, to set aside the method of induction. For,
> when they propose to establish the universal from the particulars
> by means of induction, they will effect this by a review either of all
> or of some of the particular instances. But if they review some, the
> induction will be insecure, since some of the particulars omitted in the
> induction may contravene the universal; while if they are to review all,
> they will be toiling at the impossible, since the particulars are infinite
> and indefinite. Thus on both grounds, as I think, the consequence is
> that induction is invalidated.

For example, consider that "no matter how many instances of white swans
we may have observed, this does not justify the conclusion that all swans
are white."[61] The existence of black swans is logically possible, even if all
swans observed so far are white—in fact, black specimens were discovered
in 1697 in Western Australia.

In his work *An Enquiry Concerning Human Understanding*, a revision
of *A Treatise on Human Nature*, Hume argues that inductive reasoning
requires assuming the uniformity of nature, a belief taken as true without
any possibility for rational or logical justification:

> For all inferences from experience suppose, as their foundation, that
> the future will resemble the past, and that similar powers will be
> conjoined with similar sensible qualities. If there be any suspicion,
> that the course of nature may change, and that the past may be no
> rule for the future, all experience becomes useless, and can give rise
> to no inference or conclusion.[62]

Even the claim that "induction has worked pretty well in the past, therefore
induction will work well in the future" is an inductive judgment itself,
rendering any efforts to justify induction into circular arguments. Hume's
critique also extends to probabilistic reasoning, where the iid assumption is
necessary to guarantee that the observed frequencies about an event converge
to their expected probabilities. In sum, Hume argues that any inductive
generalization of particulars into laws traps us in circular reasoning.

Hume's attack dealt a significant blow to the Enlightenment program, which aimed to replace religious dogmatism with scientific reasoning. The Scottish philosopher's insights, which likewise permeate the pages of this book, continue to deprive contemporary philosophers of sleep— and perhaps will continue to do so in the future.[63] For example, C. D. Broad (1887–1971) considered induction "the glory of science and the scandal of philosophy"[64] and Stanford's *Encyclopedia of Philosophy* does not shy away from acknowledging Hume's problem:

> Many have regarded it [Hume's problem of induction] as one of the most profound philosophical challenges imaginable since it seems to call into question the justification of one of the most fundamental ways in which we form knowledge. Bertrand Russell, for example, expressed the view that if Hume's problem cannot be solved, "there is no intellectual difference between sanity and insanity."[65]

All of this threatens a dire situation. While Aristotle's deductive reasoning is logically sound, it does not expand our understanding of the world. Bacon's method of induction, one with hopes to furnish science and prediction, was decisively slayed by David Hume as lacking justification. It took two centuries to glimpse a way out of this impasse.

Fearing the annexation of Austria by Nazi Germany, Karl Popper (1902–1994) wrote *The Logic of Scientific Discovery* in 1934 as an academic interview of sorts, in hopes of securing a job in some country safe for Jewish professors. Popper's first thoughts on the problem of induction echo the exposition so far:

> I had become interested in the problem of induction in 1923. ... Hume, I felt, was perfectly right in pointing out that induction cannot be logically justified. He held that there can be no valid logical arguments allowing us to establish "that those instances, of which we have had no experience, resemble those, of which we have had experience." Consequently "even after the observation of the frequent or constant conjunction of objects, we have no reason to draw any inference concerning any object beyond those of which we have had experience." ... In other words, an attempt to justify the practice of induction by an appeal to experience must lead to an infinite regress. As a result we can say that theories can never be inferred from observation statements, or rationally justified by them. I found Hume's refutation of inductive inference clear and conclusive.[66]

To address the problem of induction, Popper introduced the philosophical system of critical rationalism. He characterized scientific theories as propositions that, while impossible to verify, allow for numerous experiments to falsify them:

> I think that we shall have to get accustomed to the idea that we must not look upon science as a "body of knowledge," but rather as a system of hypotheses; that is to say, as a system of guesses or anticipations which in principle cannot be justified, but with which we work as long as they stand up to tests, and of which we are never justified in saying that we know that they are "true" or "more or less certain" or even "probable."[61]

Falsifiability here replaces induction as the new foundation of science; in Popper's words, "In so far as a scientific statement speaks about reality, it must be falsifiable: and in so far as it is not falsifiable, it does not speak about reality."[61] Accordingly, Popper would consider unfalsifiable questions, such as the existence of God, outside the realm of science:

> I shall certainly admit a system as empirical or scientific only if it is capable of being tested by experience. These considerations suggest that not the verifiability but the falsifiability of a system is to be taken as a criterion of demarcation ... it must be possible for an empirical scientific system to be refuted by experience.[61]

Popper's critical rationalism promotes a *survival of the fittest* model for scientific hypotheses, not so different from mutations evolving or extinguishing within the arena of Darwin's natural selection. By replacing induction with falsification, Popper offered a logically valid, yet non-ampliative epistemological tool to evaluate scientific progress. Falsification is formalized in table 2.1 as the fourth figure of the implicative syllogism.

However, a major challenge to Popper soon joined the conversation: How shall we choose between two mutually exclusive theories that have resisted all attempts at falsification so far? In the words of Wesley Salmon (1921–2001):

> Typically there will be an infinite array of generalisations which are compatible with the available observational evidence, and which are therefore, as yet, unrefuted. If we were free to choose arbitrarily from among all the unrefuted alternatives, we could predict anything whatever.[67]

Popper attempted to cut himself free of these criticisms using Occam's razor:

> Above all, our theory explains why simplicity is so highly desirable. To understand this there is no need for us to assume a "principle of

economy of thought" or anything of the kind. Simple statements, if
knowledge is our object, are to be prized more highly than less simple
ones because they tell us more; because their empirical content is
greater; and because they are better testable.[61]

Simple theories are preferable, Popper argues, because they enjoy fewer
degrees of freedom to explain data and resist falsification. (Preferring simple
theories is an epistemological bias reaching back to Newton, who thought of
Nature as "always simple and ever consonant with itself.") Another tool
to choose among unrefuted theories is to prefer the ones that provide us
with *riskier* predictions. Borrowing an example from Paul E. Meehl (1920–
2003),[68] a meteorological theory successfully predicting that "it will rain this
April" would generate little if any serious interest. However, an alternative
theory rightly proposing the *riskier* prediction "it will rain 4mm this 12th
of April" could draw our attention. This is because the second theory could
have been falsified more easily and—paraphrasing Wesley Salmon—it would
be a *damn strange coincidence* that a false theory provides predictions so
precise.

Recognizing that all models have their flaws, Popper eventually acknowledged that some scientific theories possess higher degrees of *verisimilitude*—
an ontological measure distinct from epistemological concepts like evidence,
probability, and belief. Historically, we have continued to rely on theories
despite their falsification by near-miss predictions. Building on these intuitions, Imre Lakatos (1922–1974) offered a strategy to defend theories with
high yet imperfect verisimilitude. His approach, known as a Lakatosian
defense,[69] treats theories as conjunctions of premises:

$$T = T_C \wedge A_T \wedge A_I \wedge C_P \wedge C_N,$$

where T_C represents the *hard core* of the theory, and the remaining terms
constitute its *protective belt*. The latter group includes auxiliary theories
A_T, auxiliary instruments A_I, *ceteris paribus* clauses C_P, and miscellaneous
experimental conditions C_N. Let $T \rightarrow (O_1 \supset O_2)$ denote that theory
T implies that O_2 is obtained when observing O_1. Assume further that
$(O_1 \supset O_2)$ is a very low probability event in the absence of T. If the
logical implication $O_1 \supset O_2$ fails to hold under the theory T, this does not
necessarily falsify the hard core of the theory T_C, but rather the conjunction
forming T as a whole. In such a scenario, the Lakatosian defense seeks
issues within the protective belt, aiming to preserve the integrity of the hard
core of the theory. Lakatosian defenses parallel the Duhem-Quine thesis,
which asserts the impossibility of testing any theory in pristine isolation. In
sum, it contends, all inductive generalizations are local and sustained by an
unjustifiable network of background conditions.

In his *Philosophical Psychology* lectures, Paul Meehl illustrates the Lakatosian defense by mean of two examples. Firstly, Van der Waals amended the ideal gas law by introducing additional parameters to account for otherwise unusual behaviors at small volumes and low temperatures. This adjustment allowed the law (ϕ) to be refined without abandoning its basic use under standard conditions. Secondly, the orbit of Uranus initially appeared inconsistent with the laws of gravitation. This discrepancy led to the discovery of Neptune, thereby necessitating a revision of the initial conditions (X, the list of planetary bodies) while upholding the fundamental principles of gravitational laws.

2.3   Empirical Risk Minimization

When Popper retired from academic life in 1968, Soviet mathematicians Vladimir Naumovich Vapnik and Alexey Yakovlevich Chervonenkis were hard at work at the opposite side of the Iron Curtain. They were on the brink of a scientific breakthrough that would justify the principle of minimizing training error using simple machines—bringing formal clarity to Hume's problem of induction and Popper's theory of risky falsification. To better understand their work, we shall first introduce the framework of empirical risk minimization (ERM) developed at Bell Labs during the early 1960s by Bill Highleyman, a productive intern at the time, who also created the first machine learning benchmark and proposed the train-test splitting of datasets.[70]

The canonical object of study in ERM is the population risk:

$$R_P(f) = \mathop{\mathbb{E}}_{(x,y)\sim P(X,Y)} \left[\ell(f(x), y)\right]. \tag{2.1}$$

This expression measures the error of a machine f over the entire distribution P of examples (x, y). Each example (x, y), drawn iid from the distribution P, is a pair containing one input x and its corresponding target y. The *loss function* ℓ, appropriately chosen for the task at hand, translates discrepancies between predictions $f(x)$ and desired targets y into a numerical error or loss value $\ell(f(x), y) \in \mathbb{R}$. Then, the learning problem is to find a machine $f^\star \in \mathcal{F}$ that minimizes the population risk (2.1), namely:

$$f^\star \in \arg\min_{f\in\mathcal{F}} R_P(f). \tag{2.2}$$

In the equation above, the set of candidate predictors $\mathcal{F}$ is known as the *function class*. It must contain carefully selected predictors with a taste for the patterns structuring our training data, hoping (inductively) that future test cases will also contain those patterns.

In practical situations, however, we do not have direct access to the entire probability distribution of examples P. Instead, we assume ownership of a finite *training set* of examples (x_i, y_i), all of them independently and identically distributed (iid) according to P. By invoking the law of large numbers, we approximate the unknown population risk (2.1) by the observed empirical risk:

$$R_{P_n}(f) = \frac{1}{n} \sum_{i=1}^{n} \ell(f(x_i), y_i). \tag{2.3}$$

We call the process of minimizing (2.3) *empirical risk minimization*. Following the same steps as in the population case, in machine learning we are interested in finding an empirical risk minimizer:

$$\hat{f} \in \arg\min_{f \in \mathcal{F}} R_{P_n}(f). \tag{2.4}$$

It is difficult to overstate the importance of ERM in machine learning—in fact, one would be hard-pressed to find examples of AI systems that do not perform ERM to learn from data. In general, ERM is difficult because the target function of interest can be high-dimensional, nonlinear, and nondeterministic, and because the training data at hand are often scarce and arranged irregularly. To make matters concrete, let us describe two practical implementations of the ERM principle that will feature recurrently throughout this book.

2.3.1 Linear and Logistic Regression

Consider a training dataset $\{(x_i, y_i)\}_{i=1}^{n}$ with d-dimensional inputs $x_i \in \mathbb{R}^d$ and c-dimensional *continuous* targets $y_i \in \mathbb{R}^c$. Define the input matrix $X \in \mathbb{R}^{n \times d}$ with rows x_i, and the target matrix $Y \in \mathbb{R}^{n \times c}$ with rows y_i. In *linear regression*, a linear machine f predicts $f(x_i) = x_i \cdot F$ about x_i, where $F \in \mathbb{R}^{d \times c}$ represents the regression coefficients learned to minimize the empirical risk (2.3). One common loss function for regression is the mean-squared error $\ell(f(x_i), y_i) = \frac{1}{2}\|f(x_i) - y_i\|^2$, which trains our machine to approximate the conditional expectation $\mathbb{E}[Y \mid X = x]$. The resulting setup is known as linear least-squares, where the empirical risk minimizer (2.4) has a closed form solution. To see this, write down the empirical risk (2.3), now taking this form:

$$R_{P_n}(f) = \frac{1}{n} \sum_{i=1}^{n} \ell(f(x_i), y_i) = \frac{1}{2n}\|XF - Y\|^2.$$

Taking the gradient with respect to the parameter F, we obtain:

$$\frac{\partial R_{P_n}(f)}{\partial F} = \frac{1}{n} X^\top (XF - Y) = \frac{1}{n} X^\top X F - \frac{1}{n} X^\top Y.$$

By setting this gradient to zero and solving, we arrive at the linear least-squares estimate:

$$\hat{F} = (X^\top X)^{-1}X^\top Y. \tag{2.5}$$

Linear least-squares estimates assume residuals $y_i - x_i\hat{F}$ that are independently and identically distributed with respect to a Gaussian distribution with zero mean and constant variance. Therefore, practitioners often look at plots of (1) predictions versus residuals, and of (2) example index versus residuals, as diagnostics for goodness-of-fit.

Some additional properties of the linear least-squares estimate admit closed form formulae. By letting predictions $\hat{y}_i = x_i\hat{F}$, we call $V = X(X^\top X)^{-1}X^\top$ the *hat matrix*, which maps Y into $\hat{Y}$, that is, $\hat{Y} = VY$. The hat matrix allows expressing the sum of squared errors as $Y^\top(I - V)Y$. The diagonal elements of the hat matrix $v_i := V_{ii}$ satisfy $1/n \leq v_i \leq 1$, $v_i = \sum_j V_{ij}^2$, allowing the identification of *high leverage* examples. Some authors call $1/v_i$ the *number of effective cases* necessary to build the prediction $\hat{y}_i$. Notably, when $v_i = 1$, it follows that $\hat{y}_i = Y_i$ and one parameter is devoted to that example. Conversely, large v_i may indicate that the example (x_i, y_i) is (1) an outlier with large $\|x_i\|$ and/or (2) memorized. Since v_i is nondecreasing in the number of input dimensions d and nonincreasing in the number of training examples n, the study of outliers and memorization becomes more difficult as the dimension increases and the sample size decreases.

The hat matrix is also a helpful device to estimate the influence of training examples on regression coefficients. Let $\hat{R}_i = y_i - \hat{y}_i$ be the residual on (x_i, y_i) when using all the training examples. Then, the expression

$$\hat{F}_{(-I)} = \hat{F} - (X^\top X)^{-1}X_I^\top(I - V_I)^{-1}\hat{R}_I$$

describes what the regression coefficients would have been if we omitted a subset of examples (X_I, Y_I) from our training data. When holding out a single point (x_i, y_i), its held-out residual follows the expression $\hat{R}_{-i} = \hat{R}_i/(1-v_i)$. Consequently, $\sum_i \hat{R}_{-i}^2$ is a leave-one-out cross-validation statistic useful for model selection.

So far, the analysis above has assumed the invertibility of $X^\top X$. When this is not the case—such as when $n > d$ or some features are linear combinations of one another—it is common to minimize the regularized empirical risk $R_{P_n}^\lambda(f) := \frac{1}{2n}\|XF - Y\|^2 + \frac{\lambda}{2}\|F\|^2$, resulting in this optimal solution:

$$F_n^{\star,\lambda} = (X^\top X + \lambda \cdot I)^{-1}X^\top Y.$$

This regularization technique—sometimes referred to as weight decay, Tikhonov regularization, or *ridge* regression—relates to the Moore-Penrose pseudo-inverse $X^\dagger = (X^\top X + \lambda \cdot I)^{-1}X^\top$ as $\lambda \to 0$.

For classification problems, consider a training dataset $\{(x_i, y_i)\}_{i=1}^n$ with targets $y_i \in \Delta_{01}^c$, where Δ_{01}^c is the set of c-dimensional *one-hot vectors*. One-hot vectors are vectors with one element equal to one and all others equal to zero. Here, they describe classification problems with c classes, where $y_{i,j} = 1$ indicates that example x_i belongs to category j. One popular model to perform linear classification is called multinomial logistic regression. Specifically, we set up a machine f producing predictions $f(x) = x \cdot F$, where $F \in \mathbb{R}^{d \times c}$ contains the parameters to be optimized to minimize the empirical risk. One common loss function for classification problems involves cross-entropy:

$$\ell(f(x_i), y_i) = -\sum_{j=1}^c y_{i,j} \log p_{i,j}, \text{ and } p_{i,j} = \text{sm}(f(x_i))_j := \frac{e^{f(x_i)_j}}{\sum_{k=1}^c e^{f(x_i)_k}}.$$

This expression shows that computing the cross-entropy loss for one example (x_i, y_i) is a composition of three steps. First, the machine accepts the d-dimensional input x_i and transforms it into a c-dimensional vector of real-valued *logits* $f(x_i) = x_i \cdot F$. Second, the vector of real-valued logits is normalized into a c-dimensional probability vector $p_i := \text{sm}(f(x_i)) \in \Delta^c$, where Δ^c is the set of c-dimensional probability vectors and *sm* stands for the softmax operation:

$$p_{i,j} = sm(f)_j = \frac{\exp(f_{i,j})}{\sum_{k=1}^c \exp(f_{i,k})}.$$

Each element in a softmax vector has values within the unit interval, and they all sum to one. Third, the predicted probability vector p_i is compared against the desired target y_i by means of the cross-entropy loss $\ell(p_i, y_i) = -\sum_j y_{i,j} \log p_{i,j}$. Because of the softmax normalization, we observe that multinomial logistic regression aligns with the assumption that each example belongs to only one out of the c categories, since increasing one coordinate necessarily pushes the remaining $c - 1$ values down to zero. Unlike linear least-squares, we do not have the luxury of a closed-form solution to our estimate $\hat{F}$, nor are continuous residuals amenable to goodness-of-fit analysis. However, binning techniques to analyze the calibration of such predictions will be studied in chapter 11.

Although regression and classification often receive separate treatments, I approach all learning tasks as regression problems. This is because the computations involved utilize real-valued predictions and losses, while the learning process is guided by real-valued gradients. In particular, these gradients take the form

$$\frac{\partial \ell(g(\phi(x) \cdot w), y)}{\partial w_{jk}} = (g(x_i \cdot w)_k - y_k)\phi(x)_j,$$

where (x, y) is a training example and ϕ is a feature representation function taken to be the identity map in the linear case. Furthermore, g is an inverse *link function* set to be the identity for regression, the sigmoid function for binary classification, and the softmax function for multi-class classification. Unifying things further, some researchers have successfully used the mean-squared error to learn classification problems.[71] Soft labels are another powerful tool that will be further examined in chapter 10.

2.3.2 Vapnik-Chervonenkis Learning Theory

We are now equipped with the necessary tools to study the learning theory of Vapnik and Chervonenkis, which is chiefly concerned with describing the generalization error of empirical risk minimizers under the iid assumption.

Vapnik and Chervonenkis had to surmount two sizable challenges to develop their ERM theory. First, because the data distribution P is unknown to us, guarantees must be valid for all possible distributions of data. Second, ERM proceeds by scanning each and every function in $f \in \mathcal{F}$, choosing one among those attaining minimal empirical risk. For this function comparison to be fair in the midst of random and finite training data, we must ensure that the empirical risks of all functions in $\mathcal{F}$ converge *uniformly* to their population risks. This can be done by controlling the convergence of the empirical risk of the *slowest* function in $\mathcal{F}$ to its population risk. Mathematically, we are interested in upper-bounding the *generalization error*:

$$R_P(\hat{f}) - R_P(\eta) = \underbrace{\left\{ R_P(\hat{f}) - \inf_{f \in \mathcal{F}} R_P(f) \right\}}_{\text{estimation error}} + \underbrace{\left\{ \inf_{f \in \mathcal{F}} R_P(f) - R_P(\eta) \right\}}_{\text{approximation error}}.$$

In the equation above, the *approximation error* describes the difference in error between the best function $f^\star \in \mathcal{F}$ and the best possible predictor η, referred to as the *Bayes predictor*. This deterministic quantity, independent of the training data at hand, encodes both the appropriateness of our function class for the learning problem at hand and the existence of irreducible sources of noise. In contrast, the *estimation error* is a random quantity expected to decrease as we collect more training data. It can be elaborated as follows:[72]

$$R_P(\hat{f}) - R_P(f^\star)$$
$$= R_P(\hat{f}) - R_{P_n}(\hat{f}) + R_{P_n}(\hat{f}) - R_{P_n}(f^\star) + R_{P_n}(f^\star) - R_P(f^\star)$$
$$\leq \sup_{f \in \mathcal{F}} |R_{P_n}(f) - R_P(f)| + \underbrace{\{R_{P_n}(\hat{f}) - R_{P_n}(f^\star)\}}_{=0} + \sup_{f \in \mathcal{F}} |R_{P_n}(f) - R_P(f)|$$
$$\leq 2 \sup_{f \in \mathcal{F}} |R_{P_n}(f) - R_P(f)|.$$

According to the last line, we may upper-bound the estimation error by controlling the difference between the empirical and population risks of the *slowest* learner in the function class. While individually bounding the convergence of each function with Hoeffding's inequality is straightforward, controlling the supremum above—guaranteeing uniform convergence across the entire function class—requires extending the Glivenko-Cantelli theorem from 1933, one of the most important results in foundational statistics.

The groundbreaking result of Vapnik and Chervonenkis (VC) takes the following form: Given any data distribution, the probability of ERM picking the best rule in the function class approaches *one* as we collect more data, *if and only if* the function class $\mathcal{F}$ has *finite complexity*. To achieve this result, VC define the complexity of a function class in terms of a combinatorial quantity called the *VC-dimension*. Specifically, a family of binary classifiers $\mathcal{F}$ has VC-dimension $v := \text{VC}(\mathcal{F})$ if (1) there exists one set of v examples *shattered* by $\mathcal{F}$ and (2) there exists no set of $v+1$ examples shattered by $\mathcal{F}$. A set S containing v examples is shattered by $\mathcal{F}$ if we can classify all 2^v possible binary labels of S using functions in $\mathcal{F}$.

Consider some illustrative examples, as shown in figure 2.2. If $\mathcal{F}$ contains only one classifier, then $\text{VC}(\mathcal{F}) = 0$. If $\mathcal{F}$ contains all threshold classifiers on the real line $f(x) = \text{sign}(x > theta)$ and $\theta \in \mathbb{R}$, then $\text{VC}(\mathcal{F}) = 1$. If $\mathcal{F}$ is the set of linear classifiers in d dimensions $f(x) = x \cdot \theta$ and $\theta \in \mathbb{R}^{d \times 1}$, then $\text{VC}(\mathcal{F}) = d$. For affine classifiers, $f(x) = x \cdot \theta + b$ it follows $\text{VC}(\mathcal{F}) = d + 1$. Interestingly, if $\mathcal{F}$ is the set of one-dimensional sinusoid classifiers $f(x) = \sin(x \cdot \theta)$ for $\theta \in \mathbb{R}$, then $\text{VC}(\mathcal{F}) = \infty$. These examples illustrate how VC-dimension is a subtler concept than simply counting the number of parameters in our function class.

Second, VC specified the *rates* at which the uniform convergence of estimation error occurs. A slight refinement[73] reads: For any $\delta > 0$, with probability at least $1 - \delta$, the following holds for all data distributions P and function classes $\mathcal{F}$ with finite VC-dimension v:

$$\sup_{f \in \mathcal{F}} |R_P(f) - R_{P_n}(f)| \leq \sqrt{\frac{2v \log \frac{en}{v}}{n}} + \sqrt{\frac{\log \frac{1}{\delta}}{2n}}. \tag{2.6}$$

This result, originally presented in three pages and without a proof, was published in Russian in 1968[74] and translated into English later that year.[75] The translation quickly garnered the attention of the international community due to the enthusiastic endorsement of Richard Dudley.[76] It was only in their longer, celebrated 1971 paper that VC provided a full proof to their theorem.[77] (To simplify exposition, I have directly upper-bounded the originally proposed *growth function* by the VC-dimension.)[78] The curious reader can learn more about the fascinating history behind VC-theory, developed

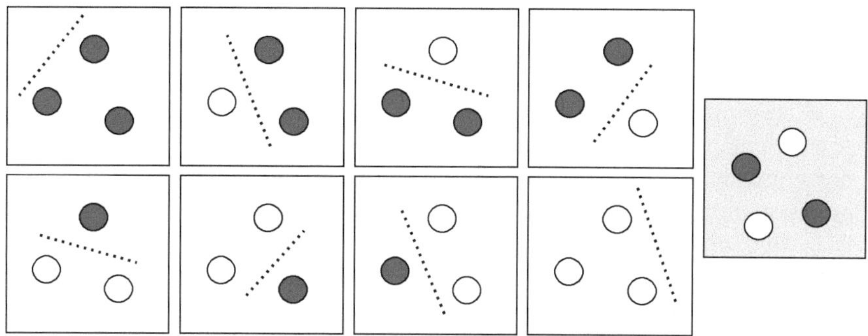

Figure 2.2: Two-dimensional affine classifiers can shatter 3 points. That is, there exists an arrangement of 3 points that can be correctly classified by an affine classifier, regardless of their binary labeling. (There are $2^3 = 8$ possible binary labels, illustrated above.) However, there exists an arrangement of 4 points that cannot be shattered by affine classifiers, highlighted in red. That is, there is a binary labeling of such arrangement of 4 points that cannot be correctly classified by an affine classifier. Therefore, the VC-dimension of two-dimensional affine classifiers is $v = 3$.

against the backdrop of the Cold War, by reading the *Festschriften* honoring the lives of Vapnik[76] and Chervonenkis.[79]) Since the publication of VC's original results, decades of intense research efforts have proven—under the *realizability* assumption that the Bayes predictor belongs to the chosen function class—that the ERM principle can achieve fast learning rates $O(n^{-1})$ with matching lower bounds.[80] In particular, *relative* bounds like

$$R_P(f) \le R_{P_n}(f) + g\left(\frac{v}{n}\right) + \sqrt{R_{P_n}(f) \cdot g\left(\frac{v}{n}\right)},$$

hold with probability $1 - \delta$, where $g(v/n) = \frac{\log(2n/v+1) - \log(\delta/4)}{n/v}$. These bounds illustrate the benefits of attaining zero training error, since machines f achieving $R_{P_n}(f) = 0$ also obtain fast convergence rates $O(n^{-1})$. To summarize, ERM is established as an optimal learning rule under the iid assumption.

Circling back to the writings of Karl Popper, we observe an interesting predecessor to the VC-dimension:

> If there exists, for a theory t, a field of singular (but not necessarily basic) statements such that, for some number d, the theory t cannot be falsified by any d-tuple of the field, although it can be falsified by certain $(d + 1)$-tuples, then we call d the characteristic number of the theory with respect to that field. All statements of the field

> whose degree of composition is less than d, or equal to d, are then
> compatible with the theory, and permitted by it, irrespective of their
> content.[61]

A closer inspection reveals that Popper's dimension and VC-dimension are
not equivalent, however. In particular, while the VC-dimension "is the
largest number of points one can shatter, the Popper dimension is one less
than the smallest number of points one can not shatter."[81] To illustrate
this discrepancy, consider the function class $\mathcal{F}$ of all d-dimensional linear
classifiers. As discussed above, the VC-dimension of such linear $\mathcal{F}$ is d.
However, Popper suggests that the dimension of linear $\mathcal{F}$ is always 2, since
no linear classifier can shatter three *collinear* points, for example, when
they are labeled $(+, -, +)$.[81]

Vapnik-Chervonenkis and Popper both had profound insights relating
the simplicity of a theory to the amount of data necessary to falsify it, which
we may summarize in two points. On one hand, theories with a small VC-
dimension are easier to falsify. Because small zero training error solutions
have less flexibility to resist falsification, we consider these predictors to
be highly informative about the phenomenon of interest. On the other
hand, theories with a large VC-dimension increase underspecification and
require more data to rule out (falsify) zero training error solutions. In the
extreme case, function classes with an infinite VC-dimension are deemed
unscientific because they cannot be falsified—these classes will always
contain zero training error solutions regardless of the amount of training
data. Collectively, these insights support selecting the simplest performant
solution when learning from iid data.

2.3.3 Universal Consistency, and the Lack Thereof

We have so far compared empirical risk minimizers in $\hat{f} \in \mathcal{F}$ to the best
predictor in their function class $f^\star \in \mathcal{F}$. Would it be possible to go beyond
the function class, and to learn the best possible predictor $\eta \in \mathcal{H} \subset \mathcal{F}$, as
we collect increasing amounts of training data? This best possible predictor,
often called the Bayes predictor, has the following expression for binary
classification problems:

$$\eta(x) = \left[\!\!\left[\Pr(Y = 1 \mid X = x) \geq \frac{1}{2} \right]\!\!\right],$$

where the Iverson bracket $[\![\text{condition}]\!]$ equals one when "condition" is true
and zero otherwise. We say that a learning algorithm is *universally consistent*
if it approaches the Bayes rule as we collect increasing amounts of training
data. One universally consistent learning algorithm is the k-nearest neighbor

classifier,[82] when we grow the number of neighbors k such that $k/n \to 0$ as $n \to \infty$. However, because universally consistent learning algorithms require an infinite VC-dimension, their test error decreases arbitrarily slowly for some distributions of training data.

In general, the acclaimed "no free lunch"[83] theorem formalizes the fact that every learning algorithm converges arbitrarily slowly for some distributions of training data. In particular, let $\varepsilon > 0$ be an arbitrarily small number, and let n be any integer. Then, for any algorithm $\mathcal{A}$ to learn binary classifiers, there exists a distribution P such that $\mathbb{E}_{D_n \sim P^n}\left[R_P(\mathcal{A}(D_n))\right] \geq \frac{1}{2} - \varepsilon$, where $D_n = \{(x_i, y_i)\}_{i=1}^n$ is a training dataset containing n examples drawn iid from P.

2.3.4 Distribution-Dependent Bounds

The practical application of VC bounds has met two substantial challenges. First, VC bounds are loose, as they provide worst-case guarantees across all possible distributions of data. Second, and despite intense research efforts, estimating the VC-dimension of modern function classes, such as deep neural networks, has proven elusive.

In an effort to derive tighter bounds, learning theorists have developed capacity measures that take into account the distribution of data. One prominent example is the *Rademacher complexity*, introduced by Koltchinksii and Panchenko to derive generalization bounds.[84] Their result reads as follows.[73] Let $\mathcal{F}$ be a family of classifiers taking values in $\{-1, +1\}$. Let $D = \{(x_i, y_i)\}_{i=1}^n$ be our training set, drawn iid from the unknown data distribution P. Then, for any $\delta > 0$, with probability $1 - \delta$ over the choice of D, it follows that:

$$\sup_{f \in \mathcal{F}} |R_P(f) - R_{P_n}(f)| \leq \hat{\mathcal{R}}_n(\mathcal{F}) + 3 \cdot \sqrt{\frac{\log \frac{2}{\delta}}{2n}}, \text{ and} \qquad (2.7)$$

$$\sup_{f \in \mathcal{F}} |R_P(f) - R_{P_n}(f)| \leq \mathcal{R}_n(\mathcal{F}) + 1 \cdot \sqrt{\frac{\log \frac{1}{\delta}}{2n}}. \qquad (2.8)$$

Inequality (2.7) uses the *empirical* Rademacher complexity:

$$\hat{\mathcal{R}}_n(\mathcal{F}) = \mathop{\mathbb{E}}_{\sigma_1, \ldots, \sigma_n} \left[\sup_{f \in \mathcal{F}} \frac{1}{|D|} \sum_{x_i : (x_i, y_i) \in D} \sigma_i \cdot f(x_i) \right], \qquad (2.9)$$

where each σ_i is a Rademacher random variable—a coin toss taking the values -1 or $+1$ with equal probability.

Rademacher complexities also aid in estimating VC-dimensions for arbitrary function classes. First off, the population Rademacher complexity in (2.8), with expression $\mathcal{R}_n(\mathcal{F}) = \mathbb{E}_{D \sim P^n}\left[\hat{\mathcal{R}}_n(\mathcal{F})\right]$, relates to the VC-dimension as

$$\mathcal{R}_n(\mathcal{F}) \leq 4 \cdot \sqrt{\frac{v \cdot \log \frac{en}{v}}{n}}. \tag{2.10}$$

The equation above allows us to recover the original VC bound (2.6) from (2.8). Specifically, the empirical Rademacher complexity in (2.7) measures the ability of functions in $\mathcal{F}$ to fit random labels to the n inputs comprising our training data. Therefore, one practical way to estimate the Rademacher complexity of our function class is to attempt learning the training data with randomized labels.

2.4 Zero Training Error in Modern Practice

Thus far, this chapter has gone to great lengths to justify the principle of minimizing training error with small learning machines. However, the recent deep learning revolution has brought about significant confusion to our understanding of learning theory. State-of-the-art AI systems are *overparameterized* deep neural networks, meaning their number of parameters exceeds, sometimes by orders of magnitude, the number of available training data. As discussed by Peter L. Bartlett and colleagues, growing the size of a deep neural network well beyond the smallest zero training error solution surprisingly improves the system's generalization error:

> The remarkable practical success of deep learning has revealed some major surprises from a theoretical perspective. In particular, simple gradient methods easily find near-optimal solutions to nonconvex optimization problems, and despite giving a near-perfect fit to training data without any explicit effort to control model complexity, these methods exhibit excellent predictive accuracy.[85]

In fact, practical neural networks are so flexible that they achieve zero training error on large amounts of training data annotated with random labels.[86] This voids of meaning the bounds (2.7) and (2.8), since the corresponding Rademacher complexity attains its maximum value of one. Given this dilemma, the rest of this section reviews efforts to reconcile the theoretical preference for small learning machines versus with the practical success of very large models.

To date, attempts to explain the generalization properties of large deep neural networks have adhered to one of two strategies.[87] On one hand, we may insist on characterizing generalization by means of uniform convergence bounds, such as those discussed in previous sections. In this case, to avoid trivial bounds, we must argue that the capacity of the function class is somehow *effectively reduced* as we employ more training data, potentially due to hidden regularization forces at play. On the other hand, we may forsake uniform convergence bounds altogether, instead developing deeper insights into what aspects of the empirical risk minimizer determine its generalization abilities. I will now examine these two approaches.

2.4.1   Controlling Effective Capacity

In an effort to salvage learning theories based on uniform convergence, we could argue that our empirical risk minimization routine does not explore the entire function class, but only a much smaller *effective* function class, whose complexity scales inversely with the number of training data. Take neural networks as an illustrative example. They are trained by following a finite amount of stochastic gradient descent iterations, using a small learning rate, and deploying regularizers to ensure small weights. In practice, all of these factors significantly constrain the reachable set of neural networks implementable by the learning algorithm— in other words, the Rademacher complexity of the function class and its ability to memorize random labels.

To make matters concrete, consider limiting the effective capacity of a neural network function class by upper-bounding the distance that the optimization process travels from its random initialization.[88] Denote by f_0 a random initialization, and let f be the solution obtained by the learning process. Then, a first-order Taylor expansion of the excess risk reads:

$$R_P(f) - R_{P_n}(f) = R_P(f) \approx R_P(f_0) + [\nabla_f R_P(f_0)]^\top (f - f_0)$$
$$= \frac{1}{2} + [\nabla_f R_P(f_0)]^\top (f - f_0)$$
$$\approx \frac{1}{2} + [\nabla_f R_{P_n}(f_0)]^\top (f - f_0).$$

In these equations, we have assumed zero training error ($R_{P_n}(f) = 0$), negligible second-order terms, a random initialization with random chance performance ($R_P(f_0) \approx \frac{1}{2}$), and that empirical gradients estimate their population counterparts well. The equations above help us drive three points home. First, while the test error of the learning machine is known at random initialization, we gradually lose sight of it after each gradient step. Second, random initializations with small weights are desirable, as they often increase the smoothness of the machine, described mathematically by $\|\nabla_f R_{P_n}\|$. Third, the possible test error of the learning machine is inversely proportional to the distance between the random initialization f_0 and the final solution f. In this sense, machines that learn faster generalize better.[89]

This analysis suggests that we could constrain the VC-dimension of our function class a priori by either choosing a distribution of random initializations with small weights or setting a limit on the distance the optimization process can traverse. Within this framework, we might reconsider modern neural network training strategies—such as increasing model size, making residual connections, and various forms of normalization—as techniques to attain zero training error in shorter walks from random initialization. In fact, empirical evidence suggests that larger models require shorter walks from initialization, which may explain why they generalize better.[88] Likewise, the distance from random initialization increases with label noise, supporting the notion that more complex function classes are necessary to fit random targets. However, similar experiments show that distance from random initialization grows with the number of training data. This is an unfortunate result that falsifies our hypothesis, as it wrongly suggests that generalization error worsens as we collect more training data. In conclusion, uniform convergence remains unable to describe the generalization properties of state-of-the-art, large neural networks.[90,91]

2.4.2 Characterizing the Learned Minimizer

Uniform convergence guarantees are excessively pessimistic because they assess the generalization error of the worst possible machine in the function class, over all possible data distributions. In practice, our empirical risk minimizer does not need to be the slowest learner, and natural data represents a very restricted subset from all possible distributions. Accordingly, the research community is devoting growing efforts to develop theories of generalization beyond uniform convergence, in order to explain the uncanny generalization abilities of large deep neural networks on real-world data. Many of these theories examine the characteristics of the learned empirical risk minimizer on the training data at hand, rather than considering the entire function class for any possible distribution.

Two significant research findings have reignited interest in the generalization properties of large learning machines. First, Zhang and colleagues demonstrated that large deep neural networks can memorize random labels for extensive real-world datasets.[86] This suggests that modern neural networks have unit empirical Rademacher complexities, rendering uniform convergence bounds such as (2.7) meaningless. Second, Belkin and colleagues[92] showed that test error decreases as the size of modern neural networks grows in the over-parameterized regime. This counter-intuitive result is vividly illustrated by the *double descent* phenomenon.[92,93]

To observe a double descent curve, consider training a classifier on a dataset of n handwritten digit images $x_i \in \mathbb{R}^d$. In particular, separate the ten digits into a negative group (containing digits 0, 3, 6, 8, and 9, labeled as $y_i = -1$) and a positive group (containing the remaining digits, labeled as $y_i = +1$). Configure our function class $\mathcal{F}_k$ to contain all linear classifiers on top of a fixed set of k random features:[94]

$$\mathcal{F}_k := \mathcal{F}_k(w, b) = \left\{ f : f(x) = \sum_{j=1}^{k} \alpha_j \cos(xw_j + b_j), \alpha \in \mathbb{R}^k \right\}, \quad (2.11)$$

where the parameters of the random features are $w_k \sim \text{Gaussian}(0, \sigma^2 I_d)$ and $b_k \sim \text{Uniform}[0, 2\pi]$. In this experiment, we employ the mean-squared error loss $\ell(f_{\hat{\alpha}}(x_i), y_i) = (f_{\hat{\alpha}}(x_i) - y_i)^2$ to measure the discrepancy between the prediction $f_{\hat{\alpha}}(x_i)$ about digit x_i and the desired target $y_i \in \{-1, +1\}$. Under this setup, linear-least squares (2.5) provides a closed form solution for the optimal vector of coefficients $\hat{\alpha}$.

The experiment proceeds by training classifiers for an increasing amount of random features k. Figure 2.3 depicts the final training loss, testing loss, and norm of $\hat{\alpha}$ for each classifier. In this plot, the phenomenon of double descent appears in three distinct phases. During the first phase, known as the under-parameterized regime, both the training and testing error decrease as the number of random features grows. This phase concludes with a local minimum in test error, described in classic textbooks as the *sweet spot* that optimally balances training error and model capacity.[95] During the second phase, training error continues to decrease while test error increases, signaling *overfitting*. The second phase concludes at the *interpolation threshold* $k = n$ with a spike in test error and weight norm. This interpolation threshold is the first value of k guaranteeing the machine will achieve zero training *loss*, and it marks the beginning of the *over-parameterized regime*. During the third phase, the test error and weight norm undergo a second descent despite the absence of training errors, which have been already dealt with since the interpolation threshold. Remarkably, the lowest test error and weight norm occur during this second descent.

The double descent phenomenon goes against conventional wisdom. For instance, in their famous *Elements of Statistical Learning*, Hastie et al. claim that "a model with zero training error is overfit to the training data and will typically generalize poorly."[95] Prominent statistician Leo Breiman similarly pondered, "Why don't heavily parameterized neural networks overfit the data?"[96] However, learning theorists were baffled at similar observations in the context of boosting, over twenty-five years ago:

> Ordinarily, as classifiers become more and more complex, we expect their generalization error eventually to degrade. Yet these curves reveal that test error does not increase for either method even after

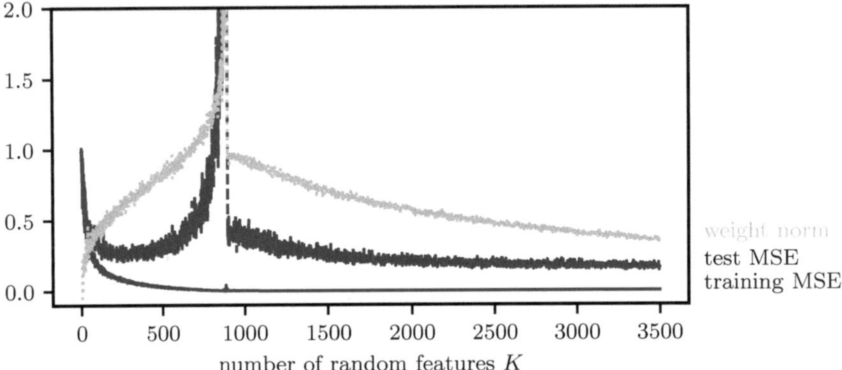

Figure 2.3: Training linear classifiers on top of k fixed random features to classify n handwritten digits into two classes. As we increase k—the capacity of the function class—we monitor the final training loss, testing loss, and weight norm of each classifier. A *double descent* in test loss emerges in three phases. During the first phase, the test loss descends until its first *sweet spot* local minima around $k = 250$. During the second phase, classifiers achieve zero training error at the interpolation threshold $k = n$, while their test loss increases to its maximal value. During the third phase, the classifier is no longer subject to the pressure of minimizing training errors, so the minimum-norm regularization effect of linear least-squares yields a second, deeper descent of the test loss.

1000 trees have been combined (by which point, the combined classifier involves more than two million decision-tree nodes). How can it be that such complex classifiers have such low error rates? ... After just five trees have been combined, the training error of the combined classifier has already dropped to zero, but the test error continues to drop. ... The results of these experiments seem to contradict Occam's razor, one of the fundamental principles in the theory of machine learning. This principle states that in order to achieve good test error, the classifier should be as simple as possible.[97]

What is really happening during the second descent of test error?

As it turns out, the main factor determining in-distribution generalization error is the smoothness of the predictor. As we grow our function class from $\mathcal{F}$ to $\mathcal{F}'$, it follows that $\min_{f \in \mathcal{F}'} \|f\| \leq \min_{f \in \mathcal{F}} \|f\|$, meaning that the smoothest function in $\mathcal{F}'$ is equally smooth as or smoother than the smoothest function in $\mathcal{F}$. In the case of boosting, additional weak learners *iron out* random fluctuations in the overall function, decreasing test error even if there are no remaining training errors to correct. In the case of deep learning, enlarging the size of our neural networks provides us with a larger set of zero training error solutions, some of them with increased smoothness. Perhaps surprisingly, increasing the number of parameters can result in learning a simpler (smoother) function. Consequently, "we are back to an Occam's razor argument in which instead of arguing that the classification rule itself is simple, we argue that the rule is close to a simple rule."[97]

To understand why large models have a natural inclination toward smoothness, let us revisit the digit classification problem discussed earlier. We are interested in finding

$$\hat{\alpha} = \min_{\alpha \in \mathbb{R}^{k \times 1}} \|\Phi\alpha - y\|_2, \tag{2.12}$$

where $\Phi \in \mathbb{R}^{n \times k}$ is the input matrix of random features with entries $\Phi_{i,j} = \cos(\langle w_j, x_i \rangle + b_j)$, and $y \in \mathbb{R}^{n \times 1}$ is the column vector of targets. The solution to this problem is $\hat{\alpha} = \Phi^\dagger y$, where $\Phi^\dagger \in \mathbb{R}^{k \times n}$ is the Moore-Penrose inverse of Φ, uniquely defined for any matrix Φ in one out of two possible manners:

- When $\Phi^\top \Phi$ is invertible, the Moore-Penrose inverse is $\Phi^\dagger = (\Phi^\top \Phi)^{-1}\Phi^\top$. This is the under-parameterized case $k \leq n$ where zero training error may not be possible. Among all solutions minimizing (2.12), $\hat{\alpha} = \Phi^\dagger y$ is the one with minimum norm.

- When $\Phi\Phi^\top$ is invertible, the Moore-Penrose inverse is $\Phi^\dagger = \Phi^\top(\Phi\Phi^\top)^{-1}$. This is the over-parameterized case $k \geq n$ where zero training error is possible. Among all solutions achieving zero training error, $\hat{\alpha} = \Phi^\dagger y$ is the one with minimum norm.

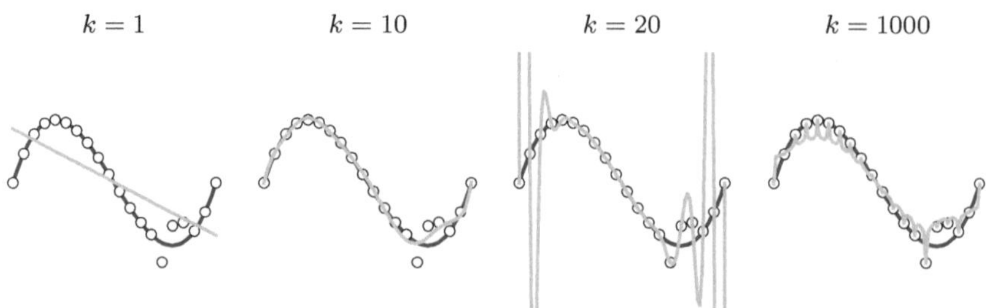

Figure 2.4: Training polynomials of degree k to fit a noisy cubic function. We observe a first descent in test error from $k = 1$ (norm of estimated coefficients 0.8) to $k = 10$ (norm of estimated coefficients 1.4). We observe a second descent in test error from $k = 20$ (norm 44) to $k = 1000$ (norm 1.2).

The previous formulæ provide us with the following intuitions to explain the two descents observed in figure 2.3:

- During the first descent the machine has insufficient capacity, and the explicit force of minimizing training error dominates at the expense of stressing the implicit minimum-norm regularization force. The learning machine twists and turns to fit the data, maximally so just before the interpolation threshold—where a maximum amount of points are correctly predicted and zero training loss is finally achieved.

- From then on, and during the second descent, the learning machine has enough capacity to be freed from the explicit force of training error minimization, so the implicit minimum-norm regularizing force dominates. Other effects, such as grokking,[98] also emerge during this phase.

Figure 2.4 illustrates the double descent phenomenon when fitting polynomials of various degrees k to a noisy cubic function. Some refer to cases like $k = 1000$ in the figure as *benign overfitting*, where the model memorizes each training example without compromising the global structure and smoothness of the estimated function.

In summary, the number of parameters in a predictor does not determine its ability to generalize; rather, it depends on its training error and the smoothness of the function it implements. These lessons can be neatly summarized into *Belkin's razor*:

> Select the smoothest function, according to some notion of functional smoothness, among those that fit the data perfectly.[99]

Such a function is sometimes referred to as the minimum-norm interpolant.[85] (As a counter-example to Belkin's razor, consider the 1-nearest neighbor classifier, which achieves zero training error only by means of memorization, therefore lacking smoothness.) In light of this principle, advances in neural network architectures, optimizers, and regularization schemes may be evaluated in terms of their pull for smoothness. Although functional smoothness can be measured in various ways, some studies advocate the use of Jacobian norms.[100,101] A notion similar to smoothness is the one of *compressibility*. Andrew Gordon Wilson argues:

> Even large models with many parameters that represent hypotheses with a low empirical risk and a small compressed size can achieve strong generalization guarantees. ... Increasing the number of parameters also increases a compression bias: that is, models with more parameters can be stored with less total memory after training than models with fewer parameters after training.[102]

Arguably, smoother models should be able to compress, as there are less high-frequency fluctuations to consider.

2.5 Simplify-and-Memorize

The pursuit of smoothness heralded in previous sections turns out to be a double-edged sword, as it can enforce an excessive bias for simplicity.[103,104] Typically, large learning machines often follow a two-step shortcut, the *simplify-and-memorize* strategy, to achieve zero training error with maximal smoothness.[6] First, the learning machine quickly identifies and latches onto a simplistic feature able to correctly classify most of the training examples. Unfortunately, the learning machine *grips* this simplistic feature so early and so tightly that it starves[105] the learning process from acquiring more complex patterns, perhaps of better quality. This results in a *malign* type of overfitting, precluding the learning of invariant solutions with better generalization properties.[106] Second, the learning machine uses its remaining capacity to memorize those few examples that do not comply with the simplistic feature. At this point, the machine has reduced training error to zero while maximizing smoothness, albeit only by acquiring a very superficial understanding of the problem at hand. (In situations without capacity necessary to "memorize," the machine can still lack the necessary learning signals to escape the simplistic explanation—we could refer to this case as *simplify-and-stuck*.) As Sam Bell and Levent Sagun argue, this limited comprehension has downstream implications for the performance of the learning system:

When a model finds one group easier than another (even if sample sizes of each group are balanced), it will prioritize the easy group at the expense of the difficult, resulting in a greater performance disparity when compared to training each group separately.[107]

2.5.1 The Cow-on-the-Beach Problem

To better understand the *simplify-and-memorize* bias, let's revisit the idealized binary classification problem commonly known as *cow-on-the-beach*.[29] This problem involves classifying pictures x_i of cows with a positive label $y_i = 1$, while classifying pictures of camels with a negative label $y_i = 0$. In the training data, cows are much more likely to appear in grasslands, while camels mostly appear in beige sandy beaches. Occasionally—say, in five percent of total instances—cows amble on beaches and camels graze in meadows. To solve this classification problem, we have access to a training dataset $\{(x_i, y_i)\}_{i=1}^{n}$ of such pictures, each produced according the following data generating process:

$$
\begin{aligned}
y_i &\sim \text{Bernoulli}(1/2), \\
c_i &\sim \text{Bernoulli}(p^e), \\
x_i^{\text{fg}} &\sim \text{Gaussian}(0.2, \sigma^2) \cdot (2 \cdot y_i - 1), \\
x_i^{\text{bg}} &\sim \text{Gaussian}(1, 0.1^2) \cdot (2 \cdot [\![y_i = c_i]\!] - 1), \\
x_i^{\text{noi}} &\sim \text{Gaussian}(\text{vec}_{d-2}(0), \text{Diag}_{d-2}(1)), \\
x_i &\leftarrow \text{Concat}(x_i^{\text{fg}}, x_i^{\text{bg}}, x_i^{\text{noi}}).
\end{aligned}
\tag{CoB}
$$

In words, to generate one example (x_i, y_i), (1) choose at random between cow ($y_i = 1$) and camel ($y_i = 0$), (2) determine whether the animal appears in its natural ($c_i = 1$) or unnatural ($c_i = 0$) habitat, (3) draw a value for the d-dimensional foreground or *animal* feature x_i^{fg}, (4) draw a value for the d-dimensional background or *landscape* feature x_i^{bg}, (5) draw a value for the d'-dimensional noise feature x_i^{noi}, and (6) construct the observed input by concatenating these three features. Background features, here representing landscape, are also known as *shortcuts* or *distractors*.[108] The $d - 2$ noise features increase or decrease the level of over-parameterization (also referred to as underspecification) of the learning problem, formalized by the ratio d/n.

This family of problems (CoB) has four parameters: the number of training examples n, the number $d - 2$ of noise features, the strength σ^2 of the foreground feature, and the percentage p^e of animals appearing in their usual context. By default, we consider *Pezeshki's problem*, comprising a training dataset with $n = 1000$ examples and

$$p^e = 0.9, \sigma^2 = 0.02^2, d = 1200.$$

Given these parameters, (1) the foreground feature bears a total correlation with the target and small variance, (2) the fast feature bears only 90% correlation with the target but has a variance five times larger, and (3) the $d - 2 = 1198$ noise features—while statistically independent in the population sense—jointly bear total empirical correlation with the target, since $d > n$. See algorithm 2.1 for PyTorch code on how to generate this data, and the top-left plot in figure 2.7 for a visualization of its first two features, animal x^{fg} and background x^{bg}.

```
import torch

def cob_base(num_samples=1000, num_dimensions=1200,
             p_e=0.9, sig2=0.02):
  y = torch.zeros(num_samples, 1).bernoulli_(0.5)
  c = torch.zeros(num_samples, 1).bernoulli_(p_e)
  m = (y == c).float().view(-1, 1)
  x1 = (torch.randn(num_samples, 1) * sig2 - 0.2) * (2*y-1)
  x2 = (torch.randn(num_samples, 1) * 0.10 - 1.0) * (2*m-1)
  xn = torch.randn(num_samples, num_dimensions - 2) * 1
  return torch.cat((x1, x2, xn), -1), y

def cob(train=True): # equation (CoB) in main text
  return cob_base(pe=0.9 if train else 0.1, sep=0.02)

def cob_p(train=True): # equation (CoB-P) in main text
  return cob_base(
      num_dimensions=2,
      pe=0.9 if train else 0.1,
      sep=0.3)

# Illustrate generalization failures
from sklearn.linear_model import LogisticRegression as LR
print(LR().fit(*cob(train=True)).score(
  *cob(train=False)))
print(LR().fit(*cob_piif(train=True)).score(
  *cob_piif(train=False)))
```

Algorithm 2.1: PyTorch code to generate CoB and CoB-P data.

Figure 2.5 illustrates the simplify-and-memorize learning strategy on the over-parameterized cow-on-the-beach problem. During the *simplify* phase, the learning machine quickly absorbs the fast feature x_2 to learn a simplistic rule that classifies the *majority* of training examples. This tight grip on the fast feature starves all gradient signals from the slow, invariance-inducing feature x_1. Because the fast feature does not afford zero training error, the machine implements a *memorize* phase to store the *minority* of classification errors into the weights associated with the noise features.

Two remarks are in order. First, it is common to accept that linear models treat all examples equally, according to the fixed dot product $x \cdot w$. However, linear models implement surprisingly intricate behaviors in the over-parameterized regime, simplifying some training examples and memorizing others. Second, the variance of the noise features determines the memorization and overfitting behaviors that the machine implements. Figure 2.6 illustrates these non trivial behaviors for a one-dimensional nonlinear regression task, approached by a predictor with 30 noise features of varying variance σ_ϵ, and 1000 training examples. This learning problem is one of many examples in this book advocating against Occam's razor. (Francis Crick, co-discoverer of the helical structure of DNA, is credited with saying that "many men have slit their throats with Occam's razor.") Namely, the simplest explanation—in terms of smoothness or weight norm— is undesirable as it latches onto spurious correlations and overlooks the invariant patterns of interest.

In conclusion, the machine is not at fault: In search of minimal *average* error, the system prioritizes simple patterns able to correctly classify a majority of examples. Thus, background information is absorbed first, addressing $100 \cdot p^e = 90\%$ of training errors. At this stage, the noise dimensions serve two purposes. First, they are a route to zero training error, which we set as the machine's objective. Second, since minimizing the cross-entropy loss of a linear model under separable data converges to the maximum-margin classifier,[109] the noise dimensions are also useful to increase the margin of the resulting separating hyper-plane. With more data, we would transition from the over-parameterized regime ($d > n$) to the under-parameterized regime ($d < n$), making noise dimensions insufficient for memorization and leaving the slow feature as the sole path to zero training error. It is now appropriate to close this chapter by highlighting that the pitfalls of the simplify-and-memorize learning strategy only worsen when considering the chief learning setup in this book: out-of-distribution (ood) test data.

2.6 Failing to Generalize Out-of-Distribution

Applying ERM to (CoB) yields a machine with zero training error and maximum smoothness, by virtue of following a simplify-and-memorize learning strategy. While this is an optimal recipe under the iid assumption, what

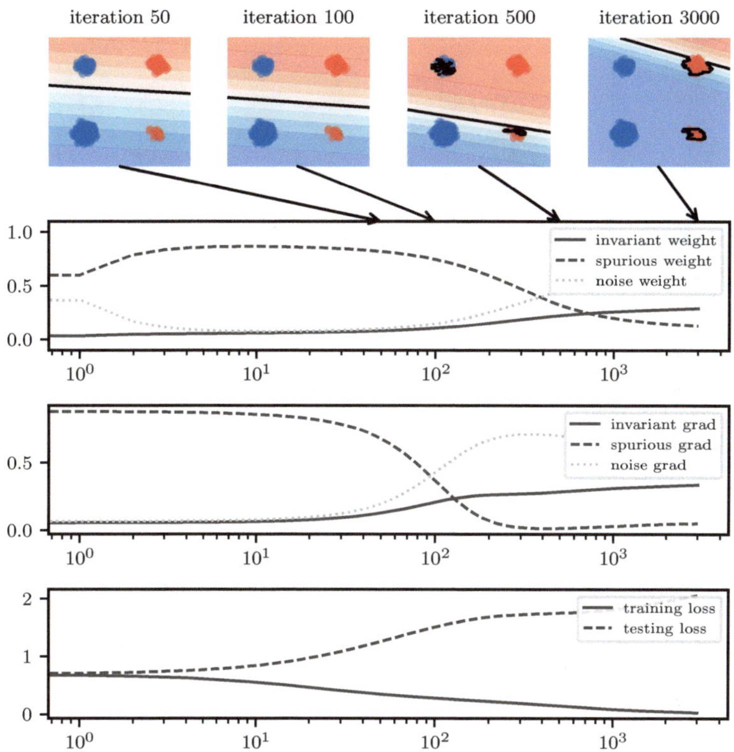

Figure 2.5: Illustration of the *simplify-and-memorize* learning strategy on (CoB). This problem contains 1000 examples with a one-dimensional slow feature of unit variance and perfect correlation (x-axis), a one-dimensional fast feature with a variance of 5 and 90% label correlation (y-axis), and 1198 noise features that jointly bear a perfect label correlation with the target (not visualized). To start, the learning machine grips quickly and tightly the higher-prominence fast feature. As the fast feature is insufficient to achieve zero training error, the machine looks for alternatives. Unfortunately, the tight grip starves all incoming gradient signals from the lower-variance invariant feature. So the machine resorts to using the storage provided by the noise dimensions to memorize the remaining mistakes, and thus achieves zero training error.

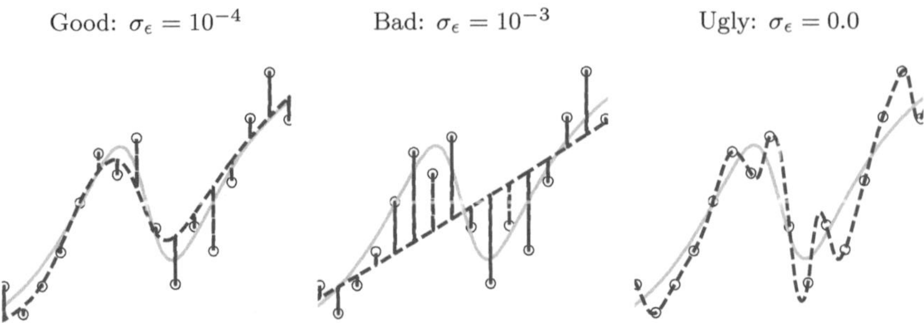

Figure 2.6: *Memorization, the Good, the Bad, and the Ugly.*[6] The variance σ_ϵ of noise features is proportional to the memorization storage of a nonlinear machine. Depending on σ_ϵ, various memorization behaviors occur, which influence how well the machine regresses a target function (y-axis) of a scalar core feature (x-axis). *Good* memorization happens when noise features provide capacity to store only the noise in the training data, allowing proper learning of its overall structure. *Bad* memorization happens when noise features provide sufficient storage to memorize each training example relative to a global mean, precluding the learning of its overall structure. *Ugly* memorization happens when noise features provide no storage, so the machine must interpolate the noisy training examples using the core feature alone.

is the performance of such a machine on out-of-distribution test data? To understand the important ood case, allow the parameter p^e in (CoB) to vary between training and testing data. In particular, let $p^e = 0.9$ for training data so that animals appear in their usual habitat happen 90% of the time. In contrast, let $p^e = 0.1$ for testing data, yielding pictures of animals appearing in their usual habitat only 10% of the time. The minority in training has become the majority in testing: While most animals appeared in their natural habitat during training, the test data depicts specimens mostly out of context. Such out-of-distribution test data is illustrated in the bottom-left plot of figure 2.7. Under this train-test distribution shift, we may rebrand the animal and background features as *invariant* and *spurious* features, where spurious is but a technical term for *variant*. The more important fact is that the background-target *correlation* is spurious, changing from 0.9 to 0.1 between training and testing distributions, while the animal-target correlation is invariant, remaining stable at 1.0 across training and testing data. This distributional shift is an instance of the "fully informative invariant features"[110] (fiif) problem, where the invariant correlation is able to address the classification problem perfectly, yet it is difficult to capture because the spurious correlation offers a simpler (smoother) explanation to attain zero training error.

The machine that simplifies-and-memorizes, as well as the one using invariant features, both achieve zero training error on (CoB), but they perform drastically differently under the testing environment. Specifically, the machine relying on spurious and noise features crumbles to 90% test error, while the one leveraging the invariant pattern maintains perfect classification accuracy. Therefore, training error is a myopic proxy to learning success, as finite datasets can only impose a limited amount of constraints and underspecify the learning problem at hand.[111,112] In Popperian terms, to falsify all but one zero training error solutions, one must (1) collect more diverse training data, (2) reduce the capacity of our function class, or (3) place additional assumptions about the invariant structures in the data generating process.

In some other cases, invariant features do not afford zero training error. To see this, consider a second version of the cow-on-the-beach problem, CoB-P, illustrated in figure 2.7 and implemented in algorithm 2.1. The CoB-P problem is two-dimensional—there are no noise features—and the two classes overlap slightly when taking only the invariant feature into account ($\sigma^2 = 1/9$). The invariant feature provides 75% training and testing accuracy, while the spurious feature enables 90% training accuracy and 10% testing accuracy. In this setup of partially informative invariant features (piif),[110] machines have no choice but to rely on spurious correlations to attain zero training error, even if these patterns can subsequently lead to large out-of-distribution errors. In contrast, the machine must sacrifice training accuracy to learn the invariant predictor, so the ERM principle is not appropriate for this type of learning problem.

A central conclusion of this chapter is that attaining zero training error does not imply learning the true input-target mechanisms. This idea is well known to philosophers of science. In her famous book *How the Laws of Physics Lie*, Nancy Cartwright articulates this perspective:

> There is no reason to think that the principles that best organize will be true, nor that the principles that are true will organize much ... The fundamental laws of physics do not describe true facts about reality. Rendered as descriptions of facts, they are false; amended to be true, they lose their fundamental, explanatory force.[113]

Cartwright further criticizes epistemologies that focus solely on minimizing training error:

> For any given set of phenomena, in principle there will always be more than one equally satisfactory explanation, and some of these explanations will be incompatible. Since not all them can be true, it is clear that truth is independent of satisfactoriness for explanation.[113]

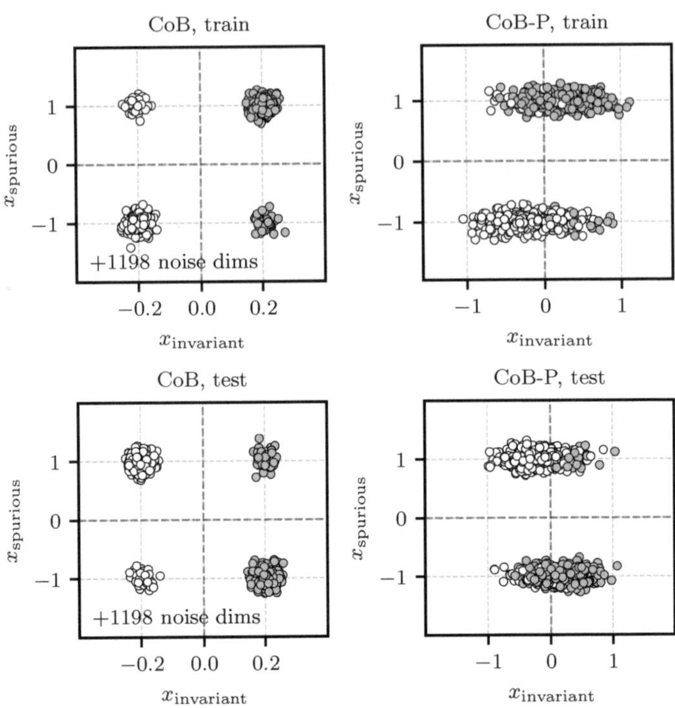

Figure 2.7: Illustration of *cow-on-the-beach* variations. On the left plots are the original cow-on-the-beach (CoB) problem. This is a problem with fully informative invariant features where the animal or foreground feature admits affords zero training error for both the training and testing distributions of examples. However, learning machines tend to simplify-and-memorize in this problem because the landscape, background, or spurious feature has five times more variance and it is learned first as a simplistic explanation. The remaining 1198 noise dimensions provide enough storage to memorize the training examples that do not comply with the spurious feature, thus achieving zero training error. On the right plots, we see a second version of the cow-on-the-beach problem, CoB-P. This is a problem with partially informative invariant features (piif), since the animal or foreground feature affords only 75% accuracy on both the training and testing distributions of examples. Conversely, the landscape, background, or spurious feature provides 90% training accuracy and therefore is preferred by the learning machine. However, the spurious feature provides only 10% test accuracy, while the invariant feature yields a predictor with a stable test accuracy of 75%. In sum, and for these two examples, ERM fails to capture the invariant pattern—either because it is easier to capture or because it provides better training performance—and discard the spurious correlation, yielding poor out-of-distribution performance in novel, yet relevant, distributions of test examples.

Next, we shall begin our exploration of alternatives to ERM for learning predictors with stronger generalization capabilities. The natural first stop on this path is to review the main framework that historically has been proposed to build robust predictive systems: the theory and practice of estimating causation from data.

Chapter 3

Theories of Causation

3.1   Introduction

We have an intimate relationship with cause and effect, the basic ingredients
of our daily ruminations, explanations, and plans. Can I still pay rent if
I quit my job? Why did the Federal Reserve raise interest rates? What
would have happened otherwise? Would I have been on time to my job
interview yesterday if I had taken the route Google Maps suggested? These
questions are causal because their answers involve predicting the outcomes
of our actions or the ones by others.

Causation is our language to categorize patterns of dependence. As
we'll see, the nuances of causation allow us to understand and communicate
various types of associations, each useful in different circumstances. In
fact, Turing awardee Judea Pearl argues that our ability to reason about
causation is what makes us human and sets us above other species:

> Historians of Homo sapiens such as Yuval Noah Harari and Steven
> Mithen are in general agreement that the decisive ingredient that
> gave our ancestors the ability to achieve global dominion about forty
> thousand years ago was their ability to create and store a mental
> representation of their environment, interrogate that representation,
> distort it by mental acts of imagination, and finally answer the "What
> if?" kind of questions. Examples are interventional questions ("What
> if I do such-and-such?") and retrospective or counterfactual questions
> ("What if I had acted different?"). No learning machine in operation
> today can answer such questions.[114]

Many other thinkers join Pearl in praising our abilities as causal thinkers.
Konrad Lorenz describes thinking as "acting in an imagined space;" novelist

Salman Rushdie calls humans "the storytelling animal;" and philosopher James Woodward adds that "in talking about causation, we cannot avoid employing categories and modes of thinking that reflect characteristically human concerns ... our goals lead us to care about certain sorts of relationships, those that support manipulation." Much, much earlier, the pre-Socratic philosopher Democritus (460–370 BC) was credited with "preferring to discover one true cause than gain the kingdom of Persia," while most medieval thinkers equated the concept of causation with God.

The primary purpose of causal language is to distinguish between spurious and invariant patterns of association. Spurious correlations dissolve when we intervene in the system of variables under study, making them valuable for prediction only under passive observation. In contrast, invariant patterns persist under intervention, offering greater potential for constructing systems that can predict and operate in dynamic environments.[115]

Spurious correlations have animated philosophical debates since the times of Karl Pearson and his student Udny Yule.[116] One vivid example of a *post hoc ergo propter hoc* fallacy—since this followed that, then that causes this—comes from Elliot Sober:

> Consider the fact that the sea levels in Venice and the cost of bread in Britain have both been on the rise in the past two centuries. Both, let us suppose, have monotonically increased. Imagine that we put this data in the form of a chronological list; for each date, we list the Venetian sea levels and the going price of British bread. Because both quantities have increased steadily with time, it is true that higher than average sea levels tend to be associated with higher than average bread prices. The two quantities are very strongly positively correlated.[117]

The previous quote suggests that the price of British bread is a good prediction of the Venetian sea levels. While most of us would deem this association strange and delusive, learning machines unabashedly exploit correlations like these when minimizing their error across the provided training data, as explained in the previous chapter.

A study published in *Nature* established a strong statistical dependence between children developing myopia and their exposure to nighttime ambient light, leading to the claim that "the absence of a daily period of darkness during early childhood is a potential precipitating factor in the development of myopia."[118] However, it was later revealed that the association was due to a *common cause*, parental myopia, that simultaneously influenced both observed factors. More specifically, parents with lower visual acuity tend to leave some lights on in their infants' nurseries, and they also pass on their myopia genes to their children.

These two examples describe spurious correlations rather than causal relations, because they would not remain stable against *interventions* in the variables under study. When passively observing the level of the Venetian seas (increasing due to global warming), we obtain a strong correlation with British bread prices (increasing due to inflation). However, if we were to actively intervene by draining all water from the Venetian seas, we would not expect our manipulation to cheapen British bread. Similarly, a strong correlation obtains when passively observing which children develop myopia and which children sleep with their lights on. To assert that "nighttime ambient light causes children myopia," however, would require performing an experiment or intervention that leaves night lights on for a random selection of children. If the incidence of myopia remains higher for the random subset of children with lights on, we would take this fact as evidence of a causal relation.

In contrast to spurious correlations, causal patterns hold invariant under manipulations on the system of variables under study. When we say "an increase in elevation causes a decrease in temperature," we expect the relationship from elevation to temperature to remain stable across changes in elevation. As we climb up, temperatures drop. (At least until we reach the tropopause. This pedantic comment illustrates that no causal relation remains invariant across all possible interventions.) Conversely, we do not expect the relationship from temperature to elevation to remain stable under interventions. For instance, if we light a fire at base camp, the temperature rises without affecting elevation. Causation therefore refines association, mapping the structure of the world as a network of directed relations that are stable under intervention. Thus, it feels natural to assert that humanlike AI systems will need to understand the language of causation to predict and act in a changing world.

Despite much praise and promise, causation has proven to be a slippery concept, perplexing philosophers since before Socrates. Dictionary definitions are overly generic (a reason for an action or condition) or circular (something that *brings about* an effect or a result). Causation has a distinctly temporal aspect—causes precede their effects in time—yet most theories in physics are invariant to time-reversal. Bertrand Russell, one of the most distinguished philosophers in the twentieth century, led a pack of intellectuals who grew frustrated with the notion of causation:

> All philosophers, of every school, imagine that causation is one of the fundamental axioms or postulates of science, yet, oddly enough, in advanced sciences such as gravitational astronomy, the word "cause" never occurs. Dr. James Ward, in his *Naturalism and Agnosticism*, makes this a ground of complaint against physics: the business of

science, he apparently thinks, should be the discovery of causes, yet physics never even seeks them. To me it seems that philosophy ought not to assume such legislative functions, and that the reason why physics has ceased to look for causes is that, in fact, there are no such things. The law of causality, I believe, like much that passes muster among philosophers, is a relic of a bygone age, surviving, like the monarchy, only because it is erroneously supposed to do no harm.[119]

Even earlier, Ernst Mach (1838–1916) expressed similar doubts in *The Science of Mechanics*:

> In speaking of cause and effect we arbitrarily give relief to those elements to whose connection we have to attend in the reproduction of a fact in the respect in which it is important to us. There is no cause nor effect in nature; nature has but an individual existence; nature simply is ... Much of the authority of the ideas of cause and effect is due to the fact that they are developed instinctively and involuntarily, and that we are distinctly sensible of having personally contributed nothing to their formation. We may, indeed, say, that our sense of causation is not acquired by the individual, but has been perfected in the development of the race. Cause and effect, therefore, are things of thought, having an economical office.[120]

Some prominent philosophers of causation, such as Nancy Cartwright, abandon all hopes in reducing causation to a single primitive notion, instead resorting to a pluralistic view where causation is relinquished as

> a concept with rough, shifting, porous boundaries, a congestion of different ideas and implications that can in various combinations be brought into focus for different purposes and in different contexts.[121]

Notably, causation depends on context—when reading "Socrates' drinking hemlock at dusk caused his death," we can easily identify "drinking hemlock" and not "at dusk" as the cause of death.[63] By using sports as an example, Stephen Mumford and Rani Lill Anjum illustrate how causal judgments are subjective and depend on the point of view:

> If we ask how a footballer's leg was broken, a physiotherapist might say it was due to the player's foot being twisted outwards when his body weight was all on that leg. A referee might say that the break was caused by a reckless tackle by an opponent who slid in from the side. And a fan might say that the leg was broken in a desperate late attempt to stop a goal. These are three different candidate explanations and all could be valid and true within a certain context.

However, this makes the question of what caused what at least partly an epistemological matter.[122]

Debates about the nature of causation continue in full force to this day,[123] with philosophers producing numerous theories about the subject.[63] These theories differ in several aspects, such as the *relata* involved: Some view causes and effects as events, while others propose that substances, objects, processes, facts, mental states, or symbolic variables constitute the causal relation. Similarly, some theories posit that causation operates at the *token* or instance level, while others consider that causal relations link variables at the *type* level. Token-level theories regard statements like "My granddad's habit of smoking four packs a day caused him lung cancer" as fundamental. Philosopher of causation Nancy Cartwright, an advocate of token-level causation, asserts:

> single cases of causings in the world are primary in an ontological sense: what exist are single cases of smoking causing lung cancer in different people at different times. The generic level is in a sense only derived, or resultant, due to repeated instances of single-case causes.[124]

Type-level theories consider a causal relation as the product of clustering single cases into general claims, such as "smoking causes cancer." Theories of causation also differ in their *level of abstraction*: While physicists believe that causation operates at the elementary particle level, for instance, social scientists adopt a broader perspective to study the effects of policies. Certain philosophers argue for *downward causation*, where high-level systems influence low-level systems, such as mental events affecting physical events. While *primitivists* regard causation as an irreducible concept, *reductionists* distill it to more basic concepts, and *pluralists* abandon such projects to consider causation, in words of Bryan Skyrms, as an "amiable jumble" of concepts that we use interchangeably as demanded by context. Stephen Mumford and Rani Lill Anjum, who also adopt the pluralist position, contend that causation leaves behind a plurality of symptoms, including probability raising, regularity, energy transference, manipulability, and difference making.[122] Finally, Nancy Cartwright argues that causal relations operate at the case level in terms of capacities—sometimes referred to by others as powers, tendencies, or dispositions.[125]

To make sense of this vast literature, this chapter reviews the most prominent theories of causation in terms of how they might help us build robust AI systems. As we tour different theories, it will become apparent that all philosophical theories of causation share a common feature with great predictive import: the invariance or stability of the causal relationship across relevant circumstances or environments. While this can be challenging material, it is my hope that reviewing the philosophy of causation will unearth valuable insights about what causation is (ontology), how it operates (metaphysics), and the manner in which we learn about it (epistemology), all of which help us predict the dynamic world we live in.

3.2 Classic Theories of Causation

3.2.1 Ancient and Rationalist Philosophers

The dialogues of Plato (428–348 BCE) contain the earliest inquiries about the epistemology of causation. Prominent examples include the *Timaeus* (which states that "everything which becomes must of necessity become owing to some cause"), and the *Phaedo*. In the latter text, a dialogue unfolding during the final hours of Socrates' life, Socrates reflects:

> When I was young, Cebes, I was tremendously eager for the kind of wisdom which they call investigation of nature. I thought it was a glorious thing to know the causes of everything, why each thing comes into being and why it perishes.

For Plato, causation inhabits the world of Forms, where essences—the necessary and sufficient conditions of all things—exist prior and independently of their earthly manifestations as substances. The cause of a pyramid (*what is it?*), Plato would argue, is the timeless, absolute, unchangeable tetrahedron.

Aristotle (384–322 BCE), a student of Plato, developed a finer theory of causation in his *Physics*, covering the four explanatory principles (*aitiai*) of something: material (*what is it made of?*), formal (*what is it?*), efficient (*what is its origin?*), and final causes (*what is its good?*). In contrast to Plato, who considered causation a relation found in the eternal world of Forms, Aristotle's worldly causation descended to Earth to propose a substance ontology where "we do not have knowledge of a thing until we grasped its cause." For example, a statue may be made of bronze (material cause), embody the shape of Socrates (formal cause), be crafted by an sculptor (efficient cause), and serve an aesthetic purpose (final cause). These are four perspectives on the statement "*X* causes *Y*," each providing a viewpoint about how "*Y* is understandable in the light of *X*."

Therefore, the Greeks understood causation as explanatory in character, with the etymological roots of *aitia* being on accusation, blame, and guilt, as used in a court of law. The Stoics later developed the notion of causal *necessity* by adopting an organic view of the cosmos ruled by *logos* or divine reason. Stoics were first to posit that nothing happens without a cause, and that causal relations leave as footprints an "exceptionless regularity."[126]

With the rise of Christianity after the fall of the Roman Empire, medieval philosophers developed various versions of causal necessity with a theological taste. These include biblical conservationism (God intervenes only as the first cause and later only through miracles), the occasionalism of Nicolas Malebranche (God is the sole cause behind all effects), the concurrentism of Thomas Aquinas (substances can be causes, but God contributes to the production and potency of their effects), and the preestablished harmony of Gottfried Leibniz (substances affect only themselves, with God instantiating the initial array of substances such that they appear to interact causally and harmoniously).

While Aristotle considered causation to be a feature of substances helpful for explanatory purposes, medieval philosophers shifted their focus and considered causation to be a footprint of deterministic laws. Menno Hulswit highlights this paradigm shift:

> Whereas the formal cause was thought to explain the stability of the world by explaining the structure of things, the laws of nature were thought to explain the stability of the world by explaining the *relations* between things.[126]

This new perspective, to which I will adhere in chapter 5, is a recurring theme in this book. Namely, causation and invariance are not attributes of observable substances, but attributes of the hidden mechanisms governing their evolution.

Later on, rational philosophers also embraced theological determinism as a key feature of causation—if we rewind an MP3 and hit play once more, we shall hear the same song. Two major rationalists of the sixteenth and seventieth centuries, René Descartes and Baruch Spinoza, restricted the domain of causation to the locomotion of physical bodies (a subset of Aristotle's efficient causation) and proposed appropriate refinements of causal necessity. Empiricist philosophers of the same period—such as Thomas Hobbes, John Locke, and Isaac Newton—gravitated instead toward the notion of causal possibility. Necessity is a feature manifested in a past causal relation, the empiricist would argue, while possibility is the causal power that a substance may or may not exert in the future. Newton made this distinction particularly vivid with his First Law of Motion, where inertia detaches causation from law-like behavior, denying that every event must have a cause.[126]

3.2.2 David Hume

David Hume (1711–1776) is the starting point of most discussions on the philosophy of causation. He considered causation to be nothing less than "the cement of the Universe," and he built his philosophical program around the epistemological question: *How do we acquire causal knowledge?* As we have seen in chapter 2, Hume proposes that we are a tabula rasa upon which all knowledge is imprinted from sense experience. However, Hume continues, no amount of sense experience can provide us with the knowledge to leap from particulars to laws—nor causal relations. In the Humean world, "events seem entirely loose and separate. One event follows another; but we never can observe any tie between them. They seem conjoined, but never connected."[62] Therefore, empirical data cannot bridge the insurmountable gap between the observed *constant conjunction* and the theorized *necessity*, the key to discover causal relations. Ludwig Wittgenstein (1929–1947) expressed similarly skeptical arguments in his *Tractatus Logico-Philosophicus*, where statement 5.1361 reads: "The events of the future cannot be inferred from those of the present. Superstition is the belief in the causal nexus."[127]

Hume presents his well-known skeptical argument about causal inference in this passage from *A Treatise of Human Nature*:

> Thus we remember to have seen that species of object we call flame, and to have felt that species of sensation we call heat. We likewise call to mind their constant conjunction in all past instances. Without any farther ceremony, we call the one cause and the other effect, and infer the existence of the one from that of the other.[60]

We infer causal relations, Hume argues, by unjustifiably summarizing past constant conjunctions into generalizable laws. This inductive reasoning requires the uniformity of nature: What has been will continue to be. However, attempting to logically justify this uniformity, Hume argues in his latter *Enquiry Concerning Human Understanding*, falls prey to circular reasoning:

> We have said, that all arguments concerning existence are founded on the relation of cause and effect; that our knowledge of that relation is derived entirely from experience; and that all our experimental conclusions proceed upon the supposition, that the future will be conformable to the past. To endeavour, therefore, the proof of this last proposition by probable arguments, or arguments regarding existence, must be evidently going in a circle, and taking that for granted, which is the very point in question.[62]

Despite his epistemological skepticism, Hume investigated how we estimate causal relations in everyday live, concluding that our assessments rest on two pillars. The first is regularity: observing the constant conjunction of two events, where one precedes another, and both happen within a reasonable degree of spatiotemporal contiguity. As he put it,

> An object precedent and contiguous to another, and where all the
> objects resembling the former are placed in like relations of precedence
> and contiguity to those objects that resemble the latter.[60]

The second element is anticipation, the *custom* or *habit* of the mind where,
upon sufficient repetition, we become psychologically acquainted with a
pattern and declare it a causal relation within the confines of our own
subjectivity:

> An object precedent and contiguous to another, and so united with
> it, that the idea of the one determined the mind to form the idea of
> the other, and the impression of the one to form a more lively idea of
> the other.[60]

Similar notions would appear much later in Eastern thought, notably in the
teachings of Nisargadatta Maharaj:

> Causality is in the mind, only; memory gives the illusion of continuity
> and repetitiveness creates the idea of causality. When things repeat-
> edly happen together, we tend to see a causal link between them. It
> creates a mental habit, but a habit is not a necessity.[128]

The second ingredient, which Hume believed to be "so necessary to the
subsistence of our species, and the regulation of our conduct, in every
circumstance of human life"[62] anticipated discussions about the subjective
character of causation, reviewed below.

3.2.3   Immanuel Kant

Immanuel Kant (1724–1804), who admitted that it was David Hume who
"first interrupted my dogmatic slumber and gave my investigations in the
field of speculative philosophy a completely different direction,"[129] offered in
Critique of Pure Reason[130] a reply to radical skepticism. As a philosopher
who in his inaugural dissertation claimed that "causation is nothing less
than the most fundamental principle of the form of the world," Kant found
himself caught in a philosophical battle between the skeptical empiricism of
David Hume and the dogmatic rationalism of René Descartes. As we have
just seen, Hume believed that all knowledge stems from experience, making
necessary or universal judgments impossible. But rational philosophers
like Descartes considered all experience doubtful, and defended rational
speculation as the only path toward necessary and universal knowledge. Kant
synthesized empiricism and rationalism into *transcendental idealism*, whereby
knowledge arises at the meeting point between the subject's predefined
mental structures and the world's raw sensory content.

Understanding Kant requires defining two types of judgments: analytic a priori and synthetic a posteriori. Analytic judgments are those true by definition, such as "Bachelors are unmarried." As with deductive reasoning, all the information in the conclusion of an analytic judgment is contained in its premise. Therefore, analytic judgments are universal, since their truth is noncontingent and verified regardless of the state-of-affairs in the external world. However, analytic arguments are non-ampliative, as they do not extend our knowledge. Synthetic judgments, on the other hand, rely on experience and are ampliative, being novel observations about the world that extend our knowledge. For example, the synthetic judgment "Bachelors age badly" provides no necessary or universal relation between "bachelor" and "aging badly," apart from the observed cases. Because particular cases cannot justify inductive generalizations into laws, synthetic judgments are ampliative but not universal. Neither analytic nor synthetic judgments alone can support the scientific program, which seeks to extend our knowledge through universal judgments, often involving new causal relations.

To bridge this gap, Kant's major innovation introduced synthetic a priori judgments, which he defined as *both* ampliative and universal. These judgments are possible, Kant argues, because our experience is facilitated through a collection of a priori mental structures, called the categories of knowledge. In his own words, Kant's solution

> rescues the a-priori origin of the pure concepts of the understanding
> and the validity of the general laws of nature as laws of the under-
> standing, in such a way that their use is limited only to experience,
> because their possibility has its ground merely in the relation of the
> understanding to experience, however, not in such a way that they
> are derived from experience, but that experience is derived from them,
> a completely reversed kind of connection which never occurred to
> Hume.[129]

As an example, if our brain were only able to perceive colors in grayscale, we could make this ampliative and universal judgment about all future observations: They will all be grayscale.

Kant considered his advance a Copernican revolution in epistemology. While Hume contended that our experience is mainly shaped by the external world, Kant argued that our experience is mainly shaped by the internal structures of our mind. And because these mental structures (or "prepro-cessing modules," or "user interfaces") are fixed, we can arrive at synthetic a priori judgments that are both universal and ampliative:

> Up to now it has been assumed that all our cognition must conform
> to the objects; but all attempts to find out something about them

> a-priori through concepts that would extend our cognition have, on this presupposition, come to nothing. Hence let us once try whether we do not get farther with the problems of metaphysics by assuming that the objects must conform to our cognition, which would agree better with the requested possibility of an a-priori cognition of them, which is to establish something about objects before they are given to us. This would be just like the first thoughts of Copernicus, who, when he did not make good progress in the explanation of the celestial motions if he assumed that the entire celestial host revolves around the observer, tried to see if he might not have greater success if he made the observer revolve and left the stars at rest.[130]

Quoting Irish Murdoch, "I can only choose within the world I see:" Our cognitive apparatus imposes certain restrictions about the catalog of stimuli that can possibly percolate into our consciousness. By carving out what cannot be possibly perceived, we obtain certain universal judgments about future data—by assuming invariances *in*, we obtain invariances *out*.

For Kant, knowledge arises out of the encounter between the a priori categories of knowledge of the subject and the a posteriori sense data from the world. In a parallel to Plato's model of *form* and *matter*, Kant argues that we never access the naked *noumena* or *thing-in-itself*, but instead experience the *phenomena* as preprocessed by our mental structures. Unlike Plato, however, Kant determines that Forms do not reside in some external realm but are provided by the subject's a priori mind structures. All knowledge is mind-dependent or, as Kant himself would perhaps say today, there is no such thing as *raw data*. Trading places with a confused moth, Alex Broadbent summarizes our discussion neatly:

> A moth bangs into a pane of glass, and cannot simply fly through it; the pane of glass constrains it. But clearly the moth's perceptual modalities also constrain what kind of thing it takes the pane of glass to be. Otherwise, it would not keep flying into the glass.[131]

Similarly, by filtering a vast potion of the combinatorially explosive amount of information rushing in from the world (invariance in), our cognitive apparatus lets us experience patterns and generalizations helpful for survival (invariance out). Consequently, different organisms perceive reality differently; for instance, mantis shrimps have up to sixteen photoreceptors that can see ultraviolet, visible, and polarized light.

To grasp Kant's perspective on causation, we must first understand the basics of his multilayered epistemological system. On a first layer, the transcendental aesthetic, the raw and chaotic data of the world is arranged into the a priori intuitions of space and time. For Kant, space and time are not constituents of the world, but human "user interfaces"[132] affording only partial access to reality. This spatiotemporal data is then processed by the transcendental analytic, a second layer containing the twelve categories of knowledge. These are the necessary conditions of our experience, enabling a priori judgments and classifying the quantity, quality, relation, and modality of objects. One of these categories is causation, which Kant asserts should "either be grounded completely a priori in the understanding, or must be entirely given up as a mere phantom of the brain." (Schopenhauer, a contemporary of Kant, would argue that causation is indeed the *only* category of knowledge.) Paralleling Newton's laws of motion, Kant built a theory of causation by asserting three *analogies of experience*. They establish that space and time are permanent, that every event has a cause, and that all phenomena are causally interconnected. Thus, Kantian causation is a mind-dependent tool that arranges the vast incoming data from the noumenal world into our familiar conscious experience.

Kantian knowledge, in essence, arises at the meeting point between a priori mental structures and a posteriori worldly content. (One millennium before Kant, Buddhist monk and philosopher Vasubandhu also proposed that the objects of experience are only representations about the unknowable things-in-themselves.) This *togetherness principle* is summarized in the most quoted passage in the entire *Critique*:

> *Thoughts without content are empty; intuitions without concepts are blind.* It is thus just as necessary to make the mind's concepts sensible (that is, to add an object to them in intuition) as it is to make its intuitions understandable (to bring them under concepts). Further, these two faculties or capacities cannot exchange their functions: the understanding is not capable of intuiting anything, and the senses are not capable of thinking anything. Only from their unification can cognition arise.[130]

I would like to argue that Kant's *togetherness principle* enjoys a natural interpretation in the context of learning machines, for two reasons. First, I see a parallel between Kantian categories and function classes. These two are chosen initially and independently, determine the structure of possible experience, and are *empty* in the absence of training examples. Second, Kantian sense intuitions are analogous to training data, since both are beyond understanding (*blind*) without a function class. Therefore, we may paraphrase Kant as "function classes without data are empty; data without function classes are blind." Pushing the analogies a bit further, Hume's force of habit resembles the empirical risk minimization learning algorithm, whereby we estimate relations by repeatedly observing input-output conjunctions.

3.3 Regularity Theories

The regularity theory of causation, spearheaded by David Hume, considers the causal relation as a summary of constant conjunctions. Regularity theories are metaphysically lean, with extreme versions subscribing to what is known as *Humean supervenience*:

> the doctrine that all there is to the world is a vast mosaic of local matters of particular fact, just one little thing and then another. ... For short: we have an arrangement of qualities, and that is all. There is no difference without difference in the arrangement of qualities. All else supervenes on that.[133]

In the words of Stathis Psillos, these theories assume that the world is indeed "regularities all the way down." That is, regardless of our efforts, the inescapable ingredient used to describe causal relations is statistical regularity. While causation is often intuitively understood as a productive force leaving statistical regularities as footprints, Humeans consider regularities as fundamental, with causation being a derived language used to discuss patterns of association.

Regularity theories are excessively stringent if *constant* conjunction is taken as literal *necessity*. While we assert that "smoking causes cancer," for instance, some lifelong smokers do not develop the disease. Philosophers of causation, such as Nancy Cartwright and James Woodward, argue that it is a mistake to catalog regularities as either laws followed *sans* exception or as mere accidents. Instead, invariance comes in gradations, where *law* is an honorific title granted to those generalizations with a particularly wide range of application. Woodward argues, in fact, that no scientific law is without exceptions: The law of gravitation breaks apart in very strong fields, and the equations of general relativity are not expected to apply below Planck length scales.[134]

One refinement to regularity, less stringent than necessity, is to define a cause as an *Insufficient but Necessary part of a condition which is itself Unnecessary but Sufficient for the effect*, or INUS.[135] Phyllis Illari and Federica Russo illustrate the INUS condition with the following example:

> The idea is that when we say that the short-circuit caused the fire, it is insufficient to cause the fire, because it needs other conditions too, such as oxygen. However, it is nonredundant, because in this particular type of set of conditions, it in fact produces the spark. This set of conditions, which includes the short-circuit and oxygen, is unnecessary for fire, because fires can start other ways. However, that whole set of conditions, together, on this kind of occasion, is sufficient to start the fire.[124]

The INUS condition, also known as NESS for *Necessary Element of a Sufficient Set* in the court of law,[63] facilitates a regularity treatment in cases of *overdetermination*. For instance, consider a company board where four out of five members vote to replace their president. None of the four votes is decisive, but each belongs to at least one subset of three votes in favor that is sufficient for the outcome. Thus, INUS and NESS tests would consider each of the four votes as causal in the decision to replace the president.

Another relaxation of constant conjunction, pioneered by Hans Reichenbach (1891–1953), is to consider causal relations as probabilistic. Reichenbach developed two distinct theories of probabilistic causation. His early theory treated probability as an epistemological tool, suggesting that observations increase the likelihood of certain causal laws, which themselves are not reducible to probabilistic relations. Proposing an interesting predecessor to Belkin's razor, Reichenbach favored smooth and simple rules to select among laws explaining the observed data. In his later theory, Reichenbach gave ontological priority to probability and did not regard causal relations as primitive. Reichenbach's later work framed the direction of time in terms of causal relations, and the direction of causal relations in terms of frequentist conditional probabilities.[136]

Within his later theory of causation, Reichenbach's major contribution is the *principle of common cause* (PCC), reading "if an improbable coincidence has occurred, there must exist a common cause [for the correlated events]."[136] More formally, the PCC states that if two random variables X and Y are statistically dependent, then there exists a third variable Z—which may or may not coincide with either X or Y—that causally influences both.[137] Epistemologically, common explanations Z are evidence against the existence of a direct causal relation between two events X and Y:

> If an improbable coincidence has occurred, there must exist a common cause. In our daily life we often employ inferences of this kind. Suppose both lamps in a room go out suddenly. We regard it as improbable that by chance both bulbs burned out at the same time, and look for a burned-out fuse.[136]

Figure 3.1 illustrates Reichenbach's PCC, enumerating four potential reasons behind the observed statistical dependence between X and Y. These are (a) X causes Y, (b) Y causes X, (c) there exists a *fork* structure, where an unobserved variable or *confounder* Z causes both X and Y, or (d) there exists a *collider* structure, where an unobserved variable Z conditions the examples we observe from X and Y and produces a selection bias. As discussed in the next chapter, Reichenbach's PCC is a useful tool for understanding certain statistical paradoxes—such as Simpson's and Berkson's—and for developing causal discovery methods.

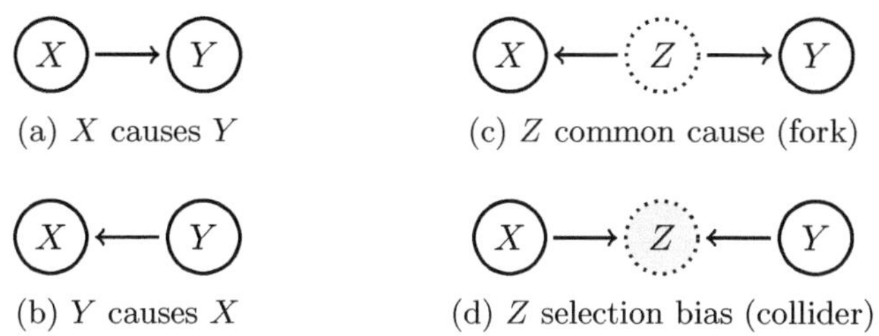

(a) X causes Y

(c) Z common cause (fork)

(b) Y causes X

(d) Z selection bias (collider)

Figure 3.1: Reichenbach's principle of common cause (PCC). Any statistical dependence between two random variables X and Y can be explained because either (a) X causes Y, (b) Y causes X, (c) there exists an unobserved variable or confounder Z that causes both X and Y, or (d) there exists an unobserved variable Z conditioning the collection of paired data from X and Y.

Reichenbach's PCC is a central result that formalizes the oft-cited mantra "correlation does not imply causation." Without prior knowledge at our disposal, the PCC states that we cannot identify which of the four causal structures in figure 3.1 accounts for the observed statistical dependence between X and Y. This underscores why causal inferences from observational data must either rely on additional assumptions or take a leap of faith. One example of a common cause structure follows when we let Z denote *drop in atmospheric pressure*, X denote *drop in the mercury level of a barometer*, and X denote *occurrence of a storm*. Here, Z is a common cause or confounder that influences both X and Y, resulting in the causal structure $X \leftarrow Z \rightarrow Y$. The absence of a causal connection from X to Y is relevant information for an acting agent who, if interested in preventing a storm, should abandon all hopes of achieving so by tampering with the barometer. This is because, as we will see in the next section, the relationship from *drop in the mercury level of a barometer* to *occurrence of a storm* is not invariant under intervention.

Regularity theories are not without their critics. First, statistical dependencies may arise by chance in small samples, resulting in amusing spurious correlations,[138] such as the relation between Venetian seas and British bread prices described at the beginning of this chapter. Second, lawfulness does not imply causation. To exemplify, the law of identity ($X = X$)—dating back to Plato's *Theaetetus*—is void of any causal significance. Third, despite Reichenbach's preference for smoothness, the simplest explanation is not always the causal one. For instance, consider $X = f(Z) + N$ and $Y = f(Z) + N'$, where f is an intricate nonlinear function and (N, N') are some independent noise random variables. In this case, the two causal relationships from $Z \rightarrow X$ and $Z \rightarrow Y$ both describe complex patterns, while the noncausal statistical dependence between X and Y exhibits a simple linear pattern. Fourth, both deterministic and probabilistic regularity theories of causation struggle with token causation: It is acceptable to say that "Martin's letter caused Paula's joy" in the absence of regularity, since Martin only mailed Paula once. To escape this issue, singularist theories of causation, espoused by philosophers such as Nancy Cartwright, Elisabeth Anscombe, and Curt John Ducasse, posit that causation happens at the token level, but clustering similar instances allows causal reasoning via regularity. In the words of Ducasse:

> The causal relation is essentially a relation between concrete individual events; and it is only so far as these events exhibit likeness to others, and can therefore be grouped with them into kinds, that it is possible to pass from individual causal facts to causal laws.[139]

The framework of structural equation models introduced in the next chapter offers a mathematical formalization to unify token-level and type-level causation. Fifth, low-probability events happen all the time. While rare events are difficult to analyze in terms of statistical regularity, they are often most informative to support theories (in terms of accumulating Salmonian *damn strange coincidences*) or refute them (by falsifying their invariances).

3.4 Interventionist Theories

For the interventionist, causation is valuable because it serves as a tool to control the environment. For this control to be effective, the causal relation must "hold as we change the system whose behavior we are trying to explain." Therefore, causal patterns are "invariant relationships that are potentially exploitable for purposes of manipulation and control."[140] Invariance, philosopher of causation James Woodward argues, is not an all-or-nothing concept, as it inhabits the entire spectrum from accidental to lawful behavior:

> Invariance is the key feature a relationship must possess if it is to count as causal or explanatory. Intuitively, an invariant relationship remains stable or unchanged as various other changes occur. Invariance, as I understand it, does not require exact or literal truth; I count a generalization as invariant or stable across certain changes if it holds up to some appropriate level of approximation across those changes. ... I urge that we should relativize the notion of invariance and recognize that a relation can be invariant under some changes and interventions but not under others ... When we say that a relation

is invariant, we have said something incomplete; we need to specify under which changes the relation is (or is not) invariant.[140]

Similarly, statistician Paul Holland summarized the interventionist account as "no causation with manipulation."[141] Sociologists Donald Campbell and Thomas Cook argued that "X causes Y" means "I could vary Y by means of varying X."[142] Woodward suggested that causal explanations "tell us how, if we were able to change the value of one or more variables, we could change the value of anther variables."[140] Similar notions of causal invariance have appeared in scholarly literature from other fields of knowledge. For instance, Kevin Hoover defines the causal relation as follows:

> X causes Y if control of X renders Y controllable. A causal relation, then, is one that is invariant to interventions in X in the sense that if someone or something can alter the value of X, the change in Y follows in a predictable fashion.[143]

Philosopher of physics Michael Redhead argued that causal relations display a feature he called *robustness*:

> a necessary condition for stochastic causality, that sufficiently small disturbances of the cause do not affect the functional form of the causal connection. ... $P(Y|X)$ is robust iff that probability is insensitive to extremely small changes in how X comes about.[144]

British econometrician David Hendry considered that "X causes Y if and only if the parameters of $P(Y \mid X)$ stay fixed as we vary the parameters of the distribution of X." All these examples illustrate the rich history of invariance in defining the causal relation under the interventionist account.

3.4.1 Example: Hooke's Law

Consider Hooke's law $F = -kx$, illustrated in figure 3.2a. This law describes the restoration force F of a spring with a characteristic constant factor k when elongated at a distance x from its rest position. Under the interventionist account, Hooke's law qualifies as a causal relationship: For a certain range of interventions, Hooke's formula describes the behavior of the system under manipulation. For instance, the law allows us to understand the restoration force of a spring as we elongate it to different positions, or the behavior of another spring with a different characteristic constant factor. These are all successful predictions to *what-if-things-had-been-different* questions. However, Hooke's law is not universal, as this first-order formula would be invalid if we subject our spring to extreme temperatures or elongations, or if we use spring materials with nonlinear elasticity.

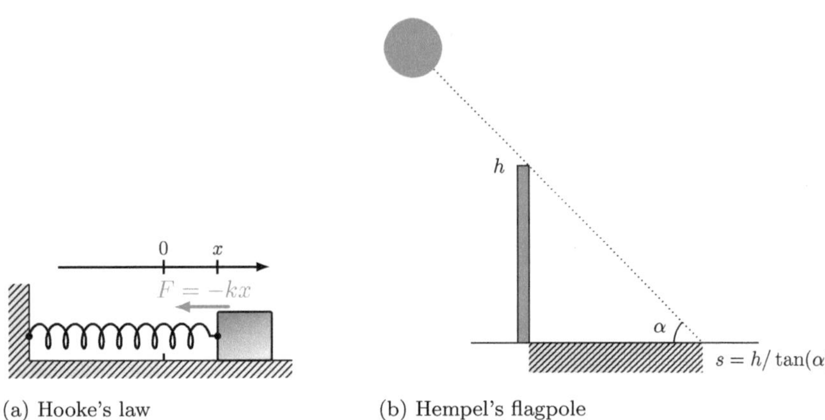

(a) Hooke's law   (b) Hempel's flagpole

Figure 3.2: (a) Hooke's law describes the restoring force $F = -kx$ of a spring with constant k when elongated at a distance x from its rest position. Hooke's law qualifies as a causal relation, since it allows us to answer several *what-if-things-had-been-differently* questions about the behavior of the spring. In particular, we can use Hooke's law to predict the outcome of certain interventions or manipulations on the system, such as the restoration force of the spring at different positions, or the change in force by replacing the spring with another one with a different constant. However, Hooke's law is not universal, since it breaks down under very hot or cold temperatures, extreme elongations damaging the spring, or materials with nonlinear elasticity. (b) Hempel's flagpole, where it is equally simple to explain the length of the flagpole's shadow s in terms of its height h and the elevation of the sun α, or to explain the height of the flagpole in term's of the length of its shadow and the elevation of the sun. However, we only consider the first of these two explanations as causal, because the prediction of the *explanandum* (shadow length) is invariant across interventions on the *explanans* (pole height).

3.4.2 What Is an Intervention?

We may go about building a system of variables with two different attitudes. One approach is to passively observe the system at work. The resulting observational data reveal correlations useful as basic ingredients to construct predictive rules. In statistics, predicting certain variables from others by using observational data amounts to *conditioning*. For example, we may enjoy watching pedestrians from our fourth-floor office window and conclude that the likelihood of rain R is much higher when people carry open umbrellas U. This correlation is captured by the observational conditional distribution $P(R \mid U)$. That is, the collected observational data helps to predict likelihood of rain U from number of open umbrellas U.

A second approach to understanding a system is to actively manipulate or intervene in its variables. Returning to our model predicting rain from umbrellas, we could perform an intervention to instruct all pedestrians to close their umbrellas. This experiment is represented by the interventional conditional distribution $P(R \mid \mathrm{do}(U \leftarrow 0))$. As it turns out, the rain does not subside and everyone ends up drenched in water, proving that our predictive model going from umbrellas to rain is *not invariant* under intervention. To the interventionist, the absence of correlation in the interventional distribution suggests that there is no causal relationship from umbrellas to rain. Conversely, a predictive model from rain to umbrellas would likely be invariant under intervention—if we could stop the rain at will, most people would close their umbrellas to enjoy the sun. Woodward summarizes as:

> A necessary and sufficient condition for a generalization to describe a causal relationship is that it be invariant under some appropriate set of interventions ... an intervention on X with respect to Y changes the value of X in such a way that if any change occurs in Y, it occurs only as a result of the change in the value of X and not from other source when a relationship is invariant under at least some interventions in this way, it is potentially usable for purposes of control—in the sense that, though it may not as a matter of fact be possible to carry out an intervention on X, it is nonetheless true that if an intervention on X were to occur, this would be a way of manipulating or controlling the value of Y.[140]

In summary, observing umbrellas is effective for *diagnosing* weather conditions and deciding whether to carry an umbrella. However, tampering with the number of open umbrellas is an ineffective *treatment* to control the weather. This distinction arises because a diagnosis involves observation, while a treatment requires intervention—two distinct modes of understanding a system of variables.

3.4.3 Range of Interventions

By stating that a causal relation is invariant across a certain *range* of interventions, we are distinguishing the conditions under which the relationship is invariant from those under which the relation breaks apart. Drawing this boundary is a different exercise from listing the causal variables of interest or the functional forms relating each other. Typically, demarcating the range of interventions or relevant environments $\mathcal{E}$ is done approximately rather than precisely:

> Imprecision is allowable in the specification of the domain over which an explanatory generalization holds but not acceptable when specifying the generalization itself ... we can operate perfectly well with domains with vague boundaries, because often we can know that we are within those boundaries even if we don't know exactly what they are ... Those who appeal to explanatory generalizations that are not exceptionless laws typically are able to recognize that they are within the domain of invariance of those generalizations and are able to see how they can be used to answer a range of what-if-things-had-been-different questions. Information that is not epistemically accessible to users, such as information about the exact boundaries of domains of invariance or the full range of circumstances in which a generalization will break down, is not information that is needed to successfully explain.[140]

Therefore, and as put forward by Curt John Ducasse, all causal relations are local: "X causes Y over the range of interventions $\mathcal{E}$."[139] Similarly, Ellery Eells considered that causal relations are contingent with respect to the population of cases under study.[145] The issue of developing algorithms that are aware of their operating conditions will be addressed in chapter 11, which focuses on uncertainty estimations.

Perhaps surprisingly, none of our best-regarded physical laws are invariant across all ranges of interventions. For example, the law of ideal gases breaks down under extremely high pressures, Maxwell's equations are invalid at scales where quantum-mechanical effects dominate, Newton's Law of Gravitation does not apply in very strong fields, and Einstein's General Relativity is not expected to apply below Planck scales where quantum gravitational effects arise.[140] While not universal, these theories deserve the honorific title of *law* because they answer *what-if-things-had-been-different questions* about their phenomena across a remarkably wide range of interventions.

3.4.4 Autonomy of Interventions

Causal relations do not exist in isolation—they are ingredients of larger systems, each feeding information to one another. To ease the study of big causal structures, the interventionist must assume a second invariance condition: When performing an intervention in one causal relation, the manipulation must not affect other causal relations. The central notion of *modular* or *autonomous* causal mechanisms originated in econometrics with the work of Ragnar Frisch[146] in 1938, and it was further developed in 1944 by his assistant and later Nobel laureate, Trygve Haavelmo.[147]

Drawing on the everyday experience of driving a car, Haavelmo argues that good representations of causal systems are *autonomous*:

> If we should make a series of speed tests with an automobile, driving on a flat, dry road, we might be able to establish a very accurate functional relationship between the pressure on the gas throttle (or the distance of the gas pedal from the bottom of the car) and the corresponding maximum speed of the car. And the knowledge of this relationship might be sufficient to operate the car at a prescribed speed. But if a man did not know anything about automobiles, and he wanted to understand how they work, we should not advise him to spend time and effort in measuring a relationship like that. Why? Because (1) such a relation leaves the whole inner mechanism of a car in complete mystery, and (2) such a relation might break down at any time, as soon as there is some disorder or change in any working part of the car. ... We say that such a relation has very little autonomy, because its existence depends upon the simultaneous fulfillment of a great many other relations, some of which are of a transitory nature. On the other hand, the general laws of thermodynamics, the dynamics of friction, etc., etc., are highly autonomous relations with respect to the automobile mechanism, because these relations describe the functioning of some parts of the mechanism irrespective of what happens in some other parts.[147]

Understanding car acceleration in terms of gas pedal depression, Haavelmo argues, is a brute portrayal of how cars work. In particular, this *coarse* representation fails to answer relevant what-if-things-had-been-differently questions, for instance concerning vehicles that are out of gas or missing an engine. In contrast, a *fine* representation of the car in terms of mechanics and thermodynamics yields a representation with a higher degree of autonomy and ability to predict under intervention. As Woodward suggests, autonomy, invariance, and prediction under intervention are deeply intertwined, where "the degree of autonomy of a relationship has to do with whether it would remain stable or invariant under various possible changes."[140] In essence, we value autonomous or *disentangled* representations because they pull apart complex systems into pieces that can be manipulated and understood in isolation.

The seminal work of Haavelmo placed autonomy at the heart of discussions about causation. Over time, Haavelmo's autonomy evolved into various notions, including Skyrm's resiliency (1977),[148] Wigner's independence between laws and their initial conditions (1979),[57] Redhead's robustness (1987),[144] Aldrich's autonomy (1989),[149] Mitchell's stability (1997),[150] Hendry's exogeneity,[151] Pearl's Causal Markov assumption (2000),[152] and Schölkopf's independence of causal mechanisms (2012).[153] Assuming autonomy is a *ceteris paribus* clause (everything non intervened remains the same) related to the Duhem-Quine thesis, which asserts the impossibility of testing any hypothesis in isolation without assuming certain background conditions. Rephrasing the Duhmen-Quine thesis in causal language, we arrive to the "No cause in, no cause out" aphorism of Nancy Cartwright:

> Without antecedent information it is no more possible to establish a causal claim via a regularity than it is to demonstrate a singular cause directly; and in both cases the inputs must include causal information. ... Singular claims are not just input for inferring causal laws; they are the output as well.[125]

Throughout the rest of this book, I would like to extend Cartwright's aphorism to claim "No invariance in, no invariance out."

The concepts of autonomy and invariance under intervention are closely related. In one sense, when asserting that a causal relation $X \to Y$ is invariant across interventions on X, we imply the joint probability distribution factorization

$$P(X,Y) = P(X) \cdot P(Y \mid X).$$

This factorization suggests that tampering with the distribution of the cause $P(X)$ does not affect or influence the cause-to-effect conditional distribution $P(Y \mid X)$. Conversely, stating that two causal relations $X \to Y$ and $X' \to Y'$ are autonomous introduces a similar invariance assumption, whereby tampering with one relation does not affect or influence the other.

These two assumptions about invariance are encompassed by the principle known as the independence of causal mechanisms (ICM):[154]

> The causal generative process of a system's variables is composed of autonomous modules that do not inform or influence each other. In the probabilistic case, this means that the conditional distribution of each variable given its causes (its mechanism) does not inform or influence the other mechanisms.[154]

As an example, consider the joint distribution $P(A, T)$ of altitudes and temperatures of cities worldwide.[137] Assuming that an increase in altitude causes a decrease in temperature, the joint distribution follows the natural or causal factorization

$$P(T, A) = P(T \mid A) \cdot P(A).$$

According to the ICM assumption, the marginal distribution $P(A)$ of altitudes does not contain any information about and does not influence the invariant causal relation implemented by the conditional distribution $P(T \mid A)$ of temperatures given altitude values. The factorization $P(T \mid A) \cdot P(A)$ is in that sense disentangled—if we intervene in altitude, nature would render the appropriate temperature using the same invariant mechanism $P(T \mid A)$. In contrast, the anti-causal factorization $P(A \mid T)P(T)$ disrupts autonomy. Specifically, an intervention in atmospheric pressure would simultaneously require adjusting the anti-causal conditional distribution $P(T \mid A)$ to model what would really happen in the physical world—namely, the altitude would remain unaffected by our manipulation of atmospheric pressure.

As with any assumption, autonomy can fail in certain situations. Such failures abound in psychology and economics, where interventions are *fat-handed* or *structure-altering*, meaning their impact extends beyond the mechanism under intervention.

3.4.5   Criticisms

The interventionist account has been subject to multiple criticisms. First and foremost, the *ability* to manipulate is a largely subjective, agent-dependent definition of causation. In discussing the work of Robin G. Collingwood,[155] Menno Hulswit gives an example where the causal narrative shifts depending on the subject's interventional reach:

> According to Collingwood, however, this selection is by no means arbitrary: "for any given person, the cause of a given thing is that one of its conditions which he is able to produce or prevent" ... For example, from the driver's point of view, the cause of a car accident may be that he drove too hard, while from the county surveyor's point of view, it may be a defective road surface, and from the motor manufacturer's point of view, it may be a defective design. In this sense of the word cause, only persons that are *practically* concerned with certain kinds of event can form opinions about their causes. "For a mere spectator there are no causes."[126]

This duality between intervener agent and intervened world, the critic would push on, is a matter of point of view. It is reasonable to argue that the world has a unified existence, and that the separation between subject and object is merely an artifact from our conscious experience. Just as blurry is is the dividing line between observation and intervention. According to your present experience, isn't observation all there is? Interventions are a special kind of observation, often accompanied by proprioception or haptic perception, that we imbue with particular significance and physical grounding. Observation is, from the perspective of the world, impossible without intervention: A mercury-in-glass thermometer must absorb some of the temperature from the measuring body, and some interpretations of quantum mechanics suggest that conscious observers determine how wave functions collapse. An act of observation is always an *act*, an intervention into the world. Causation, when understood in terms of interventions, is inescapably subjective: My interventions are your observations, and your interventions are my observations.

Second, the interventionist account requires the existence of *free* agents.

> An event X is a cause of a distinct event Y just in case bringing about the occurrence of X would be an effective means by which a free agent could bring about the occurrence of Y.[156]

The freedom of the agent is crucial because if their interventions were correlated with other external factors, it would be impossible to disambiguate the impact of the (no longer freely chosen) intervention from its confounders. If agency theories rely on our "direct personal experience of doing one thing and thence achieving another,"[156] does this imply that causation did not exist before humans?

Third, the interventionist account faces criticism for being circular, as argued by Menno Hulswit:

> Another important objection against the agency approach is that it begs the question. The idea of producing or preventing one thing by producing or preventing another thing appears to presuppose the concept of causation. The concepts of producing, preventing, manipulating, controlling, bringing about, and so on, are all causal concepts. And thus, it does not make us any wiser.[126]

Woodward elaborates on the circularity argument with a more technical tone:

> At least for the purposes of defining the notion of an intervention the notion of a causal mechanism or direct cause is taken as primitive and the notion of an intervention is defined in terms of it ... If, as Pearl apparently intends, we understand this to include the requirement that an intervention on X_i must leave intact the causal mechanism

if any, that connects X_i to its possible effects Y, then an obvious
worry about circularity arises, if we want to use the notion of an
intervention to characterize what it is for X_i to cause Y.[63]

Issues of circularity also arise when discussing autonomous causal relations,
since "for a relation to be causal, it has to be invariant under changes in
other causal relations, thus referring to causes in the *definiens* as well as
in the *definiendum*."[63] In essence, we are launched into an infinite regress
because all interventions must be themselves caused—a dilemma medieval
philosophers sidestepped by invoking God as an *unintervened intervener.*

In *Phenomenological Causality*, Janzing and Garrido-Mejia tackle the
issue of circularity by embracing subjectivity. The authors consider that
causal structures derive from the *elementary* actions that an agent can
perform. Specifically, their work suggests that "X causes Y" when the
elementary actions in the system (1) change $P(X)$ while preserving $P(Y \mid X)$,
or (2) preserve $P(X)$ while changing $P(Y \mid X)$. To illustrate how causation
arises from elementary actions, the authors present a simple example of
four *micro-variables* $X_1 \rightarrow Y_1$ and $X_2 \leftarrow Y_2$ aggregating into two *macro-
variables* $X = X_1 + X_2$ and $Y = Y_1 + Y_2$. Then, for agents with elementary
manipulating X_1 and Y_1, we obtain the casual relation $X \rightarrow Y$. In contrast,
for agents with elementary actions manipulating X_2 and Y_2, the reverse
causal relation $Y \rightarrow X$ is true.

Fourth, the interventionist account relies on the feasibility of interventions. How do we study the outcomes of interventions that we cannot
implement due to practical, ethical, or economical constraints? How could
we judge causal statements where interventions are expensive, unethical,
or impossible, such as "The 1989 San Francisco earthquake was caused by
friction between continental plates?"[63] Interventionist accounts often evade
this critique by arguing that we should be able to reason about manipulations that, while impossible to implement, can be conceived and theorized
about. These mental experiments, imagining what could happen in different
worlds, are the signature of the counterfactual theory of causation, reviewed
next.

3.5 Counterfactual Theories

The counterfactual—contrary to the fact—theory of causation, pioneered by
David Lewis,[157] evaluates the truth of causal statements "X causes Y" as
the truth of the counterfactual statements "If X hadn't occurred, Y would
not have occurred:"

> We think of a cause as something that makes a difference, and the
> difference it makes must be a difference from what would have hap-

pened without it. Had it been absent, its effects—some of them, at least, and usually all—would have been absent as well.[157]

Evaluating the truth of counterfactual statements hinges upon (1) the existence of a *possible world* where X and Y occur, and (2) that world being closer to the actual world than any world where X does occur but Y does not occur. Consider, for instance, the causal statement "My alarm clock running out of batteries caused me to be late to the job interview," together with its counterfactual translation "If my alarm clock had not run out of batteries, I would not have been late to the job interview." That counterfactual statement is true if, among all possible worlds where "My alarm clock had not run out of batteries" the closest one to the actual world is one where "I was not late to the job interview." Therefore, *grosso modo*, the counterfactual theory considers the causal relation as invariant across relevant possible worlds.

To find the closest possible world, Lewis introduces the concept of a *miracle*, which acts as a surgical intervention on the course of events. In the example from the previous paragraph, we construct the closest possible world by (1) running the original history of events until the very moment where the alarm clock was supposed to ring, (2) performing a miracle to ring the battery-depleted clock, and (3) allowing the intervened world to continue its course of events thereafter. If I am not late to my job interview in this closest possible world, then the aforementioned counterfactual and causal statements are true. Therefore, miracles intervene in the *difference that makes the difference* so we can verify or falsify putative causal claims.

As a brief historical note, some scholars argue that David Hume conceived the counterfactual theory of causation in the following passage from the *Enquiry*:

> We may define a cause to be an object, followed by another, and where all the objects, similar to the first, are followed by objects similar to the second. Or in other words, where, if the first object had not been, the second never had existed.[62]

However, I interpret these two sentences as expressing the conditional probability statements $P(E \mid C) = 1$ and $P(E \mid \neg C) = 0$, respectively. These statements do not reference other possible worlds but rather describe the necessity condition of causal relations commonly accepted under the regularity theory.

3.5.1 Criticisms

Counterfactual dependence is sufficient but not necessary for causation. This insight led to several critiques of the counterfactual theory of causation, which I review next. First and foremost, the counterfactual theory of causation demands *modal realism*. This philosophical stance contends that all possible worlds are *as real as* the actual world, that each world is causally isolated, and that the difference between worlds is a matter of indexing. Without modal realism, the counterfactual theory would encounter the *paradox of material implication*: Since the putative cause X never happened in the actual world, the counterfactual material implications "**not** X **or** Y" are vacuously true. The lofty proposal of modal realism has been criticized as unscientific, since there are no experiments possible in the real world that could falsify a causal claim happening in some other, isolated counterfactual world. We never learn about the destiny of roads not taken.

Second, evaluating counterfactual statements requires a similarity metric between possible worlds. According to philosophers Phyllis Illari and Federica Russo, "our causal views are structuring the similarity judgments that we use to ground the counterfactual dependence that was supposed to explain causation."[124] This is a key concern about circularity: The similarity metric used to define causation is itself built on top of causation, as it must be sensitive to miracle interventions. Two cases help drive this point home. On one hand, the similarity metric must push possible worlds infinitely apart based on certain causal structures. For instance, *backtracking counterfactuals* describing backward causation, such as "Had X_{t+1} not occurred, X_t would not have occurred," are prohibited and thus maximally dissimilar to the observed world. On the other hand, the similarity metric must coarsen reality into events that are sufficiently distinct from one another. As an example, we would not say that typing `I-n-v` on my keyboard caused me to type `I-n-v-a-r-i-a-n-c-e`, while the counterfactual statement "Had I not typed `I-n-v`, I wouldn't have typed `I-n-v-a-r-i-a-n-c-e`" is indeed true. To avoid these problems, the similarity metric should not consider the typing of different characters as distinct events.

Computing distances between worlds brings up another issue: The similarity metric must trim an immense number of counterfactuals into a few relevant alternatives, all by means of sorting through a vast number of features. In the context of building AI systems, this need to confront a combinatorially explosive amount of factors to make decisions under a limited computational budget is known as the *frame problem*. Lewis, who was well aware of this problem, argued that "the vagueness of similarity does infect causation, and no correct analysis can deny it."[158] Henry Nelson Goodman (1906–1998), who famously called the notion of similarity "a pretender, an impostor, a quack," elaborates:

> Comparative judgments of similarity often require not merely selection
> of relevant properties but a weighting of their relative importance,

> and variation in both relevance and importance can be rapid and
> enormous. Consider baggage at an airport check-in station. The
> spectator may notice [the] shape, size, color, material, and even make
> of luggage; the pilot is more concerned with weight, and the passenger
> with destination and ownership. Which pieces of baggage are more
> alike than others depends not only upon what properties they share,
> but upon who makes the comparison, and when.[159]

Since two objects "can be infinitely similar of dissimilar,"[160] any metric
for distinguishing causal structures presupposes the notion of causation,
revealing a circular argument.

Third, counterfactual theories of causation struggle to differentiate between causes and enabling conditions. While the statement "the short-circuit
caused the fire" seems reasonable, we would be perplexed to hear that "the
presence of oxygen in the room caused the fire." This is because most
individuals would consider the short-circuits to be a cause of the fire, and
deem the presence of oxygen in the room an enabling condition. Cognitively,
we distinguish between causes and enabling conditions by attributing the
latter to events abnormal from the statistical (causes are rare events), moral
(causes are deviant), or functional (causes are instances of malfunctions)
perspectives.[161] Judea Pearl elaborates on this point:

> In 1982, psychologists Daniel Kahneman and Amos Tversky investi-
> gated how people choose an "if only" culprit to "undo" an undesired
> outcome and found consistent patterns in their choices. One was
> that people are more likely to imagine undoing a rare event than a
> common one. For example, if we are undoing a missed appointment,
> we are more likely to say, "If only the train had left on schedule,"
> than "If only the train had left early." Another pattern was people's
> tendency to blame their own actions (striking a match) rather than
> events not under their control.[162]

However, abnormality itself is context-dependent. In a highly controlled
laboratory experiment to test the resilience of electronic equipment to short-
circuits, one may indeed conclude that the presence of oxygen caused the
fire. Philosopher of causation Ned Hall expands:

> When delineating the causes of some given event, we typically make
> what are, from the present perspective, invidious distinctions, ignoring
> perfectly good causes because they are not sufficiently salient. We say
> that the lightning bolt caused the forest fire, failing to mention the
> contribution of the oxygen in the air or the presence of a sufficient
> quantity of flammable material. But in the egalitarian sense of "cause,"

a complete inventory of the fire's causes must include the presence of oxygen and of dry wood.[163]

On the same topic, John Stuart Mill (1806–1873) said, "Nothing can better show the absence of any scientific ground for the distinction between the cause of a phenomenon and its conditions, than the capricious manner in which we select from among the conditions that which we choose to denominate the cause."[164] Hillary Putnam expressed a similar view, noting that "one man's background condition can easily be another man's cause." Since both elements are necessary for the effect to appear, the counterfactual account struggles to distinguish between causes and enabling conditions.

A fourth criticism of the counterfactual theory is its inadequate treatment of omissions. Consider a familiar example:[63] Upon arriving home after a well-deserved holiday, you are horrified to discover that most plants in your apartment are dry and dead. Most would identify your failure to water the plants as the cause of their death. This claim is acceptable under the counterfactual account, since the counterfactual statement "Had you watered the plants, they would not have died" holds true. Rather amusingly, the counterfactual statement "Had the Queen of England watered the plants, they would not have died" is equally valid. Are we to blame the British monarchy for the death of your plants? Doubtfully so. While omissions may sound like a pastime for philosophers, they are taken into account in the court of law, where statements such as "but-for the omission of treatment by the medical staff, the patient would not have died" are commonplace.

Fifth, counterfactual dependence does not effectively model cases of preemption and over determination. To discuss preemption first, consider a famous vignette from Ned Hall:[163]

> Billy and Suzy throw rocks at a bottle. Suzy throws first so that her rock arrives first and shatters the glass; Billy's rock sails through the air where the bottle had stood moments earlier. Without Suzy's throw, Billy's throw would have shattered the bottle. However, Suzy's throw caused the bottle to shatter, while Billy's throw is merely a preempted potential cause. This is a case of late preemption because the alternative process (Billy's throw) is cut short by the main process (Suzy's throw) running to completion.[121]

In the previous example, we would all agree that "Suzy's throw caused the bottle to shatter." However, this causal judgment does not translate into the counterfactual statement "Had Suzy not thrown a rock, the bottle would have not shattered" because, in that counterfactual world, Billy's upcoming throw would have hit the target. (We could, perhaps, try to salvage the counterfactual analysis by considering a sufficiently fine description about how the bottle shatters. This highlights how variable selection and coarsening influence causal judgments, a matter we will revisit in the next chapter.) The case of overdetermination is simply symmetric preemption, where both rock throws arrive simultaneously to shatter the bottle. In both the preemption and overdetermination versions of the story, Suzy's throw lacks the "difference-making" character commonly associated with causation in the counterfactual account. Instead, Ned Hall argues, Suzy's throw has a "causal production force," where the physical transmission of bottle-shattering energy gives Suzy's throw causal priority over Billy's.[163] Lewis' frustration with preemption and overdetermination cases led him to revise the counterfactual theory of causation to incorporate *alterations*—if Suzy throws her rock one millisecond later, the bottle shatters one millisecond latter, but the same is not true of Billy's nonproducing throw. Alas, Lewis' new theory was also subject to various forms of criticism.[121]

Sixth, counterfactual dependence is transitive, whereas our everyday understanding of causation is not necessarily so. For example, the counterfactual statement "Had the Big Bang not occurred, I would not be writing this chapter" translates into the causal judgment "The Big Bang caused me to write this chapter." While the counterfactual statement is true due to transitivity, I would not accept the causal judgment because the Big Bang lacks sufficient salience in the causal chain leading to my writing these words. One particular example of nontransitivity, known as double prevention, gives special trouble to the counterfactual analysis of causation:

> A hiker is walking along a mountain trail, when a boulder high above is dislodged and comes careening down the mountain slopes. The hiker notices the boulder and ducks at the appropriate time. The careening boulder causes the hiker to duck and this, in turn, causes his stride to continue. (This second causal link involves double prevention: ducking prevents the collision between hiker and boulder which, had it occurred, would have prevented the hiker's continued stride.) However, the careening boulder is the sort of thing that would normally prevent the hiker's continued stride and so it seems counterintuitive to say that it causes the stride.[121]

Stephen Mumford presents another example:[122] A fire triggers sprinklers, which then extinguish the fire—can we say that the fire caused its own cessation? James Woodward identifies an example of double prevention in biology,[134] involving the synthesis of enzymes for the metabolization of lactose in *Escherichia coli*.

Seventh and finally, overly generic counterfactuals statements lead to bizarre causal judgments. Consider the following example from Woodward's *Causation with a Human Face*: "My writing of this very chapter was caused by my not being hit by a large meteor prior to beginning it."[134] This causal judgment translates into the counterfactual statement: "If I were not struck by a large meteor prior to beginning it, I would have written this very chapter."[134] This counterfactual statement is awkward because it is not invariant across relevant background changes. Meteors aside, I could have not written this chapter because I felt lazy about it, some family emergency came about, or I regarded it as irrelevant for the book at large. In all these relevant counterfactual worlds the counterfactual statement is false because, even when meteors do not happen, the chapter remains unwritten. I will expand on this idea in chapter 5 by discussing how explanations that are *easy to vary* often yield invariances that lack robust generalization and diverge from causation and truth.

3.6   Causation and Explanation

Philosophical discussions of causation often emphasize its crucial role in explanation. To understand how causation helps explain nature beyond prediction, consider the following example cited by Cartwright:

> God tells you that Schroedinger's equation provides a completely satisfactory derivation of the phenomenological law of radioactive decay. You have no doubt that the derivation is correct. But you still have no reason to believe in Schroedinger's equation. On the other hand, if God tells you that the rotting of the roots is the cause of the yellowing of the leaves ... Then you do have reason, conclusive reason, to believe that there is water in the tub.[113]

Hempel's flagpole example, illustrated in figure 3.2b and often used to invalidate the deductive-nomological model of explanation,[165] helps us review some of the concepts in this chapter under the lens of explanation. The example seeks to explain the relationships between the height of a flagpole, the length of its shadow, and the position of the sun. On one hand, we may explain the length of the shadow by referencing the height of the pole, the sun's position, and some basic trigonometry. On the other hand we could, with similar ease, explain the height of the pole in terms of the length of its shadow and the position of the sun. Yet, we would only accept the height of the pole as an explanation about the length of its shadow. This is because good explanations follow a causal blueprint and enjoy invariance under intervention. In this example, we accept that manipulating the height of the pole or the position of the sun effects a change in the length of the pole's shadow. The anti-causal explanation does not enjoy this property, as it is unfeasible to change the height of the pole by manipulating the length of its shadow (for instance, by inclining the terrain), or by tampering with the position of the sun.

Some explanations, particularly in mathematics, do not rely on causation. Consider this fact: There is always a pair of antipodal points along Earth's equator with matching temperatures.[166] For a proof, let $t(x)$ be the temperature at location x along the equator, and let $t(a(x))$ be the temperature at the antipodal location $a(x)$. Assume without loss of generality that these starting conditions satisfy $t(a(x)) - t(x) > 0$. Now, move x westward until $x' = a(x)$, effectively reversing the two starting locations so that $t(a(x')) - x' < 0$. Assuming that surface temperature is a continuous function, during our travel westbound we must encounter a point on the equator where the temperature matches at both antipodal points. This explanation does not invoke any interventions on the causal structure of the world, but rather rests on a *mathematical constraint*—in this case, Bolzano's theorem—which is the strongest type of invariance.

3.7   Causation and Time

The relationship between causation and time has stimulated endless philosophical debates. The major puzzling fact is that physical laws appear to be time symmetrical—that is, they can describe equally well the evolution of the universe forwards or backward in time. For example, in the ideal gas law $PV = nRT$, does pressure P cause temperature T, or vice versa? What is the causal structure governing force, mass, and acceleration in Newton's second law $F = ma$? For the interventionist, determining cause and effect depends on what variables are manipulable. While many would agree that force causes acceleration, for cellular agents only able to manipulate their mass by importing or exporting fluids into their system, mass could be seen as the cause of acceleration. Some physicists, however, see this as a feature and not as a bug. Moritz Schlick—the founding father of logical positivism and the Vienna Circle—defended the uniformity of nature by arguing that space-time coordinates should not appear in the laws of nature.[167]

Reichenbach proposed that time's asymmetry arises from the abundance of fork structures and the rarity of collider structures in nature. This asserts that causal structures are fundamental, with time emerging from them. In contrast, the concept of *Granger causality* suggests that causation derives from time, where X causes Y if the past of X helps predict the future of Y better than using the past of Y alone.[168] For interventionists, time and causation are aligned with the direction of agency: We cannot act to change the closed past, but we can manipulate the open future.[63] Claude Shannon (1916–2001) shared a similar view:

> This duality can be pursued further and is related to a duality between past and future and the notions of control and knowledge. Thus we may have knowledge of the past but cannot control it; we may control the future but have no knowledge of it.[169]

For David Lewis, pioneer of the counterfactual theory, the arrow of time reflects the fact that the future is much more overdetermined than the past—there are a myriad of ways things can play out, but only one manner in which the past has already happened.

In the context of machine learning, prediction does not always align with the arrow of causation. Forensics and medical diagnosis are good examples of *anti-causal prediction*. The detective inspects wounds in the victim (effect) to conclude they were shot (cause). Similarly, the doctor inspects a tumor to recognize the presence of cancer. Finding cloven hoof prints in the sand leads us to suspect that a cow was on the beach. We purchase car insurance today because of the likelihood of an accident tomorrow. Science, to a large extent, is anti-causal—we observe effects, and walk our way back to causes by means of proposing and refuting theories. All these are problems that, despite being noncausal, are relevant to navigate the world because they afford largely invariant predictors.

Some researchers categorize supervised learning problems as either *causal* (predicting effects from causes, such as estimating atmospheric pressure from terrain elevation) or *anti-causal* (predicting causes from effects, such as diagnosing cancer from histological evidence).[153] A different view considers all supervised learning problems as *causal*, as they emulate the cognitive processes of human annotators who produce labels from the observation of inputs. Back to our detective, when she enters the crime scene and discovers a body with gunshot wounds, the relation $P(\text{firing} \mid \text{gunshot wound} = 1, e)$ is so invariant across relevant environments $\mathcal{E}$ that it is safe to conclude that the victim was shot. Conversely, the predictive model $P(\text{gunshot wound} = 1 \mid \text{firing}, e)$, which follows the temporal sequence of events, is arguably less invariant across environments—such as when the shooter misses the target. I argue that the detective employs the invariant, counter-to-time, counter-to-causation rule, to explain the crime scene.

These are examples of *supervised learning*, where the machine learns to imitate a labeling cognitive process happening forward in time. In contrast, the goal of unsupervised learning, illustrated in figure 3.3, is to reverse-engineer the latent variables of nature from observable features. Therefore, unsupervised learning does not rely on imitating a labeling cognitive process, and it counters the arrows of both time and causation.

Causal structures also influence other popular learning paradigms, such as semi-supervised learning and meta-learning. On one hand, consider the

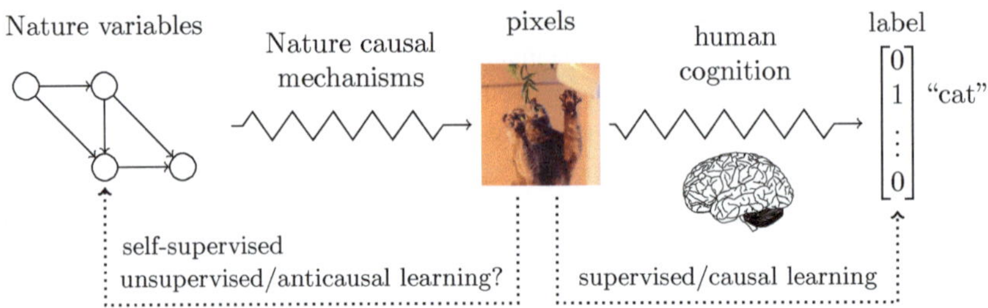

Figure 3.3: All learning problems use empirical observations, here exemplified as *pixels*. Following a causal and cognitive process, humans produce labels. Therefore, supervised learning problems predicting annotations from observations often yield invariant conditional distributions $P(\text{label} \mid \text{pixel})$. Conversely, unsupervised learning reverse-engineers causal factors of variation (nature's variables) by reversing the data generation process (nature's mechanisms). This is an anti-causal learning problem that often yields variant conditional distributions—an opportunity to leverage multiple interventions and data environments to reveal statistical invariance. Cat picture by `https://www.flickr.com/photos/pustovit/15867520885/`.

supervised learning of a causal mapping transforming some inputs X into some label Y. Under the ICM assumption, the cause distribution $P(X)$ and the causal mechanism $P(Y \mid X)$ do not contain any information about each other. This would render semi-supervised learning—the use of additional unlabeled inputs X to better our classifier—ineffective. In contrast, learning semi-supervisedly may be advantageous in anti-causal $X \leftarrow Y$ problems, since an unlabeled input X may contain information about the mechanism $P(Y \mid X)$ of interest.[153] On the other hand, causal structures can influence the adaptation speed of predictors in meta-learning.[170] When interventions affect only a sparse subset of mechanisms within the causal structure, models that align more closely with causation should need less adaptation to perform under novel interventions.[171]

3.8   Causation and Cognition

Humans are (so far) the best demonstration of intelligence, so it is worth investigating the role of causal reasoning in our own cognition. A pioneering exploration on this topic is *La perception de la causalité* from Albert Michotte (1881–1965).[172] Using an ingenious arrangement of rotating cardboard disks, Michotte depicted different sequences of squares bouncing into each other, revealing that our perception of causation is highly correlated with certain spatiotemporal features.[173] (For a related investigation on the perception of complex emotions and roles in simple polygons, I suggest watching Heider and Simmel's animations.[174]) One of the most famous examples is Michotte's *launching effect*, which involves five events: (e_1) a red square sits at the center of the screen, (e_2) a blue square appears from the left edge of the screen, moving toward the red square, (e_3) the blue square contacts the red square, (e_4) the blue square stops moving, and (e_5) the red square starts moving to the right. Both human and nonhuman primate infants perceive a causal connection in sequences like this, inferring that the blue square caused the red square to move. However, this causal perception vanishes as we introduce small delays between events e_3 and e_4, or if movement is substituted by change in color. Subjects were also sensitive to environmental noise, since "whether an image sequence is perceived causally can thus change depending on seemingly irrelevant events elsewhere in the visual field, and even infants are affected by these sorts of contextual changes."[63]

Michotte's seminal experiments showed that humans follow strong inductive biases to identify causal relationships. Our causal sense grants certain invariances—those useful for the purposes of manipulation and control—special status, since "the capacity to control rather than just react to the environment that provided the impetus for the evolution of a mind and a nervous system capable of representing causation."[175] Otherwise, Woodward and others argue, we may have developed a very different kind of cognition, perhaps one not so adept in describing the world in terms of causal structures:

> If we had been unable to manipulate nature—if we had been, in Michael Dummett's example, intelligent trees capable only of passive observation—then it is a reasonable conjecture that we would never have developed the notions of causation and explanation and the practices associated with them that we presently possess.[140]

Similarly, Eugene Wigner once remarked that "our consciousness could hardly differ from that of plants if we were unable to influence the events, and if these had no structure or if we were not familiar with some of this structure, we could not influence them."[57] All of these arguments echo Kant, since they suggest that causation is not an ontological ingredient of the world, but a principle of our minds to organize sense data.

Non-human primates "appear to understand very little about why their successful actions are effective" and "operate entirely within a framework of properties that can be readily perceived, and this underlies their lack of causal understanding."[134] Human infants are, in addition, capable of counterfactual thinking, since they "spontaneously invoke what would have happened under alternative possibilities in arriving at causal judgments, even when those alternatives are not explicitly mentioned in or prompted by the scenarios they are given."[134] Preschoolers, as Alison Gopnik explains, "test hypotheses against data and make causal inferences; they learn from statistics and informal experimentation, and from watching and listening to others."[176] Based on these differences, Woodward catalogues three types of increasingly sophisticated causal learners.[134] First, *egocentric proto-causal learners* relate their own actions to their corresponding outcomes—Pavlov's classical conditioning, as well as Skinner's operant conditioning, fall within this category. Second, *agent-causal learners* learn and replicate the outcomes of actions of other members of their own species. Third, *observation-action causal learners* estimate causal relations from patterns of covariance occurring in nature—such as the wind shaking a fruit down from a tree. Within this taxonomy, nonhuman primates are proto-causal learners and human toddlers are agent-causal learners. Finally, adult humans are observation-action causal learners, capable of the most sophisticated causal cognition. This involves disentangling representations of actions and outcomes, understanding causal relations *as* causal, and modeling the world in terms of increasingly autonomous relations.[134]

All the evidence above supports the key role of causal reasoning as an ingredient of animal and human intelligence. But what features of the world do these learners identify as causal? As Patricia Cheng and colleagues argue, "The psychological literature shows that people spontaneously assume causal invariance in their causal judgments."[177] Causal reasoning uses statistical invariance as an aspiration, default belief, and criteria for revising our representations of the world.[177] Humans, in particular, tolerate increasingly complex causal theories if they provide invariant prediction rules across a wider range of contexts:

> One of the lessons we may extract from Cheng's experiments is that a model according to which people represent causal relations in terms of causal power based on some relatively simple invariance assumptions seems to provide a good fit with at least some aspects of lay causal judgment. This suggests that some substantial number of people operate with assumptions about or representations of causation in which some invariance-based notions play an important role ... As an empirical matter, features of causal relationships having to do with invariance influence ordinary subjects' judgments (as expressed in responses to various causal strength probes) about how "strong" or "good" those relationships are or about the extent to which the subjects find it appropriate to describe those relationships as causal.[134]

Lastly, humans excel at learning invariant relationships from both an observational and an interventional stance.[134] Rats and nonhuman primates understand their own voluntary actions as interventions,[63] but only humans are capable of identifying exogenous actions—those happening due to natural processes or other beings—as interventions that we could replicate to achieve our goals.[63] By observing the wind tearing a branch off the tree, only humans understand that we can ourselves exert the same force to obtain the same result.

Chapter 4

Practice of Causation

4.1 Introduction

Our next topic of study is the algorithmic implementation of some of the causation theories covered in the previous chapter. The exposition is organized as follows. First, I discuss the issue of variable selection and coarsening. Several times in the previous chapter, I alluded to the fact that causal judgments depend upon the choice of representation. So, which variables should we design to describe the system under study? Good representations are conducive to autonomy, which determines the range of interventions over which a set of putative causal relations remain invariant. In particular, describing our system with fine variables will allow us to describe more patterns in our training data, increasing overfitting (also called fragility) and generalization error. On the contrary, describing our variables using a coarse representation would render the putative causal relations only true at the probabilistic level but would enable better generalization across novel contexts.

Second, I will review structural equation models (SEMs), a widely used mathematical formalization of the interventionist account. Given a predefined set of variables, SEMs produce a list of equations, each describing how one variable in the system takes its values as a function of the values taken by its causal parents. Building a SEM requires borrowing domain knowledge and making unverifiable assumptions, but it equips us with the tools necessary for unbiased causal inferences. More broadly, SEMs allow the study of the causal structures governing our data by means of observational, interventional, and counterfactual statistics—thereby serving as a common framework to the three major theories of causation we reviewed in the last chapter.

Third, this chapter offers a short discussion of causal *discovery*, the task of estimating the structural equation models from their observational data. While Reichenbach's principle of common cause (PCC) warns that this task is in general impossible, causal discovery methods impose various invariance assumptions about the data generation process to enable a degree of identifiability about the underlying causal relations.

Fourth and finally, the chapter concludes with an overview of the potential outcomes framework by Neyman and Rubin, a model-free approach to estimate the strength of causal relationships. Using the example of a study of aspirin's efficacy to relieve headaches, the canonical implementation of the potential outcomes framework involves conducting a randomized control trial (RCT). In this case, we distribute a collection of participants randomly into a treatment group (receiving aspirin) and a placebo group (receiving a sugar pill). While it is impossible to estimate the effect of aspirin on any particular individual—since each participant *either* takes the aspirin *or* the placebo—random treatment-control assignment enables the estimation of *average* treatment effects. Unfortunately, true randomization is a rare privilege in practice, requiring us to condition our analysis on a set of covariates to reduce discrepancies between the treatment and control groups. These covariates must satisfy what is known as conditional *exchangeability* or *ignorability*, which are conditions tightly related to the Invariance Principle introduced in the following chapter.

As this chapter will reveal, causal relations are highly valuable assets because of their invariance properties. This fact prompts us to explore whether invariance is itself a more primitive concept than causation, and whether it serves as a superior epistemological tool to avoid spurious correlations and seek true patterns. Although it is challenging to conceive of causation without invariance, examples abound where invariance can be examined without invoking causation. This chapter is therefore an invitation to reconsider the often-repeated mantra "correlation does not imply causation," and instead wonder whether correlation does imply causation *when observed under the right distributions*.

4.2 Variable Selection

The first and most significant challenge in the study of causation is the design of variables that best describe the phenomenon of interest.[178] If good variables are those affording good predictions across relevant environments and interventions, their definition is necessarily task-dependent and impossible to specify a priori. When we're building intelligent systems, choosing the relevant variables out of a combinatorially explosive pool of possibilities—using a limited computational budget—is known as the *frame problem*. Consequently, as Patrick Suppes advanced half a century ago, variable selection is unavoidably limited and subjective, and certainly influences our causal judgments.[179] The curious reader can consult the work of Arthur S. Goldberger, who analyzed how different representations of the problem of salary discrimination[180] led various authors to opposite conclusions about the same data.

Variable selection must occur at the appropriate level of abstraction or granularity.[181–183] While the quantum physicist seeks to understand the fine structures of nature below the atomic scale, for instance, the thermodynamicist is concerned with coarser variables such as temperature, pressure, and volume. As a more familiar example, consider studying the impact of blood cholesterol on health at two different levels of abstraction. On one hand, we may parameterized our study in terms of the two fine variables of LDL and HDL cholesterol types. This would reveal that LDL cholesterol is harmful to health, while HDL cholesterol is beneficial. On the other hand, examining cholesterol in terms of the coarser variable of total cholesterol—LDL minus HDL—would reveal no clear impact on health. Nancy Cartwright provides a parallel example, where "ingesting an acid poison may cause death; so too may the ingestion of an alkali poison. But ingesting both may have no effect at all on survival."[113] In sum, choosing an appropriate level of abstraction or granularity is a problem-dependent balancing act: Finer representations explain more training data, while coarser representations offer broader predictive power.

As Woodward argues, our choice of variables and level of abstraction both influence the questions we may pose and answers we may obtain about the phenomena of interest:

> Different choices of variables for theorizing are associated with different
> ways of carving up nature into possible alternatives, answers to
> different w-questions, and hence different explanations.[140]

While the fundamental forces of nature apply at the particle level, causal patterns of dependence obtain at all levels of abstraction, from quarks to societies. Woodward continues:

> Some will hold that even if there are facts about what would happen
> if rocks strike windows or aspirin is ingested, these cannot be part of
> the "fundamental ontology" of the world. ... What matters for my
> purposes is that whatever may be the constituents of nature at more
> fundamental levels ... certain claims about what would happen if
> certain interventions were to occur turn out to be true and others
> turn out to be false. ... It is these that we represent and reason
> about when we engage in causal inference and judgment.[134]

In this view, the causal relation is an epistemological tool about the chosen level of abstraction, rather than a mind-independent and ontological constituent of the world.

The chosen variables and their level of abstraction both impact the robustness of causal relations. When using a long list of fine-grained variables, one obtains *fragile* causal relations. These relations explain all past observations deterministically, but fail to predict future cases—in statistical terms, fragile causal relations achieve zero training error by overfitting. As Cartwright argues, causal relations such as "Smoking a daily pack of cigarettes, living in a highly polluted city, working as a painter, and eating processed foods daily for dinner causes cancer" are fragile because, while they may explain all of our past observations, they fail to obtain useful data for future cases:

> The principle "same cause, same effect," which philosophers imagine to be vital to science, is utterly otiose. As soon as the antecedents have been given sufficiently fully to enable the consequent to be calculated with some exactitude, the antecedents have become so complicated that it is very unlikely they will ever recur.[113]

One such philosopher was John Stuart Mill, who considered necessity central to the causal relation and defined the *total cause* of an event as "the antecedent, or the concurrence of antecedents, on which a given phenomenon is invariable and unconditionally consequent."[164] According to Mill, statements such as "day follows night" do not necessarily obtain because they omit a vast amount of factors from the total cause, such as "the sun is burning."

Rules built on top of coarse variables, such as "smoking causes cancer," explain only probabilistically past observations but predict future cases better. On the extreme, "within an interventionist account, causation disappears when we consider the entire universe, since there is nothing left out of it to carry the intervention."[63] Judea Pearl lingers on this case:

> If you wish to include the entire universe in the model, causation disappears because interventions disappear—the manipulator and the manipulated lose their distinction. However, scientists rarely consider the entirety of the universe as an object of investigation. In most cases the scientist carves out a piece from the universe and proclaims that piece *in*—namely, the focus of investigation. The rest of the universe is then considered *out* or background and is summarized by what we call boundary conditions. This choice of ins and outs creates asymmetry in the way we look at things, and it is this asymmetry that permits us to talk about "outside intervention" and hence about causation and cause-effect directionality.[152]

Alan Watt entertains a similar point of view in this excerpt from his *The Book on the Taboo Against Knowing Who You Are*:

> Here is someone who has never seen a cat. He is looking through a narrow slit in a fence, and, on the other side, a cat walks by. He sees first the head, then the less distinctly shaped furry trunk, and then the tail. Extraordinary! The cat turns round and walks back, and again he sees the head, and a little later the tail. This sequence begins to look like something regular and reliable. Yet again, the cat turns round, and he witnesses the same regular sequence: first the head, and later the tail. Thereupon he reasons that the event head is the invariable and necessary cause of the event tail, which is the head's effect. This absurd and confusing gobbledygook comes from his failure to see that head and tail go together; they are all one cat.[184]

Causation not only disappears as we consider wider regions of space as antecedents—it also dissolves as we consider infinitesimal slices of time where past and future meet in the instantaneous present moment.

As discussed in section 3.4.4, one guide to selecting variables is to build representations satisfying the principle of autonomy. For instance, studying the causal structure of natural images in terms of pixels makes little sense, whereas understanding the causal relations among visual objects is a fundamental goal in computer vision.[185] Autonomous variables are valuable because they expose invariant mechanisms that can be manipulated independently, providing answers to numerous amounts of what-if-things-had-been-different questions. More generally, autonomy is crucial to scientific variable naming and distinguishes empirical (phenomenological, low-autonomy) models from theoretical (substantial, fundamental, high-autonomy) models.[113,125] Although this chapter assumes variable selection as a given, the fertile literature in causal representation learning[171] offers algorithmic solutions to discover causal variables from raw data.

4.3   Structural Equation Models

Structural equation models are the leading framework to formalize causal structures between random variables. SEMs were introduced by Sewall Wright (1889–1988),[186] who ideated causal graphs as a tool to understand the factors determining guinea pig coat color.[162] The further development of the SEM framework owes much to the work of Judea Pearl,[152] who was awarded the Turing Award in 2011 "for fundamental contributions to artificial intelligence through the development of a calculus for probabilistic and causal reasoning."

The SEM governing a system of variables $X = \{X_1, \ldots, X_d\}$ is a list of d causal relations, each describing how the values of a variable X_i are determined by others. Since the true causal mechanisms at play in nature are unobservable, constructing a SEM is a modeling exercise that allows practitioners to explicitly state their domain knowledge and assumptions. As Pearl notes,

> Unlike correlation and most of the other tools of mainstream statistics, causal analysis requires the user to make a subjective commitment. She must draw a causal diagram that reflects her qualitative belief— or, better yet, the consensus belief of researchers in her field of expertise—about the topology of the causal processes at work.[162]

Therefore, SEMs assume that all relevant variable selection issues discussed in the previous section have already been addressed.

More formally, the structural equation governing the values of X_i is

$$X_i \leftarrow f_i(\mathrm{Pa}(X_i), N_i), \tag{4.1}$$

where $\mathrm{Pa}(X_i) \in X \setminus X_i$ denotes the *parents* of X_i, $N_i \sim P(N_i)$ is an independent *noise term*, and f_i is the *mechanism* transforming parents and noise into the value taken by X_i. Therefore, given the SEM, X_i stands for known factors to the theory, while N_i stands for unknown factors. Note how the equation above employs an asymmetric assignment operator. This is akin to programming languages, where the left-hand side takes, receives, or listens to the value of the right-hand side. Therefore, the equation $X_2 \leftarrow 2X_1$ cannot be rearranged into an equation $X_1 \leftarrow X_2/2$ where X_1 would take, receive, or listen to X_2.

Structural equation models separate structure, contained in the mechanisms f_i, from random initial conditions, provided by the independent noise terms N_i. As argued by Eugene Wigner, physicists have long relied on a similar separation to advance physical theories:

> The world is very complicated and it is clearly impossible for the human mind to understand it completely. It has therefore devised an artifice which permits the complicated nature of the world to be blamed on something which is called accidental and thus permits him to abstract a domain in which simple laws can be found. The complications are called initial conditions, the domain of regularities, laws of nature. Unnatural as such a division of the world's structure may appear from a very detached point of view, and probable though it is that the possibility of such a division has its own limits, the underlying abstraction is probably one of the most fruitful ones that human mind has made. It has made science possible.[187]

Causal discovery algorithms, reviewed in section 4.4, build upon a similar insight to search for causal models as those producing independent residuals.

4.3.1 The Causal Graph

We can summarize a SEM into a *causal graph*, where each variable X_i instantiates a graph node, and each functional relationship $X_i \in \mathrm{Pa}(X_j)$ instantiates a graph edge $X_i \to X_j$. The SEM equations furnish in this way a causal structure, yielding "X_i causes X_j" if and only if $X_i \in \mathrm{Pa}(X_j)$. Figure 4.1 shows the causal graphs induced by three different linear SEMs. Taking figure 4.1a, the associated SEM is the list of structural equations:

$$
\begin{aligned}
I &\leftarrow N_I, \\
C &\leftarrow N_C, \\
X &\leftarrow \beta_c \cdot I + \gamma_c \cdot C + N_X, \\
Y &\leftarrow \alpha_c \cdot X + \delta_c \cdot C + N_Y,
\end{aligned}
\tag{4.2}
$$

where $N_I, N_C, N_X, N_Y \sim P(N)$. These equations show that SEMs have three types of variables: independent *noise* terms N_i, *exogenous* variables X_i with $\mathrm{Pa}(X_i) = \emptyset$ (such as I and C above), and *endogenous* variables X_i with $\mathrm{Pa}(X_i) \neq \emptyset$ (such as X and Y above). These roles depend on variable selection: A variable X_i can be exogenous in one SEM, but endogenous in a larger SEM that includes its causal parents $\mathrm{Pa}(X_i)$.

Research and practice on SEMs often constrain the space of causal graphs in two ways. First, most studies only consider SEMs that produce directed *acyclic* causal graphs, to avoid complications related to feedback loops and backward causation. Second, the assumption of *sufficiency* ensures that there are no *hidden confounders*, meaning all relevant nodes appear in the causal graph. Mathematically, hidden variables yield *dependent* noise variables in the SEM, similar to the problem of dependent residuals in regression analysis. By assuming sufficiency, residuals are independent under the right SEM model, enabling a host of causal discovery methods, discussed below in section 4.4.

Figure 4.1 shows three important structural equation models. First, figure 4.1a illustrates the confounding structure. Confounder structures lurk behind *Simpson's paradox*, where a correlation observed for several groups of data reverses or disappears when combining all groups together. In other words, empirical correlations may reverse when stratifying the data into subgroups. A popular example[188] considers the correlation between daily exercise and blood cholesterol. When looking at age groups separately, daily exercise is negatively correlated to blood cholesterol, suggesting the benefits of sports on health. However, when combining all age groups, the correlation between exercise and cholesterol turns positive. This is easy to explain using the SEM in figure 4.1a, where we let X denote exercise, Y cholesterol, and Z age group. By conditioning on the valid adjustment set Z, we reveal a positive and invariant causal effect from exercise to cholesterol.

Second, the collider structure in figure 4.1b is helpful to understand *Berkson's paradox*, where a spurious correlation arises due to selection bias. For example, even though attractiveness and talent are two statistically independent traits in people, they appear negatively correlated when examining only celebrities. The selection creates a spurious correlation because individuals who are neither attractive nor talented are less likely to achieve fame. Given the ubiquity of selection bias, it is wise to remember that our training data are always drawn from the *conditional* distribution $P(X, Y \mid \text{training} = \text{True})$.

Third, figure 4.1c shows a causal mediation case. In mediated causal structures, the influence of some independent variable X on some dependent variable Y decomposes into one direct causal effect $X \to Y$ and one indirect causal effect $X \to M \to Y$, where M is called the *mediator*.

4.3.2 Observational Distribution

Structural equation models provide a framework for acquiring three types of knowledge about a system of variables governed by a causal structure. This is often illustrated by Pearl's *ladder of causation*, which features three rungs demanding increasingly sophisticated inferences to obtain observational, interventional, and counterfactual knowledge.

By passively observing the structural equations of a SEM at play, we can collect samples from its associated *observational distribution*. To do so, we walk through the list of variables, following the topological order of the associated causal graph. For each variable X_i, sample its value x_i by (1) drawing an independent noise sample $n_i \sim P(N)$, (2) reading the values of the parents $\mathrm{Pa}(X_i)$, and (3) plugging both of these values into the mechanism f_i, obtaining our sample X_i. By repeating this process for all variables, we obtain the observational data point $(x_1, \ldots, x_d)$, which is a sample drawn from the observational distribution $P(X_1, \ldots, X_d)$ associated to the SEM under study. Although this approach may seem unnecessarily complex compared to sampling conditional distributions, it brings about significant modeling clarity:

> We played around with the possibility of replacing the parents-child relationship $P(X_i \mid \mathrm{Pa}(X_i))$ with its functional counterpart $X_i \leftarrow f_i(\mathrm{Pa}(X_i), N_i)$ and, suddenly, everything began to fall into place: We finally had a mathematical object to which we could attribute familiar properties of physical mechanisms instead of those slippery epistemic

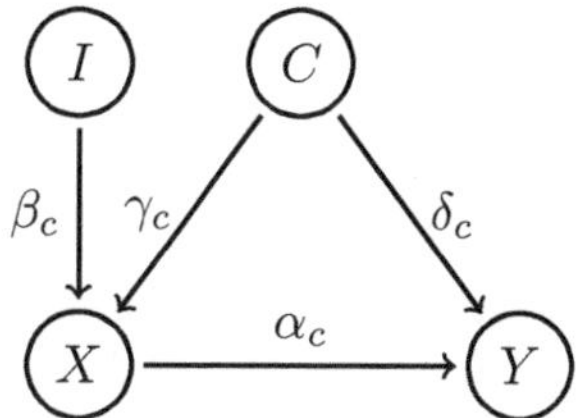
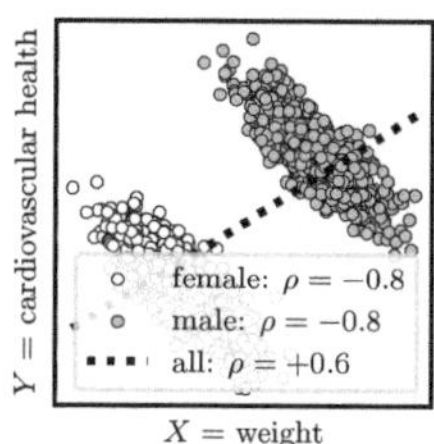

(a) Confounding SEM, where the *common cause* C confounds the causal relation $X \to Y$. Adjusting for C decreases the confounding between X and Y. When C is unobserved, adjusting can be done via an instrumental variable I. On the right, confounded SEMs are responsible for Simpson's paradox. Confounder values are good invariance environments.

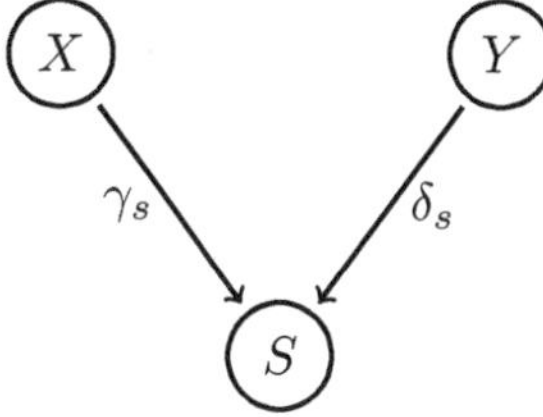
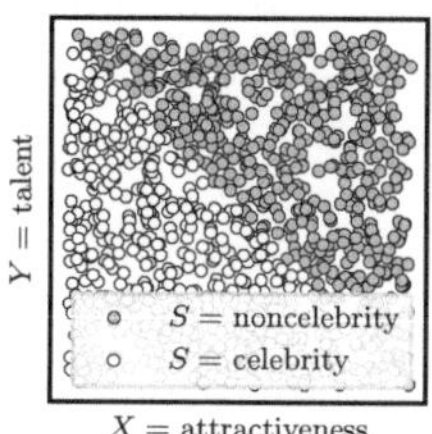

(b) Selection bias SEM, where collecting data about X and Y is conditioned on the value of a *collider* or *fork* S confounds the causal relation $X \to Y$. Adjusting for S increases the confounding between X and Y. Thus, we would like to collect data for X and Y unconditionally from the value of S. On the right, selection bias SEMs are responsible for a Berkson's paradox. Collider values are bad invariance environments.

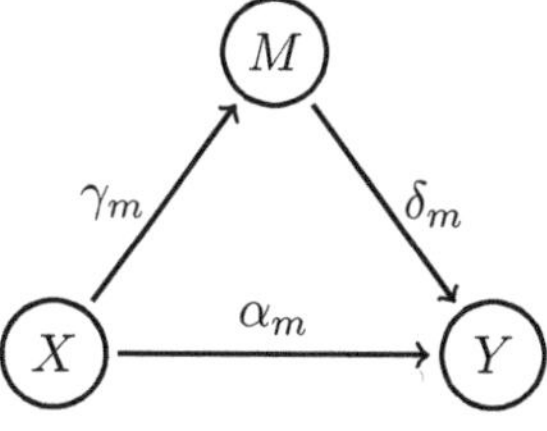
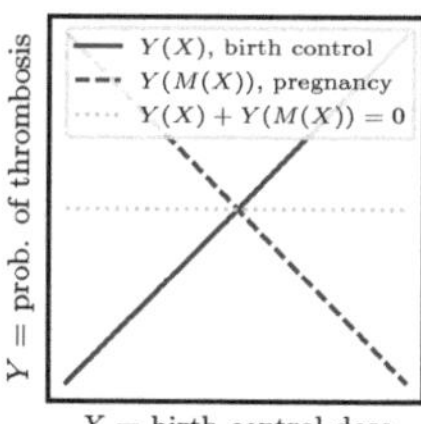

(c) Mediation SEM, where the total causal effect from X to Y decomposes into a direct causal effect $X \to Y$ and an indirect causal effect $X \to M \to Y$. Adjusting for M results in underestimating the total causal effect from X to Y. Thus, we would like to fix the mediator to a fixed value. On the right, mediation SEMs can induce faithfulness violations. Mediation values are good invariance features.

Figure 4.1: Three important structural equation models.

probabilities $P(X_i \mid \mathrm{Pa}(X_i))$ with which we had been working so long in the study of Bayesian networks.[152]

As noted earlier, expressing conditional distributions as structural equations helps separate the deterministic structure in the laws of nature from the randomness arising from initial conditions.

Two important conditions relate a SEM's observational distribution to its underlying causal graph. First, the *Markov condition* states that the observational distribution factorizes into the conditional distributions prescribed by the causal graph:

$$p(X_1, \ldots, X_d) = \prod_{i=1}^{d} p(X_i \mid \mathrm{Pa}(X_i)). \tag{4.3}$$

The Markov condition guarantees that the conditional independences implied by the causal graph are obtained in the observational distribution. While we could factorize the joint distribution in any arbitrary order, the Markov assumption provides sparse conditionals. In particular, the Markov assumption establishes that each variable is conditionally independent of its nondescendants, given its parents. The Markov condition also determines the Markov blanket of each variable X_i, denoting the minimal set of conditioning variables rendering X_i statistically independent from all other variables. Specifically, the Markov blanket of X_i contains the parents, the children, and the coparents of X_i. Finally, the Markov assumption enables us to determine conditional independences from analyzing the graph, using a tool known as d-separation.[7]

Second, the *faithfulness* assumption guarantees that no conditional independences, other than those implied by the graph, appear in the observational distribution. The faithfulness assumption rules out the existence of *canceling paths* in the causal graph. To understand the difficulties that canceling paths pose, let us interpret the SEM in figure 4.1c as illustrating the relationship between birth control pills X, probability of pregnancy M, and probability of thrombosis Y. In this example, birth control pills increase the likelihood of thrombosis by a factor of α_m along the causal relation $X \to Y$. Pregnancy also increases the risk of thrombosis by a factor of δ_m, encoded in the causal relation $M \to Y$. However, birth control pills inhibit pregnancy by a factor of $\gamma_c = -\alpha_m/\delta_m$ along the causal relation $X \to M$. This results in an indirect causal influence of birth pills on thrombosis, *mediated by* pregnancy. In sum, the structural equation for thrombosis reads

$$\begin{aligned}
Y &\leftarrow \alpha_m \cdot X + \delta_m \cdot M + N_Y \\
&= \alpha_m \cdot X + \delta_m \cdot (-\alpha_m/\delta_m)X + N_X + N_Y, \\
&= 0 + N_X + N_Y.
\end{aligned}$$

This equation violates the faithfulness assumption because the SEM does not admit any intervention on X or M *alone* to control Y, despite the causal graph showing arrows from both X and M into Y. Violations of faithfulness demonstrate the non-transitivity of causation within the interventionist account.

4.3.3 Interventional Distributions

We have seen how to use the framework of structural equation models to study the observational distribution of causal structures. However, as noted by David Freedman (1938–2008), "fitting an equation to an existing data set is one activity; predicting the results of an intervention is quite another, and the crucial issue is getting from here to there."[189] SEMs equip us with tools to bridge this gap. Broadly speaking, studying the interventional distributions of a SEM requires (1) performing an intervention on the SEM, and (2) studying the observational distribution of the intervened SEM. First, performing an intervention requires modifying one or more of the SEM's structural equations. To show the mechanics of this step, consider once again the SEM depicted in figure 4.1a. We'll manipulate it to hold the variable X constant and equal to zero. Let's replace the structural equation for X in equation (4.2) by:

$$\sout{X \leftarrow \beta_c \cdot I + \gamma_c \cdot C + N_X.}$$
$$X \leftarrow 0,$$

thereby removing the influence of I and C on X. Similar to editing lines of code, interventions modify structural equations, typically breaking all arrows in the causal graph pointing to the variable under intervention. Thus, in our example, all the arrows toward X are wiped out.

Predicting a target variable Y under intervention requires further assumptions. Technically, *valid* interventions to predict Y produce SEMs with acyclic causal graphs, invariant conditional expectations $\mathbb{E}\left[Y \mid \mathrm{Pa}(Y)\right]$, and finite conditional variances $\mathbb{V}\left[Y^e \mid \mathrm{Pa}(Y)\right] < \infty$. One simple yet powerful result is that the causal conditional expectation

$$\mathbb{E}\left[Y \mid \mathrm{Pa}(Y)\right] \tag{4.4}$$

is invariant across valid interventions. Therefore, causation implies invariance under valid interventions, making the causal relation a valuable tool to build robust prediction systems. Conversely, one must avoid *fat-handed* or *structure-altering* interventions, which disrupt the target structural equation of Y and render prediction efforts futile.

4.3.4 Counterfactual Distributions

In addition to observational and interventional distributions, the SEM framework allows us to compute *counterfactual* distributions about *individual* examples. These counterfactual distributions describe how the observed individual example would have been different, had some intervention occurred in the system.[154] To illustrate, consider again the SEM in figure 4.1c, with coefficients $(\gamma_m, \delta_m, \alpha_m) = (2, 1, 3)$, and noise terms taking the values $\{-1, 0, 1\}$ with uniform probability. Assume that we observe the example $(x, m, y) = (1, 1, 4)$. Following some algebraic manipulations, we can reply to the counterfactual question "What would the value of Y have been, had M been intervened and held constant to 5?" as

$$\mathbb{E}[Y \mid \mathrm{do}(M \leftarrow 5), X = 1, M = 1, Y = 4] = 8.$$

Such counterfactual reasoning calls for three steps:

(a) (abduction) solve for the noises, which must have been $(n_x, n_m, n_y) = (1, -1, 0)$; this replicates the environmental conditions (random seed) the world was in at the time of observation;

(b) (action) construct an intervened SEM where M is held constant to 5, wiping out the causal arrow $X \to M$ and

(c) (prediction) run the equations of the intervened SEM using (n_x, n_m, n_y) and holding $M = 5$, revealing that the value of Y would have been 8.

Due to autonomy, all non-intervened equations are assumed to remain invariant. Note that, in some cases, abduction may produce a *collection* of potential noise configurations, leading to a collection of feasible counterfactual answers. Figure 4.2 offers some examples of observing, intervening upon, and asking counterfactual questions about a structural equation model.

According to Reichenbach's principle of common cause, two different SEMs can produce matching observational distributions, yet react differently to the same intervention. Going further, two different SEMs may produce matching observational *and* interventional distributions, yet answer differently to the same counterfactual question. This illustrates Pearl's ladder of causation: Computing observational, interventional, and counterfactual distributions requires increasingly sophisticated knowledge about the SEM.

4.3.5 Instrumental Variables

In many practical applications, reasons abound to suspect the existence of hidden variables not appearing in our SEM. Of particular importance is the issue of hidden *confounders*. A hidden confounder C is the common cause

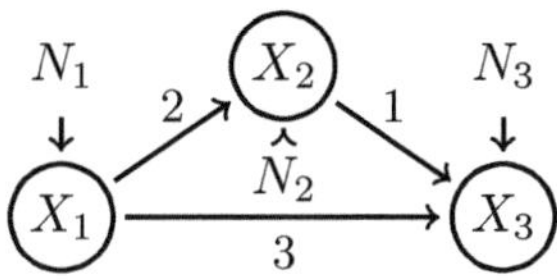

(a) Observing

```
1  x1 = n()
2  x2 = 2 * x1 + n()
3  x3 = 3 * x1 + 1 * x2 + n()
4  E(x2, x3, 5) # 11
```

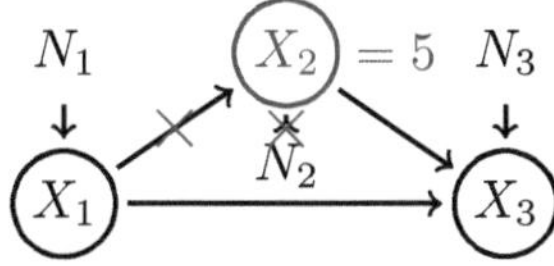

(b) Intervening

```
1  x1 = n()
2  x2 = 2 * x1 + n()
3  x2.fill_(5) # do(X2 <- 5)
4  x3 = 3 * x1 + 1 * x2 + n()
5  E(x2, x3, 5) # 5
```

```
1  # observations
2  x1, x2, x3 = 1, 1, 4
3  # abduce noises from
      observation
4  n1, n2, n3 = 1, -1, 0
5  # use noises in intervened SEM
6  x1 = n1
7  x2 = 5 # do(X2 <- 5)
8  x3 = 3 * x1 + 1 * x2 + n3 # 8
```

(c) Asking a counterfactual question

Figure 4.2: Observing, intervening, and answering counterfactual questions from a SEM, where n = lambda: torch.randn(1000, 1) samples exogenous noise, and E = lambda x, y, x0: torch.linalg.lstsq(x, y).solution * x0 computes the expected value $\mathbb{E}\left[Y \mid X = x_0\right]$.

of two observed variables $X \to Y$, such that ignoring the existence of C biases our estimation of the causal effect of X on Y. To illustrate, consider estimating the causal effect α_c from X to Y in SEM from figure 4.1a when the common cause C is unobserved. The true structural equation for the target is:

$$Y = \alpha_c \cdot X + \delta_c \cdot C + N_Y. \tag{4.5}$$

To estimate α_c in the absence of C, we may try a simple linear least-squares regression from X to Y:

$$\frac{\mathrm{cov}(X,Y)}{\mathrm{var}(X)} = \frac{\alpha_c \cdot \mathrm{var}(X) + \delta_c \cdot \gamma_c \cdot \mathrm{var}(H)}{\mathrm{var}(Y)} = \alpha_c + \frac{\delta_c \cdot \gamma_c \cdot \mathrm{var}(H)}{\mathrm{var}(X)}.$$

The previous estimate of the causal effect is biased, because the linear least-squares regression erroneously considers $\delta_c \cdot C + N_Y$ to be an *independent* additive noise term—in reality, though, the hidden confounder introduces a dependence between these putative residuals and X.

Instrumental variables are one method to consistently estimate the causal effect α_c. A variable I is an instrument for the causal relation $X \to Y$ if and only if (1) I is independent of C, (2) I is (strongly) dependent to X, and (3) I influences Y only through X. Because these three assumptions are unverifiable, choosing appropriate instruments requires domain expertise and merits several pages of justification in scientific articles.

As an example, we could be interested in demonstrating that smoking X causes cancer Y. We must do so thanks to the tireless efforts of tobacco companies and Ronald Fisher to convince us that the observed relation is due to a hidden confounder C, perhaps a genetic predisposition that makes individuals simultaneously more likely to enjoy smoking and develop lung cancer. Reusing the SEM from figure 4.1a, one valid instrument I would be a tax on cigarettes, as it is (1) independent of the hidden confounder C, (2) influences X, and (3) influences Y only through X. Instrumental variables are one instance of the Invariance Principle presented in chapter 5, since their condition (3) above translates into the conditional independence statement $Y \perp I \mid X$. By considering instruments as environments, their discovery relates to the machinery described in chapter 7.

To estimate α_c using a valid instrument I, it is common to follow a *two-stage least squares* approach. To start, consider the structural equation for X:

$$X = \beta_c \cdot I + \gamma_c \cdot C + N_X.$$

Because of the SEM structure figure 4.1a, the term $\gamma_c \cdot C + N_X$ is an independent additive noise for X. Consequently, we can consistently estimate the regression coefficient β_c as $\hat{\beta}_c$ with a *first* linear least-squares regression from I to X. By substituting X with its estimate $\beta_c \cdot I + \gamma_c \cdot C + N_X$ in the structural equation of Y, we obtain

$$
\begin{aligned}
Y &= \alpha_c \cdot X + \delta_c \cdot C + N_Y \\
&= \alpha_c \cdot (\beta_c \cdot I) + (\alpha_c \cdot \gamma_c + \delta) \cdot C + N_Y \\
&\approx \alpha_c \cdot (\hat{\beta}_c \cdot I) + (\alpha_c \cdot \gamma_c + \delta_c) \cdot C + N_Y.
\end{aligned}
$$

Because the term $(\alpha_c \cdot \gamma_c + \delta_c) \cdot C + N_Y$ is an independent additive noise for Y, we can now safely estimate the causal effect α_c using a *second* linear least-squares, this time from $\hat{\beta}I$ to Y.

4.3.6 Do-Calculus

Confounding—from the Latin confundō or mix together—occurs when any factor produces discrepancies between the observational distribution $P(Y \mid X)$, describing the statistical association between X and Y, and the interventional distribution $P(Y \mid \mathrm{do}(X \leftarrow x))$, describing the causal effect from X to Y. In essence, confounding has a clear invariance taste: Two variables are de-confounded if their conditional observational and interventional distributions match. De-confounding a causal relation $X \to Y$ consists in expressing the interventional distributions $P(Y \mid \mathrm{do}(X \leftarrow x))$ in terms of observational distributions. Pearl's *do-calculus* analyzes the causal graph of a given SEM to find a *valid adjustment set* of variables Z that allow us to express interventions on the causal relation $X \to Y$ in terms of observational distributions:

$$
P(Y = y \mid \mathrm{do}(X \leftarrow x)) = \sum_z P(Y = y \mid X = x, Z = z) \cdot P(Z = z).
$$

In particular, Z is a valid adjustment set if Z contains no descendant of any node on a directed path from X to Y (except for descendants of X that are not on a directed path from X to Y) and Z blocks all nondirected paths from X to Y.[137] Do-calculus is a more nuanced approach than the often recommended "control for all pre-treatment variables," which may lead to biased estimations in some scenarios.[162]) To cite some examples based on figure 4.1, adjusting for a confounder or common cause can alleviate confounding, adjusting for a mediator may reduce the causal effect, and adjusting for a collider or its descendant may increase confounding.

One important example of a valid adjustment set is $Z = \mathrm{Pa}(Y)$, leading to the simple and powerful conclusion that the structural equation $f_Y(\mathrm{Pa}(Y), N_Y)$ is invariant under all interventions not targeting Y.[137] In essence, many efforts to perform causal inference reduce to choosing the right set of features (a valid adjustment set) to deploy supervised learning algorithms.

By way of summary, do-calculus is a tool to express causation (the presence of do-operators) in terms of correlation (the absence of do-operators). According to Pearl, when using do-calculus,

> the ultimate goal is to calculate the effect of an intervention, $P(Y \mid do(X \leftarrow x))$, in terms of data such as $P(Y \mid X, A, B, Z, \ldots)$ that do not involve a do-operator. If we are completely successful at eliminating the do's, then we can use observational data to estimate the causal effect, allowing us to leap from rung one to rung two of the Ladder of Causation.[162]

Therefore, we may say, correlation *does* imply causation *if* measured under the right distribution! This brings us back to David Hume: We cannot observe causation directly, so all attempts to estimate it reduce to the study of regularities and their invariance across interventions. Methods in causal discovery, reviewed next, double down on this idea.

4.4   Causal Discovery

So far, we have treated the structural equation model as a given entity. The problem of *causal discovery*, described next, addresses the challenge of inferring structural equation models directly from observational data.

The fundamental challenge in causal discovery is Reichenbach's principle of common cause: Observational data is, in general, insufficient to determine whether the association between two random variables X and Y is due to (1) a causal relation from X to Y, (2) a causal relation from Y to X, or (3) the existence of a common cause. Higher dimensions bring about additional issues, since the amount of possible causal structures grows super-exponentially with the number of variables. To illustrate, there are twenty-five causal graphs on three variables, but the number escalates to 4175098976430598143 for ten variables. Clark Glymour adds other warnings to the practitioner interested in discovering causal structures from observational data:

> There are a great many hazards to correct causal inference from nonexperimental data, for example: (1) missing values of variables for cases; (2) unmeasured confounding variables; (3) measurement errors; (4) sample selection bias; (5) autocorrelation, in which values of variables for a sample unit influence values of variables in other sample units; (6) probability distributions and functional dependencies that are not among the familiar examples; (7) samples that are formed

of sub-populations with distinct probability distributions and even distinct qualitative causal relations; (8) the data may be described best by a cyclic graph, and for reasons noted above, the causal content of such models is ambiguous and their discovery from data alone seemed implausible; (9) sometimes the causal relations of interest are among variables that are not measured, but whose effects or manifestations are measured, and it seemed implausible—some claimed impossible (Bartholomew and Knott 1999)—that data-driven methods could provide the information required.[63]

Moreover, causation leaves diverse imprints in observational data, calling for tailored causal discovery methods for different problems. For instance, in the context of epidemiology, a classic 1965 paper by Sir Austin Bradford Hill documented nine criteria to collect support that an observed association is causal: strength, reproducibility, specificity, temporality, dose-response, plausibility, laboratory-world coherence, experimental evidence, and analogy to other studies.[190] (For a similar set of criteria, the reader may consult Koch's postulates.) Despite these challenges, there is a rich body of literature about causal discovery methods that place smart assumptions on the data generation process (invariances in) to reduce the number of candidate causal graphs (invariances out) that could explain the data. Let's review two examples.

First, consider the case of *additive noise models*, where the causal relation from X to Y follows the structural equation model

$$Y \leftarrow f_Y(X) + N_Y. \tag{4.6}$$

In the equation above, $f_Y : \mathbb{R} \to \mathbb{R}$ is a deterministic mechanism and N_Y is an *independent* additive noise term. Assuming (4.6) and barring some corner cases explained below,[191] it is not possible to find an *anti-causal* additive noise model with the form

$$X \leftarrow f_X(Y) + N_X.$$

In particular, it is not possible to find an *independent* additive noise term N_X for any deterministic mechanism $f_X : \mathbb{R} \to \mathbb{R}$. It follows that the anti-causal model exhibits a spurious correlation between X and N_X, detectable by means of an statistical independence test.[192]

A simple algorithm enables us to estimate the causal direction between X and Y under the additive noise model assumption. This process, illustrated in figure 4.3 in panels (c) and (d), involves fitting two regression models, one in each direction, and declaring as causal the model rendering independent residuals. However, panels (a) and (b) highlight a challenging scenario where (1) the causal mechanism f is linear, (2) the cause variable X is Gaussian,

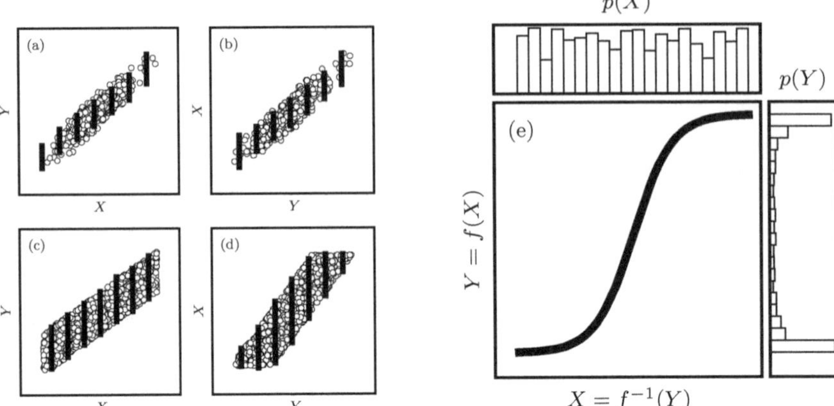

Figure 4.3: Panels (a-d) detect the causal direction of a linear additive noise model $Y \leftarrow \alpha X + N$. Here, X denotes the cause, Y the effect, and N is an independent additive noise term. On panels (a) and (b), both the cause X and the noise term N follow a Gaussian distribution, rendering a joint Gaussian distribution on (X, Y). Since Gaussian distributions are symmetrical, the causal direction between X and Y is unidentifiable. On panels (c) and (d), the cause X and the noise term N follow a uniform distribution. In this case, the causal direction is identifiable—in particular, we can conclude $X \rightarrow Y$ because, under the wrong hypothesis $X \leftarrow Y$, the resulting additive noise term is not independent. In particular, the variance of the noise, depicted as vertical bars, varies for different values of Y. Panel (e) detects the causal direction of a deterministic mapping. This is done by the IGCI method, which prefers the causal direction under which the marginal distribution of the cause $p(X)$ is independent of the slope of the putative mechanism f. This is the case for the correct causal direction $X \rightarrow Y$. However, the wrong hypothesis $Y \rightarrow X$ would require us to believe in a spurious correlation between the shape of $p(X)$ and the shape of f^{-1}.

and (3) the additive noise term N is also Gaussian. In this case, the joint distribution of (X, Y) is symmetric, both regressions yield independent additive noise terms, and the causal direction remains unidentifiable even under the additive noise model assumption.

A second algorithm for causal discovery, called the *information geometric causal inference method (IGCI)*,[193] studies two distinct scalar variables X and Y related by a deterministic mechanism $Y \leftarrow f(X)$. Given that f is invertible, the anti-causal model $X = g(Y)$ with $g = f^{-1}$ also explains the observed data. To simplify, assume that the cause variable X follows a uniform distribution $p(X)$ on the unit interval. As illustrated in figure 4.3, the density function $p(Y)$ of the effect variable Y would then grow in regions where the deterministic causal mechanism f is flat. Then, according to the independent causal mechanisms (ICM) assumption, the spurious correlation between $p(Y)$ and $g'(Y)$ challenges the anti-causal hypothesis $X \leftarrow Y$. Instead, we should favor the causal hypothesis $X \rightarrow Y$, since the independence of $p(X)$ and $f'(X)$ satisfies the ICM assumption.

Discovering causal structures beyond the bivariate case poses formidable challenges, as the required number of conditional independence tests grows exponentially with the number of variables.[188] Most alternatives for multivariate causal discovery build on this recipe: If no subset of variables $X_K \notin \{X_i, X_j\}$ induces the conditional independence $X_i \perp X_j \mid X_K$, then there is a link—with a potentially undecidable orientation—between X_i and X_j. Alas, the necessary assumptions to identify or evaluate the estimated causal graph of any realistic multivariate system—sometimes affectionately called a *hair ball*—are insurmountable.

Like machines, humans also struggle with the challenges of multidimensional causal discovery. Seminal works in psychology show that our short-term memory can manage only about seven variables,[194] and that we often experience an *illusion of explanatory depth*, where we overestimate our mechanistic understanding of the world.[195] For example, Rebecca Lawson asked participants to draw a bicycle,[196] finding that even regular riders often produced impossible designs. Similarly, Arthur S. Reber showed that participants who engaged in implicit learning from input-target pairs—similar to machine learning—outperformed those pursuing explicit learning that required outlining the problem's causal structure.[197] Cartwright argues that we build *simple models of a complex world*, where their utility resides in predicting well under various interventions:

> It is important that the models we construct allow us to draw the right conclusions about the behavior of the phenomena and their causes. But it is not essential that the models accurately describe everything that actually happens.[113]

All models are wrong, some are useful: Our cognition does not operate on top of complex causal structures, but through identifying patterns that are roughly invariant across a wide range of circumstances.

4.5 Potential Outcomes Framework

The potential outcomes framework, first appearing in Jerzy Neyman's 1923 master's thesis[198] and later refined by Donald Rubin,[199] is a widely used approach to studying causation from experimental data. Over time, the potential outcomes framework has become the gold standard for analyzing causal effects in randomized controlled trials across various fields, including econometrics, medicine, political science, and psychology.[178]

To elucidate the framework of potential outcomes, let us consider the causal effect of attending college on an individual's first-job salary.[200] Collect a vector of features x_i for each individual i, which may include their ability, family background, geographical location, interests, and so on. For each individual, hypothesize about the outcomes in two potential worlds. In the first world the individual goes to college, a fact denoted by setting *treatment* variable to $t_i = 1$, and obtains the first salary y_i^1 on their first job. In the second world, the individual does not go to college ($t_i = 0$), and obtains the salary y_i^0. We call y_i^1 and y_i^0 the two *potential outcomes* associated with individual i with features x_i. We refer to individuals associated with $t_i = 1$ as the *treated group*, whereas we say individuals associated with $t_i = 0$ form the *control group*.

For each individual i, we get to observe only the *factual outcome*

$$y_i := y_i^{t_i} = (1 - t_i) \cdot y_i^0 + t_i \cdot y_i^1. \tag{4.7}$$

Taking this expression for granted is referred to as the *stable unit treatment value assumption* or SUTVA, whereby there are only two treatments that each individual can receive (known as consistency), and the potential outcomes of one individual do not depend on the treatment assignment of others (noninterference). (Amusingly, the expression (4.7) requires committing to the modal realism of Lewis, since the sum would otherwise remain undefined.) One could violate consistency, for instance, by offering the same surgery treatment at different facilities and by different surgeons. As a common example of the violation of noninterference, consider a vaccination study where my probability of contracting the disease is influenced by whether other members in my household have been vaccinated. We shall also assume that interventions do not alter the structure of the world. As an example of a structure-altering intervention, consider providing fishing nets to some fishers in a village. While the productivity of fishers with nets could improve, giving fishing nets to all the fishers could reduce the productivity per capita, as the total amount of fish remains fixed.

Although we always observe factual outcomes y_i, we never get to explore the road not taken, the *counterfactual outcome*:

$$\tilde{y}_i := y_i^{1-t_i} = t_i \cdot y_i^0 + (1 - t_i) \cdot y_i^1.$$

The difference between factual and counterfactual outcomes $y_i - \tilde{y}_i$ defines the causal effect for individual i. Since the counterfactual outcome is unobservable, Paul Holland famously stated that "the fundamental problem of causal inference" is one of missing data imputation.[141] Many algorithms, some of which are discussed below, address this issue by estimating the *average* causal effect across populations instead of individuals.

4.5.1 Naïve Difference Estimator

So, does attending college cause individuals to achieve higher salaries on their first job, *on average*? Technically, the purpose of this question is to estimate the *average treatment effect* (ATE) expressed by the quantity $\mathbb{E}[y_i^1 - y_i^0]$. As a first approach, let us compare the average salary of individuals who attended college to the average salary of those who did not. This is denoted by the difference of observational expectations $\mathbb{E}[y_i \mid t_i = 1] - \mathbb{E}[y_i \mid t_i = 0]$. Given a dataset of triplets (x_i, t_i, y_i), the naïve difference ATE estimate is:

$$\hat{\text{ATE}}^{\text{naïve}} = \frac{1}{|i : t_i = 1|} \sum_{i:t_i=1} y_i - \frac{1}{|i : t_i = 0|} \sum_{i:t_i=0} y_i. \tag{4.8}$$

Although simple, this expression often provides a biased estimate of the ATE. Upon closer inspection and by virtue of (4.7), the naïve difference estimator (4.8) decomposes as[200]

$$\mathbb{E}[y_i \mid t_i = 1] - \mathbb{E}[y_i \mid t_i = 0] = \underbrace{\mathbb{E}[y_i^1 \mid t_i = 1] - \mathbb{E}[y_i^0 \mid t_i = 1]}_{\text{ATE}}$$
$$+ \underbrace{\mathbb{E}[y_i^0 \mid t_i = 1] - \mathbb{E}[y_i^0 \mid t_i = 0]}_{\text{selection bias}}.$$

The first braced term is the average causal effect on treated individuals—this is the quantity of interest describing whether college attendance leads to better-paid first jobs. However, this term is impossible to compute, as we never get to observe the counterfactual expectation $\mathbb{E}[y_i^0 \mid t_i = 1]$. The second braced term is called the *selection bias*. In the fortunate situation when selection bias is zero, the naïve difference estimator matches the average causal effect of interest. Alas, selection bias is, in most applications, far from zero. In these situations, the naïve difference estimator can be far from the average causal effect, and even have the opposite sign. For example, individuals who attend college might be wealthier and have better networking opportunities, leading to better-paid first jobs regardless of holding a college degree.[200]

4.5.2 Eliminating Selection Bias by Randomization

The preferred approach to combat selection bias is *complete randomization*: Assign each participant in the study to either the control group or the treated group *at random*. The resulting design, known as a randomized controlled trial (RCT) or A/B test,[178] ensures that treated and control groups follow the same distribution, and is widely considered as the gold standard for causal inference. One of the earliest RCTs is credited to James Lind (1716–1794), who sought to cure scurvy in British sailors at a time when the connection between the disease and vitamin C deficiency was unknown. Peters et al. recall the story:

> They all in general had putrid gums, the spots and lassitude, with weakness of the knees ... Two were ordered each a quart of cyder a day. Two others took twenty-five drops of elixir vitriol three times a day ... Two others took two spoonfuls of vinegar three times a day ... Two of the worst patients were put on a course of sea-water ... Two others had each two oranges and one lemon given them every day ... The two remaining patients, took ... an electuary recommended by a hospital surgeon ... The consequence was, that the most sudden and visible good effects were perceived from the use of oranges and lemons; one of those who had taken them, being at the end of six days fit for duty.[137]

Technically speaking, randomization is highly prized because it entails the *exchangeability* or *ignorability* condition:

$$(Y^1, Y^0) \perp T, \tag{4.9}$$

whereby both potential outcomes—actual and counterfactual—become independent of the treatment assignment. This independence removes selection bias, since the naïve difference estimator now can be expressed as

$$\begin{aligned}
\mathbb{E}[y_i \mid t_i = 1] - \mathbb{E}[y_i \mid t_i = 0] &= \mathbb{E}[y_i^1 \mid t_i = 1] - \mathbb{E}[y_i^0 \mid t_i = 0] \\
&= \mathbb{E}[y_i^1 \mid t_i = 1] - \mathbb{E}[y_i^0 \mid t_i = 1] \\
&= \mathbb{E}[y_i^1 - y_i^0 \mid t_i = 1] = \mathbb{E}[y^1 - y^0].
\end{aligned}$$

In the previous equations, randomization allows (1) switching from $t_i = 0$ to $t_i = 1$ in the second line and (2) dropping the conditioning on t_i in the third line. Overall, randomization ensures that the difference in observed average differences matches the causal effect, giving validity to the naïve estimate (4.8). One metaphor to understand randomization and exchangeability within our running example is as follows: If we were to rewind the world, exchange those individuals who went to college with those who did not, and let events unfold again, then the average causal effect on earnings would remain unchanged.

4.5.3 Reducing Selection Bias by Valid Adjustment

Complete randomization is a rare privilege. Control groups may be unethical (consider studying the effectiveness of parachutes), designing placebos may be impossible (think of psychedelic-assisted psychotherapy), and subjects in vaccination programs may quit the study at different rates depending on whether they feel relief after their first injection. In these and many other cases, there is a distributional discrepancy between the individuals in the control group and the individuals in the treated group. Technically, this is formalized in terms of the *propensity score* $\pi(x_i) = P(T = 1 \mid X = x_i)$, which describes the probability of individual i belonging to the treated group. Under the blessings of complete randomization and equally sized treated and control groups, we would expect constant propensity scores $\pi(x_i) = \frac{1}{2}$ for all individuals. Conversely, when deviating from complete randomization, propensity scores can range across the entire unit interval. Such situations demand understanding the treatment assignment mechanism—formalized in terms of the propensity score function—to de-bias the our causal inferences.

A common method to narrow treated-control group discrepancies is to condition the study on certain features x_i that describe the individuals i involved. More specifically, we aim to construct a feature representation X that induces *conditional exchangeability*, denoted by the conditional independence statement

$$(Y^0, Y^1) \perp T \mid X. \tag{4.10}$$

If X meets the condition above, then it is a valid adjustment set that de-confounds the observed association between the potential outcomes and treatment assignments. In other words, control for the causes X you know about, and attempt randomization for the rest. Conditioning on X results in a study that satisfies the *exchangeability* condition discussed in section 4.5.2, enjoys all the benefits of a randomized controlled trial, and allows for the use of the naïve difference estimator to infer the causal effect. Looking forward, equation (4.10) is one incarnation of the Invariance Principle that will be proposed in chapter 5 to learn statistical invariances from different collections of observational data.

In addition to conditional exchangeability, we must assume that our feature vectors X satisfy *positivity*. This condition means that the propensity scores $\pi(X)$ are bounded away from their extreme values of zero and one. Randomization ensures positivity, because in these cases $\pi(x) = \frac{1}{2}$ for all x. However, having treated and control groups with disjoint supports complicates causal inference. For instance, if all individuals in the treated group of a medical study are men, we cannot infer causal effects on women. Conditional exchangeability and positivity are often in tension: Adding features to X can improve conditional exchangeability, but it can also diminish positivity. (Methods such as regression discontinuity designs leverage further knowledge about the treatment assignment to address the absence of positivity.[178]) On the other hand, bad controls—akin to bad adjustment sets in the context of SEMs—are those that increase confounding between treatment assignment and outcome. Angrist and Pischke suggest the following recipes to select good controls:

> Some variables are bad controls and should not be included in a regression model ... Bad controls are variables that are themselves outcome variables in the notional experiment at hand ... Good controls are variables that we can think of as having been fixed at the time the regressor of interest was determined.[200]

However, some exceptions to this rule of thumb exist,[162] and do-calculus offers an exact procedure for selecting good controls when the structural equation model is known.

Assume that we have identified a valid adjustment set X containing features that induce both conditional exchangeability and positivity. To explore the various methods available to control for X, it will be helpful to decompose the ATE as the average of *individual treatment effects*:

$$\hat{\text{ATE}} = \frac{1}{n} \sum_i^n \hat{\text{ITE}}_i, \text{ where } \hat{\text{ITE}}_i = y_i^1 - y_i^0,$$

where $\hat{\text{ITE}}_i$ describes the effect of the treatment on individual i.

One popular technique for correcting treated-control differences is to construct a dataset containing matched pairs of examples from both groups. The purpose of *matching methods* is to satisfy the positivity constraint by increasing the shared support between treated and control individuals:

> The objective of matching is to find in the population individuals that are similar in all possible respects, the only difference being the administration of the "treatment." Statisticians have formally shown that in the case of perfect matching, the results are equivalent to randomization ... Once we have the cases and the matched controls (rather than experimental controls), we can compute the average response for the two groups, and then the difference, thus obtaining the average causal effects.[200]

For instance, the *nearest-neighbor* estimator pairs each example (x_i, t_i, y_i) to the closest example $(x_{j(i)}, 1 - t_i, y_{j(i)})$, defining the individual treatment effect

$$\hat{\text{ITE}}_i^{\text{nn}} = y_i - y_{j(i)}, \text{ where } j(i) = \underset{j : t_j = 1 - t_i}{\arg\min} \| \phi(x_i), \phi(x_j) \|^2.$$

To find the closest example, one must choose a representation $\phi(x)$ of feature vectors x. To that end, three alternatives are most popular. First, engineer a representation ϕ by hand, in most cases the identity function $\phi(x) := x$. Second, learn a representation ϕ that minimizes the distributional discrepancy between the treated and control groups, while retaining reasonable predictive power about the factual outcomes.[201] Third, propensity scores, defined as $\phi(x_i) := \hat{\pi}(x_i)$, are another popular representation for matching. Propensity score matching is justified by a celebrated theorem, credited to Paul R. Rosenbaum and Donald B. Rubin,[202] ensuring that if adjusting on X induces conditional exchangeability, then adjusting on $\pi(X)$ does so too.

$$(Y^0, Y^1) \perp T \mid X \Rightarrow (Y^0, Y^1) \perp T \mid \pi(X). \tag{4.11}$$

In practice, practitioners estimate $\pi(x)$ using a binary classifier, then perform matching on some quantization of the estimated propensity scores. Propensity score matching is appealing because it eliminates the need to engineer a representation ϕ, while reducing the matching problem from the high-dimensional feature space X to the one-dimensional scores $\pi(X)$. However, the capacity of π must be carefully controlled to avoid propensity scores near zero or one, as these would breach the positivity assumption.

A second strategy to perform propensity score matching is the *inverse probability weighting* estimator. By noting that

$$\mathbb{E}\left[Y^1\right] = \mathbb{E}\left[\frac{Y \cdot T}{\pi(X)}\right] \text{ and } \mathbb{E}\left[Y^0\right] = \mathbb{E}\left[\frac{Y \cdot (1 - T)}{1 - \pi(X)}\right],$$

it follows:

$$\hat{\text{ITE}}_i^{\text{ipw}} = \left(\frac{[\![t_i = 1]\!]}{\hat{\pi}(x_i)} - \frac{[\![t_i = 0]\!]}{1 - \hat{\pi}(x_i)}\right) y_i,$$

where positivity is required to avoid near-zero denominators. Because of this reason, it is common practice to discard individuals with propensity scores near zero or one.

In the *g-computation* framework, we model the relationship from feature vectors X and treatment indicators T to outcomes Y directly.[178] Two common implementations of this approach are the s-learner and the t-learner:

$$\hat{\text{ITE}}_i^{\text{g,s}} = \hat{g}(x_i, 1) - \hat{g}(x_i, 0)$$

$$\hat{\text{ITE}}_i^{\text{g,t}} = \hat{g}_1(x_i) - \hat{g}_0(x_i).$$

In the first equation above, the s-learner estimates one function from feature-treatment pairs (X, T) to outcomes Y using the entire dataset (x_i, t_i, y_i). In the second equation, the t-learner estimates two separate functions $\hat{g}_1$ and $\hat{g}_0$, trained on the data from the control and treated groups, respectively.

All these alternatives have their own strengths and weaknesses. Choosing one over another depends on the available assumptions to either design a relevant similarity metric ϕ, model the propensity score function π, or model the potential outcome functions g directly.

4.5.4 Exploring a Linear Case

A linear example allows closed-form expressions for some of the quantities discussed above. Consider a potential outcome study with the form

$$y_i = w_x^\top x_i + w_t^\top t_i + w_0 + \varepsilon_i.$$

Because the residuals ε_i are independent, the feature vectors x_i induce conditional exchangeability. Therefore, regressing from (x_i, t_i) to y_i yields the true causal effect w_t. However, excluding x_i from our regression produces a biased causal effect. The difference between the true and biased causal effects is quantified by the *omitted variable bias* (OVB) formula:[200]

$$\frac{\text{cov}(y, t)}{\text{var}(t)} = w_t + \underbrace{w_x^\top m}_{\text{bias}},$$

where m is the regression coefficient from x to t. The OVB formula, considered by Joshua Angrist and Jörn-Steffen Pischke as the "most important result in regression theory,"[200] tells us that "coefficients on included variables are unaffected by the omission of variables when the variables omitted are uncorrelated with the variables included."[200] An important corollary of the OVB formula is the propensity score theorem, instructing us that "the only covariate you really need to control for is the probability of treatment itself."[200] Moreover, the OVB formula allows interpreting the framework of instrumental variables as a technique to decrease omitted variable bias,[200] and identifies the statistical signature of hidden confounders: correlated residuals.

4.5.5 Limitations

RCTs remain a valuable tool in causal inference, but they are best used in combination with domain knowledge and observational data. (Jin Tian and Judea Pearl offer some formulas on how to combine these two types of knowledge.[203]) The lack of assumptions in RCTs can be seen as "an advantage when persuading distrustful audiences, but it is a disadvantage for cumulative scientific progress, where prior knowledge should be built upon, not discarded."[204] In fact, three influential publications argue that most breakthroughs in medical science have been due to observational studies:

> Moreover, to attain some of the medical community's most significant insights, historical and observational methods were used and RCTs were not later needed (and at times not possible), ranging from most surgical procedures, antibiotics and aspirin, to smallpox immunisation, anaesthesia, immobilising broken bones, smoking inducing cancer, among many other examples.[205]

> We found little evidence that estimates of treatment effects in observational studies reported after 1984 are either consistently larger than or qualitatively different from those obtained in randomized, controlled trials.[206]

> The results of well-designed observational studies (with either a cohort or a case-control design) do not systematically overestimate the magnitude of the effects of treatment as compared with those in randomized, controlled trials on the same topic.[207]

When discussing the role of randomization, Deaton and Cartwright point out that "many experiments, including many of the most important (and Nobel Prize-winning) experiments in economics, do not and did not use randomization"[204] and that "randomization is an alternative when we do not know enough to control, but is generally inferior to good control when we do." We shall add that randomization is in fact infeasible in many domains of science, such as those involving large-scale phenomena like public health, policy, and biology.[205]

The framework of potential outcomes is limited to estimating *average* treatment effects due to the linearity property of the expectation operator. Estimating treatment effects for statistics that do not decompose linearly, such as the *median* treatment effect, would be much more laborious and call for additional assumptions. This focus on average treatment effects comes with its own limitations. As illustrated in figure 4.4b, large individual treatment effects can aggregate into near-zero average treatment effects.

Throughout a process that necessarily involves many human beings and complex decisions, there are countless insidious manners under which post-randomization spurious correlations may arise. Based on their own private characteristics, patients may comply with medical instructions to a different degree, drop out of the study at different stages, and be treated in different facilities by different practitioners.[205] Treatments can be *structure-altering* when implemented at a larger scale. Because randomization happens only once, the confidence intervals in our study may turn out excessively large in

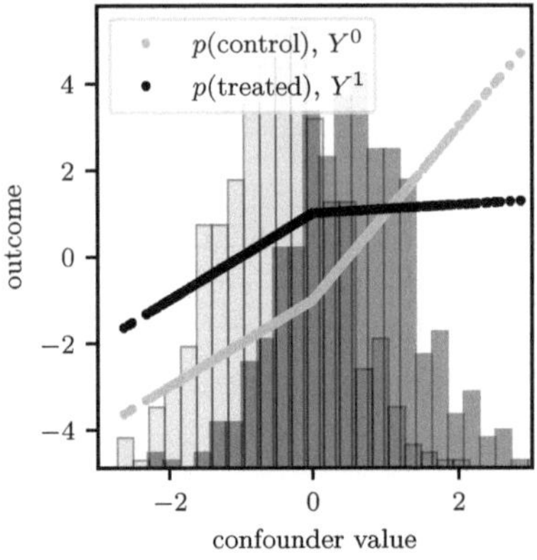

(a) POs for control and treated groups.

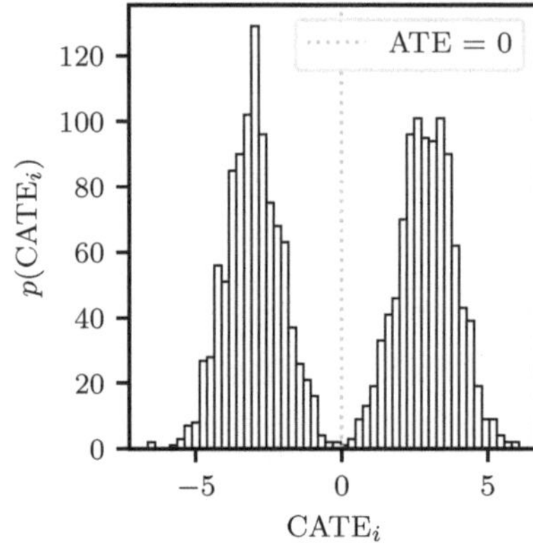

(b) Zero ATE $\not\Rightarrow$ zero ITE$_i$.

Figure 4.4: On the left, a study where the control and treated groups share only partial support overlap. In this example, our knowledge about the outcome functions for negative values of the confounder is given mostly by the control group. Analogously, we observe the outcome functions for positive values of the confounder mostly on treated individuals. Therefore, we lack differential data to estimate the outcome function in regions far away from zero. The right panel illustrates a situation where the average treatment effect is zero, regardless of the fact that the treatment has a large impact on every single individual.

i	deity	gender	kingdom	T	Y^0	Y^1	Y
1	Amun	Male	New	1	1	1	1
2	Nut	Female	New	1	0	0	0
3	Nephthys	Female	Old	0	0	0	0
4	Horus	Male	Old	1	1	1	1
5	Bastet	Female	New	0	0	0	0
6	Ptah	Male	New	1	1	1	1
7	Sekhmet	Female	Old	0	0	0	0
8	Seth	Male	Old	1	1	1	1
9	Khnum	Male	New	0	1	1	1
10	Isis	Female	Old	0	0	0	0
11	Ma'at	Female	Old	0	0	1	0
12	Tefnut	Female	New	0	0	0	0
13	Hathor	Female	Old	0	0	0	0
14	Osiris	Male	Old	1	1	1	1
15	Anubis	Male	Old	1	1	1	1
16	Thoth	Male	New	1	1	1	1
17	Wadjet	Female	New	0	0	1	0
18	Sobek	Male	New	1	1	1	1
19	Ra	Male	Old	1	1	1	1
20	Mut	Female	New	0	0	0	0

Table 4.1: Toy study under the potential outcomes framework. In truth, the treatment has no causal effect. However, the observable naïve difference estimator is:

$$P(Y = 1 \mid T = 1) - P(Y = 1 \mid T = 0) = 0.8.$$

The (unverifiable) assumption of exchangeability does not hold in this example, since:

$$\max_{t \in \{0,1\}} \left(P(Y^t = 1 \mid T = 1) - P(Y^t = 1 \mid T = 0) \right)^2 = 0.8.$$

Gender is a good control, since it brings us closer to the situation where the (unverifiable) assumption of conditional exchangeability will hold:

$$\max_{t \in \{0,1\}, g \in \{f,m\}} \left(P(Y^t = 1 \mid G = g, T = 1) - P(Y^t = 1, G = g \mid T = 0) \right)^2 = 0.22.$$

Kingdom is a bad control, as it exacerbates the violation of exchangeability:

$$\max_{t \in \{0,1\}, k \in \{o,n\}} \left(P(Y^t = 1 \mid K = k, T = 1) - P(Y^t = 1, K = k \mid T = 0) \right)^2 = 1.0.$$

those situations where the number of participants is small.[204] Even under the companion of prefect randomization, Crabbe et al. admit that "despite our efforts to equate laboratory environments, significant and, in some cases, large effects on site were found for nearly all variables."[208]

Even under complete randomization, extrapolating RCT results to broader populations is "a long and tortuous path."[204] For example, subjects behave differently when they know they are part of a study—a phenomenon called Hawthorne's effect. This raises the question: How can I ensure the external validity of my RCT to the population at large? To bridge the gap between the laboratory and the real world, Deaton and Cartwright argue, "there is no option but to commit to some causal structure if we are to know how to use RCT evidence out of the original context … And because RCTs tell us so little about how results happen, they have a disadvantage over studies that use a wider range of prior information and data to help nail down mechanisms."[204] RCTs provide statistical estimates about the parameters of a presupposed causal structure. Extending or falsifying the presumed causal structure is the task of science, and it transcends all statistical analysis. To transform statistical insights into scientific theories, additional assumptions are necessary: Without invariance in assumptions, there is no invariance in conclusions.

4.6 Conclusion

Arguing for the existence of causation, we have seen, is a debate confined to metaphysics. Moreover, discovering causation from data, I have argued in this chapter, is fraught with pitfalls and complexities. Therefore, the rest of this book turns the epistemological program upside-down: Rather than searching for causation to find invariance, we shall seek to uncover what is meant by causation. This new approach gives ontological priority to the *how* described by invariant mechanisms over the subjective, circular, and slippery *why* of causal language. Interestingly, Fritz Perls, the founder of *Gestalt* therapy, described a similar shift in psychiatry during the 1960s:

> In his time, the scientific approach was that of causality, that the trouble was caused by something in the past, like a billiard cue pushing a billiard ball, and the cue then is the cause of the rolling of the ball. In the meantime, our scientific attitude has changed. We don't look to the world any more in terms of cause and effect: We look upon the world as a continuous ongoing process. We are back to Heraclitus, to the pre-Socratic idea that everything is in a flux. We never step into the same river twice. In other words, we have made—in science, but unfortunately not yet in psychiatry—the transition

from linear causality to thinking of process, from the why to the how. If you ask how, you look at the structure, you see what's going on now, a deeper understanding of the process. The how is all we need to understand how we or the world functions. The how gives us perspective, orientation. The how shows that one of the basic laws, the identity of structure and function, is valid. If we change the structure, the function changes. If we change the function, the structure changes. I know you want to ask why, like every child, like every immature person asks why, to get rationalization or explanation. But the why at best leads to clever explanation, but never to an understanding.[209]

In all likelihood, I would like to suggest, nature disregards the teleological *why* and embraces the mechanistic *how*. If the goal of science is to explain the laws of nature, should we not attempt to reverse engineer from their statistical invariances, as statistical invariances? This is the road taken next, to propose the Invariance Principle.

Part III

Invariance Setups

Chapter 5

The Invariance Principle

5.1   Introduction

In the exposition so far, I've laid out two main arguments. First, large neural networks that emphasize minimizing training error adopt a *simplify-and-memorize* strategy vulnerable to spurious correlations. The resulting predictors lack robustness, leading to large predictive errors when the distributions of the training and testing examples differ. Second, the framework of causation, though often proposed as the gold standard to build AI systems, is fraught with complexities that hinder its application to real problems. Despite these obstacles, most accounts of causation focus on the stability or invariance of causal relations. To engage both these arguments, this central chapter proposes taking *statistical invariance* as the primary target of learning, which will align with the causal structure of the data when the target obtains across manipulations of the phenomena of interest. In other words, it is time to turn the epistemological problem upside-down: Instead of seeking causation to find invariance, we should seek invariance to—at times—discover causation.

The main learning tool introduced in this book is the *Invariance Principle*, informally stated as:

Frame your question so its answer matches across situations.

(IP)

This principle invites us to focus on those aspects of a learning problem that yield the same predictors despite varying background circumstances. Predictions based on these invariant solutions should be more robust to novel configurations of external factors like time, location, experimental protocol, and interventions. For example, a self-driving car should be able to detect

127

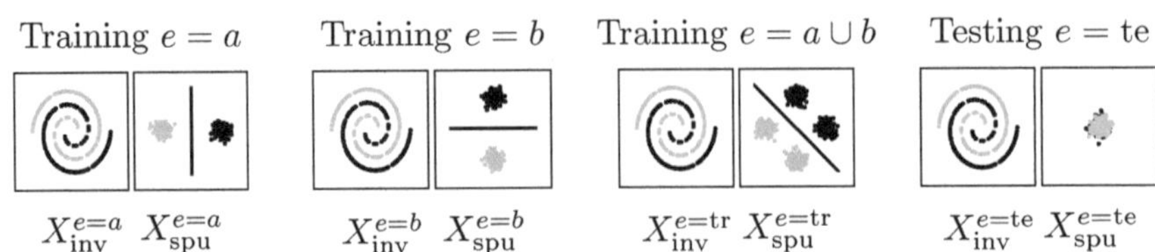

Figure 5.1: Learning a binary classifier from two training environments $e = \{a, b\}$, as illustrated in "Learning Explanations That Are Hard to Vary".[210] Each environment has two features: a two-dimensional spiral feature X_{inv}^{e}, and a two-dimensional blob feature X_{spu}^{e}. The spiral feature induces an invariant yet complex nonlinear decision boundary, shown in gray. The blob feature induces a linear, large-margin, zero training error decision boundary, for any mixture of training environments. However, this simple decision boundary changes in orientation for each environment, and it is unable to classify correctly points in the testing environment $e = \text{te}$. The goal of learning invariances across environments is, in many cases, to discard easier-yet-varying solutions in favor of complex-yet-invariant patterns.

pedestrians regardless of environmental conditions such as location, weather, or traffic conditions. Toward the end of this chapter, I will argue that this principle of invariance has been a crucial component of scientific discoveries in mathematics, physics, and philosophy, especially in areas like relevance realization and metaphysics. In the context of machine learning, the primary task of this chapter is to reformulate (IP) as a more practical recipe, "find a feature representation such that the optimal classifier matches across data distributions," yielding the algorithm of invariant risk minimization.

In their work "Learning Explanations That Are Hard to Vary," Parascandolo and colleagues offer a useful example to ground our discussion. As illustrated in figure 5.1, it involves the binary classification of gray and black points based on four real-valued features. The first two features (x_1, x_2) separate the two classes by means of a nonlinear spiral pattern. The second two features (x_3, x_4) separate the classes neatly into two Gaussian blobs, by means of a linear decision boundary. To train our binary classifier using ERM, we are given examples from a mixture of two training environments $\text{tr} = a \cup b$. After training, the predictor is deployed in a novel test environment te.

There are plenty of reasons why ERM tends to learn the decision boundary afforded by the Gaussian blob features. In particular, "the boundary is linear, it has a large margin, it can be expressed with small weights, it is fast to learn, robust to input noise, and has perfect accuracy and no iid generalization gap."[210] However, this simple decision boundary *varies* across the two environments that comprise our training data. When robust learning matters, this should be taken as a warning signal: The decision boundary could change once again, in unexpected ways, under the test environment. In those cases, predictors that rely on changing or spurious correlations could incur large out-of-distribution errors.

In contrast, the nonlinear decision boundary afforded by the spiral features is observed to be *invariant* across training environments, promising greater predictive robustness. However, finding the spiral decision boundary "is a fiddly process and arguably a much slower path towards small loss"[210] than the one provided by the Gaussian blobs. Reasoning about invariance is challenging for ERM, since the learning algorithm is agnostic to the existence of two distinct environments within the training data, and this knowledge is necessary to decide which decision boundaries are invariant. This is where moving beyond ERM, by means of the Invariance Principle, shows potential to learn robust predictors. Paraphrasing the principle, we would like to frame our question (choose the spiral features) so its answer (the decision boundary) matches across situations (training environments).

The previous example illustrates how learning with the Invariance Principle must balance two opposing forces. On one hand, we shall recruit correlations to improve our predictive accuracy across training environments. On the other hand, we shall discard correlations to improve our extrapolation toward all relevant environments. As we will see, the patterns learned by the Invariance Principle often relate to the causal structures governing our data. Further, as philosophers like Robert Nozick suggest, they may be the constituents of what we define as truth.[211]

5.2   What Is an Environment?

A fundamental concept in the study of invariance is the *environment*, which describes different variations of a data collection process concerning the same system of variables. Environments may differ in location, time, experimental details, the identity of the data collector or annotator, measurement device, external interventions, contextual circumstances, background conditions, and nuisance factors. Using the cow-on-the-beach problem as an example, photographers may collect pictures of cows and camels in a handful of countries (environments), yielding various distributions of landscapes. Because our learning goal is to build a cow-camel classifier that generalizes across the globe, we must focus on animal patterns invariant across observed environments, while discarding spurious landscape correlations.

More formally, consider a large collection of *relevant environments* $\mathcal{E}$, each describing a different condition where the relationship between an input

setup	training inputs	test inputs
generative learning	U^1	$\emptyset$
unsupervised learning	U^1	U^1
supervised learning	L^1	U^1
semi-supervised learning	L^1, U^1	U^1
transductive learning	$L_1^1 U_1^1$	U_1^1
multitask learning	$L^1, \ldots, L^{e_{\mathrm{tr}}}$	$U^1, \ldots, U^{e_{\mathrm{tr}}}$
continual (or lifelong) learning	$L^1, \ldots, L^{\infty}$	$U^1, \ldots, U^{\infty}$
domain adaptation	$L^1, \ldots, L^{e_{\mathrm{tr}}}, U^{e_{\mathrm{tr}}+1}$	$U^{e_{\mathrm{tr}}+1}$
transfer learning	$U^1, \ldots, U^{e_{\mathrm{tr}}}, L^{e_{\mathrm{tr}}+1}$	$U^{e_{\mathrm{tr}}+1}$
learning across environments	$L^1, \ldots, L^{e_{\mathrm{tr}}}$	$U^{e_{\mathrm{tr}}+1}$

Table 5.1: Different learning setups. L^e and U^e denote labeled and unlabeled data from environment e, respectively.

variable X and a target variable Y remains invariant. Among the set of the relevant environments, assume we have access to examples collected from a handful of *training environments* $\mathcal{E}_{\mathrm{tr}} \subset \mathcal{E}$. These training environments provide the data to learn our machine, later deployed to perform in a variety of unobserved *testing environments* $\mathcal{E}_{\mathrm{te}} = \mathcal{E} \setminus \mathcal{E}_{\mathrm{tr}}$. While environments can relate to each other by means of rich structures—for instance, countries may relate to each other in terms of geographical distance or spoken languages—for now we'll ignore such information and index environments using natural numbers $e \in \mathcal{E} \subset \mathbb{N}$. However, we'll come back to the issue of leveraging rich environmental information in chapter 8.

Each environment $e \in \mathcal{E}$ produces a joint probability distribution $P^e(X, Y)$ over the inputs and targets, sometimes denoted as X^e and Y^e. These distributions help us formalize the problem of learning across multiple training environments as estimating a predictor with minimal worst-case performance over the relevant environments:

$$f = \arg\min_{\tilde{f}} \sup_{e \in \mathcal{E}} R_{P^e}(\tilde{f}). \tag{5.1}$$

The population risk $R_{P^e}(f)$, defined in chapter 2, measures the error of predictor f on environment $e \in \mathcal{E}$ by integrating the loss ℓ across the distribution P^e. The relationship between (5.1) will become apparent as the chapter unfolds, following several previous scholarly studies.[212,213] For a comparison between the problem of learning across multiple environments and other learning setups, see table 5.1.

From a practical standpoint, learning across multiple training environments is a doubly underspecified problem. First, we do not observe all the relevant environments $\mathcal{E}$ but only a small subset of training environments $\mathcal{E}_{\mathrm{tr}} \subset \mathcal{E}$. Second, for each of the observed training environments $e \in \mathcal{E}_{\mathrm{tr}}$, we do not observe the distribution P^e but only a finite dataset $D^e = \{(x_i^e, y_i^e)\}_{i=1}^{n^e}$ containing iid examples from P^e. These two underspecifications force us to approximate the population risk (5.1) with the empirical counterpart

$$f = \arg\min_{\tilde{f}} \ \sup_{e \in \mathcal{E}_{\mathrm{tr}}} \ R_{P_n^e}(\tilde{f}),$$

where the empirical risk $R_{P_n^e}(f)$ measures the error of the predictor f across the examples D^e collected from training environment $e \in \mathcal{E}_{\mathrm{tr}}$. While training seeks to improve performance on the worst of training environments $\mathcal{E}_{\mathrm{tr}}$, we must not lose sight of our interest in obtaining a predictor performing well on the worst of all relevant environments $\mathcal{E}$.

The second underspecification arises from observing limited data in each training environment, yielding similar estimation issues to those studied in chapter 2. To address this, we (1) place an iid assumption within each environment, and (2) wield Belkin's razor to carve out the smoothest predictor attaining zero training error. The first underspecification, resulting from observing only a limited number of relevant environments, is the technical challenge explored in this chapter. Our main tool to tackle the first underspecification will be the Invariance Principle, assuming that correlations invariant across training environments will persist across testing environments. Challenges related to model selection, here due to our ignorance about the test environment, will be discussed in chapter 7.

These two levels of underspecification translate into a hierarchy of two uniformity principles. In particular, learning from multiple environments assumes that the future will resemble the past in two ways: Each environment generates iid data, and there exists a collection of correlations invariant across all environments. David Cox (1924–2022) places more emphasis on this second type of underspecification, commonly analyzed in external validity studies:

> The success of a theory is best judged from its ability to predict in new contexts; often the prediction is under quite different conditions from the data.[214]

This uniformity principle is also our chief subject of study in this chapter.

To predict well in new contexts, one must steer away from spurious correlations and rely on invariant patterns. Spurious correlations are specific to a subset of training environments and form patterns unfit for robust prediction, as they may change in unpredictable manners throughout test environments. In contrast, input-output patterns that are invariant across training environments hold more promise as constituents of robust predictions. Therefore, the goal of the Invariance Principle is to serve as a learning tool to distinguish between these two types of patterns.

Correlations are always invariant or spurious in relation to a collection of environments. All correlations are invariant across a single environment and spurious across all *possible* environments. Therefore, as Woodward argued in the context of causation,[140] invariance is a concept that comes in gradations. In particular, patterns are *accidental* when they obtain only in one environment, while we consider them *laws* when they hold invariant across a wide array of environments. Just as it happens with scientific theories, invariances are never demonstrated; rather, they resist increasing attempts at falsification, where each attempt entails the collection of one additional training environment. Scientific theories exhibit convergence when they explain many past observations, and likewise show power when they allow the prediction of many future cases. Similarly, useful invariances exhibit convergence when they hold across many training environments and show power when they extrapolate to many testing environments.

When learning robust predictors, we are interested in learning correlations that are invariant across *relevant* environments. These environments should exemplify the variations expected to happen between the training and testing data. To achieve so, Federica Russo suggests, relevant environments should cover a *diverse* range of circumstances about the prediction problem:

> There is no "golden recipe" for the selection of the most appropriate environments. The reason is apparent: a major challenge in social science research is precisely to define the population of reference and the appropriate subpopulations for the purpose of invariance tests ... It is worth noting that these partitions of the data set are not randomly sampled subpopulations. If they were, we would expect to find approximately the same values of the parameters, but with a larger confidence interval. Instead, different environments—adequate partitions of the data set—must be chosen such that successful invariance tests allow us to say that (1) the parameterization and (2) the causal structure are stable across the partition.[215]

That is, diverse environments reveal relevant correlations, while identical environments make every correlation look like it's invariant.

5.2.1 Interventions as Environments

The signature of a causal relation, we have seen in chapter 3, is its invariance across interventions. For example, Hooke's law remains invariant as we manipulate body mass, spring constants, and elongation distances—enabling us to answer an array of what-if-things-had-been-different questions. However, the concept of environment introduced in this chapter encompasses not only causal interventions but also passive variations, under which we can examine a system of variables. Woodward provides an example concerning the incidence of lung cancer across different socioeconomic groups:

> There is evidence of a higher frequency of lung cancer among smokers than among nonsmokers, when potentially confounding variables are controlled for, among both men and women, among people of different genetic backgrounds, across different diets, different environments, and different socioeconomic conditions. The precise level and quantitative details of the association do vary; for example, the incidence of lung cancer among smokers is higher in lower socioeconomic groups, but the fact that there is some stable association or other is stable or robust across a wide variety or different groups and background circumstances.[140]

Russo reaches similar conclusions in a study on factors influencing self-rated health in Baltic countries:

> It turned out that the chosen factors (alcohol consumption, physical health, psychological health, psychological distress, education, locus of control, and social support) had a remarkably stable impact on self-rated health across the different Baltic countries, across the time frames analysed, across gender, ethnicity, and age groups.[215]

In these studies, the authors do not actively intervene or manipulate the variables; instead, they passively observe natural changes that reveal both spurious and invariant patterns.

Russo identifies the benefits of broadening the criteria of *invariance across interventions* common in causation to the more encompassing notion of *invariance across environments*:

> I argued that, in nonexperimental contexts, invariance properties are tested across changes of the environment. This means partitioning the population of reference into relevant subpopulations, contexts, or environments, and testing a causal structure across them. Invariance tests concern, on the one hand, the stability of the parameters (their sign and values), and, on the other hand, the stability of the "arrangement" of the variables across the chosen different partitions.[215]

In this quote, Russo does not only emphasize searching for stable correlations; she also calls attention to the importance of variable selection for the discovery of invariance. Later in the text, Russo defends two main advantages from considering environments beyond interventions. To start with, causal interventions are in many cases unethical or downright impossible. For instance, lethal medical studies contravene morality, while switching off the Sun is wholly unrealizable. Furthermore, the notion of environment is metaphysically lean and free from circularity. This is in contrast to the causally laden notion of intervention, as criticized in chapter 3.

As another example of invariance without causation, Nancy Cartwright discusses the concept of exogeneity put forward by David Hendry:[151]

> Hendry adds a constraint and defines: X causes Y if and only if the parameters of $P(Y \mid X)$ stay fixed as we vary the parameters of the distribution of X ... The logic is simple. We have an association. We assume it to be invariant under a particular kind of manipulation. So we are able to use that association to predict what happens under the specified kind of manipulation. This logic works no matter whether the starting association is causal or not. Hendry's proposal is a case in point. What good is causation then? ... Causation without invariance will not do the job, and any invariant relation will provide reliable predictions regardless of whether it is causal.[216]

According to Cartwright, invariant relations are valuable because they enable robust predictions across relevant environments, regardless of whether these environments correspond to active manipulations. While this general stance does not rule out finding causation by searching for invariance across interventions, it suggests a leaner epistemological program: Search directly for observable invariance, because it will in all cases afford robust predictions, and sometimes align with causation.

5.2.2 Environments as Domains, Attributes, and Groups

To simplify the nomenclature, consider environments and *domains* synonymous, two inclusive terms to describe different data collection circumstances surrounding the same system of variables. Slightly different is the concept of *attribute*, which is often aligned with one known spurious correlation in the data. Lastly, each attribute-label combination yields one data *group*.

To illustrate, consider two training environments (or domains) for the cow-on-the-beach problem, a binary classification task to distinguish between cows ($y_i = 0$) and camels ($y_i = 1$). The first environment produces a collection of triplets ($x_i, y_i, e_i = 1$) containing 80% of cows in grasslands, 20% of cows in beaches, 80% of camels in beaches, and 20% of camels in grasslands. The second environment yields another collection of triplets ($x_i, y_i, e_i = 2$), this time with a 90%/10% blend. With these two training environments at hand, we could identify that intrinsic animal-target correlations (those on top of horns, hoofs, and humps) are invariant, while background-target correlations (those on top of grass and sand) are spurious. When using attributes, the usual arrangement is a single collection of triplets (x_i, y_i, a_i), where a_i is a binary attribute indicating whether the background appearing on the image x_i is a grassland or a beach. We may transform the attribute dataset into a group dataset, containing triplets (x_i, y_i, g_i), by assigning group indices $g_i = n_a \cdot y_i + a_i$, where n_a is the number of distinct attributes. Therefore, annotating a dataset with attributes assumes additional supervision—not only do we need to annotate the background appearing on each individual image, we also need to *know* that the background-target correlations are spurious and not worth attending to.

The literature on *subpopulation shift* considers that the set of training environments encompasses all relevant environments, meaning $\mathcal{E}_{\mathrm{tr}} = \mathcal{E}$. Therefore, in subpopulation shift problems, the second source of underspecification is absent. However, the amount of data available from the training environments can vary significantly, so learning algorithms that minimize average training error often perform poorly on the environments with the smallest training data. As an example, if training examples concern cows appearing 90% in grassy backgrounds and 10% in sandy landscapes, but these percentages reverse during test time, a subpopulation shift problem arises. Notably, subpopulation shift problems evaluate learning machines with respect to their worst-case performance across relevant environments.

5.3 Invariant Risk Minimization

One interpretation of the Invariance Principle (IP) for supervised learning problems, known as Invariant Risk Minimization (IRM), reads as follows:

Learn a feature representation such that the optimal classifier [regressor] matches across environments.

(IP-IRM)

Mathematically, this principle translates into the following bi-level optimization problem:

$$
\min_{\substack{\phi:\mathcal{X}\to\mathcal{H} \\ w:\mathcal{H}\to\mathcal{Y}}} \quad \sum_{e\in\mathcal{E}_{\mathrm{tr}}} R_{P^e}(w \circ \phi) \tag{IRM}
$$

$$
\text{subject to} \quad w \in \arg\min_{\tilde{w}} R_{P^e}(\tilde{w} \circ \phi), \text{ for all } e \in \mathcal{E}_{\mathrm{tr}}.
$$

The outer optimization problem performs ERM over the union of training environments $\mathcal{E}_{\mathrm{tr}}$, to find predictors that perform well across all training examples. Each constraint in this outer ERM problem is itself an *inner* optimization problem, encouraging feature representations that induce the same optimal classifier for every training environment.

Following conventions in deep learning, consider predictors $f = w \circ \phi$, where the featurizer $\phi : \mathcal{X} \to \mathcal{H}$ maps inputs into feature representations, while the classifier $w : \mathcal{H} \to \mathcal{Y}$ maps feature representations into target predictions. We say that $f = w \circ \phi$ is *an invariant predictor* across the training environments $\mathcal{E}_{\text{tr}}$ if there is no further risk minimization possible, with respect to the classifier w, at any environment $e \in \mathcal{E}$. Note that this is a claim about the invariance of the classifier function w, and not about the distributions of feature representations, nor distributions of errors.[217] These notations help us reveal the parallel between (IRM) and the more general (IP): We are framing (ϕ) our question (predict Y from X) so its answer (w) matches across situations (environments $\mathcal{E}_{\text{tr}}$).

When learning with loss functions such as the mean squared-error and the cross-entropy, invariant predictors satisfy

$$\mathbb{E}\left[Y^{e_1} \mid \phi(X^{e_1}) = h\right] = \mathbb{E}\left[Y^{e_2} \mid \phi(X^{e_2}) = h\right], \tag{5.2}$$

for all pairs of environments $e_1, e_2 \in \mathcal{E}$ and representation values h. By relaxing the requirement from invariant conditional distributions to invariant conditional expectations, the Invariance Principle can be summarized as the conditional independence statement:

$$Y \perp E \mid \phi(X). \tag{IP-Cond}$$

The characterizations (5.2) and (IP-Cond) match for classification problems learned using the cross-entropy loss, where conditional expectations contain all information about conditional distributions. The attentive reader will notice that the conditional independence statement (IP-Cond) has appeared repeatedly throughout previous chapters, under names such as conditional exchangeability, instrumental variables, propensity scores, and invariance across interventions. Consequently, the central equation (IP-Cond) underscores many of the similarities between invariance and causation. For completeness, the ERM terms (2.1) and (2.3) admit their formulation as the conditional independence statement $f(X) \perp Y \mid f$, where $f = w \circ \phi$ denotes a probabilistic representation of the predictor weights.

The study of regression coefficients as an alternative to correlations dates back a century. In his seminal *Statistical methods for research workers*, Ronald A. Fisher (1890–1962) writes:

> The idea of regression is usually introduced in connection with the theory of correlation, but it is in reality a more general, and, in some respects, a simpler idea, and the regression coefficients are of interest

and scientific importance in many classes of data where the correlation coefficient, if used at all, is an artificial concept of no real utility.[218]

Three decades later, John W. Tukey (1915–2000) remarked on the importance of obtaining *reasonably invariant* regression coefficients:

> One of the major arguments for regression instead of correlation is potential stability. We are very sure that the correlation cannot remain the same over a wide range of situations, but it is possible that the regression coefficient might. We have next to inquire, "When will it remain reasonably constant?" ... We are seeking stability of our coefficients so that we can hope to give them theoretical significance.[219]

Just a few passages later, Tukey underlines the importance of feature representation when searching for invariance:

> We have just inquired into the effect of changing the population. We need next inquire about the effect of adding new variables ... If we are to obtain stable coefficients from multiple regression, we must enforce some restrictions on the variables to be considered ... under the appropriate and relevant causal scheme.[219]

Together, these quotes form an antecedent to the Invariance Principle, where the invariant relationship is defined in terms of (1) an phenomenon Y, (2) some initial conditions X and their representation $\Phi(X)$, (3) an unobserved law w translating initial conditions into the observed phenomenon, and (4) an array of experimental conditions $\mathcal{E}$ over which invariance obtains.

5.3.1 A Linear Example

To understand how IRM operates, consider a linear regression problem with two inputs $(X_1^e, X_2^e) =: X^e$ and one target Y^e. For each environment $e \in \mathcal{E}$, let these three real-valued variables take values as governed by the following structural equation model:

$$
\begin{aligned}
X_1^e &\leftarrow \text{Gaussian}(0, \sigma_e^2), \\
Y^e &\leftarrow X_1^e + \text{Gaussian}(0, \sigma_e^2), \\
X_2^e &\leftarrow Y^e + \text{Gaussian}(0, 1).
\end{aligned}
\tag{Example1}
$$

Next, consider two training environments $\mathcal{E}_{\text{tr}} = \{e_1, e_2\}$. The first training environment e_1 provides data where $\sigma_e^2 \leftarrow \sigma_1^2 = 0.1$, while the second training environment produces examples where $\sigma_e^2 \leftarrow \sigma_2^2 = 10$. Consequently, X_1^e is the most predictive feature for environment e_1, while X_2^e is the better signal for environment e_2.

What are the invariant predictors in equation (Example1)? To answer this question, let us represent our inputs by means of the featurizer

$$\phi(X_1^e, X_2^e) = (\phi_1 \cdot X_1^e, \phi_2 \cdot X_2^e),$$

where the two binary parameters $\phi_1, \phi_2 \in \{0, 1\}$ select or ignore each of the two raw inputs.

Using the representation above, our predictor takes the form

$$f(X^e) = \alpha_1^e \cdot \phi_1 \cdot X_1^e + \alpha_2^e \cdot \phi_2 \cdot X_2^e,$$

Next, we employ linear least-squares to determine the optimal regression coefficients (α_1^e, α_2^e) for each environment $e \in \mathcal{E}_{\mathrm{tr}}$. Because of the two binary parameters involved in our feature representation, there are four possible regressions we could consider. First, we could set $(\phi_1, \phi_2) = (1, 0)$ to discard X_e^2 and regress from X_e^1 alone to Y^e, leading to the predictor

$$f_1(x) = 1 \cdot X_1^e + 0 \cdot X_2^e. \tag{5.3}$$

Second, we could set $(\phi_1, \phi_2) = (0, 1)$ to regress only from X_e^2 to Y^e, obtaining the regressor:

$$f_2(x) = 0 \cdot X_1^e + \frac{\sigma_e^2}{\sigma_e^2 + \frac{1}{2}} \cdot X_2^e. \tag{5.4}$$

Third, we could take the usual machine learning route and set $(\phi_1, \phi_2) = (1, 1)$, to regress from all available inputs to our target variable. This results in the empirical risk minimizer:

$$f_{1,2}(x) = \frac{1}{\sigma_e^2 + 1} \cdot X_1^e + \frac{\sigma_e^2}{\sigma_e^2 + 1} \cdot X_2^e. \tag{5.5}$$

The fourth alternative, discussed later below, would be to set $(\phi_1, \phi_2) = (0, 0)$ to consider *no* inputs.

Among the three regressions above, only the predictor (5.3) is invariant across training environments $e \in \mathcal{E}_{\mathrm{tr}}$. More formally, the predictor (5.3) satisfies the Invariance Principle (IP-IRM) because the optimal regressor on top of the representation $\phi(X_1^e, X_2^e) = (1 \cdot X_1^e, 0 \cdot X_2^e)$ is $w = (1, 0)$ for all training environments $e \in \mathcal{E}_{\mathrm{tr}}$. Furthermore, this invariant solution solves the out-of-distribution generalization problem of learning across multiple environments, as stated in equation (5.1). The resulting predictor $w \circ \phi$ is invariant because it admits no further risk minimization with respect to the regressor w at any training environment.

Because the environments in equation (Example1) arise due to interventions, the invariant predictor (5.3) relates to the causal structure governing the data. In particular, this predictor forecasts Y^e by employing the same causal process as the ground truth structural equation model, and it would react to interventions on its inputs in the same manner as the ground-truth system. This example highlights two important conclusions. First, invariance across interventions leaves behind observable statistical footprints. Second, searching for invariance does, in those cases, unearth causation.

In contrast, predictors (5.4) and (5.5) are not invariant, as their coefficients vary across training environments. Relying on these predictors for out-of-distribution generalization is a risky strategy, since we cannot estimate their coefficients in novel test environments. In contrast to the invariant predictor (5.3), these two predictors have unbounded error across valid interventions—to see this, tend $X_2^e \to \infty$. On the flip side, the ERM solution (5.5), training on all features on environment $e \in \mathcal{E}_{tr}$, is optimal for that same environment. This example reveals the difficulty of learning invariance: Because predictive power does not always align with truth, learning invariant predictors sometimes requires incurring training error.

To conclude with this example, let me discuss the fourth possible regression hinted at above. This involves regressing on top of the *null* feature representation with parameters $(\phi_1, \phi_2) = (0, 0)$. This null representation has two properties worth noticing. On one hand, null representations induce explanations (here, regressors) that are *easy to vary*. In particular, *any* regressor founded on the null representation results in an invariant predictor. On the other hand, null representations offer little or no predictive power. However, and because the objective (IRM) involves an ERM term, it is unlikely that we will encounter null representations when training IRM predictors in practice.

5.4   IRMv1, a Tractable Approximation

For general function classes, the objective (IRM) is a constrained nonconvex optimization problem, where each constraint is itself a nonconvex optimization problem. The resulting computational challenges are formidable and call for tractable approximations to the IRM paradigm. The remainder of this section discusses one such approximation, known as IRMv1.

5.4.1   Posing IRM as a Regularized ERM

We start by transforming the bi-level hard-constrained optimization problem (IRM) into a single-level soft-constrained optimization problem:

$$\sum_{e \in \mathcal{E}_{tr}} R_{P^e}(w \circ \phi) + \lambda \cdot \text{Inv}_{P^e}(w \circ \phi),$$

where the invariance penalty $\mathrm{Inv}_{P^e}(w \circ \phi) \in [0, \infty)$ should reach zero if and only if w is an optimal classifier on top of the feature representation ϕ across training environments $\mathcal{E}_{\mathrm{tr}}$.

What form should the invariance penalty take? Recall that the classifier w is optimal in environment e if there is no gradient available to further reduce the risk $R_{P^e}(w \circ \phi)$ with respect to w. To formalize this intuition, define gradient updates on R_{P^e} starting at w as follows:

$$\mathrm{opt}^0(w, P^e) = w,$$
$$\mathrm{opt}^{t+1}(w, P^e) = \mathrm{opt}^t(w, P^e) - \alpha \cdot \nabla_w \left[R_{P^e}(\mathrm{opt}^t(w, P^e) \circ \phi) \right],$$

Then, the current classifier w is optimal at environment e if the following invariance penalty is zero:

$$\mathrm{Inv}_{P^e}^\infty(w \circ \phi) = \| w - \mathrm{opt}^\infty(w, P^e) \|^2. \tag{5.6}$$

This is a meta-learning expression,[220,221] in the sense that the penalty *peeks* into the future of the optimization process to provide a regularization signal to the current state of the objective function.

Before proceeding further, let us examine the invariance penalty (5.6) on the linear least-squares problem:

$$\mathrm{Inv}_{P^e}^\infty(w \circ \phi) = \left\| w - \underset{X^e}{\mathbb{E}} \left[\phi(X^e)^\top \phi(X^e) + \lambda \cdot I \right]^{-1} \underset{X^e, Y^e}{\mathbb{E}} \left[\phi(X^e)^\top Y^e \right] \right\|^2. \tag{5.7}$$

Simplifying even more, apply this penalty to (Example1) using the feature representation

$$\Phi(X_1^e, X_2^e) = [1 \cdot X_1^e, \phi_2 \cdot X_2^e], \tag{5.8}$$

where the parameter $\phi_2 \in \mathbb{R}$ determines the weight placed on the feature X_2^e inducing spurious correlation. In this setup, the goal is to learn a feature representation with $\phi_2 = 0$, thus revealing the desired invariant predictor (5.3).

As illustrated in figure 5.2 with a solid line, the penalty (5.7) reaches zero for $\phi_2 = 0$, but it violently shoots up to infinity in the immediate neighborhood. This occurs because the matrix inversion in (5.7) can assign a very large weight to *fully* recover partial occlusions of X_2^e due to very small ϕ_2, unless ϕ_2 is *exactly* zero. Additionally, the invariance penalty (5.7) decays to zero for non-invariant predictors as long as $|\phi_2| \to \pm\infty$. In sum, the penalty (5.7) exhibits two undesired behaviors: It is highly convex and it achieves its minimum for certain non-invariant predictors.

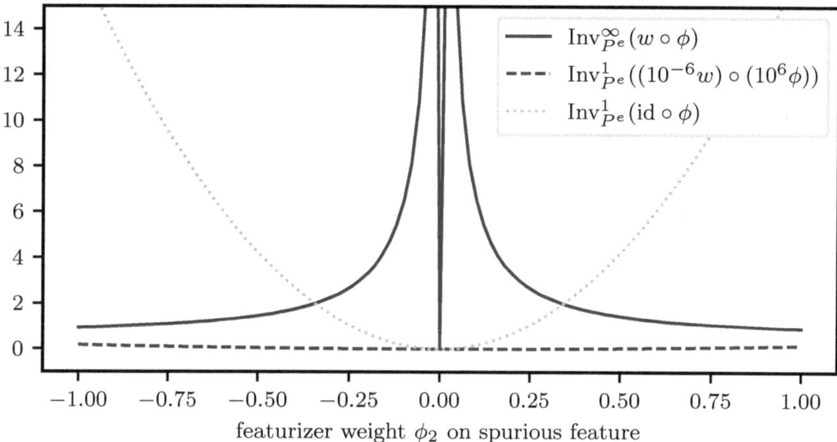

featurizer weight ϕ_2 on spurious feature

Figure 5.2: Behavior of different invariance penalties discussed in section 5.4 when learning a predictor $f(x) = w(\phi(x))$, where the featurizer $\phi(x) = x \cdot ((1,0),(0,c))$, and the classifier $w(z) = z \cdot (1,0)$. The "exact penalty" Inv$_{Pe}^{\infty}(w \circ \phi)$ correctly assigns zero invariance penalty to the invariant solution $c = 0$, but it shoots to infinity as soon as there is a nonzero mass placed on the spurious feature, resulting in a very challenging optimization landscape. Also, it tends to zero as we place a larger coefficient on the spurious feature. The *first-order penalty* Inv$_{Pe}^{1}(w \circ \phi)$, allowing a learnable classifier w, exhibits an over-parameterization problem where it tends to zero everywhere, as the weights of the featurizer increase. Finally, the *fixed-classifier first-order penalty* Inv$_{Pe}^{1}(\text{id} \circ \phi)$ does not have any of the aforementioned problems, providing us—in this example—with a convex invariance penalty that achieves its global minimum at the desired solution $c = 0$.

5.4.2 Controlling the Capacity of the Classifier

The undesired *shooting up* numerical behavior of (5.6) arises when we allow an infinite amount of gradient updates to measure the optimality of the classifier w, incarnated as a full matrix inversion in the linear least-squares case (5.7). This powerful operation can entirely restore unwanted inputs, such as X_2^e, even when they are multiplied by near-zero representation weights ϕ_2. To temper the strength of the penalty, consider a first-order approximation taking only one gradient step:

$$
\begin{aligned}
\mathrm{Inv}^1_{P^e}(w \circ \phi) &= \|w - \mathrm{opt}^1(w, P^e)\|^2 \\
&= \|w - w + \nabla_w [R_{P^e}(w \circ \phi)]\|^2 \\
&= \|\nabla_w [R_{P^e}(w \circ \phi)]\|^2 .
\end{aligned}
$$

Returning to the linear least-squares case as a sanity check, the expression for this single-step penalty indeed no longer involves a full matrix inversion:

$$
\mathrm{Inv}^1_{P^e}(w \circ \phi) = \|\phi(X^e)^\top \phi(X^e)w - \phi(X^e)^\top Y^e\|^2.
$$

While this first-order penalty does mitigate the shooting up behavior, it presents another issue. Namely, multiplying ϕ and dividing w by a small positive number yields the exact same predictor, yet at a significantly cheaper invariance penalty. As illustrated by the dashed line in figure 5.2, this creates an opportunity to minimize the invariance penalty *for free* by artificially decreasing the magnitude of the representation weight ϕ_2.

5.4.3 Controlling the Capacity of the Representation

To address the problem of over-parameterization, we fix the classifier w to a reference value $\tilde{w}$ and delegate all learning responsibilities to the feature representation ϕ:

$$
\mathrm{Inv}^{1,\tilde{w}}_{P^e}(\phi) = \left\|\nabla_{w|w=\mathrm{id}} [R_{P^e}(\tilde{w} \circ \phi)]\right\|^2. \tag{5.9}
$$

The fixed classifier $\tilde{w}$ is no longer an argument for the invariance penalty, yet the learning gradients still propagate to ϕ as a regularization force. In our running example, the penalty (5.9) alleviates over-parameterization because learning a large ϕ_2 can no longer be compensated by the classifier in order to produce an performant predictor. This is illustrated in figure 5.2 with a dotted line, where the penalty (5.9) is a convex function reaching its global minimum at the desired solution $\phi_2 = 0$. Nonetheless, it is important to note that for general scenarios, the penalty (5.9) is nonconvex and will therefore be sensitive to random initialization.

To simplify further, we can reshape our representation ϕ to map directly into the target space, yielding the "dummy" or identity classifier $\tilde{w}(z) = 1.0 \cdot z$. If the output of ϕ is multidimensional, multiply each output by the same "dummy" classifier. For all the above results in IRMv1, this is a tractable approximation to IRM:

$$\min_{\phi:\mathcal{X}\to\mathcal{Y}} \sum_{e\in\mathcal{E}_{\mathrm{tr}}} (1-\lambda) \cdot R_{P^e}(\phi) + \lambda \cdot \left\| \nabla_{w|w=1.0} \left[R_{P^e}(w \cdot \phi) \right] \right\|^2 \qquad \text{(IRMv1)}$$

Algorithm 5.1 offers PyTorch code to implement (Example1) and solve it with (IRMv1).

We close with some comments about IRMv1 from contemporary work. The IRMv1 objective is related to calibration based on temperature scaling.[106,222] In particular, we may read (IRMv1) as "Find a feature representation such that the optimal calibration temperature is one for each and every environment," an interpretation that has motivated the use of IRMv1 for model selection.[106] To stabilize training, Kartik Ahuja and colleagues suggest regularizing the output variance of ϕ to implement an information bottleneck from X to Y.[110] As a final remark, it is possible to monitor the invariance of arbitrary neurons in a deep network by multiplying their outputs by the same scalar classifier $w = 1.0$, subject to regularization.

5.4.4 Empirical Performance of IRMv1

The original work on IRM introduced the ColoredMNIST benchmark, a variant of the popular handwritten digit classification task MNIST. ColoredMNIST describes a binary classification problem, where the class label $y = 1$ conveys digits $\{0, 1, 2, 3, 4\}$ and $y = 0$ otherwise. Furthermore, we inject 25% noise on labels y by computing $y := y \oplus \text{Bernoulli}(\frac{1}{4})$ on each example, where "$\oplus$" stands for the logical XOR operation. The 60000 MNIST training digits are divided into two training environments containing 25000 examples each, alongside one testing environment containing 10000 examples. For environment e, color each digit red if $z = 1$ and green if $z = 0$, where $z = y \oplus \text{Bernoulli}(p^e)$. In particular, $p^1 = 0.1$ for the first training environment, $p^2 = 0.2$ for the second training environment, and $p^{\mathrm{te}} = 0.9$ for the test environment. The resulting dataset is illustrated in figure 5.3.

The ColoredMNIST benchmark resembles a cow-on-the-beach problem with partially informative invariant features. In this dataset, the spurious digit color feature is more informative and easier to learn than the invariant digit shape feature. Although the color-target correlation is strong and positive in the two training environments, it turns negative in the test environment. However, this spurious correlation shifts subtly across training environments (from 0.1 to 0.2), signaling invariance learning algorithms

```python
1  import torch
2  from torch.autograd import grad
3
4  def compute_penalty(losses, w):
5      g1 = grad(losses[0::2].mean(), w, create_graph=True)[0]
6      g2 = grad(losses[1::2].mean(), w, create_graph=True)[0]
7      return (g1 * g2).sum() # unbiased estimate of squared
       norm
8
9  def example_1(n=10000, d=2, env=1):
10     x = torch.randn(n, d) * env
11     y = x + torch.randn(n, d) * env
12     z = y + torch.randn(n, d)
13     return torch.cat((x, z), 1), y.sum(1, keepdim=True)
14
15 envs = [example_1(env=0.1), example_1(env=1.0)]
16
17 phi = torch.nn.Parameter(torch.ones(envs[0][0].size(1), 1))
18 w = torch.nn.Parameter(torch.Tensor([1.0]))
19
20 opt = torch.optim.SGD([phi], lr=1e-3)
21 mse = torch.nn.MSELoss(reduction="none")
22
23 for iteration in range(10000):
24     error, penalty = 0, 0
25     for x_e, y_e in envs:
26         p = torch.randperm(len(x_e))
27         error_e = mse(x_e[p] @ phi * w, y_e[p])
28         penalty += compute_penalty(error_e, w)
29         error += error_e.mean()
30     opt.zero_grad()
31     (1e-5 * error + (1 - 1e-5) * penalty).backward()
32     opt.step()
33
34     print(" ".join([f"{x:.3f}" for x in phi.view(-1)]))
```

Algorithm 5.1: PyTorch code to learn (IRMv1) on (Example1).

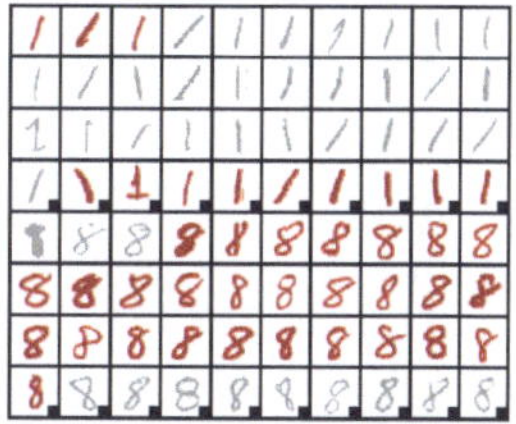

(a) Training env. $p^e = 0.1$.

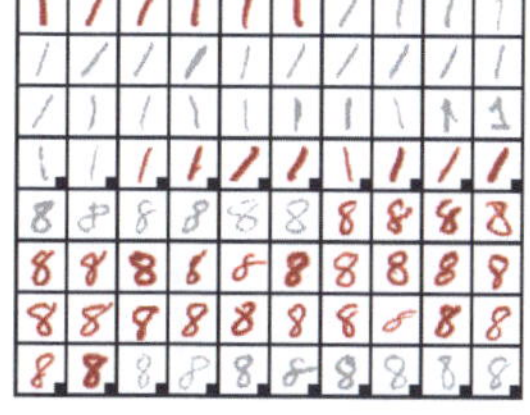

(b) Training env. $p^e = 0.2$.

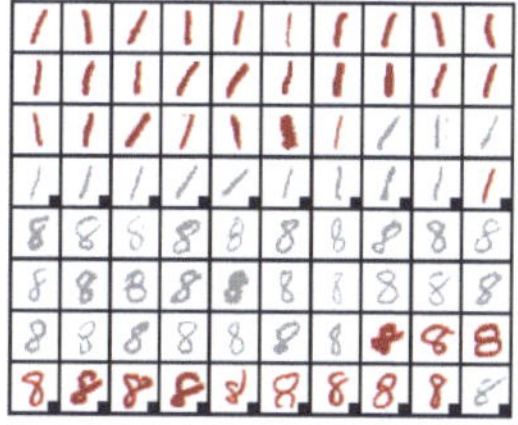

(c) Test env. $p^e = 0.9$.

Figure 5.3: The ColoredMNIST dataset. For simplicity, this figure only shows two digits, where *1* belongs to the positive class, and *8* belongs to the negative class. I associate color *red* with dark digits and color *green* with gray digits. In each image, 25% of the examples have the wrong label, here denoted with a white square. Therefore, shape features induce a correlation that is indicative of the label for 75% of examples for all environments. Color features induce a correlation that is indicative of label for 90% of examples for the first training environment, and 80% for the second training environment. The color-label correlation is stronger yet spurious, and is therefore preferred by ERM. The shape-label correlation is weaker yet invariant, and is therefore preferred by IRM. The color-label correlation changes direction in the test environment, while the shape-label correlation remains invariant. Therefore, only the latter affords generalization across all relevant environments.

to pursue the less informative and more difficult shape-target invariant correlation.

An ERM baseline on ColoredMNIST achieves 17% test error, while an ERM *oracle*—grayscaling images to remove the spurious color-target correlation—achieves 73% test error. A simple implementation of IRMv1 sits in between these two, achieving 67% test error. Other applications of IRM include wildlife classification from camera traps,[223] toxicity classification,[224] removal of spurious correlations in natural language processing,[225] language modeling,[226] the discovery of causal factors for liver dysfunction during spaceflight,[227] and competitive performances in standard datasets such as Waterbirds and CivilComments[228] or WILDS' Camelyon17 and PovertyMap.[229]

5.4.5 Theoretical Analyses of IRMv1

The original work on IRMv1 provided three remarks about its geometrical structure, all based on the following result.

Theorem 5.1. *For all $e \in \mathcal{E}$, let $R_{P^e} : \mathbb{R}^d \to \mathbb{R}$ be convex differentiable cost functions. A predictor $f \in \mathbb{R}^{d \times 1}$ can be written $f = \Phi \cdot w$, where the*

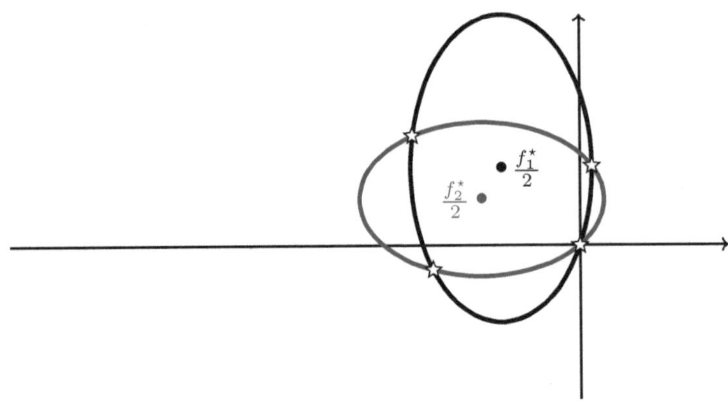

Figure 5.4: Learning a two-dimensional invariant linear least-squares predictor across two training environments. Each training environment e proposes its empirical risk minimizer $f_e^\star/2$. In addition, each training environment poses an orthogonality condition, in the form of a quadratic equation whose solutions form an ellipsoid. The intersections of the ellipsoids determine the set of invariant solutions. In this example, these are a manifold with four disconnected components (depicted as stars) containing the null predictor.

featurizer $\Phi \in \mathbb{R}^{d \times p}$ and the classifier $w \in \mathbb{R}^{p \times 1}$ simultaneously minimize $R_{P^e}(\Phi \cdot w)$ for all $e \in \mathcal{E}$, if and only if $f^\top \nabla_f[R_{P^e}(f)] = 0$ for all $e \in \mathcal{E}$. The matrices Φ for which such a decomposition exists are the matrices whose nullspace $\mathrm{Ker}(\Phi)$ is orthogonal to f and contains all the $\nabla_f[R_{P^e}(f)]$.

First, theorem 5.1 shows that any linear invariant predictor can be expressed using a representation $\Phi \in \mathbb{R}^{d \times p}$, for any choice of p. Therefore, we may conveniently restrict our search to $p = 1$, justifying our choice for a scalar *dummy* classifier $w(z) = 1.0 \cdot z$ in IRMv1.

Secondly, theorem 5.1 shows that each training environment e imposes an orthogonality condition $f^\top \nabla_f[R_{P^e}(f)] = 0$ that defines a one-dimensional manifold in $\mathbb{R}^d$. When these environmental constraints are orthogonal, the intersection of the resulting manifolds is a non-empty manifold of dimension $d - m$ that *always* contains the null predictor $f = 0$. Figure 5.4 illustrates these concepts for the linear least-squares case.

Thirdly, theorem 5.1 shows that the null space of the representation contains the m environment gradients $\nabla_f[R_{P^e}(f)]$. This implies that these m vectors are linearly dependent, meaning there exists a nonzero vector λ such that $Q := \sum_{e=1}^m \lambda_e \nabla_f[R_{P^e}(f)] = 0$. Since the coefficients λ_e can be negative, IRM implements an objective function Q that *extrapolates* beyond the convex hull of the training environment risks, as shown in figure 5.5.

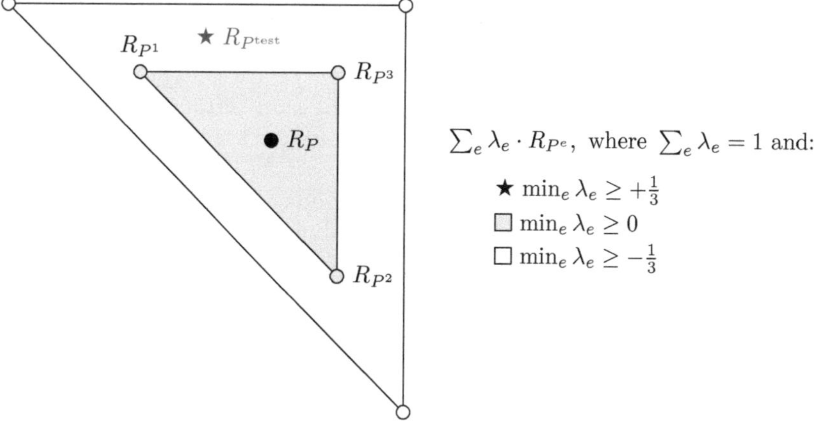

Figure 5.5: Illustration of learning from three training environments, with associated population risks R_{P1}, R_{P2}, and R_{P3}, respectively. $\bullet$ ERM optimizes the average loss across environments. This gives equal weight $\lambda_1 = \lambda_2 = \lambda_3 = \frac{1}{3}$ to each environment, focusing efforts to minimize the risk $R_P = \frac{1}{3}R_{P1} + \frac{1}{3}R_{P2} + \frac{1}{3}R_{P3}$. $\square$ Risk interpolation minimizes a convex combination of the three environment risks, where the importance of the training environment e is given by $\lambda_e \geq 0$. $\square$ Risk extrapolation minimizes an affine combination of the three environment risks, allowing for negative coefficients. Risk extrapolation allows us, for the right choice of $(\lambda_1, \lambda_2, \lambda_3)$, to optimize for performance in test environments $\bigstar\ R_{P\text{test}}$ outside the convex hull of the training environments. As an example, solving equation (Example1) requires risk extrapolation, because all risk interpolations place a nonzero coefficient on the spuriousness-inducing variable.

This capacity to extrapolate is the reason behind the success of IRMv1 in equation (Example1), where the invariant solution is not a minimizer of any convex combination of training environment risks.

The original work on IRMv1 provided some theoretical guarantees in the linear case, where inputs $X^e \in \mathbb{R}^d$, targets $Y^e \in \mathbb{R}$, and the predictor $f(X^e) = X^e \cdot \Phi \cdot w$ employ a representation matrix $\Phi \in \mathbb{R}^{d \times d}$ of rank r. In this situation, the performance of IRMv1 relies on having access to a sufficient number of training environments in *general position*. We say that a collection of environments lays in general position if they are not collinear, and if each of the environments removes one degree of freedom from the space of invariant predictors.[49] The number of necessary training environments in general position relates to the rank of the true representation matrix Φ. More specifically, if one finds a representation Φ of rank r eliciting an invariant predictor $w \circ \Phi$ across $d - r$ training environments in general position $\mathcal{E}_{\text{tr}}$, then such a predictor is invariant across relevant environments $\mathcal{E}$. Consequently, IRMv1 requires fewer training environments to learn invariant predictors founded on high-rank representation matrices. This is a fortunate situation, as high-rank representations retain most of the predictive power about the inputs. In contrast, IRMv1 requires $d - 1$ training environments in general position for those cases where $r = 1$.[230] Little is known about the performance of IRMv1 (and most methods of invariance) beyond the linear case, apart from some praise for polynomial predictors[231,232] and some criticisms in the absence of sufficient train-test environment support overlap, as described in the next section.[230,233] Recently, the compositional risk minimization (CRM) method[234] has provided both nontrivial out-of-distribution generalization performance and guarantees in the nonlinear case.

5.5   Trade-offs and Pitfalls

Learning invariant predictors from data requires navigating three challenges in mutual tension:[235]

- *Maximizing the accuracy of the predictor $w \circ \phi$*, implemented by the ERM term, and resulting in *recruiting* information about the inputs.

- *Maximizing the invariance of the optimal classifier w*, implemented by the IRM constraints, and resulting in *discarding* information about the inputs.

- *Maximizing environment support overlap* between $\phi(X^e)$ and $\phi(X^{e'})$, or positivity, implemented by means of data collection across diverse environments $e, e' \in \mathcal{E}_{\text{tr}}$. To maximize support overlap, representations *discard* information about the inputs, converting extrapolation into interpolation and raising the probability of rare examples. Unlabeled data is helpful to maximize support overlap.

IRM balances these objectives to search for a predictor $f = w \circ \phi$, where the featurizer ϕ and classifier w assume roles adversarial to each other. During learning, ERM dominates the learning of the featurizer by promoting the absorption of patterns to minimize training error, while the IRM constraints dominate the learning of the classifier by discarding features to increase invariance, at the expense of training error.

Examining support overlap is an important task when building invariant predictors. If we don't enforce support overlap between the representations $\phi(X^e)$ and $\phi(X^{e'})$ of two training environments $e, e' \in \mathcal{E}_{\text{tr}}$, we leave the door open to learning *spuriously invariant* predictors. In such cases of disjoint support, IRM could be learning a classifier w that models the empirical risk minimizer of environment e across $\phi(X^e)$, and similarly for e'. Alas, this is not really modeling invariance *across* training environments, and the resulting predictor will likely not generalize out-of-distribution. Instead, if we enforce support overlap between $\phi(X^e)$ and $\phi(X^{e'})$, as requested by the Invariance Principle statements (IP-Cond) and (5.2), these spuriously invariant predictors do not arise. The issue of support overlap does not only pertain to pairs of training environments, but also extends to test environments. After all, the invariance program—finding the feature representation $\phi^\star$ such that the conditional distribution of the targets given featurized inputs is stable—can only be successful given some support overlap across *all relevant* environments.

Marco Federici and colleagues[236] formalize how out-of-distribution performance depends on the three forces described above. For any relevant environment $e \in \mathcal{E}$, the error induced by the representation ϕ follows the expression

$$\mathrm{Error}^e(\phi) = I(X^e, Y^e \mid \phi(X^e)) + \mathrm{KL}(P(Y^e \mid \phi(X^e)) \,\|\, P(Y \mid \phi(X))). \tag{5.10}$$

To minimize error in environment $e \in \mathcal{E}$, we should therefore learn a representation yielding (1) maximum accuracy and (2) maximum invariance as given by the IRM constraint (5.2). In the equation above, the information-theoretic terms are estimated from the training environments $\mathcal{E}_{\mathrm{tr}}$ but evaluated on test environments $\mathcal{E}_{\mathrm{te}}$. To grant these estimates meaning, we must also encourage representations that (3) maximize environment support overlap.

Equation (5.10) admits the following practical implementation:

$$\sum_{e \in \mathcal{E}_{\mathrm{tr}}} R_{P^e}(w \circ \phi) + \lambda \cdot \Omega(\phi), \tag{5.11}$$

where the two terms represent an ERM objective and an invariance regularizer, respectively. Federici and colleagues discuss several alternatives for choosing Ω, reviewed below.

- The *information bottleneck criterion* sets $\Omega(\phi) = I(X, \phi(X))$, with one example being weight decay. Removing information is a necessary yet insufficient condition to maximize invariance.

- The *independence (or parity) criterion* sets $\Omega(\phi) = I(E, \phi(X))$. Enforcing this criterion may *increase* invariance when the distribution of the target variable $P(Y^e)$ varies across environments.

- The *separation criterion* sets $\Omega(\phi) = I(E, \phi(X) \mid Y)$, enforcing a class-conditional independence or parity criterion.

- The *sufficiency criterion* $\Omega(\phi) = I(Y, E \mid \phi(X))$ is the Invariance Principle (IP-Cond) proposed in this chapter.

While the work of Federici and colleagues provides a full characterization of out-of-distribution generalization, the literature offers two additional taxonomies concerning patterns of distribution shift. One taxonomy differentiates between covariate and correlation shifts based on the factorization $P(X^e, Y^e) = P(Y^e \mid X^e) \cdot P(X^e)$ of the environment joint probability distribution. Covariate shifts, or diversity shifts, occur when environments share the same input-target mapping $P(Y \mid X)$ but the distributions of inputs $P(X^e) \neq P(X^{e'})$ differ across the environments, leading to insufficient support overlap on raw inputs. Concept shifts, or correlation shifts, happen when environments exhibit matching input distributions $PX^e)$ but differing labeling mechanisms $P(Y^e \mid X^e) \neq P(Y^{e'} \mid X^{e'})$, leading to insufficient invariance on raw inputs. Another taxonomy, discussed in section 2.6, distinguishes between learning problems with invariant features admitting zero training error and those spurious correlations necessary to minimize the empirical risk.[110] Fully informative invariant features (fiif) are difficult to discover when spurious patterns are simpler or faster to learn,[237] as happens in the cow-on-the-beach problem. Partially informative invariant features (piif) are difficult to capture when (potentially more complex) spurious patterns offer zero training error, as happens in the ColoredMNIST problem. This taxonomy explains why Occam's razor is not a silver bullet to learn invariances—the pattern of interest may or may not be the simplest explanation of the learning problem at hand.

5.5.1 Null Invariance

The rest of this section presents two scenarios where predictors satisfying the Invariance Principle offer minimal or no predictive power. First, let us consider a *null* representation, which destroys all information contained in the raw inputs:

$$\phi_\emptyset(x) = \vec{0}. \tag{5.12}$$

It is evident that null representations yield predictors with no generalization capabilities. But, perhaps surprisingly, null representations do afford invariance in many problems, because they can combine with any classifier to yield an invariant predictor. This is the phenomenon of null invariance.

To illustrate, consider estimating a linear function $f(x) = x \cdot \Phi \cdot w$. Then, if one sets Φ to be the null representation—hereby incarnated as a zero matrix—then all candidate classifiers w are deemed invariant by (IRMv1). In particular, the penalty (5.13) becomes

$$\mathrm{Inv}^1_{P^e}(w \circ \phi_\emptyset) = \|\phi_\emptyset(X^e)^\top \phi_\emptyset(X^e) w - \phi_\emptyset(X^e)^\top Y^e\|^2 = 0. \tag{5.13}$$

The resulting predictor $f(x) = 0$ is probably not able to forecast the target variable for any relevant environment. To make matters worse, the null representation is in certain situations the only choice inducing an invariant predictor. Let's reconsider the prior setup for linear regression, but assume this time that the true data generation process is $Y^e = (X^e)^2$ across environments, where $X^e = \text{Gaussian}(0, \sigma_e^2)$. Then, the only *linear* invariant predictor is the one built on top of the null representation.[49] In sum, insufficient capacity in ϕ can lead to null invariances, which we shall take as a warning signal that the resulting predictors are easy to vary.

Two strategies are helpful to address the example above. First, consider a quadratic representation $\Phi^e = \theta_\phi \cdot (X^e)^2$ and a linear classifier $w(\Phi^e) = \theta_w \cdot \Phi^e$. In this case, letting $\theta_\phi = 1$ elicits the invariant classifier with $\theta_w = 1$, both combining into the desired invariant predictor. On the other hand, consider a linear representation $\phi(X^e) = \theta_\phi \cdot X^e$ and a quadratic classifier $w(\Phi^e) = \theta_w \cdot (\Phi^e)^2$. In that case, the desired invariant predictor also obtains. But wait, there's more! If we use *both* a quadratic representation and a quadratic classifier, we run into the same predicament as before, as the null representation is the only one inducing an invariant classifier.

5.5.2   Delta Invariance

Delta invariances, also a trivial solution to the invariance learning problem, occur when the learning machine has sufficient capacity to memorize every training example from every training environment. To illustrate, consider two training environments producing the input-target datasets $\{(x_i^1, y_i^1)\}_{i=1}^{n_1}$ and $\{(x_i^2, y_i^2)\}_{i=1}^{n_2}$. Using these data, construct the $(n_1 + n_2)$-dimensional nonparametric *delta representation*:

$$\phi_\delta(x) = \big[y_1^1 \cdot [\![x = x_1^1]\!], \ldots, y_{n_1}^1 \cdot [\![x = x_{n_1}^1]\!],$$
$$y_1^2 \cdot [\![x = x_1^2]\!], \ldots, y_{n_2}^2 \cdot [\![x = x_{n_2}^2]\!]\big]. \tag{5.14}$$

Assuming binary labels $y_i^e \in \{-1, +1\}$ and unique inputs, the representation above is a one-hot vector for every example x_i^e across the two training environments, where the nonzero element equals to the label y_i^e. Therefore, any linear classifier $w \in \mathbb{R}^{(n_1+n_2) \times 1}$ with positive weights induces a zero training error invariant predictor $f_\delta(x) = \phi_\delta(x) \cdot w$, since $\text{sign}(f_\delta(x_i^e)) = y_i^e$ for all training examples (x_i^e, y_i^e). Delta representations are in this manner akin to conspiracy theories that allow the incorporation of more degrees of freedom as we observe more data.

Due to the underspecification of invariance penalties, delta representations lead to undesirable *delta invariances*. Mathematically, invariance penalties such as (IRMv1) consider as invariant any predictor achieving zero training error:

$$R_{Pe}(w \circ \phi) = 0 \Rightarrow \mathrm{Inv}_{Pe}^{\infty}(w \circ \phi) = \mathrm{Inv}_{Pe}^{1}(w \circ \phi) = \|\nabla_w[R_{Pe}(w \circ \phi)]\|^2 = 0,$$

where this equation obtains for any predictor built on top of the delta representation. Delta invariances are difficult to falsify in the Popperian sense, because they yield predictors that are easy to vary. In some cases, delta invariances also violate Belkin's razor, as they yield nonsmooth predictors.

5.6 The Invariance Principle in Other Fields of Knowledge

According to the original authors of IRM, the Invariance Principle "clarifies common induction methods in science:"

> Indeed, some scientific discoveries can be traced to the realization that distinct but potentially related phenomena, once described with the correct variables, appear to obey the same exact physical laws. The precise conservation of these laws suggests that they remain valid on a far broader range of conditions. If both Newton's apple and the planets obey the same equations, chances are that gravitation is a thing.[49]

Philosopher of science Nancy Cartwright anticipated this idea over thirty years ago, nothing that

> when we present a model of a phenomenon, we prepare the description of the phenomenon in just the right way to make a law apply to it[113]

I also contend that the Invariance Principle $Y \perp E \mid \phi(X)$ is pivotal in scientific discovery. As discussed in chapter 2, finding a better representation ϕ helped Van der Waals improve the ideal gas law, while updating the initial conditions X allowed scientists to explain the orbit of Uranus after the discovery of Neptune. Reevaluating invariances after conducting new experiments $\mathcal{E}$ is the main process to falsify scientific theories, such as happened with Newtonian gravity after the observations of Arthur Eddington.

Just like causal relations, invariances can be thought of as scientific theories. Following Popper, invariances are never shown true—however, when falsified, they are falsified for good. This is why scientific experiments, as Nancy Cartwright recounts below, are set up to falsify a certain null hypothesis only once:

> The bulk of experiments that support the gigantic edifice of twentieth-century physics are never repeated, and they involve no statistics.

> The trick of the outstanding experimenter is to set the arrangements
> just right so that the observed outcome means just what it is intended
> to mean; and that takes repeated efforts, usually over months and
> sometimes over years. But once the genuine effect is achieved, that is
> enough. The physicist need not go on running the experiment again
> and again to lay bare a regularity before our eyes. A single case, if it
> is the right case, will do.[125]

The rest of this section deepens on these interplays between the Invariance
Principle and various domains of knowledge, including mathematics, physics,
metaphysics, relevance realization, and the philosophy of truth.

Due to space and knowledge constraints, I must leave out some of the
potentially infinite topics this section could touch upon. For instance,
consider the invariance flavor of Kant's categorical imperative, as presented
in his *Groundwork of the Metaphysics of Morals*:

> Act only according to that maxim whereby you can at the same time
> will that it should become a universal law.

Similarly, Henry Hazlitt's (1894–1993) *Economics in One Lesson* includes
a close-to-verbatim statement of the Invariance Principle:

> The art of economics consists in looking not merely at the immediate
> but at the longer effects of any act or policy; it consists in tracing
> the consequences of that policy not merely for one group but for all
> groups.[238]

Finally, the curious reader can find my thoughts about the role of invariance
in topics related to spirituality, psychology, and religion in the parting—and
nonscientific—chapter of this book.

5.6.1   Invariance in Mathematics

In mathematics, "a symmetry of an object or system is a transformation that
leaves a certain property of said object or system unchanged or invariant."[239]
A basic formalization of invariance in mathematics is possible by virtue
of group theory. A group is a set $\mathcal{G}$ along with a composition operation
$\circ : \mathcal{G} \to \mathcal{G}$ satisfying (1) associativity $(g \circ h) \circ l = g \circ (h \circ l)$ for all $g, h, l \in \mathcal{G}$,
(2) existence of identity $e \in \mathcal{G}$ satisfying $e \circ g = g \circ e$ for all $g \in \mathcal{G}$, (3)
existence of inverse $g^{-1} \in \mathcal{G}$ such that $g \circ g^{-1} = g^{-1} \circ g$ for all $g \in \mathcal{G}$, and
(4) closure under composition, namely $g \circ h \in \mathcal{G}$ for all $g, h \in \mathcal{G}$.

Further, group elements act on elements of the set by means of group
actions. We call $T_g : \mathcal{X} \to \mathcal{X}$ the action of the group element $g \in \mathcal{X}$,
producing $T_g(x) \in \mathcal{X}$ for all $x \in \mathcal{X}$. Similarly, let $T'_g : \mathcal{X} \to \mathcal{X}$ be the action

of the same group on a second space of data $\mathcal{Y}$. A function $f : \mathcal{X} \times \mathcal{Y}$ is $\mathcal{G}$-invariant if $f(T'_g(x)) = f(x)$ for all $g \in \mathcal{G}$. For example, in computer vision, image classifiers f are often translation-invariant. A function $f : \mathcal{X} \times \mathcal{Y}$ is $\mathcal{G}$-equivariant if $f(T_g(x)) = T'_g(f(x))$, being $\mathcal{G}$-invariant if T'_g is the identity. In the language of learning across multiple environments, we are often concerned with learning an equivariant function where group actions describe environmental changes.

5.6.2 Invariance in Physics

Examples abound to justify that invariance is the signature of a good theory in physics. Paul Anderson famously said that "it is only slightly overstating the case to say that physics is the study of symmetry,"[240] where symmetry refers to an object (possibly an equation) remaining invariant under certain transformations. Physicists, such as Caspar Jacobs, have their own versions of the Invariance Principle:

> a quantity is physically real only if it is invariant under the symmetries of our theories ... [Q]uantities that vary under a theory's symmetries are physically unreal. The Invariance Principal codifies so-called "symmetry-to-(un)reality inferences:" inferences from the variance of some quantity to its non-reality. For example, (absolute) positions vary under shifts, and hence the Invariance Principle rejects them as unphysical.[241]

Prior to Jacobs, Paul Dirac said that "the important things in the world appear as the invariants ... of these transformations."[242] Herman Weyl suggests that "objectivity means invariance with respect to the group of automorphisms."[243] Steven Weinberg argues that "out of the fusion of relativity with quantum mechanics there has evolved a new view of the world, one in which matter has lost its central role. This role has been usurped by principles of symmetry."[244] Simon Saunders concludes that "physically real quantities are invariant under exact symmetries—this is the general lesson."[245] David J. Baker likewise suggests:

> It follows that physical situations related by symmetries must be qualitatively identical. And if this is right, then physical quantities that change under symmetry transformations (not invariant) must not be fundamental quantities. Qualitatively identical objects or worlds cannot disagree about the fundamental quantities.[246]

Over a century ago, a celebrated theorem by Emmy Noether revealed that for every continuous symmetry (invariance) in a Lagrangian of a physical system, there is a conserved quantity along all trajectories satisfying the equations of motion.[247] For instance, spatial translation invariance in the Lagrangian relates to conservation of momentum, time translation invariance relate to conservation of energy, and rotational invariance relates to conservation of angular momentum.

While this is already better company than expected when defending any point of view, no survey of physicists working on invariance would be complete without Eugene P. Wigner (1902–1995). In his Nobel prize lecture in 1963, Wigner argued that "a law of nature can be accepted as valid only if the correlations which it postulates are consistent with the accepted invariance principles."[248] In his latter *Symmetries and Reflections*, Wigner recounts how Einstein's work on relativity elevated the role of invariance, making it the central epistemological aim in physical theories:

> There is a structure in the laws of nature which we call the laws of invariance. This structure is so far-reaching in some cases that laws of nature were guessed on the basis of the postulate that they fit into the invariance structure. It is not necessary to look deeper into the situation to realize that laws of nature could not exist without principles of invariance. ... If the correlations between events changed from day to day, and would be different for different points of space, it would be impossible to discover them. Thus the invariances of the laws of nature with respect to displacements in space and time are almost necessary prerequisites that it be possible to discover, or even catalog, the correlations between events which are the laws of nature. ... The significance and general validity of these principles were recognized, however, only by Einstein. His papers on special relativity also mark the reversal of a trend: until then, the principles of invariance were derived from the laws of motion. Einstein's work established the older principles of invariance so firmly that we have to be reminded that they are based only on experience. It is now natural for us to try to derive the laws of nature and to test their validity by means of the laws of invariance, rather than to derive the laws of invariance from what we believe to be the laws of nature. ... The progression from events to laws of nature, and from laws of nature to symmetry or invariance principles, is what I meant by the hierarchy of our knowledge of the world around us.[57]

Therefore, while ontological order progresses from events to laws to invariance, Wigner's hierarchical epistemology unfolds in the opposite direction.[57]

Wigner also considered invariance a helpful guide to distinguish between laws of nature and irrelevant initial conditions:

> However, the possibility of isolating the relevant initial conditions would not in itself make possible the discovery of laws of nature. It is,

> rather, also essential that, given the same essential initial conditions, the result will be the same no matter where and when we realize these. This principle can be formulated, in the language of initial conditions, as the statement that the absolute position and the absolute time are never essential initial conditions. The statement, that absolute time and position are never essential initial conditions, is the first and perhaps the most important theorem of invariance in physics. If it were not for it, it might have been impossible for us to discover laws of nature ... The irrelevant initial conditions must not enter in a relevant fashion into the results of the theory. Second, once the fundamental equations are given, the principles of invariance furnish, in the form of conservation laws and otherwise, powerful assistance toward their solution.[187]

In particular, Wigner suggests that the laws of nature should account for all structure in phenomena, delegating all randomness to initial conditions:

> The existence of the regularities in the initial conditions is considered so unsatisfactory that it is felt necessary to show that the regularities are but a consequence of a situation in which there were no regularities.[248]

We may draw a parallel between the quotes above and the framework SEMs, where mechanisms f_i describe laws of nature, the causal variables X_i stand for relevant initial conditions, and the exogenous random noise terms N_i account for irrelevant initial conditions. The quotes above also admit, I would like to argue, a summary of the Invariance Principle that reads "Find the relevant conditions $\phi(X)$ such that the law of nature w is invariant across irrelevant conditions $\mathcal{E}$."

Nobel laureate Max Born (1882–1970) argued that understanding the physical world often involves realizing that some observed property of an object is actually a property of its relationship to a more fundamental invariant quantity.[249] Born illustrates this with the example of determining the radius of a cardboard circle (the invariant quantity) by examining the length of its ellipsoidal shadow (the observed or relational property) cast by a light source. By studying the length of the shadow under multiple orientations (analogous to diverse environments), we ascertain that the original shape must be a circle. Then, by assuming that the observed shadows are related to a more fundamental invariant quantity, we can deduce its radius. Born contends that "the idea of invariant is the clue to a rational concept of reality, not only in physics but in every aspect of the world," and that "reality is always some kind of invariance of a structure independent of the aspect, the projection." "Whenever possible,"

Bertrand Russell concludes similarly, "substitute constructions out of known entities [states] for inferences to unknown entities [mechanisms]." (The terms in brackets are mine, to highlight the similarities to the process ontology and epistemology espoused by the Invariance Principle.) In the context of learning systems, Born goes on to conclude that "power of the mind to neglect the differences of sense impressions and to be aware only of their invariant features seems to me the most impressive fact of our mental structure."

5.6.3   Invariance and Metaphysics

Metaphysics is a vast branch of philosophy investigating the structure of reality. The succinct comments in this section focus on ontology, the part of metaphysics interested in listing the basic components of reality. A common taxonomy distinguishes between *substance ontologies* and *process ontologies*. Substance ontologies are those that, when considering equations such as $y = f(x)$, regard the states x and y as the fundamental constituents in the world. This stance is appealing because events or states (x, y) are directly observable—we see the caterpillar x become a butterfly y, but the intricate biological process f remains hidden from plain sight. However, all states are transitory. This is why *process ontologies* grant ontological priority to invariant mechanisms f—such as the physical laws yielding a storm following a drop in atmospheric pressure—even if they are not directly perceptible to our senses. The Invariance Principle presented in this chapter subscribes to such process ontologies.

Interestingly, we find echoes of the Invariance Principle in previous literature on metaphysics. Shamik Dasgupta argues:

> The definition of symmetry as "invariance under a specified group of transformations" allowed the concept to be applied much more widely, not only to spatial figures but also to abstract objects such as mathematical expressions.[250]

Invariances are revealed, Dasgupta continues, by finding a "operations on entire physicals systems that leave some aspects of the theory unchanged."[250] To paraphrase, finding representations ϕ on environments $\mathcal{E}$ that leave some pattern w invariant has been our aim all along.

Dasgupta illustrates the use of invariance in determining real quantities through an example involving Galilean boosts, or changes in absolute velocity.[250] More specifically, imagine a world of moving particles m operating according to the Newtonian laws of physics. Consider also a second world m', obtained from m by uniformly adding the same constant absolute velocity vector to every particle. This uniform velocity boost is a symmetry of Newtonian physics, because the laws cannot distinguish between the worlds m and m'. Dasgupta argues that this invariance serves as a metaphysical clue to suggest that absolute velocity is superfluous, not objective, redundant, undetectable, unknowable, and physically insignificant: unreal.

Dasgupta later discusses another source of invariance, arising from our limited epistemological capabilities:

> There is another reason why symmetries might be seen as being primarily epistemological. As we have mentioned, there is a close connection between the notions of symmetry and equivalence, and this leads also to a notion of irrelevance: the equivalence of space points (translational symmetry), for example, may be understood in the sense of the irrelevance of an absolute position to the physical description. There are two ways that one might interpret the epistemological significance of this: on the one hand, we might say that symmetries are associated with unavoidable redundancy in our descriptions of the world, while on the other hand we might maintain that symmetries indicate a limitation of our epistemic access—there are certain properties of objects, such as their absolute positions, that are not observable.[251]

In other words, our cognition remains invariant to factors we overlook. This idea resonates with Kant, in the sense that the invariances in our cognitive apparatus (invariances in) shape the invariances that we can predict about (invariances out). Finally, Dasgupta warns about representations of physical systems that induce trivial invariances:

> I said that a dynamical symmetry is an operation that preserves the laws, and operations can do that while changing how the world looks: just consider an operation that maps each physical system to the "null" system containing nothing whatsoever, in which the laws are true vacuously. Still, I also said that merely preserving the truth of the laws doesn't suffice for being a dynamical symmetry. More conditions must be added. To generalize the symmetry argument, then, one must show that these extra conditions entail that systems related by a dynamical symmetry are observationally equivalent.[250]

In the quote above, these extra conditions parallel the requirement of retaining predictive power, as to avoid the null and delta invariances discussed in section 5.5.

5.6.4   Invariance and Relevance

At the beginning of this chapter, I made a distinction between the set of *possible* environments and the set of *relevant* environments. The set of

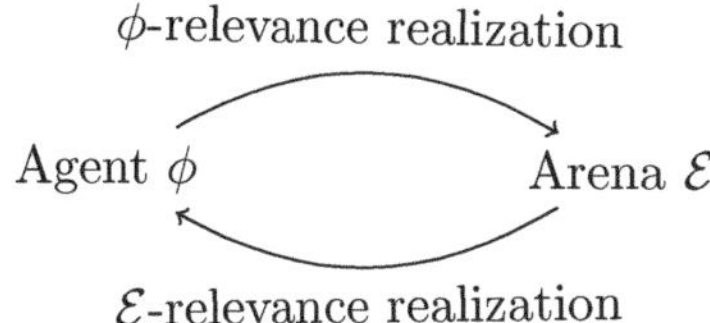

Figure 5.6: Illustration of relevance realization, or the reciprocal disclosure of the agent-arena relationship. The agent's experience of environments shapes their representation of the world in a process called ϕ-relevance realization; a subjective, vertical, or evidence-based process. The agent's exploration and acting on the world demarcates the set of relevant environments in a process called $\mathcal{E}$-relevance; an objective, horizontal, or model-based process. Following Kant's epistemology, the learning of relevant invariances happens at the meeting point between agent and environment.

possible environments encompasses all imaginable experimental conditions, in the broadest sense, that one could expose the mechanism of interest to. However, and as discussed in chapter 3, there is ample evidence to suggest that no mechanism is invariant across all possible environments. For example, Hooke's law fails under extreme temperatures, Newton's law of gravitation does not obtain in very strong fields, Einstein's theory of general relativity breaks down below Planck scales where quantum gravitational effects arise, and day does not follow night if the Sun has burnt out. The much smaller set of *relevant* environments includes those experimental conditions that are reasonable, fall within the expected operating regime of the phenomena under study, and cover most of the likely test environments one might encounter in the future. But this definition is rather vague—what do we exactly mean by *relevant*?

The following comparison between relevance and invariance is heavily inspired by the work of John Vervaeke and his colleagues on *relevance realization*.[160,252] Their main thesis, illustrated in figure 5.6, defines relevance as the reciprocal disclosing between the learning agent ϕ and its environments $\mathcal{E}$, composed itself of two processes. On one hand, the learning agent shapes its representation given the observed environments in a process called ϕ-relevance realization. On the other hand, the learned representation leads the agent to navigate and act upon the world in a process termed $\mathcal{E}$-relevance realization. In the context of learning invariance, this agent-arena reciprocal disclosure implicitly defines the set of *relevant* patterns for the agent to trade off specialization and generalization across the observed environments.

Relevance and invariance realization share many features, discussed next. First off, they are two processes guided by sparsity. For instance, consider my decision-making process regarding the best route to the laboratory this morning. Unpleasant weather ruled out cycling, traffic conditions made the bus unworthy, and a lack of time prevented a leisurely stop at my favorite breakfast place. So, as on many other mornings, I took the metro. In making such a decision, I ignored irrelevant factors such as the color of my shirt, which of my friends has a longer first name, or whether the current day of the month is divisible by seven. How does the sparse set of relevant variables come into focus? How is this selection performed without the prohibitive enumeration of the combinatorially explosive many factors hiding behind each decision? Zooming in to the very sparse set of relevant variables amidst a vast panorama of possibilities, all at the expense of limited cognition, is known as the frame problem:

> The frame problem refers to a cognitive agent's ability to intelligently ignore irrelevant information and zero in on those aspects of the world that are relevant to their goals. The relevance realization framework suggests that the brain achieves this feat by attempting to balance the competing goals of remaining efficient in the current environment while also being resilient in the face of environmental perturbations.[253]

> This is the paradox, it sounds like a Zen Koan: you are intelligent because of your ability to ignore so much information, in a way that makes obvious to you the relevant information enough of the time, so that you are a very good problem solver in very many domains.[254]

In terms of the importance of removing information to reveal invariance, Vervaeke and colleagues explain that "[e]specially important are finding patterns that are invariant across many different contexts and are multiply realized in many different causal processes."[252] William James (1842-1910), considered the father of American psychology, reached a similar conclusion and stated that "the art of being wise is the art of knowing what to ignore." Chapter 8 formalizes how context can be amortized, by means of invariant zooming-in mechanisms, to dynamically construct the representation appropriate for dealing with a learning problem.

Both relevance and invariance are implicitly-defined tools that aid us in finding the correct level of abstraction to deal with various learning situations. In a talk at Yale University, Brian Cantwell Smith argued that dynamically adjusting the level of abstraction is a key feature of intelligent systems:

> Because what happens is we people, maybe other creatures too, live in a continuous creative tension between the incredible richness of the world and the long distance utility of language abstraction and inference on the other. When we engage with the world, we want to do the operative abstraction, we want to kind of reconcile or concretize our ideas with respect to reality to let more of the world's ineffable details fill our representations in order to be appropriately responsive in action to the world's fine grain detail. But when we want to travel long distances ... when we do science, we have to let go of a lot of detail and employ more efficient methods purposefully designed for inferential travel. And if we're clever, and we're damn clever—I think there's nothing more important about AI than it teaches you humility—we must in fact do both ... Basically, living in this middle realm between engaging with the detail, letting go of the detail. And what's magic about us is that we live this dance between them, among them, so as to both live and be able to think.[255]

Vervaeke and colleagues also comment on the importance of this trade off:

> Should an organism focus on the particularities of specific situations (as in a "microscope") or zoom out to produce more generalizable machinery (as in a "telescope")? The optimal solution to this trade-off depends on the volatility of the environment. Whereas specialists will tend to thrive in highly stable environments, generalists will do (relatively) better in highly volatile situations.[160]

These quotes are in line with the Invariance Principle, whereby invariant representations are better performing in volatile situations.

Relevance and invariance both elude explicit definition, as these concepts are difficult to define—absent conditions and environments—without getting trapped in argumentative circles. Vervaeke and colleagues exemplify this challenge by analogy with the concept of *fitness* in biological evolution. While intuitive, defining *fitness* is only possible implicitly and in terms of the ever-changing environment:

> What evolutionary theory provides is not an account of the biological features that define fitness, but a mechanism by which fitness is realized in a contextually sensitive manner. Therefore, by strong analogy with the centrality of natural selection in biology, we do not really want a theory of relevance. We want instead a theory that articulates a mechanism for how relevance is realized in a contextually sensitive manner.[160]

Relevance, invariance, and fitness are thus best understood as ongoing processes that balance multiple opposing forces at play.

In the case of relevance, Andersen and colleagues describe the associated process of relevance realization as

> a cognitive agent's ability to intelligently ignore irrelevant information and zero in on those aspects of the world that are relevant to their goals. The relevance realization framework suggests that the brain achieves this feat by attempting to balance the competing goals of remaining efficient in the current environment while also being resilient in the face of environmental perturbations.[253]

Examples of these trade offs include the efficiency-resiliency, exploration-exploitation, specialization-generalization, and intension-extension compromises. These all relate to learning and using invariances across shifting environments.

Relevance and invariance are also dependent on context and environment. As argued in multiple occasions, "it is commonly acknowledged that the truth or falsity of causal propositions is relative to context."[63] The same context-dependence applies relevance, as Vervaeke and colleagues argue,

> relevant information cannot simply be always identical to frequent, or invariant, or prototypical information, because relevance is context sensitive.[160]

Similar remarks follow for invariance, which is defined only after deciding upon a collection of relevant environments.

The processes of relevance and invariance realization are both nonconvex and vulnerable to local minima. In cognitive science, local minima are compared to self-deception, defined as "a self-imposed lack of the cognitive flexibility needed for depth insights, so that we trap ourselves in illusion."[252] Vervaeke and colleagues argue that "the very same processing that makes us intelligent also makes us vulnerable to foolishness," and that wisdom is nothing but "seeing through illusion and by implication seeing into reality."[252] Similarly, large learning machines are able to capture intricate patterns but also get lost in spurious correlations. To escape from self-deception and local minima, one often injects entropy into the system to reframe the situation under a different point of view that affords more powerful invariances.[256]

> Attaining insight requires discovering an effective problem representation, and that performance on insight problems can be predicted from the availability of generators and constraints in the search for such a representation. ... Noticing properties of the situation that remained invariant during solution attempts ... proved to be a particularly powerful means for focusing search.[257]

The Copernican Revolution, a radical reframing of the solar system that placed the sun at its center, is a canonical example of insight. Paul Churchland offers a visceral exercise to experience a similar insight, where one triangulates two celestial bodies in a starry night to realize our relative angle with respect to the ecliptic plane of the solar system.[258]

5.6.5 Invariance and Truth

By stretching our metaphysical investigations further, we may inquire about the relationship between invariance and truth. In his last book *Invariances*, Robert Nozick (1938–2002) argued that "what constitutes the objectivity of facts is invariance under certain transformations."[211] More precisely, "once we possess the covariant representation under which the equations stay the same for all coordinate systems, the quantities in the (covariant) equations are the real and objective quantities."[211] Using our notations, the previous quote implies that a feature ϕ_j describes a real and objective quantity if and only if the optimal classifier invariant across relevant environments $\mathcal{E}$ has a nonzero coefficient w_j. Vervaeke and Ferraro also connect invariance-inducing representations to truth from the angle of cognitive science, whereby

> the word "real" is being used here in a comparative sense, which means a general enhancement of problem-solving abilities. In this sense, seeing into reality is seeing into the nature of our problems, to be able to understand the challenges before us in a manner that facilitates their solution.[252]

As a counterpoint to this argument, in his book *The Case Against Reality*, Donald Hoffman argues that, while the representations we learn are helpful for survival, they hide from us vast aspects of reality.[132] Because the main interest of living agents is to survive, we must process a combinatorially explosive amount of information using a finite computational budget, ignoring vast amounts of information.

In physics, many researchers highlight the role of invariance in establishing objectivity. For instance, Katherine Brading writes,

> It is widely agreed that there is a close connection between symmetry and objectivity, the starting point once again being provided by space-time symmetries: the laws by means of which we describe the evolution of physical systems have an objective validity because they are the same for all observers ... Debs and Redhead (2007) label as "invariantism" the view that "invariance under a specified group of automorphisms is both a necessary and sufficient condition for objectivity" ... They point out ... a natural connection between "invariantism" and structural realism.[251]

Structural realism considers that revisions of scientific theories retain more invariance in structure (mechanism) than content (states). When discussing the transition from Fresnel's elastic solid theory to Maxwell's electromagnetic field in the explanation of optics, John Worrall notes:

> There was an important element of continuity in the shift from Fresnel to Maxwell—and this was much more than a simple question of carrying over the successful empirical content into the new theory. At the same time it was rather less than a carrying over of the full theoretical content or full theoretical mechanisms (even in *approximate* form) ... There was continuity or accumulation in the shift, but the continuity is one of form or structure, not of content.[259]

While all structural realists give priority to mechanisms over states, one must distinguish two particular strands in this philosophical tradition. Epistemic structural realism suggests that all we know is relations between things, and never the things themselves. In contrast, ontic structural realism asserts that relations are all that there exists—a position echoed in James Ladyman's "it's relations all the way down"[260] and aligning with the Invariance Principle.

Invariantism also relates to the philosophical tradition of *pragmatism*. The pragmatic maxim of Charles Sanders Peirce states:

> Consider what effects, which might conceivably have practical bearings, we conceive the object of our conception to have. Then, our conception of these effects is the whole of our conception of the object.[261]

The pragmatic maxim states that the meaning of a concept is determined by its practical effects. When arguing that a glass vase is fragile, we mean that it will likely shatter when dropped. Therefore, the meaning of *fragility* is understood through this anticipated practical effects. Pragmatism is similar to the invariance principle: They both focus meaning on practical consequences, consider the idea of truth as a contextual construct, assume knowledge as essentially unverifiable but subject to falsification, allows multiple perspectives and solutions to a problem, and have an empirical preference to understanding nature. From the point of view of pragmatism, all of the philosophical approaches to causation surveyed in chapter 3 are merely tools to perform useful work. The pragmatist is free to choose the interpretation or combination of interpretations of causation most useful to accomplish the task at hand—or even abandon the concept of causation altogether. One could argue that these theories, together with others by Popper and Salmon, subscribe to some sort of *prediction maximalism*: The evaluation of theories and beliefs should be done in terms of the precision (error) and width (invariance) of the predictions that they afford.

Chapter 6

Domain Generalization Algorithms

6.1   Introduction

This chapter reviews the literature in domain generalization, which is also interested in learning robust predictors that generalize across multiple data environments. One notable example is invariant causal prediction (ICP), the predecessor algorithm to invariant risk minimization (IRM). Other solutions for domain generalization discussed in this chapter include distributionally robust optimization, data subsampling and reweighting, matching feature representations, and common environment loss gradients. The recent survey by Kaddour and colleagues[262] is a great companion to this chapter, as it explains a variety of algorithms for domain generalization with a focus on causation and invariance. The chapter concludes with some reflections about the inherent difficulties of model selection in the doubly underspecified problem of domain generalization, setting the stage for the following chapter.

Later chapters will dig deeper into specific domain generalization algorithms. In particular, chapter 8 reviews approaches that adapt on the fly while performing in a test environment. Chapter 9 discusses methods for learning a diverse set of features, including ensemble techniques and self-supervised learning. Finally, chapter 10 studies how to use covariant data augmentation protocols to combat spurious correlations and improve out-of-distribution performance.

6.2 Invariant Causal Prediction

IRM is a successor to Invariant Causal Prediction (ICP),[212,263] a pioneering work that founded the algorithmic path from invariance to causation. ICP seeks to identify the subset of variables within an input vector $X^e \in \mathbb{R}^d$ that are direct causes of the target variable Y^e. In each environment $e \in \mathcal{E}$, these two variables follow this linear structural equation model:

$$Y^e \leftarrow X^e \cdot \mathrm{Diag}(\phi_{01}^{\star}) \cdot w^{\star} + \varepsilon, \text{ where } X^e \perp \varepsilon. \tag{6.1}$$

The binary representation $\phi_{01}^{\star} \in \{0,1\}^d$ determines the subset $S^{\star} = \{j : \phi_{01,j}^{\star} = 1\}$ of input variables X^e directly influencing the target Y^e. The value of Y^e is therefore the combination of variables $X_{S^{\star}}^e$, their corresponding regression coefficients $w_S^{\star}$, and some independent, additive, and homoskedastic noise ε. While the distribution of the input vector X^e is allowed to vary across environments, the binary representation $\phi_{01}^{\star}$, the optimal regression coefficients $w^{\star}$, and the distribution of the independent additive noise ε are assumed to be invariant.

ICP estimates the causal variables $S^{\star}$ as $\hat{S}(\mathcal{E}_{\mathrm{tr}})$ from a collection of training environments $\mathcal{E}_{\mathrm{tr}}$ as follows. For each subset $S \subseteq \{1, \ldots, d\}$:

- Let X_S^e be the subset of variables S from the input vector X^e. Let f_S be the linear regression from X_S^e to Y^e on the union of training environments.

- Accept the set S if the distribution of the regression residuals $R^e = Y^e - X_S^e \cdot f_S$ matches for all the training environments $e \in \mathcal{E}_{\mathrm{tr}}$. Make this decision by performing two-sample tests on the regression residuals from each environment against all others, then aggregating these multiple tests using a Bonferroni correction.

Finally, let the estimated set of causal variables $\hat{S}(\mathcal{E}_{\mathrm{tr}})$ be the intersection of all accepted subsets S. Provided that all assumptions hold and the two-sample test is valid, this ICP routine ensures that $S(\mathcal{E}) \subseteq S^{\star}$. Therefore, ICP is a conservative method: Those variables estimated as causal are likely to be so, but the method may exclude some other causal variables. For instance, $\hat{S}(\mathcal{E}) = \emptyset$ when $|\mathcal{E}| = 1$, that is, observational data is insufficient to declare any variable as causal. Conversely, when training environments encompass interventions on all variables, ICP recovers the true set of causal variables $\hat{S}(\mathcal{E}) = S^{\star}$.[263]

ICP has several limitations, some of which inspired the development of IRM. First, ICP's computational complexity is prohibitive for large dimensions d, as it involves solving 2^d regression problems. Second, ICP is limited to axis-aligned, binary representations that either accept or discard individual inputs. This limits its application to problems where the observed inputs are nontrivial transformations of the underlying structural equation model governing the data. Third, ICP is reserved for linear problems with homoskedastic noise, an unrealistic assumption for nonlinear problems with prediction difficulty—the level of irreducible noise—varying across environments. Fourth, ICP is excessively conservative, as the estimated set of causal variables is the intersection over many hypothesis tests. While variables declared as causal by ICP should be so, it often happens that the estimated set of causal variables returns as empty.

The conservativeness of ICP is justified in the context of causal discovery. As noted in section 5.3.1, only those predictors that rely on the direct causes of the target achieve finite out-of-distribution error levels across valid interventions.[264] Therefore, accepting noncausal variables as such would automatically result in unbounded errors across some interventions. In contrast, methods such as IRM may only achieve very small nonzero regression coefficients on noncausal variables. When learned across interventional distributions, these softer predictors estimate what Peter Buhlmann calls *diluted* causality.[265] Thus, IRM treats causation and invariance as concepts with gradations rather than as binary conditions.

6.2.1 Methods Related to ICP and IRM

Several successors to ICP and IRM benefit from the risk extrapolation interpretation illustrated in figure 5.5.[266,267] To understand these methods, recall how empirical risk interpolation minimizes the convex sum of training environments risks:

$$\max_{\substack{\sum_e \lambda_e = 1 \\ \lambda_e \geq 0}} \sum_{e \in \mathcal{E}_{\text{tr}}} \lambda_e R_{P^e}(f).$$

In addition, risk extrapolation allows negative risk coefficients to explore distributions of data beyond the convex hull of training risks:

$$\max_{\substack{\sum_e \lambda_e = 1 \\ \lambda_e \geq \lambda_{\min}}} \sum_{e \in \mathcal{E}_{\text{tr}}} \lambda_e R_{P^e}(f) = (1 - |\mathcal{E}_{\text{tr}}| \cdot \lambda_{\min}) \max_{e \in \mathcal{E}_{\text{tr}}} R_{P^e}(f) + \lambda_{\min} \sum_{e \in \mathcal{E}_{\text{tr}}} R_{P^e}(f).$$

$$(6.2)$$

The previous expression reduces to risk interpolation when $\lambda_{\min} = 0$, places negative weights on the risk of all but the worst-case environment, and enforces the equality of risks when $\lambda_{\min} \to -\infty$.[266] When only two training environments are available, equation (6.2) is equal to ERM plus a penalty minimizing the absolute difference between the two risks. Based on these insights, the V-REx method[266] minimizes the pairwise mean squared error between risks, or risk variance:

$$\text{V-REx}(f) = \lambda \cdot \text{Var}(\{R_{P^e}(f)\}_{e \in \mathcal{E}_{\text{tr}}}) + \sum_{e \in \mathcal{E}_{\text{tr}}} R_{P^e}(f).$$

The V-REx objective searches for predictors with *similar* generalization errors at all training environments. One of the limitations of V-REx is its assumption that all training environments have the same baseline error. However, this assumption could be relaxed by instead minimizing the variance of baseline-adjusted risks $R_{P^e}(f) - R_{P^e}(\hat{f}^e)$, where $\hat{f}^e$ is the empirical risk minimizer for environment $e \in \mathcal{E}_{\text{tr}}$.

Several methods following IRM suggest regularizing classifiers with environment risk gradients. The inter-environment gradient alignment algorithm (IGA) defines its objective as follows:

$$\text{IGA}(f) = \lambda \cdot \text{Var}(\{g^e\}_{e \in \mathcal{E}_{\text{tr}}}) + \sum_{e \in \mathcal{E}_{\text{tr}}} R_{P^e}\left(f - \alpha \cdot \sum\nolimits_{e \in \mathcal{E}_{\text{tr}}} g^e\right),$$

where $g^e = \nabla_f[R_{P^e}(f)]$. IGA is a meta-learning objective consisting of two terms. The sum term parameterizes the local predictor at environment e in terms of a single gradient step taken from a global predictor f. The variance term enforces that such a gradient step, which translates the global predictor f into each local predictor, is similar across environments. Therefore, the IGA objective encourages machines to learn predictors with matching risk gradients across environments.

Some works adopt a game-theoretical approach to cast the IRM objective, avoiding the need for challenging bi-level optimization problems. For example, Kartik Ahuja and colleagues cast IRM as the Nash equilibrium of an ensemble game among several environments,[268] formulating the objective

$$\min \qquad \sum_{e \in \mathcal{E}_{\text{tr}}} R_{P^e}\left(\left[\sum\nolimits_{q \in \mathcal{E}_{\text{tr}}} w^q\right] \circ \phi\right)$$

$$\text{subject to} \quad w^e \in \arg\min_{\tilde{w}^e} R_{P^e}\left(\left[\tilde{w}^e + \sum\nolimits_{q \neq e} w^q\right] \circ \phi\right), \text{ for all } e \in \mathcal{E}_{\text{tr}}.$$

This game instantiates one player per training environment, each contributing an additive term toward building the classifier. Similarly, invariant rationalization[225] translates IRM into an adversarial game played between a collection of environment-aware classifiers w^e and one environment-agnostic classifier w:

$$\text{InvRat}(f = w \circ \phi) = \min_{\phi, w} \max_{w^e} \sum_{e \in \mathcal{E}_{\text{tr}}} R_{P^e}(w \circ \phi)$$

$$+ \lambda \cdot \max(R_{P^e}(w \circ \phi) - R_{P^e}(w^e \circ \phi), 0).$$

In both games, the goal is to find a classifier w that no adversary could fine-tune the results for the benefit of their own environment.

Recently, Wale Salaudeen and Sanmi Koyejo introduced a second method to isolate invariance-inducing features $\Phi = \phi(X)$ from spuriousness-inducing features $\bar{\Phi}$.[269,270] The authors argue that one must consider three distinct causal graphs, firstly introduced by Ahuja and colleagues[268] and illustrated in figure 6.1, when studying this problem. While the Invariance Principle (IP-Cond) identifies Φ for all three graphs, the first two cases also satisfy a second principle of invariance:

$$\Phi \perp \bar{\Phi} \mid Y, E. \tag{6.3}$$

Although this principle does not reveal Φ for the third graph, this case is addressable with an ERM baseline with information bottleneck regularization (section 5.5). To address the first two graphs via (6.3), the authors suggest minimizing the *target conditioned representation independence* objective:

$$\begin{aligned}
\mathrm{TCRI}(f = w \circ \phi; \bar{\phi}, \{w^e\}) = &\sum_{e \in \mathcal{E}_{\mathrm{tr}}} R_{P^e}(w \circ \phi) \\
&+ R_{P^e}(w^e \circ [\phi, \bar{\phi}]) \\
&+ \lambda \cdot [\![\phi(X) \not\perp \bar{\phi}(X) \mid Y, E]\!],
\end{aligned}$$

where the first term implements ERM, the second term absorbs spuriousness-inducing features $\bar{\phi}$ into an auxiliary environment-specific classifier w^e, and the third term is a conditional independence test promoting (6.3). Given that the conditioning variables in (6.3) are low-dimensional, discrete, and not subject to learning, the TCRI objective admits a simpler implementation than the invariant risk minimization algorithms discussed in the previous chapter.

6.2.2 Causal Concepts Related to ICP and IRM

The Invariance Principle is related to various concepts in causation reviewed in chapter 4. For example, recall that the representation $\phi(X)$ satisfies *conditional exchangeability* if

$$(Y^0, Y^1) \perp T \mid \phi(X),$$

where (Y^0, Y^1) describes a pair of potential outcomes and T is a binary treatment-control indicator. To compare, recall the conditional independence statement form of the Invariance Principle, reading $Y \perp E \mid \phi(X)$. Both statements encourage representations that render invariant their relationship

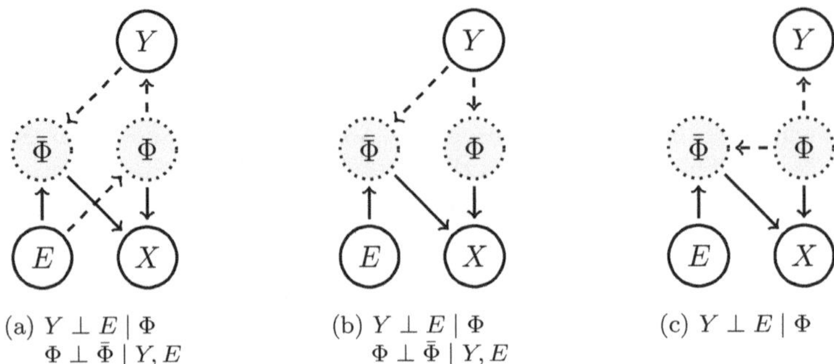

(a) $Y \perp E \mid \Phi$
  $\Phi \perp \bar{\Phi} \mid Y, E$

(b) $Y \perp E \mid \Phi$
  $\Phi \perp \bar{\Phi} \mid Y, E$

(c) $Y \perp E \mid \Phi$

Figure 6.1: Three causal graphs on the problem of learning across multiple environments. Gray dotted nodes denote unobserved variables, where Φ is the desired representation based on invariant features and $\bar{\Phi}$ is the undesired representation based on spurious features. In all three graphs, the desired representation satisfies the Invariance Principle (IP-Cond), namely $Y \perp E \mid \Phi$. In the two first graphs, Φ also satisfies a second principle of invariance, namely $\Phi \perp \bar{\Phi} \mid Y, E$, which may be easier to enforce because the conditioning variables are fixed and low-dimensional, sometimes even binary. While Φ does not satisfy the second invariance principle in the third graph, a simple ERM baseline would achieve this goal.

to the target variable Y across treatment groups T or, more generally, environments E.

Given the analogy above, a promising direction for future research is to leverage propensity scores to learn invariant predictors. Specifically, consider the binary environments $E \in \{0, 1\}$. If the Invariance Principle (IP-Cond) holds for $\phi(X)$, then it also follows for the environment propensity score $\pi(\phi(X)) = \Pr(E = 1 \mid \phi(X))$:

$$Y \perp E \mid \pi(\phi(X)).$$

This formulates the Invariance Principle in terms of a one-dimensional conditioning variable, potentially simplifying the estimation of conditional independence and increasing environmental support overlap. However, learning ϕ requires back-propagating through the optimization process necessary to build the propensity score estimate π. Related studies have used similar analogies to apply the Invariance Principle and IRM to estimate average[271] and heterogeneous[272,273] treatment effects.

The Invariance Principle (IP-Cond) also relates to the E-value, introduced by Tyler VanderWeele and Peng Ding:

The E-value is the minimum strength of association, on the risk ratio scale, that an unmeasured confounder would need to have with both the treatment and outcome, conditional on the measured covariates, to fully explain away a specific treatment-outcome association.[274]

The E-value equals $\mathrm{RR} + \sqrt{\mathrm{RR}(\mathrm{RR}-1)}$, where the risk ratio

$$\mathrm{RR} = \max_{\alpha \in \{-1,+1\}} \sum_x \left(\frac{\Pr(Y=1 \mid \phi(x), T=1)}{\Pr(Y=1 \mid \phi(x), T=0)} \right)^\alpha ,$$

and $T \in \{0,1\}$ indexes the control and treated groups, respectively. The E-value achieves its minimum value of 1 in the desirable situation when no unmeasured confounding is needed to explain away the observed association. According to the equations above, this happens when the risk ratio equals 1, so $\Pr(Y=1 \mid \phi(x), T=t)$ is invariant for all t. Taking the control and treated groups as environments, we see that representations that satisfy the Invariance Principle (IP-Cond) have minimal E-values.

6.3 Distributionally Robust Optimization

Distributional robust optimization (DRO)[275–277] aims to estimate a predictor minimizing this robust risk:

$$R_{\mathcal{P}}(f) = \sup_{\tilde{P} \in \mathcal{P}(P)} R_{\tilde{P}}(f), \tag{6.4}$$

where $\mathcal{P} := \mathcal{P}(P)$ is a set of distributions *centered* around the training data distribution P. Unlike the invariance learning setup from chapter 5, DRO considers access to only one training dataset P, from which it derives a collection of training environments $\mathcal{P}$ following a rule specified a priori. For example, some DRO implementations specify

$$\mathcal{P} = \{\tilde{P} : d(P, \tilde{P}) \le \varepsilon\},$$

where d is the distance between probability distributions chosen according to domain knowledge. Some popular choices for d include f-divergences, such as the Kullback-Liebler divergence,[278] or Wasserstein metrics.[279] Alternatively, we may implicitly construct $\mathcal{P}$ by performing data augmentation on examples from P. For instance, if $\mathcal{P}$ contains distributions obtained by translating the examples of P by a certain shift magnitude, then training over $\mathcal{P}$ imparts translational invariance to the predictors. As another example, when considering $\mathcal{P}$ to contain all valid interventions, the resulting family of distributions has an infinite radius. This is why, as described in section 5.3.1, only those predictors that rely on direct causes can attain finite robust risk.

Distributionally robust optimization implements risk interpolation, illustrated in figure 5.5. Formally, given the Karush-Kuhn-Tucker conditions and a finite $\mathcal{P}$, there exists a collection of $\lambda_{\tilde{P}} \geq 0$ such that the minimizer of (6.4) is a first-order stationary point of $\sum_{\tilde{P} \in \mathcal{P}} \lambda_{\tilde{P}} R_{\tilde{P}}(f)$. As a result, distributionally robust optimization does not generalize beyond the convex hull of the environments in $\mathcal{P}$.

6.4 Data Subsampling and Reweighting

One simple strategy to train robust predictors is to subsample or reweight training environments, both to balance the prominence of different groups of examples and to allow learning algorithms to better focus on invariant patterns. When using nonnegative environment weights, the methods in this section are limited to risk interpolation.

One surprisingly effective method to reveal invariant predictors is to subsample the training environments until they match in size. Formally, assume a training dataset consisting of n triplets (x_i, y_i, e_i), containing $n(e) = \sum_{j=1}^{n} [\![e_j = e]\!]$ examples from environment $e \in \mathcal{E}_{\text{tr}}$. The smallest training environment, also called the *minority environment*, has $n^{\min} = \min_e n(e)$ examples. Further, associate a subsampling weight $q_i \sim \text{Bernoulli}(\frac{n^{\min}}{n(e_i)})$ to each example (x_i, y_i), where q_i is more likely to be zero for bigger environments. Then, Idrissi and colleagues[280] suggest learning on the subsampled dataset by minimizing the empirical risk minimization objective:

$$\text{SUBG}(f) = \frac{1}{n} \sum_{i=1}^{n} q_i \cdot \ell(f(x_i), y_i).$$

This strategy is minimax optimal when the test environment equals one of the training environments.[281] As illustrated in figure 6.2, subsampling leads to predictors with improved margin and worst-environment accuracy in cases where the environment data distributions have heavy tails.

Although subsampling is both effective and computationally efficient, discarding a significant portion of the training data might be seen as wasteful. To preserve all training examples, one can opt to *reweight* the environments using strictly positive weights:

$$\text{RWG}(f) = \frac{1}{n} \sum_{i=1}^{n} q_i \cdot \ell(f(x_i), y_i), \text{ where } q_i = \frac{|\mathcal{E}_{\text{tr}}|}{n(e_i) \cdot \sum_e \frac{1}{n(e_i)}}.$$

The behavior of RWG is radically different from SUBG when using overparameterized models able to achieve zero training error. More specifically, any model achieving zero training loss when $q_i = 1$ for all i can also achieve zero training loss for any choice of $\{q_i\}$. In those situations, regularizing the

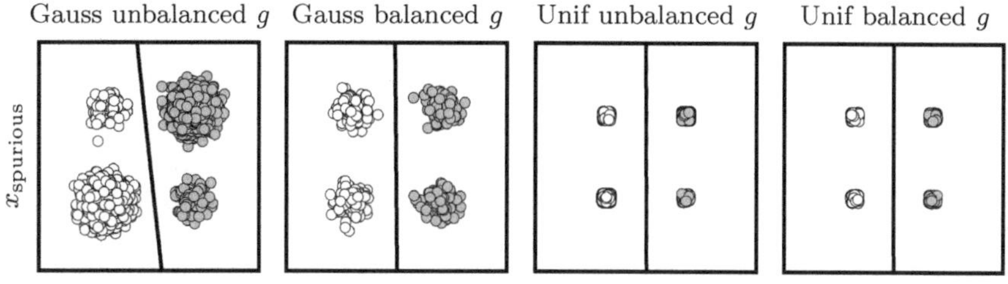

Figure 6.2: Balancing groups by data subsampling de-biases classifiers from using spurious correlations. The effect is more notable when subsampling group distributions have heavy tails.[282]

capacity of the learning machine is crucial to ensure that RWG converges to a solution different from ERM. Figure 6.3 illustrates the behaviors of ERM, SUBG, and RWG in the cow-on-the-beach problem (CoB).

Shiori Sagawa and colleagues address these issues in a seminal paper[283] by introducing a *dynamic* reweighting scheme known as group distributionally robust optimization (group DRO). The group DRO algorithm begins by randomly initializing a predictor f and a vector of environment weights $q^e = 1$, for all $e \in \mathcal{E}_{\text{tr}}$. Then, group DRO iterates the following steps until convergence:

- $q \leftarrow q \cdot \exp(\eta \cdot R_{P^e}(f))$,

- $q \leftarrow q / \sum_e q^e$,

- $f \leftarrow f - \alpha \cdot \nabla_f \left[\sum_e q^e \cdot R_{P^e}(f) \right]$.

Beyond subsampling and reweighting, a third strategy to modulate the learning of different (groups of) examples is to train on adjusted logits. While training on example x, logit adjustment (LA) adjusts logits according to

$$f(x)_c \mapsto f(x)_c + \tau \cdot \log \delta(x)_c, \tag{6.5}$$

for each class $c \in \{1, \ldots, C\}$, where $\tau > 0$ is a hyper-parameter. To understand the equation above, consider two possible adjustments made to the correct logit $f(x)_y$ for some training example (x, y).

- The adjustment $f(x) - \Delta$ where $\Delta_y \gg 0$ and $\Delta_{y' \neq y} = 0$ promoting the learning of (x, y), because the adjustment leads to a large loss value (and gradient) for the example.

- The adjustment $f(x) + \Delta$, on the other hand, preventing the learning of (x, y), because the adjustment removes all loss value (and gradient) for the example.

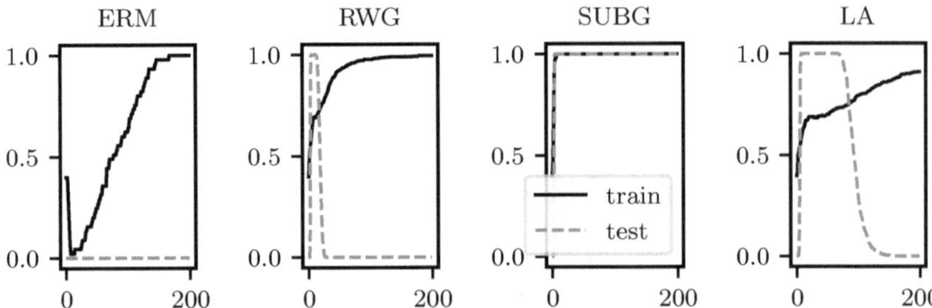

Figure 6.3: Worst-group accuracy on the cow-on-the-beach problem for three different models. ERM finds the "simplify-and-memorize" solution by using the spurious feature to discriminate between the majority examples of each class, then using the noise features to memorize the minority examples of each class (shown as small neighborhoods). This leads to poor test worst-group-accuracy. RWG also achieves good test worst-group-accuracy, but only when regularizing or early-stopping the training process carefully. SUBG throws away majority-group data to decorrelate the spurious feature and the class label. This guides the model to rely on the core feature and attains optimal worst-group-accuracy. Logit adjustment (LA), while more robust than RWG, also converges to an ERM-like solution with poor test worst-group-accuracy.

Some options to design the adjustment function $\delta(x)_c$ for a given input x include:

- $\delta_c(x) = p(c)$, the class probability for category c, where incorporating the prior distribution into the learning, allowing the model to not capture the prior distribution anymore and hence promotes the learning of small classes.[284]

- $\delta_c(x) = p(c, e(x))$ or $\delta_c(x) = p(c \mid e(x))$, the joint/conditional probability distribution of class and/given environment, promoting the learning of small groups.[285,286]

- $\delta_c(x) = \overline{p}^{ho}(c \mid x)$ where $\overline{p}^{ho}$ is a calibrated[1] predictor trained while holding-out x. This promotes the learning of examples prone to large generalization error.[6]

In the list above, options employing $e(x)$ require environment annotations or their estimation by unsupervised means.[285,286] These options can be understood as mitigating the simplify-and-memorize learning strategy. During test time the logit adjustments are discarded, so the machine produces prediction logits $f(x)$ for test inputs x.

---

[1] $\overline{p}^{ho}(c \mid x) := \sum_{c'} p(c \mid c')\, p^{ho}(c' \mid x)$

The methods in this section illustrate how ERM, applied to the right balancing of the training data, is an effective baseline to reveal invariance. These balancing techniques parallel many of the algorithms reviewed in chapter 4, which reduce causal inference to supervised learning conditioned on a valid adjustment set. This analogy further suggests that there is no free lunch when it comes to discovering the right balancing factors: Good balancing brings us closer to invariance and bad balancing steers learning away from it. While the right balancing factor is sometimes annotated in the training data (as it happens in subpopulation shift benchmarks), its discovery requires additional knowledge about the problem at hand or, as we will see in chapter 7, extra inductive assumptions.

Balancing methods in domain generalization relate to matching methods in causal inference, some of them reviewed in section 4.5.3. For instance, Yuhui Li and colleagues[287] propose matching each example (x_i, y_i) with the closest example (x_j, y_j) of a different label, indexed by $j = \arg\min_{k:y_k \neq y_i} d(f_z(x_i), f_z(x_k))$. Here, $f_z(x_i)$ is the hidden representation of the estimated propensity score mapping $\hat{e}_i = f_e(f_z(x_i), y_i)$.

As a final remark, the invariant relationship of interest may be more complex for certain regions of the input space.[107] In those cases, we should expect predictive discrepancies across groups, even after perfect balancing.

6.5 Matching Representations

The literature on domain generalization has developed numerous methods aimed at learning *invariant representations*. These techniques search for a representation ϕ such that

$$\Pr(\phi(X) = x \mid E = e) = \Pr(\phi(X) = x \mid E = e'), \text{ for all } e, e' \in \mathcal{E}, x \in \mathcal{X}. \tag{6.6}$$

There are two main implementations of this constraint. First, correlation alignment for deep domain adaptation (CORAL) enforces a representation with unit covariance in each environment:[288]

$$\text{CORAL}(f = w \circ \phi) = \sum_{e \in \mathcal{E}_{\text{tr}}} R_{P^e}(f) + \lambda \cdot \|\text{Cov}(\phi(X^e)) - I\|^2.$$

Second, domain adversarial neural network training (DANN)[289] implements the following adversarial:

$$\text{DANN}(f = w \circ \phi; g) = \sum_{e \in \mathcal{E}_{\text{tr}}} \mathop{\mathbb{E}}_{(x,y) \sim P^e} \left[\ell(f(x), y) - \lambda \cdot \ell(g(\phi(x), e)) \right],$$

where g is a classifier trying to predict the environment index from the input representation. In DANN, the representation should contain all information to predict the target, while containing no information to predict the environment index.

Learning matching representations can often impose overly rigid constraints. For instance, matching representations is unsuitable when the distribution of targets $P(Y^e)$ changes across environments, as it happens in (Example1). In such cases, efforts to match representations would steer learning away from invariance. Instead, the Invariance Principle, introduced as an epistemological tool to learn the laws of nature, promotes invariance at the mechanism or function level. This approach gives priority to unobserved mechanisms over observed states, implying a process-ontology view of reality.

To partially address these issues, representation matching methods can be extended into *class-conditional* versions.[290] Here, we aim to find a representation ϕ such that

$$\Pr(\phi(X) = x \mid Y = y, E = e) = \Pr(\phi(X) = x \mid Y = y, E = e'),$$
$$\text{for all } e, e' \in \mathcal{E}, x \in \mathcal{X}, y \in \mathcal{Y}.$$

This equation, implementing an invariance principle opposite to the one introduced in the previous chapter, loses all interpretation in terms of invariant mechanisms and causation. While matching (class-conditional) feature representations only makes sense for certain causal structures, the Invariance Principle proposed in the previous chapter is valid as long as environments arise from valid interventions.

Because predictions are also representations, we may also consider matching predictive distributions across environments:[291]

$$\Pr(f(X) = x \mid E = e) = \Pr(f(X) = x \mid E = e'), \text{ for all } e, e' \in \mathcal{E}, x \in \mathcal{X}.$$

In those cases where we have paired examples across environments—for instance, the *same* individual photographed against different backgrounds—we may regularize directly predictive variance:[292]

$$\text{CORE}(f) = \sum_{e \in \mathcal{E}_{\text{tr}}} R_{P^e}(f) + \lambda \cdot \text{Var}(f(x^e)),$$

where the penalty in the equation above enforces equal predictions across the various examples that depict the same individual.

6.6 Invariance Through Time

In sequential learning problems, such as language modeling, we may consider the following Invariance Principle through time:

$$Y \perp T \mid \phi(X), \tag{6.7}$$

where T is a continuous variable indexing time, and we assume access to a dataset of triplets (x_i, y_i, t_i). Although the continuous nature of T complicates the use of vanilla IRM, Yong Lin and colleagues[293] propose the following continuous extension:

$$\min_{w,\phi,h} \max_{g} \frac{1}{n} \sum_{i=1}^{n} \ell(w(\phi(x_i)), y_i) + \lambda \cdot \left(\|h(\phi(x_i)) - t_i\|^2 - \|g(\phi(x_i), y_i - t_i)\|^2 \right).$$

This objective states that a regressor g predicting T from $(\phi(X), Y)$ should be no better than a regressor h predicting T from $\phi(X)$ alone, when the representation $\phi(X)$ satisfies the Invariance Principle through time (6.7).

Two additional algorithms propose to enforce principles of invariance through time. First, sequential invariant causal prediction[294] assumes $Y_t = \phi(X_t) \cdot w + \mu + \varepsilon_t$, where ϕ selects a subset of the variables in X_t, and $\varepsilon_t \sim \mathcal{N}(0, \sigma^2)$ satisfies $t \perp \phi(X_t)$ for all time-steps t. A simple implementation of the sequential ICP reverts to ICP (section 6.2) by partitioning time-data into a set nonoverlapping blocks or environments $\mathcal{E}_{\mathrm{tr}}$. Then, for each ϕ inducing a candidate subset S of variables in X_t, (1) compute the rescaled regression residuals by regressing from X_t^S to Y_t, (2) compute a two-sample test statistic between the residuals within each pair of environments $e, e' \in \mathcal{E}_{\mathrm{tr}}$, (3) aggregate all pairwise test statistics, and (4) accept or reject the candidate subset S based on the null-distribution of the aggregated test statistic. Finally, return as the subset of causal variables $S^\star$ the intersection of all accepted candidate subsets.

Second, invariant subspace decomposition[295] allows the data generating process to have regression coefficients changing over time, namely $Y_t = X_t \cdot \beta_t + \varepsilon_t$, where the conditional expectation of ε_t given X_t is zero at all time-steps t. The true time-varying parameter β_t is assumed to decompose as $\beta_t = \beta + \delta_t$, where β is the time-invariant component maximizing the explained variance across time-steps, and δ_t is the time-variant component maximizing the explained variance at time-step t. While the time-varying parameter β_t belongs to $\mathbb{R}^d$, the time-invariant component β and time-variant component δ_t are assumed to inhabit orthogonal subspaces, and the method benefits from cases where the time-variant subspace is low-dimensional.

6.7 Following Common Gradients

As illustrated with IRMv1, environment risk gradients are rich in footprints about invariance. Among the various algorithms searching for those, one early and prominent example is the model agnostic meta-learning (MAML) algorithm,[220] with this objective:

$$\mathrm{MAML}(f) = \sum_{e \in \mathcal{E}_{\mathrm{tr}}} R_{P^e}(f - \alpha \cdot \nabla_f \cdot [R_{P^e}(f)]).$$

The purpose of MAML is to learn a predictor f that is fast to adapt to new environments. Its objective is achieved by learning a predictor that can be adapted to any of the training environments by taking only one gradient step down from the associated risk.

MAML relates to invariant learning algorithms and causal discovery. When facing new environments, MAML "aims to optimize the model parameters such that one or a few gradient steps on a new task will produce maximally effective behavior on that task."[220] Invariant learning algorithms, such as IRM, push adaptation speed to the limit—in fact, invariant models require no adaptation, because they are simultaneously optimal across environments.[221] Researchers have also suggested that fast adaptability is a footprint of causation, since interventions under a causal representation only modify a sparse subset of autonomous variables.[170,296]

Since MAML, several proposals have emerged to search for invariance by aligning gradients across environments. One of the simplest proposals is inter-domain gradient matching (IDGM):[297]

$$\mathrm{IDGM}(f) = \sum_{e \in \mathcal{E}_{\mathrm{tr}}} R_{P^e}(f) - \lambda \cdot \sum_{e' \neq e \in \mathcal{E}_{\mathrm{tr}}} \nabla_f [R_{P^e}(f)] \cdot \nabla_f [R_{P^{e'}}(f)],$$

where the penalty term decreases for correlated environment gradients. The more recent Fishr[298] takes IDGM one step further, aligning gradient *variances* by following the objective

$$\mathrm{Fishr}(f) = \sum_{e \in \mathcal{E}_{\mathrm{tr}}} R_{P^e}(f) + \lambda \cdot \left\| v^e - \frac{1}{|\mathcal{E}_{\mathrm{tr}}|} \sum_{e \in \mathcal{E}_{\mathrm{tr}}} v^e \right\|^2,$$

where $v^e = \mathrm{Var}(\{\nabla_f [\ell(f(x_i^e), y_i^e)]\}_{i=1}^{n^e})$. The Fishr objective (1) minimizes the variance of the environment risks similarly to V-REx[266] and (2) aligns a diagonal approximation of the environment Hessians.

The computation of second-order derivatives necessary to take the gradient of the MAML, IDGM, and Fishr objectives is computationally expensive. To address this, the research literature has proposed three main approximations. First, first-order methods such as Reptile use finite-difference approximations to second-order derivatives.[299] Second, one can compute environment gradients only with respect to a small subset of parameters—say, the last layer of the learning machine—as previously discussed for IRMv1.

Third, some methods project ERM environment gradients into a learning update, and I briefly discuss these next.

The AND-Mask method[210] updates only those gradient elements that share equal signs across most training environments:

$$f \leftarrow f - \alpha \cdot \left(\nabla_f \left[\sum_{e \in \mathcal{E}_{\mathrm{tr}}} R_{P^e}(f) \right] \odot \left[\!\left[\left| \sum_{e \in \mathcal{E}_{\mathrm{tr}}} \mathrm{sign}(\nabla_f [R_{P^e}(f)]) \right| \geq |\mathcal{E}_{\mathrm{tr}}| \cdot \tau \right]\!\right] \right),$$

where "$\odot$" denotes the entry-wise product, and the Iverson bracket creates a binary mask that zeroes gradient elements with inconsistent signs in more than a fraction $\tau > 0$ of training environments. As a result, the AND-Mask approach replaces the permissive OR operation in ERM with a more conservative AND operation to facilitate simultaneous learning across training environments. Consequently, this method reduces the amount of underspecification and zero training error solutions.

AND-Mask bears similarity to the principle "good explanations are hard to vary" articulated by physicist David Deutsch in *The Beginning of Infinity*. The preceding chapter identified a similar idea within the Invariance Principle, advocating that we learn representations admitting only a small set of classifiers to induce invariant predictors. Extending this notion to other philosophical systems already discussed in this book, explanations that are hard to vary are easy to falsify in the Popperian sense and result in what Salmon termed *damn strange coincidences*. These explanations are valuable in science, where our goal is to develop theories that are easy to falsify yet offer high-quality predictions with low uncertainty.

Gradient episodic memory (GEM)[300] is a continual learning method assuming that training environments $e = 1, \ldots, |\mathcal{E}_{\mathrm{tr}}|$ appear only once, for an undefined duration, and sequentially. While training on environment e, GEM proposes to follow the gradient update given by the quadratic program

$$\bar{g}^e = \min_{\tilde{g}^e} \|g^e - \tilde{g}^e\|^2, \text{ such that } \langle \tilde{g}^e, g^{e'} \rangle \geq 0 \text{ for all } e' < e, \qquad (6.8)$$

where $g^e = \nabla_f [R_{P^e}(f)]$, and a subset of examples from previous environments e' needs to be stored in a memory module to instantiate the objective above. The performance of GEM, like any continual learning algorithm, is partly measured by its ability to avoid the *catastrophic forgetting* of previous environments. Broadly speaking, learning invariances should alleviate catastrophic forgetting, as these should generalize across environments.

6.8 Model Evaluation and Selection

There is a wide variety of benchmark datasets on offer to evaluate the quality of domain generalization algorithms. Notable examples include

DomainBed,[301] WILDS,[302] and SubpopBench.[303] A variety of benchmarks based on ImageNet[304] have also been proposed, including ImageNet-A,[305] containing difficult in-class examples; ImageNet-C,[306] containing algorithmically corrupted examples; ImageNet-R,[307] containing artistic renditions of images; ImageNet-O,[305] containing difficult out-class examples; ImageNet-v2,[308] containing a new test set of examples; and ImageNet-X.[309]

One of the biggest challenges in learning across multiple environments is model selection. The difficulty arises from the first level of underspecification: While we learn our predictor across a set of training environments, we are interested on its worst-case performance over the much larger collection of relevant environments. In those situations, how should we choose hyperparameters (such as learning rate and number of iterations) that perform well across relevant environments, when we only get to observe performance across training environments? A multitude of empirical studies[301] confirm that bridging the gap from *performing well across all training environments* to *performing well across all relevant environments* requires a long and tortuous path, especially in those cases where the invariant features are observed in disjoint supports across environments. In particular, there exists a large gap in performance between models selected according to the worst training environment and those cherry-picked according to the worst relevant environment.

This predicament is an old problem with a new face. Because past training environments cannot justify what future relevant environments may look like, Hume's problem at the environment level tells us that no algorithm can reduce its worst-case error below one in the absence of inductive assumptions.[110] The Invariance Principle, proposing that correlations invariant across training environments should also obtain across relevant environments, is one such inductive assumption. However, the Inductive Principle does not take into consideration the chosen function class, nor does it offer guidance about how to learn robust predictors in the absence of environment annotations. These two issues, both contributing to the difficulty of model selection, are the subject matter of the next chapter.

Chapter 7

Discovering Environments

This chapter is based on Mohammad Pezeshki et al. *Discovering Environments with XRM*. arXiv, 2023.

7.1 Introduction

The primary strategy to learning invariant predictors, as discussed in chapter 5, involves identifying patterns that remain invariant across multiple training environments, while discarding changing or spurious correlations. Unfortunately, in many practical situations we only have access to one training environment, so we lack the necessary data diversity to apply the tools of invariance.

To address this problem, this chapter reviews methods to automatically discover environments from data. We expect environments to hide in most large datasets because, as Léon Bottou once remarked, "nature does not shuffle the data, we do."[311] Consequently, if we could devise a method to *un-shuffle* large pools of training examples to discover the environments within, we could apply the invariance machinery deployed throughout the previous chapters to obtain a robust predictor. In the medical literature, *hidden stratification* refers to the fact that "data contains unrecognized subsets of cases [i.e., hidden environments] which may affect model training, model performance, and most importantly the clinical outcomes related to the use of a medical image analysis system."[312] Because these "histologic image differences between submitting sites can easily be identified with deep learning,"[313] there is hope to develop algorithms that automatically discover hidden stratification in data that differ in spurious correlations and lead us to discover invariance. This is precisely the task of environment discovery.

Methods for environment discovery lean on the fact that modern learning algorithms often adopt a *simplify-and-memorize* strategy. In particular, examples correctly classified during the early *simplify* phase of learning are—because of the pressures of average training error minimization—often members of the majority group. In contrast, examples learned during the later *memorize* phase of training likely belong to the minority group. Bearing this in mind, one recipe for environment discovery is to train an auxiliary predictor for a few epochs, then construct two training environments: one composed of the correctly classified examples so far, and a second environment holding the remaining mistakes. With these two discovered environments in hand, practitioners can then apply any of the multiple environment or domain generalization techniques studied in previous chapters.

While intuitive, this line of attack suffers from one major shortcoming: How long should we train the auxiliary predictor for? If trained until convergence, the auxiliary predictor would converge to an empirical risk minimizer. (Any learning algorithm with pretensions to robustness but admitting ERM as a solution reminds us of Sisyphus arduously pushing the boulder up the mountain, only to see it roll back down.) Imagine that such a minimizer obtains 95% test accuracy on the majority group, and 70% on the minority group. Then, the recipe outlined in the previous paragraph would discover two environments encompassing a mixture of majority and minority examples. Because the test accuracy on the minority group is far from zero, none of the discovered environments would be aligned with the minority group, which is often the most informative group about spurious correlations. As a result, the invariant and spurious correlations relevant to the learning problem would not be clearly separated, reducing our hopes that any invariance algorithm could benefit from the discovered environments. Most methods resolve this conundrum by assuming access to a validation set with environment annotations. Alas, this defeats the whole purpose of the environment discovery project.

The main topic of this chapter, the Cross-Risk Minimization (XRM) method,[310] was recently proposed to overcome the aforementioned limitations. The main innovation in XRM is to bias the auxiliary predictor to maximize its reliance on spurious correlation. In this way, XRM can safely train the auxiliary predictor to convergence, discovering environments that better align with the majority and minority groups hidden in the training data. Furthermore, the XRM framework proposes model selection criteria to choose hyper-parameters and early-stopping iterations for the auxiliary predictor—removing the need for environment annotations altogether.

7.2 Environment Discovery in Humans

How do humans become aware of the various learning environments they inhabit? Admittedly, our learning experience covers a diverse array of environments encompassing factors such as geographic location, our biological age, the hour of the day, sociocultural milieu, and even varying levels of sobriety. Given our uncanny ability to function effectively across these environments, it is worthwhile to explore insights from cognitive science about the influence of context on learning and generalization performance.

In cognitive science, the relationship between environment and learning performance is established by the *encoding specificity principle*. This principle, proposed by Endel Tulving and Donald Thomson in 1973,[314] states that matching environmental factors at the encoding (training) and recall (testing) phases assists memory retrieval (performance). This is why tools such as flashcards and spaced-repetition help robust memorization of concepts across contexts. Two main types of environmental factors—external context and internal mental states—merit individual consideration.

First, context-dependent memory posits that information is better retrieved when the *external contexts* match during encoding and recall phases.[315] Many are familiar with this situation: When misplacing our car keys, physically revisiting all the places where we have recently been aids in recalling the location of the lost item. Formal studies have shown that, when subjects are asked to memorize a sequence of words in a given room, participants returning to the same room can recall more words than those tested in a different location.[316] The same applies for other contextual factors, such as level of noise: Students memorizing a list of words in a noisy environment exhibit their best recall when in equally loud environments.[316] Similarly, scuba divers memorizing a list of words underwater exhibit better recall them underwater than on land, and vice versa.[317]

Much like learning machines, humans perform better when learning tasks across multiple environments.[318] In one study, subjects instructed to memorize a list of words in various rooms recalled more than those who studied in a single room.[318] However, the researchers had to prompt the multi-room participants to pay attention to the varying environmental cues. This finding aligns with the shortcomings of ERM baselines, which fail to benefit from multiple environments because of ignoring annotations.

Three additional features of context-dependent performance for humans are worth noting. First, multiple contextual cues are most advantageous when they pertain to different senses, such as sight, smell, and hearing.[319] These multisensory cues are also transferable: Even in different rooms, we can listen to the same music to facilitate recall. (Could it be that we have developed our five senses to discover environments maximally relevant to our survival?) Second, contextual cues are ignored in the presence of prominent, noncontextual cues, a phenomenon known as the *outshining hypothesis*.[315] As shown in various experiments, these noncontextual cues often involve spurious item co-occurrences, suggesting an intriguing link between outshining and simplify-and-memorize learning strategies. Third, humans are susceptible to the *doorway effect*: We tend to forget recently relevant items immediately after crossing a boundary, such as a door between rooms.[320] Overall, there is considerable evidence that external context influences how data is memorized and compartmentalized—that is, how environments are discovered—by the human cognitive apparatus.

Another relevant concept is state-dependent memory, which posits that information is better retrieved when our *internal mental states* match during the encoding and recall phases. We find one example of this phenomenon in John Elliotson's *Human Physiology*, published nearly two centuries ago:

> "Dr. Abel informed me," says Mr. Combe, "of an Irish porter to a warehouse, who forgot, when sober, what he had done when drunk: but, being drunk, again recollected the transactions of his former state of intoxication. On one occasion, being drunk, he had lost a parcel of some value, and in his sober moments could give no account of it. Next time he was intoxicated, he recollected that he had left the parcel at a certain house, and there being no address on it, it had remained there safely, and was got on his calling for it." This man must have had two souls, one for his sober state, and one for him when drunk.[321]

Formal studies corroborate such anecdotal evidence: Recall is better when individuals are inebriated in *both* encoding and recall phases, rather than in only one of them.[322] Research involving patients with depression shows that memories are also compartmentalized by mood, as these individuals often find it overwhelmingly difficult to recall past happy experiences.[323] Furthermore, rapidly changing mental representations and environment throughout early infancy have been cited as reasons behind childhood amnesia.

Memory encoding and recall are also influenced by the *interaction* of external context and internal mental state. For example, when individuals are asked to visualize the room in which they originally memorized a list of words, their recall improves.[318] As a matter of subjective experience, in fact, both external context and internal mental state are encompassed within the same field of awareness—both the room's appearance and the thoughts experienced there are two parts of a unified conscious experience.

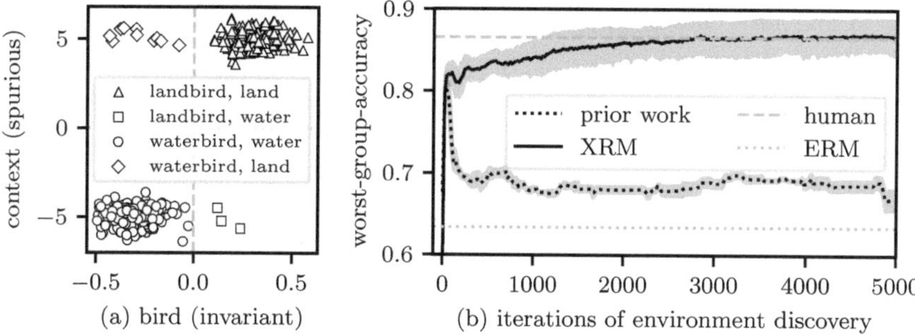

(a) bird (invariant)   (b) iterations of environment discovery

Figure 7.1: (a) The Waterbirds classification problem, containing four groups: a *majority group* of waterbirds in water, landbirds on land, waterbirds on land, and a *minority group* of landbirds in water. Learning machines latch onto the spurious feature *landscape*, as it allows the machine to classify the majority of examples, exhibits a larger signal-to-noise ratio, and yields the maximum-margin classifier among solutions with zero training error. (b) Worst-group-accuracy (minority-group-accuracy) for different methods. (Dotted gray line) An ERM baseline ignoring group annotations achieves 61%. (Dashed gray line) The GroupDRO invariance learning algorithm with human group annotations, considered our oracle, achieves 87%. (Dotted black line) Prior work to discover groups requires early-stopping with surgical precision. This is an impossible task without a validation set with human group annotations, the very information subject to discovery. Realistically, these methods would converge at 68%. (Solid black line) XRM enables an oracle performance of 87% at convergence.

7.3   Methods for Environment Discovery

As discussed in previous chapters, AI systems perform worse on underrepresented groups of data. The Waterbirds problem,[324] depicted on the left side of figure 7.1, exemplifies this issue. This task considers two class labels, landbirds and waterbirds, collected in two landscape environments, land and water. These combine into four groups: a *majority group* of waterbirds in water (73% of training examples), landbirds on land (22%), waterbirds on land (4%), and a *minority group* of landbirds in water (1%). On this problem, learning machines latch onto the spurious feature *landscape* because it effectively separates the majority of examples, exhibits a larger signal-to-noise ratio, and yields the maximum-margin classifier among those with zero training error. As shown in the right panel of figure 7.1, an ERM baseline, ignoring environment annotations, results in a worst-group-accuracy of 61%—attained, in fact, on the minority group. In contrast, the invariance learning algorithm GroupDRO achieves a worst-group-accuracy of 87%, outperforming ERM by 26 points!

While promising, invariance learning algorithms such as GroupDRO require environment annotations. These are, as argued by Sam Bell and Levent Sagun, "resource-intensive to obtain and are limited by human annotators' biases, as the biases they identify may not align with those learned by models, and vice versa."[107] In addition, and by virtue of the combinatorially explosive amount of ways in which two examples can differ,[159] the adversarial patterns that deceive a learning system could be alien or invisible to our human eyes.[27] As Kant might have put it, spurious patterns depend on the learning system under consideration, and so do the environment annotations most effective to reveal invariance.

In light of the above challenges, researchers began developing algorithms for the automatic discovery of environments from data. In broad strokes, these methods build a robust system in two phases. In phase 1, these methods learn an auxiliary predictor to *un-shuffle* the training data to distribute training examples in two environments, based on its mistakes on training data. In phase 2, an invariance learning algorithm is trained on top of the discovered environments to produce a robust system. If the environments discovered in phase 1 differ only in spurious correlation, as we would like, then the invariance learning algorithm in phase 2 should absorb invariant patterns that are more likely to generalize to the test distribution. On the unlucky side, if phase 1 produces a zero training error predictor, we would be providing phase 2 with one nonvacuous, noninformative environment—the training data itself!

Researchers have come up with a variety of phase-1 algorithms to discover invariance-inducing environments from pooled collections of training data. For example, the too-good-to-be-true prior[325] trains an auxiliary predictor with a small parameter count while correct-n-contrast (CnC)[326] applies strong weight decay regularization. Just train twice (JTT)[327] and environment inference for invariant learning (EIIL)[228] both train an auxiliary predictor for a limited number of epochs. Learning from failure (LfF)[328] biases the auxiliary predictor toward the use of *simple* features by applying a generalized version of the cross entropy loss. Other proposals, such as learning to split (LS)[329] and adversarial reweighted learning (ARL)[330] complement capacity control with adversarial games. Bias amplification (BAM)[331] incorporates per-example *slack variables* to absorb the fast learning of spurious correlations. No subclass left behind (GEORGE)[332] clusters the hidden representation of a neural network to construct different environments.

The phase-1 methods described above require controlling the capacity of the auxiliary predictor with surgical precision, so the discovered environments differ only in spurious correlations. As shown in figure 7.1, these methods discover environments yielding strong phase-2 systems only when the amount of phase-1 training iterations is tuned to a knife's edge. Only then do these algorithms provide a decent, though suboptimal, performance of 79%; otherwise, their performance reverts to an ERM-like worst-group-accuracy of 68%. Unfortunately, we lack the necessary supervision to perform such a fine hyper-parameter selection, so methods for environment discovery often require a validation set with human environment annotations. Effectively, this wraps phase 1 and phase 2 in a cross-validation envelope to select a model maximizing validation worst-group-accuracy—alas, at least in our view, this defeats the *raison d'être* of environment discovery. In fact, if we had access to a small dataset with human environment annotations, these would suffice to fine-tune the last layer of a deep neural network toward state-of-the-art worst-group-accuracy.[333] The question brought to the forefront throughout the remainder of this chapter is: Could we instead develop an algorithm for environment discovery that requires no human annotations whatsoever, but still robustly yields oracle-like phase-2 performance?

7.4 Discovering Environments with XRM

Cross-Risk Minimization (XRM)[310] is a simple method for environment discovery that requires no human environment annotations whatsoever. As opposed to the methods surveyed in the previous section, XRM comes with *batteries included*, offering a recipe for hyper-parameter tuning and a formula to annotate all training and validation data. For an implementation of XRM that complements the following description, see algorithm 7.2.

The blueprint for phase 1 with XRM is as follows. XRM trains two twin predictors, each holding one random half of the training data (section 7.4.1). During training, XRM biases each twin to absorb spurious correlations by imitating confident held-out mistakes from their sibling (section 7.4.2). XRM chooses hyper-parameters for the twins based on the number of imitated mistakes (section 7.4.3). Finally, given the selected twins, XRM employs a simple *cross-mistake* formula to discover environment annotations for all the training and validation examples (section 7.4.4). Algorithm 7.2 serves as a companion to the descriptions below; algorithm 7.2 contains a real PyTorch implementation. The runtime of phase 1 with XRM is akin to running one ERM baseline on the training data.

7.4.1 Twin Setup, Holding-out of Data

We start by initializing two twin predictors, f^a and f^b. Without loss of generality, let these predictors return softmax probability vectors over the n_{classes} classes in the training data. Next, we split our training dataset

Input: training examples $\{(x_i, y_i)\}_{i=1}^{n}$ and validation examples $\{(\tilde{x}_i, \tilde{y}_i)\}_{i=1}^{m}$.
Output: discovered envs. for training $\{e_i\}_{i=1}^{n}$ and validation $\{\tilde{e}_i\}_{i=1}^{m}$ examples.

- Fix held-in training example assignments $m_i^a \sim \text{Bernoulli}(\frac{1}{2})$ and $m_i^b = 1 - m_i^a$.
- Init twin predictors f^a, f^b at random.
- Until convergence:

  - Compute held-in softmax predictions $p_i^{\text{in}} = m_i^a f^a(x_i) + m_i^b f^b(x_i)$.
  - Compute held-out softmax predictions $p_i^{\text{out}} = m_i^b f^a(x_i) + m_i^a f^b(x_i)$.
  - Update f^a and f^b to minimize the class-balanced held-in loss $\ell(p^{\text{in}}, y)$.
  - Flip y_i into $y_i^{\text{out}} = \text{argmax}_j p_{i,j}^{\text{out}}$, with probability:

  $$(\text{softmax}(p^{\text{out}})_{i, y_i^{\text{out}}} - 1/n_{\text{classes}}) \cdot n_{\text{classes}}/(n_{\text{classes}} - 1).$$

- Define cross-mistake function

$$e(x, y) = [\![(y \notin \text{argmax}_j f^a(x)_j) \lor (y \notin \text{argmax}_j f^b(x)_j)]\!].$$

- Discover training $e_i = e(x_i, y_i)$ and validation $\tilde{e}_i = e(\tilde{x}_i, \tilde{y}_i)$ environments.

Algorithm 7.1: Cross-Risk Minimization (XRM)

```python
import torch
from torch.nn.functional import cross_entropy

def balanced_cross_entropy(p, y):
  losses = torch.nn.functional.cross_entropy(
    p, y, reduction="none")
  return sum([losses[y == yi].mean() for yi in y.unique()])

def xrm(x_tr, y_tr, x_va, y_va, lr=1e-2, max_iters=1000):
  # init twins and assign examples (Section 6.4.1)
  nc = len(y_tr.unique())
  net_a = torch.nn.Linear(x_tr.size(1), nc)
  net_b = torch.nn.Linear(x_tr.size(1), nc)
  net_a.weight.data.mul_(0.0)
  net_b.weight.data.mul_(0.0)
  ind_a = torch.zeros(len(x_tr), 1).bernoulli_(0.5).long()

  # training (Section 6.4.2)
  opt = torch.optim.SGD(
    list(net_a.parameters()) + list(net_b.parameters()), lr)

  for iteration in range(max_iters):
    pred_a, pred_b = net_a(x_tr), net_b(x_tr)
    pred_hi = pred_a * ind_a + pred_b * (1 - ind_a)
    pred_ho = pred_a * (1 - ind_a) + pred_b * ind_a

    opt.zero_grad()
    balanced_cross_entropy(pred_hi, y_tr).backward()
    opt.step()

    # label flipping, useful for model selection (Section
    6.4.3)
    p_ho, y_ho = pred_ho.softmax(dim=1).detach().max(1)
    is_flip = torch.bernoulli((
      p_ho - 1 / nc) * nc / (nc - 1)).long()
    y_tr = is_flip * y_ho + (1 - is_flip) * y_tr

  # environment discovery (Section 6.4.4)
  cm = lambda x, y: torch.logical_or(
    net_a(x).argmax(1).ne(y),
    net_b(x).argmax(1).ne(y)).long().detach()

  return cm(x_tr, y_tr), cm(x_va, y_va)
```

Algorithm 7.2: PyTorch implementation of XRM.

$\{(x_i, y_i)\}_{i=1}^n$ in two random halves, one for each twin. Formally, we construct a pair of training assignment vectors with entries $m_i^a \sim \text{Bernoulli}(\frac{1}{2})$ and $m_i^b = 1 - m_i^a$, for all $i = 1, \ldots, n$. For predictor f^a, examples with $m_i^a = 1$ are *held-in* and examples with $m_i^a = 0$ are *held-out*; a similar arrangement follows for f^b. Therefore, we will train predictor f^a on training examples where $m_i^a = 1$, and train predictor f^b on training examples where $m_i^b = 1$.

The XRM arrangement allows us to estimate the generalization difficulty of any example by looking at the accuracy of the twin that held-out that point. This contrasts with prior methods for environment discovery that consume the entire training data, and that may therefore conflate generalization and memorization. In XRM, misclassified held-out examples are suspected to belong to the minority group. Vitaly Feldman and Chiyuan Zhang[334] proposed a similar *error when holding-out* construction as a measure of memorization. In the context of label-noise robustness, CrossSplit[335] also follows a similar approach to interpret confident held-out mistakes as noisy label memorization.

7.4.2 Twin Training, Flipping Labels

As shown in figure 7.1, the test worst-group-accuracy of an ERM baseline on waterbirds is 61%. This suggests that training the twins with ERM would result in models able to correctly classify roughly one-half of the minority examples. These ERM machines, when used to discover environments based on their prediction errors, would dilute the spurious correlations evenly across the two discovered environments. As a result, phase-2 invariance learning algorithms would struggle to distinguish between invariant and spurious patterns. Although it's counterintuitive, we would like to hinder the learning process of our twins, biasing them to increasingly rely on spurious correlations. Ideally, the twins would correctly classify all majority examples and mistake all minority examples, attaining *zero* worst-group accuracy.

To this end, XRM pushes the twins away from becoming empirical risk minimizers. Let $p_i^{\text{out}} = m_i^b f^a(x_i) + m_i^a f^b(x_i)$ be the held-out softmax prediction, for example (x_i, y_i). Also, let $y_i^{\text{out}} = \arg\max_j p_{i,j}^{\text{out}}$ be the held-out predicted class label, equal to the index of the maximum held-out softmax prediction. Then, at each iteration during the training of the twins,

$$\text{flip } y_i \text{ into } y_i^{\text{out}}, \text{ with probability } (p_{y_i^{\text{out}}}^{\text{out}} - 1/n_{\text{classes}}) \cdot n_{\text{classes}}/(n_{\text{classes}} - 1), \tag{7.1}$$

and let each twin take a gradient step to minimize their held-in, class-balanced, cross-entropy loss with respect to these moving targets.

The overarching intuition is that label flipping equation (7.1) creates an *echo chamber* that reinforces the twins to rely on spurious correlations.

In such a way, the road toward discovering invariance starts by amplifying spurious correlations. Since spurious correlations are easier to capture, label flipping occurs more frequently in the early stages of training. As training progresses, label flipping converges to a vector of targets that no longer represent the original labels, but instead estimate the presence of spurious correlation. Label-flipping is a crucial novelty compared to methods that use multiple predictors to surface spurious correlations.[328,336–342] Most similarly to XRM, the CrossSplit method[335] uses a similar twin training and target correction protocol to learn under noisy labels. In the fairness community, *data massaging* methods also manipulate the labels of training examples similarly.[343,344]

7.4.3   Twin Model Selection, Counting Label Flips

Before discovering environments, we must commit to a pair of twin predictors, which come with their own hyper-parameters. Consequently, XRM would be incomplete without a phase-1 model selection criterion.[301] We propose to select the twin hyper-parameters that yield the maximum number of label flips (7.1) at the final iteration, and across the training data. To reiterate, *counting flips* compares the vector of final labels with the vector of original labels, so it does not keep track of multiple flips per label. To understand why counting flips makes sense as a model selection criterion, recall that each label flip signifies one example that is confidently misclassified when held-out. Therefore, each label flip indicates a reliance on spurious correlation, bringing us closer to identifying the minority group.

7.4.4   Environment Discovery, via Cross-Mistake Formula

Having committed to a pair of twins, we are ready to discover environments for all of our training and validation examples. In particular, consider a simple *cross-mistake* formula to annotate any example (x, y) with the binary environment

$$e(x, y) = [\![(y \notin \mathrm{argmax}_j f^a(x)_j) \vee (y \notin \mathrm{argmax}_j f^b(x)_j)]\!]. \qquad (7.2)$$

where "$\vee$" denotes logical-OR, and "$[\![\ ]\!]$" is the Iverson bracket. If operating within the group-shift paradigm, we define one group per combination of label and discovered environment. Notably, the ability to annotate both training and validation examples is a feature inherited from holding-out data during twin training. In particular, every example—within the training and validation sets—is held-out for at least one of the two twins, as implied in equation (7.2) by the logical OR operation.

While (7.2) partitions data into two environments, XRM may identify not only one spurious correlation, but a general spurious *direction*. In other words, an oracle with perfect knowledge about the test domain could reveal the statistical invariances required for generalization by partitioning the data into only two environments. To directly create multiple environments with XRM, one could quantize loss values into multiple bins or use more than two twin networks.

7.4.5   Relationship to the Invariance Principle

The XRM algorithm finds its place within the Invariance Principle as an effort to discover the environment variable E. Namely, XRM yields the estimated Invariance Principle

$$Y \perp \hat{E} \mid \phi(X), \tag{7.3}$$

where $\hat{E} = e(X, Y)$ follows (7.2). In those cases where XRM discovers environments aligned with a spurious attribute, the estimated Invariance Principle promotes robust predictions. Section 7.5.1 below includes some success and failure cases.

Two potential extensions of XRM pose interesting questions for future research. First, can we use twin disagreement for active learning purposes? In this case, XRM would begin with a small labeled dataset, plus a large pool of unlabeled examples. Twins could decide, based on their disagreement, which of the unlabeled samples to annotate. Second, could we devise an unsupervised version of XRM? For example, we could initialize all the training examples with random labels, then proceed with XRM training as described above. Since memorizing random labels requires complex features, the resulting unsupervised XRM environments could align with spurious correlations in the data. This would be handy, as we would only need to label a few examples—the minority environment and an equally sized portion of the majority environment—before proceeding with phase 2.[345]

7.5   Performance of XRM

The following experimental protocol involves three components: datasets, phase-2 invariance learning algorithms, and the source of environment annotations. Datasets include six standard subpopulation shift datasets from the SubpopBench suite.[303] These are the four image datasets Waterbirds,[346] CelebA,[347] MetaShift,[348] and ImageNetBG,[349] as well as the two natural language datasets MultiNLI[350] and CivilComments.[351] For CelebA, predictors map pixel intensities into a binary *blonde/not-blonde* label. No individual face characteristics, landmarks, keypoints, facial mapping, metadata, or any other information was used to train the CelebA predictors. The following experiments also include ColoredMNIST (section 5.4.4), where *both* the training and validation data contain two environments, with 0.8 and 0.9 label-color correlation, while the test environment shows 0.1 label-color correlation and is never used for model selection.

For each combination of dataset and phase-2 algorithm, the experiments compare group annotations from three different sources. *None* denotes class annotations (no group annotations). *Human* denotes ground-truth annotations originally provided in the datasets. *XRM* denotes group annotations discovered by XRM. Some experiments compare XRM to other environment discovery methods, such as learning from failure (LfF),[328] environment inference for invariant learning (EIIL),[228] just train twice (JTT),[327] correct-n-contrast (CnC),[326] automatic feature reweighting (AFR),[352] and learning to split (LS).[329]

The following experiments consider several phase-2 algorithms: ERM (see chapter 2, IRM (see chapter 5), GroupDRO, and SUBG (see chapter 6). When group information is available, hyper-parameters and early stopping are tuned to maximize the worst-group accuracy. In the absence of such information, we tune for worst-class accuracy. Following standard praxis, image datasets employ a pretrained ResNet-50 while text datasets use a pretrained BERT.

Table 7.1 shows that XRM enables oracle-like worst-group-accuracy across subpopulation shift datasets. The performance gains are most pronounced in the challenging ColoredMNIST dataset, where XRM excels by accurately identifying digits in minority colors, discovering two environments conducive of stronger generalization than those originally proposed by humans. For the commonly reported quartet of Waterbirds, CelebA, MultiNLI, and CivilComments, ignoring annotations leads to an average worst-group-accuracy of 67%, human annotations induce an average oracle worst-group-accuracy of 80.6%, and XRM environments close the gap at 80.4%.

Table 7.2 shows the worst-group-accuracy of GroupDRO when built on top of environments discovered by different methods. XRM achieves 80.4%, nearly matching oracle performance. JTT, the second best method with no access to environment information, falls to 58.9%. AFR, the best method accessing a validation set with human environment annotations, lags behind XRM with 78%.

Table 7.3 presents results on the DomainBed benchmark.[301] Experiments compare three settings: ERM without any environment annotations, the CORAL invariance learning algorithm[288] with human-annotated environments, and CORAL with environments discovered by XRM. CORAL is the

	ERM			GroupDRO			SUBG			IRM		
	None	Human	**XRM**	None	Human	**XRM**	None	Human	**XRM**	None	Human	**XRM**
Waterbirds	66.4	66.4	66.4	67.3	86.5	88.1	62.1	87.1	77.7	72.3	72.6	83.7
CelebA	54.3	55.1	58.6	68.4	88.3	89.1	65.9	83.9	81.1	59.4	85.6	76.3
MultiNLI	67.9	72.0	69.1	68.6	73.4	72.1	69.7	52.4	72.0	67.9	66.6	72.6
CivilComments	67.2	74.0	64.7	66.6	73.8	72.2	65.4	71.1	44.6	63.8	74.5	72.7
ColorMNIST	10.0	10.1	11.3	9.9	10.1	69.7	10.0	9.9	65.2	10.0	10.0	71.2
MetaShift	64.2	69.8	71.7	72.5	80.3	77.5	69.7	77.0	77.6	66.2	66.2	76.9
Average	55.0	57.9	57.0	58.9	68.7	78.1	57.1	63.6	69.7	56.6	62.6	75.6

Table 7.1: Worst-group-accuracies across datasets and algorithms average over ten random runs, with XRM showing oracle-level results. Class labels replace group labels when the latter are not available. ERM, while not trained with group labels, still benefits from validation group labels for hyper-parameter tuning.

e^{tr}	e^{va}		Waterbirds		CelebA		MNLI		CivComms		Average	
			Avg	Worst	Avg	Worst	Avg	Worst	Avg	Worst	Avg	Worst
✓	✓	ERM	83.8	66.4	95.5	55.1	81.6	72.0	84.3	74.0	86.3	66.9
		GroupDRO	90.2	86.5	93.1	88.3	80.6	73.4	84.2	73.8	87.0	80.5
✗	✓	ERM[†]	97.3	72.6	95.6	47.2	82.4	67.9	83.1	69.5	89.6	64.3
		LfF[†]	91.2	78.0	85.1	77.2	80.8	70.2	68.2	50.3	81.3	68.9
		EIIL[†]	96.9	78.7	89.5	77.8	79.4	70.0	90.5	67.0	89.1	73.4
		JTT[†]	93.3	86.7	88.0	81.1	78.6	72.6	83.3	64.3	85.8	76.2
		CnC[†]	90.9	88.5	89.9	88.8	—	—	—	—	—	—
		AFR[†]	94.4	90.4	91.3	82.0	81.4	73.4	89.8	68.7	89.2	78.6
✗	✗	ERM	83.5	66.4	95.4	54.3	82.1	67.9	81.3	67.2	85.6	63.9
		LfF[†]	86.6	75.0	81.1	53.0	71.4	57.3	69.1	42.2	77.1	56.9
		EIIL[†]	90.8	64.5	95.7	41.7	80.3	64.7	—	—	—	—
		JTT[†]	88.9	71.2	95.9	48.3	81.4	65.1	79.0	51.0	86.3	58.9
		LS[†]	91.2	86.1	87.2	83.3	78.7	72.1	—	—	—	—
		BAM[†]	91.4	89.1	88.4	80.1	80.3	70.8	88.3	79.3	87.1	79.8
		XRM	89.3	88.1	91.4	89.1	75.8	72.1	84.0	72.2	85.1	80.4

Table 7.2: Average and worst-group accuracies comparing methods for environment discovery. We specify access to annotations in training data (e^{tr}) and validation data (e^{va}). The symbol † denotes numbers from the original publications.

	VLCS		PACS		OfficeHome		TerraInc		DomainNet	
	Avg	Worst	Avg	Worst	Avg	Worst	Avg	Worst	Avg	Worst
ERM (None)	77.97	64.85	83.35	72.55	65.47	52.25	47.02	34.60	31.69	9.30
CORAL (Human)	77.87	65.00	84.99	77.70	67.74	53.55	48.51	37.15	41.97	13.25
CORAL (XRM)	77.66	66.15	83.81	77.30	67.01	53.90	49.60	38.00	35.87	11.60

Table 7.3: Average and worst test environment accuracies for five datasets in the DomainBed benchmark.[301] The three compared methods are ERM with no environment annotations, CORAL with human-annotated environments, and CORAL with XRM-inferred environments. Following DomainBed protocol, model selection is done following average accuracy over validation environments.

best performing single-model method in the DomainBed suite. The results indicate that the performance of XRM-inferred annotations is comparable to that of human-annotated environments.

Figure 7.2 explores some behaviors of XRM on the Waterbirds dataset. The left panel justifies the use of *percentage of label flipped at convergence* as a phase-1 model selection criterion for XRM, given its strong correlation with phase-2 worst-group-accuracy. (The Appendix of the original XRM study shows similar results for varying learning rates and weight decays.[310]) The middle panels showcase the clear separation of the minority group *landbirds/water* by XRM, as no landbirds on land are in the cross-mistake area. The right panel shows that label flipping happens almost exclusively for minority groups, and converges alongside XRM training. This stability removes the need for intricate early-stopping criteria.

Figure 7.3 illustrates the application of XRM to the CIFAR-10 dataset.[353] While CIFAR-10 does not contain environment annotations, the discovered environments by XRM for the *plane* and *deer* classes reveal that background color produces a spurious correlation in this dataset.

7.5.1 When Does XRM Work, and When Does It Fail?

Given that the problem of environment discovery has been proven impossible in the general case,[354–356] it is pertinent to explore scenarios where the XRM method is prone to failure. The problem of environment discovery is parallel to the issue of choosing a valid instrument E to de-confound a causal relation $\phi(X) \to Y$. When choosing E appropriately, this enables the Invariance Principle $Y \perp E \mid \phi(X)$. However, in environment discovery this principle has two unknowns: the environment variable E (instrumental variable) and the invariance-inducing featurizer $\phi(X)$ (what to control or adjust for). Because different invariance-inducing featurizers ϕ (causal structures) can produce the same observational data (X, Y), discovering

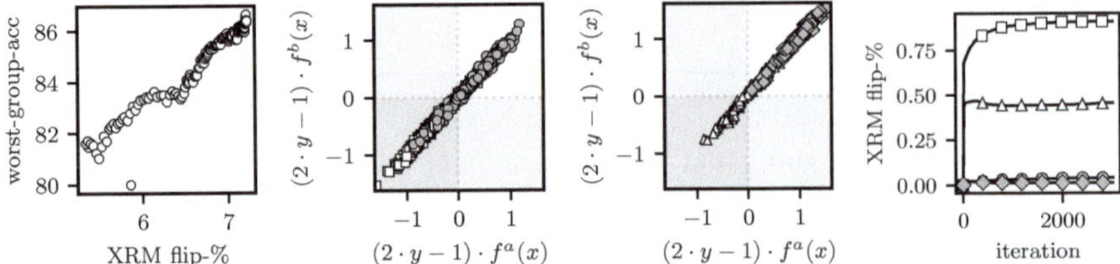

Figure 7.2: XRM on the Waterbirds problem, concerning ○ waterbirds in water, □ waterbirds on land, △ landbirds in water, and ◇ landbirds on land. The first panel shows that *percentage of XRM labels flipped at convergence* is a strong indicator of *worst-group-accuracy in phase-2*, making flips a good criterion to select twin hyper-parameters. The two middle panels show the signed margin of the twins on each ground-truth group. From each of these class-dependent plots, XRM discovers two environments: one for points in the *mistake-free* white area, and one for points in the *cross-mistake* gray areas. Notably, XRM is able to allocate the two smallest groups □△ to dedicated environments. Another notable observation is that the two middle plots appear as straight lines, indicating that the twin networks agree on their predictions. The fourth panel shows that label flipping happens almost exclusively for the two smallest groups, and that it stabilizes as training progresses.

(a) Well-classified planes   (b) Misclassified planes   (c) Well-classified deers   (d) Misclassified deers

Figure 7.3: Randomly selected images of CIFAR-10 from groups identified by XRM. For each class, well-classified examples and mistakes align with prototypical and rare background colors.

appropriate environments E requires prior knowledge or domain expertise. This is why researchers in public policy and epidemiology articles spend abundant ink justifying the validity of their chosen E as an instrument, and of $\phi(X)$ as a valid adjustment set. Since the XRM method presumes that simple features are spurious, the method should perform well in problems where the invariance-inducing environments differ in simplistic patterns, and encounter difficulties otherwise.

The ColoredMNIST dataset is a useful tool to illustrate the success and failure cases of XRM. The following analysis rests on four variations of the original ColoredMNIST dataset described in chapter 5, each involving the same colored digit classification task. The four versions differ on whether the robust feature is *digit shape* or *digit color*, and which of these two variables bears the strongest correlation to the target label. Overall, we observe generalization issues when classifiers latch onto the easier-to-learn *digit color*, but the more difficult-to-learn *digit shape* is the desired invariant feature. Table 7.4 shows the average-test-accuracy of ERM and XRM+GroupDRO for the four versions of the ColoredMNIST dataset. The table also includes the performance of a hypothetical oracle classifier that relies only on the invariant feature. In summary, ERM performs well when the invariant feature is the simplest, while XRM excels when the invariant feature is the most complex. Notably, the pair of datasets CMNIST and MCOLOR, as well as InverseCMNIST and InverseMCOLOR, are observationally equivalent from the pooled data alone. This observation, initially noted by Yong Lin and colleagues,[354] suggests that learning invariant predictors in the absence of environment annotations is impossible in full generality. For instance, it is impossible to distinguish between InverseCMNIST and InverseMCOLOR using only training data—leaving us at a loss on whether to use ERM or XRM. Nevertheless, XRM remains a state-of-the-art solution for problems where the learning machine should ignore spurious shortcuts[5,103,105] in favor of focusing on more complex, invariant patterns.

7.6 Memorization, Twin Training, and Label Flipping

In previous literature, tools similar to twin training and label flipping proved useful to study memorization in learning systems. Notably, Vitaly Feldman and Chiyuan Zhang[357] determine that an algorithm $\mathcal{A}$ has memorized the i-th example (x_i, y_i) contained in the training set D if:

$$\text{mem}(\mathcal{A}, D, i) = \Pr_{f \sim \mathcal{A}(D)}(f(x_i) = y_i) - \Pr_{f \sim \mathcal{A}(D^{-i})}(f(x_i) = y_i), \qquad (7.4)$$

	CMNIST	InverseCMNIST	InverseMCOLOR	MCOLOR
training, $e = 1$	$S \xrightarrow{0.75} Y \xrightarrow{0.80} C$	$S \xrightarrow{0.85} Y \xrightarrow{0.70} C$	$S \xleftarrow{0.80} Y \xleftarrow{0.75} C$	$S \xleftarrow{0.80} Y \xleftarrow{0.85} C$
training, $e = 2$	$S \xrightarrow{0.75} Y \xrightarrow{0.90} C$	$S \xrightarrow{0.85} Y \xrightarrow{0.80} C$	$S \xleftarrow{0.90} Y \xleftarrow{0.75} C$	$S \xleftarrow{0.70} Y \xleftarrow{0.85} C$
training, all	$S \xrightarrow{0.75} Y \xrightarrow{0.85} C$	$S \xrightarrow{0.85} Y \xrightarrow{0.75} C$	$S \xleftarrow{0.85} Y \xleftarrow{0.75} C$	$S \xleftarrow{0.75} Y \xleftarrow{0.85} C$
testing	$S \xrightarrow{0.75} Y \xrightarrow{0.10} C$	$S \xrightarrow{0.85} Y \xrightarrow{0.10} C$	$S \xleftarrow{0.10} Y \xleftarrow{0.75} C$	$S \xleftarrow{0.10} Y \xleftarrow{0.85} C$
inv. feature?	complex, weak	complex, strong	simple, weak	simple, strong
ERM	0.37 ± 0.10	0.67 ± 0.02	$\mathbf{0.75 \pm 0.01}$	$\mathbf{0.85 \pm 0.01}$
XRM	$\mathbf{0.71 \pm 0.02}$	$\mathbf{0.82 \pm 0.02}$	0.40 ± 0.01	0.57 ± 0.01
Oracle	0.75	0.85	0.75	0.85

Table 7.4: Test accuracies of ERM, XRM+GroupDRO, and Oracle classifiers on four ColoredMNIST versions. For all versions, the environment E influences digit shape S and color C, forming our input $X = (S, C)$. For each version, the figure depicts the underlying causal structure and observed correlation between variables. The invariant feature may be the complex digit shape (CMNIST versions) *or* the simple digit color (MCOLOR versions), which in turn could bear the strongest *or* weakest correlation to the target variable. The pair of datasets CMNIST and MCOLOR, as well as InverseCMNIST and InverseMCOLOR, are indistinguishable from the pooled training data alone.

where the probability runs over the randomness of the learning algorithm $\mathcal{A}$, and D^{-i} denotes the training dataset D with the i-th example held out. The expression above captures "the intuition that an algorithm memorizes the label y_i if its prediction at x_i based on the rest of the dataset changes significantly once (x_i, y_i) is added to the dataset."[357] In those cases where we may assume zero training error, we deem an example $(x_i, y_i) \in D$ memorized if $\mathrm{mem}(\mathcal{A}, D, i)$ is convincingly greater than zero. Equation (7.4) has a "meta-learning" flavor: to measure memorization, we must look ahead into the learning process, come back, and report. This makes regularizing against memorization challenging, as we would need to back-propagate gradients through multiple steps of the learning algorithm $\mathcal{A}$.

To understand how memorization precludes learning invariances,[358] let us revisit the cow-on-the-beach problem section 2.5.1. As a reminder, the first two features (x_1, x_2) represent animal shape and landscape color, while the last $d-2$ features $(x_3, \ldots, x_d)$ are independent noise terms that contain no generalizing patterns. Nevertheless, the noise features bear a total *empirical* correlation with the target variable in the over-parameterized case $d-2 > n$. Table 7.5 illustrates the effects of memorization in this example. The first row shows that the learned logistic regressor $\hat{w}$ achieves zero training error and correctly classifies all the testing examples from the majority group. However, this classifier does not generalize to the test minority group, because the examples from this group were dealt with by means of memorization. In the second row, we zero out all the logistic regression coefficients associated with the $d-2$ noise features. This action does not affect performance on the majority examples but it destroys the training accuracy on the minority group. This is because the training minority examples were memorized in the zeroed weights. Finally, in the third row, we zero the first two features associated with animal shape and background color. The classifier remains able to predict all the memorized training minority examples, but the performance on both training and test majority examples falls to level. In conclusion, the simplify-and-memorize learning strategy indeed precludes the discovery of invariant predictors in the cow-on-the-beach example.

Next, consider a learning problem containing no input pattern whatsoever. More specifically, contemplate a dataset $D = \{(x_i, y_i)\}_{i=1}^n$ where inputs $x_i \sim \mathrm{Gaussian}(0, 1_d)$, and targets $y_i \sim \mathrm{Bernoulli}(\frac{1}{2})$. In the over-parameterized case $d \geq n$, large machines can attain zero training error,[86] yet their test error would remain at the chance level $\frac{1}{2}$. Is it acceptable for a learning machine to resort to memorization—the sole strategy to attain zero training error—or should we design learning algorithms that refuse patterns that do not generalize to hold-out data? Answering this question requires additional information about the learning problem at hand. For

coefficient $\hat{w}$	$\mathrm{acc}^{\mathrm{tr}}_{\mathrm{maj}}$	$\mathrm{acc}^{\mathrm{tr}}_{\mathrm{min}}$	$\mathrm{acc}^{\mathrm{te}}_{\mathrm{maj}}$	$\mathrm{acc}^{\mathrm{te}}_{\mathrm{min}}$
$(\hat{w}_1, \hat{w}_2, w_3 \ldots, \hat{w}_d)$	1.00	1.00	1.00	0.25
$(\hat{w}_1, \hat{w}_2, 0 \ldots, 0)$	1.00	0.00	1.00	0.00
$(0, 0, \hat{w}_3 \ldots, \hat{w}_d)$	0.65	1.00	0.50	0.50

Table 7.5: Effects of memorization in the "cow-on-the-beach" problem. The estimated logistic regression achieves zero training error by dealing with the majority group using a spurious correlation and memorizing the training minority group. Zeroing the coefficients associated with noise dimensions undoes the memorization of training examples from the minority group. Zeroing the coefficients associated with animal shape and landscape color retains the memorization of training examples from the minority group, but destroys the generalization performance of all the majority examples.

instance, memorization is a reasonable strategy in those cases where the training data contains the entire population of examples, and the task at hand is to build a hash table.

Memorization is a natural part of learning that should not be shunned. *Good* memorization affords invariance and generalization by allowing us to operate in novel circumstances. For instance, we recall our passwords in every new circumstance, and remember where we parked our car each time. Conversely, *bad* memorization is a shortcut to avoid enduring the learning effort necessary to uncover complex invariant patterns—similar to machines that use a simplify-and-memorize learning strategy in the cow-on-the-beach problem. As a rule of thumb, memorization is sometimes necessary but should be a last resort to reduce training error.[6]

Memorization arises in the presence of noisy labels,[359] sometimes with surprising implications. Consider the problem in figure 7.4, where the goal is to separate two d-dimensional Gaussians, where 25% of the training and testing examples are labeled at random. We vary the input dimensionality d of this problem from 1000 to 15000, while fixing the number of training examples at $n = 1000$ for all runs. This leads to the over-parameterized regime where $d/n \geq 1$, so all runs are able to yield zero training error by memorizing the randomized labels in the training set. However, here is an interesting observation. As we increase the amount of over-parameterization— the amount of storage provided by the weights in the classifier—memorizing noisy labels happens without disturbing the learning of a generalizing predictor for the clean labels. In fact, the test accuracy of the resulting predictor approaches the best possible accuracy of 75% as we increase the input dimensionality d. We may say that the simplify-and-memorize

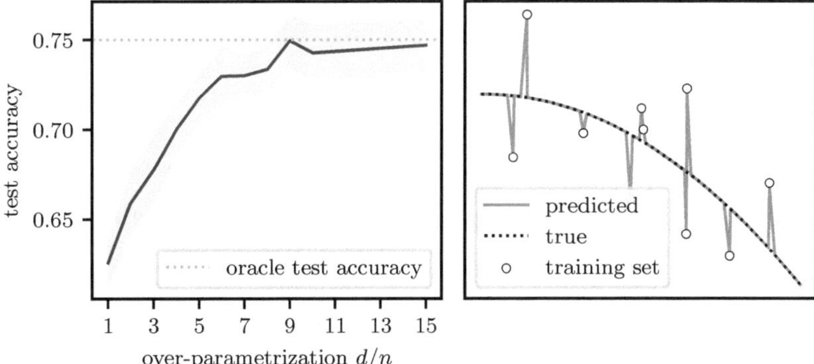

Figure 7.4: On the left, we are training linear binary classifiers to separate two Gaussians with 25% label noise and n training examples with d dimensions. All runs achieve zero training error by memorizing the noisy labels. However, as we increase the amount of over-parameterization d/n, memorizing noisy labels happens without perturbing the correct classification of test examples with clean labels. On the right, we see a similar situation where the simplify-and-memorize learning strategy overfits benignly to produce a *smooth-plus-spiky* predictor.

learning strategy is a reasonable inductive bias for this problem, because memorization is the only possible strategy to achieve zero training error and it does not preclude the discovery of an invariant predictor. Peter Bartlett and colleagues call this phenomenon "benign overfitting,"[85] whereby the predictor decomposes into a "simple component that is useful for prediction" and a "spiky component that is useful for overfitting but, in a favorable setting, does not harm prediction accuracy." The right side of figure 7.4 illustrates benign overfitting for a one-dimensional regression problem.

The research literature on learning with noisy labels[359] relies heavily on twin training, and thus relates to XRM. The de-coupling method[360] updates the twins only on disagreeing examples. In the co-teaching method,[361] each twin selects a subset of small-loss examples to train their peer. The co-teaching+ method[362] first applies de-coupling and, based on the resulting set of disagreement examples, applies the co-teaching method. The JoCor method[363] trains two networks to minimize their individual errors and agree on their predictions. In DivideMix,[364] the twins attempt to separate clean and noisy labels, sending the two subsets for training to their peer. The UniCon method[365] extends these ideas with careful class-balancing and self-supervised learning. The CrossSplit method,[335] most similar to XRM, assigns a fixed half of the data to each of the two twins, who can perturb the labels of their peer in terms of their own out-of-sample predictive confidence.

To see the relationship between memorization and the Invariance Principle, consider the statement:

$$Y \perp \text{Held} \mid \phi(X),$$

where the "Held" random variable determines whether an example is held "in" or "out" during training, producing two environments that follow the same distribution. However, certain *empirical* correlations may obtain only in the "in" environment—for instance, those necessary to memorize noisy labels across a finite dataset—but vanish in the "out" environment. In those cases, enforcing the Invariance Principle could result in learning algorithms to guard against representations that memorize training examples.

7.7 One Example, One Environment

As it happens, considering each training example as its own environment leads to interesting frameworks of invariance. For example, in the cow-on-the-beach problem, considering each training example as its own environment is arguably sufficient to realize that background features do not yield an invariant classifier across training environments (examples). In fact, following the Invariance Principle by considering each training example as its own environment should produce invariant predictors built on top of cow and camel features alone.

To grow examples into their own environments, consider a family of randomized data augmentations, such as rotations and translations. Then, we would like to "learn a feature representation such that the optimal classifier matches across applied data augmentations," leading to the Invariance Principle:

$$Y \perp \text{Aug} \mid \phi(X), \tag{7.5}$$

where each augmentation Aug indexes a different environment, with one added benefit: Augmentations produce *paired examples* across environments. For instance, if $\text{Aug}^{45}_{\text{rot}}(x_i)$ and $\text{Aug}^{90}_{\text{rot}}(x_i)$ refer to the *same* example as it appears in the environment *samples rotated by 45 degrees* and the environment *samples rotated by 90 degrees*, respectively. Paired examples enable searching for invariance by simply minimizing the predictive variance about the same example across environments.[292,366] However, determining invariance-inducing data augmentation protocols is as difficult as the learning problem itself, because we would like to vary all factors except for class identity. Furthermore, any data augmentation protocol may benefit certain classes while disadvantaging others.[367]

In the extreme case, we could consider each data point as its own environment, leading to the following Invariance Principle:

$$Y \perp \text{Index} \mid \phi(X),\tag{7.6}$$

where the example "Index" is hereby considered as a random variable. In the context of IRMv1, the equation above suggests we should "find a feature representation such that the optimal classifier is 1.0 for all training examples" or, in the language of calibration, "find a feature representation such that the optimal classifier temperature is 1.0 for all training examples." The resulting Invariance Principle is very conservative, as it would advocate for feature representations such that the optimal classifier matches for all possible environment assignment functions $E(x, y)$. In the fairness literature, searching for predictors that are simultaneously calibrated across all (groups of) examples is known as *multi-calibration*.[222]

Chapter 8

Invariance in LLMs

8.1   Introduction

Just as I started writing this book, large language models (LLMs) took the world by storm.[26,55,368,369] These enormous systems, built upon the transformer architecture,[370] are trained on vast quantities of data from the Internet to predict subsequent words in a natural language sequence. The resulting systems can hold conversations, answer queries, summarize content, draft emails, and debug code, all cases providing a natural language interface to human knowledge. This remarkable advancement in computer science has propelled many to embrace the scaling hypothesis—the notion that artificial intelligence can be achieved by training ever-larger language models on ever-larger datasets. However, little has been written about LLMs in terms of invariance.

This chapter aims to bridge that gap by examining concepts such as data mix curation, in-context learning, chain-of-thought, and multi-token prediction, specifically through the lens of invariance and the reduction of underspecification. One of the central arguments I wish to present is that, similar to standard learning machines, LLMs are trained to generate high *likelihood* outputs, which often diverge from what is *verisimilar* or true. As argued in chapter 5, verisimilitude and truthfulness are concepts related to invariance and the ability to generalize out-of-distribution widely, thereby positioning the Invariance Principle as a promising method to develop more robust and factual large language models. This chapter reviews one first step in this agenda, the in-context risk minimization (ICRM) algorithm.

8.2   The Language Modeling Task

The learning task of *language modeling* is the foundation for training LLMs.[26] Given a sequence of past words $(x_1, \ldots, x_t)$, also known as the *context* or *prompt*, the goal of language modeling is to predict the sequence of future words or *response* $(x_{t+1}, \ldots, x_T)$. Formally, this involves modeling the conditional distribution:

$$p(x_{t+1}, \ldots, x_T \mid x_1, \ldots, x_t), \tag{8.1}$$

where the sequence length T can vary from sequence to sequence.

To begin, consider the following two illustrative language modeling tasks.

- In the *induction task*, the context $(x_1, \ldots, x_{T-1})$ is a sequence of letters. The response x_T is the letter appearing right after the first occurrence of letter x_{T-1} in the context. For example, given the context (A, F, C, E, F, D, B, F), the correct response is C.

- In the *parity task*, the context $(x_1, \ldots, x_{T-1})$ is a list of zeros and ones. The response x_T equals zero if the context contains an even number of ones, and it equals one otherwise. For example, given the context $(0, 1, 1, 0, 1, 0, 1, 1)$, the correct response is 1.

However, the true power of LLMs lies in their ability to leverage language modeling as a common interface for a vast amount of learning tasks. This allows training on Internet-scale amounts of data to obtain models that can answer questions, summarize content, translate documents, draft emails, and implement code—all by expressing our requests as a prompt sequence $(x_1, \ldots, x_t)$ articulated in natural language, and allowing the model to produce a response in the form of a response sequence $(x_{t+1}, \ldots, x_T)$.

8.2.1   Next-token Prediction

Due to the curse of dimensionality, directly predicting the entire response sequence $(x_{t+1}, \ldots, x_T)$ in one step, as suggested in equation (8.1), is impractical. Instead, most language models adopt an auto-regressive prediction strategy to produce response sequences token by token. This *next-token prediction* process is represented by the equation

$$p(x_1, \ldots, x_T) = \prod_{t=1}^{T} p(x_t \mid x_1, \ldots, x_{t-1}).$$

To produce the response sequence $(\hat{x}_{t+1}, \ldots, \hat{x}_T)$, we sample the following conditional distributions:

$$\hat{x}_{t+1} \sim p(x \mid x_1, \ldots, x_t),$$
$$\hat{x}_{t+2} \sim p(x \mid x_1, \ldots, x_t, \hat{x}_{t+1}),$$
$$\ldots$$
$$\hat{x}_T \sim p(x \mid x_1, \ldots, x_t, \hat{x}_{t+1}, \ldots, \hat{x}_{T-1}),$$

where each element in the response is generated sequentially using an invariant next-token predictor, $p(x \mid \cdot)$ consuming a variable-length context sequence. While state-of-the-art LLMs are indeed next-token predictors, this simplification brings about two challenges.

First, training next-token predictors relies on *teacher forcing*. This involves training the model using segments of ground-truth response sequences, as found in the training data

$$\hat{x}_{t+k+1} \sim p(x \mid x_1, \ldots, x_t, \underbrace{x_{t+1}, \ldots, x_{t+k}}_{\text{real response}}).$$

However, at test time, such ground-truth responses are unavailable, so we must force the model to rely on its own predictions to generate next-tokens:

$$\hat{x}_{t+k+1} \sim p(x \mid x_1, \ldots, x_t, \underbrace{\hat{x}_{t+1}, \ldots, \hat{x}_{t+k}}_{\text{predicted response}}).$$

As noted by Bachmann and Nagarajan, this discrepancy between training and testing phases can lead the model to absorb spurious correlations:

> By revealing parts of the answer to the model as input [during teacher-forcing training], we allow the model to fit the data by cheating, that is, by using trivial mechanisms.[371]

That is, the ground-truth responses used as context during training may include spurious correlations that mislead the model, preventing it from learning the true, invariant processes governing token generation.

A second problem is that next-token predictors exhibit a nonzero probability of producing the wrong token at each prediction step. Once an incorrect token is generated, it becomes part of the narrative,[372] feeding a vicious circle where the model hallucinates an increasingly fictional path. As elaborated in section 8.8, hallucination occurs because next-token predictors are trained to produce *likely* tokens, in many cases distinct from *verisimilar* tokens.

8.2.2 Large Language Model Training Pipeline

The training pipeline of state-of-the-art LLMs is complex, yet it can be distilled into three primary phases:

1. During the *pretraining* phase, LLMs model tens of trillions of next-token predictions. The pretraining corpus is crawled from various sources on the Internet, including books, Wikipedia, and GitHub.

2. During the *post-training* phase, LLMs are given curated question-answer pairs, and fine-tuned to produce the desired answer for each question. The aim of post-training is to polish the general-purpose next-token predictor developed during pretraining into an adept assistant that provides coherent and well-formatted answers.

3. A final *alignment* phase uses reinforcement learning from human feedback (RLHF) to increase the factuality, safety, and usefulness of LLMs. The basic RLHF iteration (1) presents a prompt to the LLM, (2) samples two response sequences, (3) asks a human annotator to chose the preferred sequence, and (4) employs a reinforcement learning algorithm to incentivize the LLM to produce the preferred response with higher probability.

Drawing an analogy to preparing for an exam in algebra,[373] Andrej Karpathy likens the pretraining phase to studying algebra books, the post-training phase to reviewing solved exam problems, and the alignment phase to tackling new exercises with only their final answers provided. However, as of this writing, the comparison stops here, as LLMs do not yet have the innovative prowess to generate new hypotheses and scientific insights, setting them apart (in terms of the analogy) from professional mathematicians.

8.2.3 The Scaling Hypothesis

The widespread and well-deserved success of LLMs has led many to embrace the *scaling hypothesis*. This idea, closely related to Rich Sutton's *bitter lesson*, can be informally stated as:

Artificial intelligence is attainable by training increasingly large next-token predictors on increasingly large amounts of data.

However, what do these "increasingly large amounts of data" look like?

Current practices in LLM training allocate substantial resources to the curation of training data. Both the pretraining and post-training datasets must comprise a delicate blend of high-quality sources, encompassing diverse data types such as prose, code, mathematics, and multilingual examples.

These data compositions are further refined by identifying the weak areas in the LLM's performance. Commonly, additional data is gathered for the tasks in which specific models perform poorly, akin to data balancing techniques used in invariance learning (chapter 6). That is, AI scientists implement an iterative approach of worst-environment performance maximization, which leads to increasingly invariant next-token predictors. Consequently, the so-called scaling hypothesis mainly requires a human intelligence that curates the data, and invariance-inducing corpuses become the highest-prized asset in the race to AI. This approach contrasts with human learning, where individuals intuitively curate their own data and acquire complex skills from a limited number of examples.

However, if the scaling hypothesis proves true, the Invariance Principle discussed in this book might become redundant. This mirrors a concern expressed by Wigner regarding physical theories:

> However, if the universal law of nature should be discovered, the principles of invariance would lose their place in the hierarchy described before. ... If we had a complete description of all the events with which we shall ever come into contact, the correlations between these events, that is the laws of nature, would have a reduced significance, similar to that of the invariance principles when the universal law of nature is known.[57]

Essentially, with access to all possible training data, the realm deemed out-of-distribution would contract, pushing us closer to an iid scenario where ERM is an optimal learning principle. As of today, even state-of-the-art LLMs continue to struggle with sequences longer than those seen in training, are susceptible to spurious correlations, latch onto irrelevant context or distracting sentences, fail to generalize to novel compositions of known elements, and often produce nonfactual information. Principles of invariance could be useful to ground LLMs in nonspurious correlations, increasing their robustness and factuality.

8.3   The Transformer Architecture

State-of-the-art LLMs are built upon the transformer architecture,[370] here illustrated in figure 8.1. Transformers have revolutionized the field of language modeling and AI, since they are capable of (1) modeling long-term dependencies in sequences by means of an attention mechanism, and (2) optimizing GPU utilization by computing in parallel the next-token prediction losses across all tokens in a sequence. This section describes the components

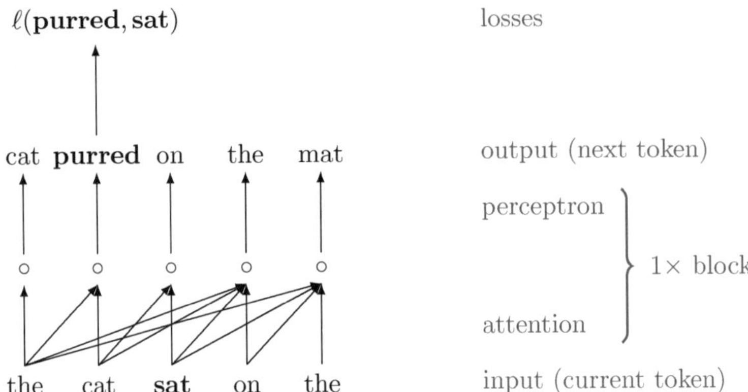

Figure 8.1: Scheme of the *transformer architecture* performing language modeling via next-token prediction. Given the sequence (the, cat, sat, on, the), the transformer is an auto-regressive architecture that produces the next-token predictions (cat, sat, on, the, mat) in parallel. The transformer architecture consists of a sequence of blocks, where each block contains an attention layer (updating each token as a function of every preceding token) and a multilayer perceptron layer (updating each token as a function of some knowledge stored in-weights). For simplicity, the scheme omits token embeddings, position embeddings, skip connections, normalization layers, and token un-embeddings; the figure also considers words as tokens, and depicts only one transformer block.

in the transformer architecture (tokenization, token embeddings, position embeddings, attention layers, multilayer perceptron layers, normalization layers, skip connections, and unembedding layers) and how they combine to form a large language model.

8.3.1 Tokenization

Most transformer architectures preprocess incoming sequences of bytes into sequences of tokens. Though there are only 256 possible bytes, some transformers employ vocabularies comprising hundreds of thousands of *tokens*. As a result, tokenization compresses long byte-sequences into shorter token-sequences, where tokens belong to a much larger vocabulary. In machine learning terms, tokenization reduces the number of predictions necessary to generate a sequence but increases the range of possible values for each token generated.

To exemplify, consider the following sequence of 51 bytes:

```
Tokenization partitions byte-sequences into tokens.
```

The GPT-4o tokenizer compresses this byte-sequence into the following sequence of nine tokens:

Tokenization partitions byte-sequences into tokens.

Notably, most English words in the sequence—together with their leading whitespace—are assigned one dedicated token. Internally, these nine tokens are encoded as the following list of integers:

$$(4421, 2860, 89097, 9239, 5460, 16559, 1511, 20290, 130),$$

representing the class-indices for each of the next-token predictions necessary to produce this sentence.

One of the most popular tokenization algorithms is known as *byte-pair encoding* (BPE). Given some byte-level training data, BPE tokenization iteratively replaces the most frequent pair of symbols with a new token, until the vocabulary reaches a prescribed size. To avoid merging words, the second merged symbol must not start with white-space.

Unfortunately, tokenization introduces a host of problems, such as spelling errors, challenges with basic string and arithmetic tasks, and reduced performance on non-English languages.[374] Consequently, there is growing interest in developing transformer architectures that can efficiently operate on long byte-sequences directly.

8.3.2 Token Embeddings

Next, we translate each token integer index $x_t \in \mathbb{N}$ into a continuous representation $e_t \in \mathbb{R}^d$, using this mapping:

$$e_t = \mathrm{emb}(x_t) = \mathrm{OneHot}(x_t) \cdot W_{\mathrm{emb}},$$

where $\mathrm{OneHot} : \mathbb{N} \to \mathbb{R}^V$ translates token integer indices into their V-dimensional one-hot vector, and the embedding matrix $W_{\mathrm{emb}} \in \mathbb{R}^{V \times d}$ is a learnable parameter. After training, the space of token embeddings is structured according to semantic similarity, admitting simple arithmetic operations such as:

$$\mathrm{emb}(\mathtt{king}) - \mathrm{emb}(\mathtt{man}) + \mathrm{emb}(\mathtt{woman}) \approx \mathrm{emb}(\mathtt{queen}).$$

Generally, word embeddings with similar meanings should have a high dot-product value.

8.3.3 Position Embeddings

The transformer architecture is equivariant with respect to input permutations. However, word ordering matters to address natural language tasks:

The two sentences "yes, the answer is no" and "no, the answer is yes" contain the same set of words, yet have opposite meanings. To account for word ordering, positional embeddings increase the similarity between nearby tokens in a sequence:

$$e_t = \mathrm{pos}(\mathrm{emb}(x_t), t).$$

An ideal positional encoding, according to Chris and Hugh Bishop, should "provide a unique representation for each position, it should be bounded, it should generalize to longer sequences, and it should have a consistent way to express the number of steps between any two input vectors irrespective of their absolute position, because the relative position of tokens is often more important than their absolute position."[7] A variety of techniques[375] exist to add positional information to a matrix of token embeddings $E \in \mathbb{R}^{t \times d}$, such as

- Learnable positional embeddings take form $E = E + W_{:t}$, where $W : \mathbb{R}^{T \times d}$ is a *learnable* parameter, and T determines the maximum sequence length. Therefore, learnable positional embeddings cannot extrapolate to test sequences of length greater than T.

- Sinusoidal positional embeddings take the form $E = E + W_{:t}$, where $W : \mathbb{R}^{T \times d}$ is a *fixed* parameter with d-dimensional rows.

$$W_t = (S_{t,1}, C_{t,1}, \ldots, S_{t,d/2}, C_{t,d/2})$$

containing entries from the sinusoid matrices

$$C_{t,j} = \cos(t \cdot 10000^{-2(j-1)/d}),$$
$$S_{t,j} = \sin(t \cdot 10000^{-2(j-1)/d}),$$

for $t = 1, \ldots T$ and $j = 1, \ldots, \frac{d}{2}$.

- Rotary positional embeddings (RoPE) rotates token embeddings an angle proportional to their position, using the two-dimensional Euler's formula:

$$E = \mathrm{concat}(E_{:,:\frac{d}{2}} \odot C_{:t,:} - E_{:,\frac{d}{2}:} \odot S_{:t,:},$$
$$E_{:,:\frac{d}{2}} \odot C_{:t,:} + E_{:,\frac{d}{2}:} \odot S_{:t,:}),$$

where "$\odot$" stands for the entry-wise product. Because the rotation mechanism is periodic, RoPE preserves relative (non-absolute) positions between tokens.

To some extent, sinusoidal and rotary positional embeddings can generalize to test sequences of length $T' > T$. This is achieved through *positional interpolation*[375] where, during test time, we employ taller sinusoid matrices $C', S' \in \mathbb{R}^{T' \times \frac{d}{2}}$ with entries

$$C'_{t',j} = \cos\left(\frac{T}{T'} \cdot t' \cdot 10000^{-2(j-1)/d}\right),$$

for $t' = 1, \ldots, T'$, and similarly for S'. These taller sinusoid matrices rescale higher test-time frequencies within the observed training-time range.

In certain transformer implementations, positional embeddings are combined with token embeddings before calculating keys and values at the start of each attention layer, as described next.

8.3.4   Attention

The cornerstone of the transformer architecture is the *attention* layer, permitting the tokens $e_1, \ldots, e_T$ to communicate with—or attend to—each other. To appreciate the necessity of such a mechanism, consider the following two sentences:[7]

- I swam across the river to get to the other *bank*.

- I walked across the road to get cash from the *bank*.

In each sentence, the word *bank* has a different meaning, depending on the preceding words. To model contextual meaning, Chris Bishop and Hugh Bishop argue, the attention layer gives

> different weights to different inputs, with weighting coefficients that themselves depend on the input values, thereby capturing powerful inductive biases related to sequential and other forms of data.[7]

Broadly speaking, and given a sequence of tokens $E = (e_1, \ldots, e_T) \in \mathbb{R}^{T \times d}$, the attention layer modifies the token e_t as a function of all others:

$$e_t = \sum_{t'=1}^{T} \alpha_{t,t'} \cdot e_{t'},$$

where in most implementations the *attention coefficients* $\alpha_{t,t'}$ depend themselves on E, are bounded between zero and one, and have unit mass $\sum_{t'} \alpha_{t,t'} = 1$ for each token x_t. Furthermore, asymmetry in attention coefficients ($\alpha_{t,t'} \neq \alpha_{t',t}$) allows "cat" to attend strongly to "animal" (because all cats are animals), while allowing "animal" to attend weakly to "cat" (because not every animal is a cat).[7]

The *scaled dot-product* attention[370] implements this communication mechanism by jointly processing the list of tokens as

$$\text{attention}(E) = \text{softmax}\left(\text{mask}\left(\frac{(E \cdot Q) \cdot (E \cdot K)^{\top}}{\sqrt{d}}\right)\right) \cdot (E \cdot V), \quad (8.2)$$

Above, the parameters $Q, K, V \in \mathbb{R}^{d \times d}$ instantiate

- a matrix $E \cdot Q \in \mathbb{R}^{T \times d}$ of *queries* describing what each token looks for;

- a matrix $E \cdot K \in \mathbb{R}^{T \times d}$ of *keys* describing what each token looks like; and

- a matrix $E \cdot V \in \mathbb{R}^{T \times d}$ of *values* describing what each token communicates.

Bishop and Bishop explain the meaning of these matrices using an example about movie recommendation:

> Consider the problem of choosing which movie to watch in an online movie streaming service. ... We could automate this by encoding the attributes of each movie in a vector called the *key*. The corresponding movie file itself is called a *value*. Similarly, the user could then provide their own personal vector of values for the desired attributes, which we call the *query*. The movie service could then compare the query vector with all the key vectors to find the best match and send the corresponding movie to the user in the form of the value file. We can think of the user "attending" to the particular movie whose key most closely matches their query.[7]

Most implementations set up *causal* and *multi-headed* attention layers. In causal attention, each token x_t attends only to itself and its precedents in the sequence. Since transformers process all sequence tokens in parallel, causal attention is essential to ensure that communication among tokens occurs exclusively from past to future. To implement causal attention, the "mask" operation sets to $-\infty$ all pairwise affinities above the main diagonal. Multi-headed attention provides multiple communication channels between tokens by concatenating the output of n_h attention *heads*:

$$\text{attention}(e) = \text{concat}(\text{attention}_1(e), \ldots, \text{attention}_{n_h}(e)) \cdot W_O. \quad (8.3)$$

In the equation above, each attention head has its own parameters, with $V \in \mathbb{R}^{d \times \frac{d}{n_h}}$. A final projection matrix $W_O \in \mathbb{R}^{d \times d}$ produces the $T \times d$ output of the multi-headed attention layer.

A few remarks on computational complexity are in order here. As illustrated in figure 8.2c, the operation $(e \cdot Q) \cdot (e \cdot K)^\top$ generates an internal matrix of size $T \times T$ containing all pairwise token affinities, incurring a $O(T^2)$ memory and computing cost. Therefore, attention layers dominate computation for long sequences. On the upside, some of the computations within these layers can be cached during test time, when tokens are generated sequentially. Specifically, generating token x_{t+1} can reuse the precomputed keys $e_t \cdot K$ and values $e_t \cdot V$ from all prior tokens x_t for each attention layer and head. This storage, referred to as the KV-cache, has a size of $O(Td)$ per attention head.

8.3.5 Multilayer Perceptrons

Multi-layer perceptrons operate on tokens *individually*, as described by the function

$$\text{perceptron}(e_t) = \text{ReLU}(e_t \cdot W_1 + b_1) \cdot W_2 + b_2 \in \mathbb{R}^d, \qquad (8.4)$$

where it is common practice to use a $4d$-dimensional hidden layer. In transformers, perceptrons serve to implement associative memories of non-contextual facts, such as answering "What is the capital of France?." Each hidden neuron can be thought of as activating the recall of a specific fact, conveyed to the token via the associated hidden-to-output weight. Multi-layer perceptrons require $O(Td^2)$ operations, so they dominate computation for short sequences.

8.3.6 Normalization

Normalization layers process tokens individually, as follows:

$$\text{normalization}(e_t) = \frac{e_t - \mathbb{E}[e_t]}{\sqrt{\mathbb{V}[e_t] + \epsilon}} \cdot \gamma + \beta,$$

where $\gamma, \beta \in \mathbb{R}^d$ are two learnable parameters and $\epsilon > 0$ is a small constant added to avoid division by zero. Most transformer architectures place *layer normalization* layers before their attention and multilayer perceptron layers, where means and variances are computed for each embedding individually across their d dimensions.

8.3.7 Skip Connections

To circumvent the challenge of vanishing gradients in the training of deep transformer architectures, both attention and multilayer perceptron layers are equipped with additive *skip connections*:

$$e_t + \text{attention}(e_t),$$

with a similar mechanism applied to the multilayer perceptron layer. This use of skip connections allows one to interpret the transformer architecture as a series of layers that modify embeddings through *additive updates*.

8.3.8   Unembedding

Finally, each embedding e_t is transformed into a logit vector $y_t \in \mathbb{R}^V$ through a linear mapping $y_t = e_t \cdot W_{\text{unemb}}$, where $W_{\text{unemb}} \in \mathbb{R}^{d \times V}$ is a learnable parameter. Applying the softmax operation to y_t yields the sampling probabilities for the next-token prediction $\hat{x}_{t+1}$. These probabilities are useful both for calculating cross-entropy losses during training and for generating next tokens during inference.

8.3.9   Putting Everything Together

The final transformer architecture, as illustrated in figure 8.2b, comprises a series of transformer *blocks*. Each block consists of an attention layer and a multilayer perceptron layer, both of which are preceded by a dedicated normalization layer and equipped with their own skip connection. Prior to these blocks, token and positional embeddings are computed; the architecture concludes with a final normalization and unembedding layers.

8.4   In-Context Learning

Certain next-token predictors, such as transformers, demonstrate a capability known as *in-context learning*.[376] This is informally stated as follows:

> In modern language models, tokens later in the context are easier to predict than tokens earlier in the context. As the context gets longer, loss goes down.[377]

To illustrate, consider the following prompt:

```
1.19:1.92, -0.13:-0.20, -0.77:-1.25, -1.44:
```

By providing the context of "x:y pairs" above, we would like the next-token predictor to realize that (1) the pairs of numbers follow the relation x:1.618*x, and (2) the correct next-token prediction should be -2.33.

However, the preceding context offers only three examples labeled with the relationship $y = 1.618x$, which may not provide enough information to

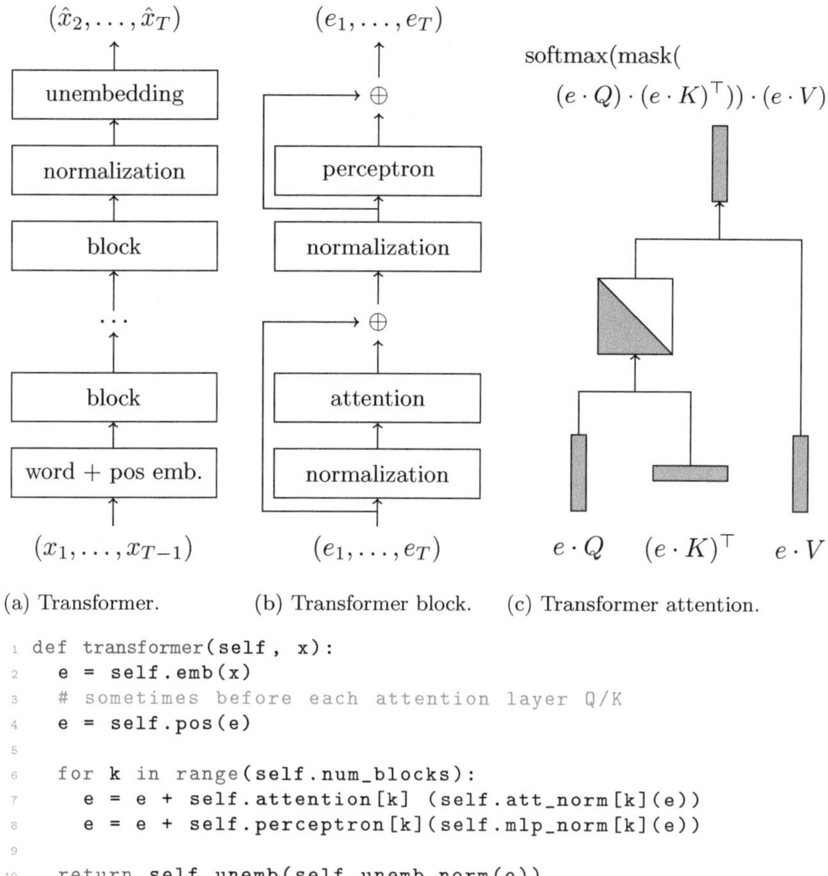

(a) Transformer.   (b) Transformer block.   (c) Transformer attention.

```python
def transformer(self, x):
    e = self.emb(x)
    # sometimes before each attention layer Q/K
    e = self.pos(e)

    for k in range(self.num_blocks):
        e = e + self.attention[k] (self.att_norm[k](e))
        e = e + self.perceptron[k](self.mlp_norm[k](e))

    return self.unemb(self.unemb_norm(e))
```

(d) PyTorch code to predict with a transformer architecture.

Figure 8.2: (a) The transformer architecture embeds each token x_t and its position t into a vector space, transforms the sequence of embeddings by means of transformer blocks, and returns a vector of logits associated with each token in the vocabulary. (b) Transformer blocks allow tokens within the sequence to communicate to each other by means of attention layers, and allow each token to perform its own individual computations by means of multilayer perceptron layers. Normalization layers and skip connections stabilize the training process by avoiding vanishing gradients. (c) A detailed view of the attention layer showcasing how each token can collect information from all the ones previously appearing in the input sequence.

predict the next-token accurately. Instead, consider the following context, which presents twice as many labeled examples to the next-token predictor:

```
1.19:1.92, -0.13:-0.20, -0.77:-1.25,
-2.10:-3.40, -0.40:-0.65, 0.40:0.65, -1.44:
```

If the prediction improves with this expanded context, we can infer that the next-token predictor is capable of learning the prediction task of interest on-the-fly, directly from in-context examples. Similarly, a well-trained LLM would complete the sequence "France-Paris Italy-Rome Spain-" with the sequence "Madrid," effectively learning, from the input itself, that the user is setting up a capital prediction task.

The ability to learn in-context suggests a degree of compositional generalization. In particular, to tackle new contexts, the next-token predictor must have learned how to *amortize* similar tasks previously appearing in the training data. This capacity for in-context learning is reminiscent of meta-learning[220,378] and test-time adaptation,[379] yet it incarnates adaptive behavior without the need of fine-tuning parameters.

Notably, in-context learning emerges without supervision, using only the natural order of words in the training corpus. This is because large language models are trained over an enormous amount of sequences, some of which share structures or partially overlapping starts. In this learning setup, the machine has the opportunity to learn and amortize across a vast amount of learning tasks, all expressed through the same natural language interface. In the upcoming sections, we will delve into how framing environments as rich and overlapping natural language prompts amortizes a greater degree of out-of-distribution generalization.

8.4.1   In-context Learning Versus in-Weight Learning

In-context learning contrasts with the usual *in-weight* learning that occurs while training the parameters of deep neural networks. I propose that these two learning modalities can serve as effective tools to differentiate between spurious and invariant correlations. While in-context learning permits the contextual use of spurious correlations, in-weight learning offers the permanent storage of invariant patterns. This mirrors biological systems that, despite having learned invariances to generalize across multiple environments, use situational awareness to extract timely spurious correlations from the changing environment.[380] (Some spurious correlations, such as geographical location, help us differentiate between visually identical species due to Batesian mimicry.) But when do current systems prefer in-context learning over in-weight learning?

Consider the problem of learning an *induction head*, a neural network module responsible for the in-context capabilities of modern language models.[377] Given the context $(\dots, a, b, \dots, a)$, an induction head predicts token b by (1) scanning across the context for the first occurrence of token a and (2) predicting what follows, in this case token b. Induction heads endow in-context learners with generalization capabilities greater than those of regular neural networks. On one hand, regular neural networks predict by matching against a fixed library of features: They predict class c if feature f is present in input x. On the other hand, in-context learners predict based on positional statistics: They predict token at index $i + j$ if the first occurrence of the query appears at index i. Here, the in-context learning rule does not depend on token values but only on their relative positions, enabling a higher degree of out-of-distribution generalization:

> Notice that induction heads are implementing a simple algorithm, and are not memorizing a fixed table of n-gram statistics. The rule [A] [B] ... [A] → [B] applies regardless of what A and B are. This means that induction heads can in some sense work out-of-distribution, as long as local statistics early in the context are representative of statistics later. This hints that they may be capable of more general and abstract behavior.[377]

Figure 8.3, inspired by the work of Albert Bietti and colleagues,[381] illustrates how two attention layers can form an induction head by implementing mechanisms to (1) attend to the previous token, and (2) copy tokens.

We are now ready to illustrate how data structure influences the predictor's preference to learn in-context or in-weights. Consider training a two-block transformer architecture on input sequences:

$$z_i := (x_{i,1}, y_{i,1}, \dots, x_{i,T-1}, y_{i,T-1}, x_{i,T}),$$

and targets $t_i := y_{i,T}$, where each $y_{i,j}$ is deterministically produced by the corresponding $x_{i,j} \in \mathcal{X}$. Furthermore, consider varying two factors in this learning problem. First, the learning problem provides us with *informative contexts* if the subsequence $(x_{i,T}, y_{i,T})$ appears in the input sequence z_i. Otherwise, the learning problem exhibits uninformative contexts. Second, the learning problem employs *the same tokens* if the vocabulary $\mathcal{X}$ remains the same during both training and testing time. Otherwise, if $\mathcal{X}$ changes from training to test time, the learning problem exhibits *new tokens*. Then, all combinations of these two factors yield four variations of the learning problem.

Figure 8.4 illustrates the generalization mechanisms of transformer neural networks under these four regimes. On one hand, the transformer employs *in-context learning* to generalize across different train-test vocabularies

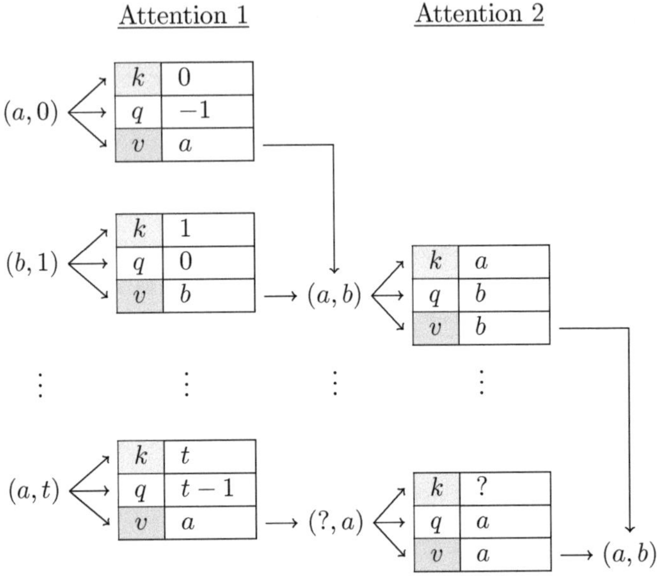

Figure 8.3: Implementation of an *induction head* with two layers of attention. The first attention layer, commonly referred to a *previous-token head*, sets the key of each token to its position embedding, the query of each token to the previous position embedding, and the value of each token to its word embedding. Therefore, the query of token $(b, 1)$ matches the key of token $(a, 0)$, propagating as the new value of $(b, 1)$ the embedding (a, b). The second attention layer, known as the *actual induction head*, sets the key of each token to the first half of its embedding, and sets both the query and value to the second half of the embedding. Therefore, the query of token $(?, a)$ matches the key of token (a, b), propagating as the new value of $(?, a)$ the embedding (a, b), and allowing the overall induction head to predict the token b at position $t + 1$.

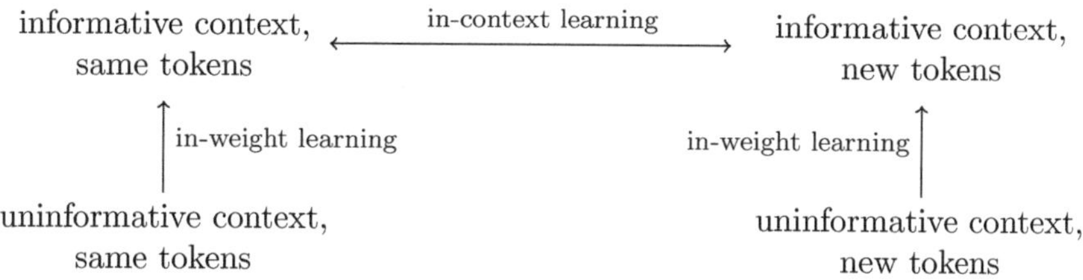

Figure 8.4: Diagram illustrating how in-context learning and in-weight learning afford different types of generalization.

when the contexts are informative. In these cases, the transformer learns an induction head to scan the context in search of $x_{i,T}$ to predict $y_{i,T}$. Notably, in-context learning enables zero-shot generalization across new vocabularies, allowing the transformer to process $x_{i,T}$ and predict $y'_{i,T}$. On the other hand, the transformer can use *in-weight learning* to learn from uninformative contexts, as long as the vocabulary remains the same from training to testing time. In these cases, when the input sequences do not contain the useful $(x_{i,T}, y_{i,T})$ subsequence, the transformer is forced to store, in its parameters, the function governing $x_{i,j} \mapsto y_{i,j}$ for each and every token. Consequently, in-weight learning does not generalize zero-shot to new tokens $x'_{i,j}$.

8.4.2 Context Is Environment

So far, this book has considered environments parameterized by indices $e \in \mathcal{E}$. Because categorical indices are disjoint, the resulting algorithms for invariance (discussed in chapter 5 and illustrated in figure 8.5a) must discard as spurious all patterns not appearing across the training environments. To illustrate, consider learning a predictor $f(x, e)$ on three training environments $\mathcal{E}_{\text{tr}} := \{e_1, e_2, e_3\}$, and evaluating it on some test environment $e \in \mathcal{E}_{\text{te}}$. Parameterizing these environments using indices leads to three shortcomings. First, the categorical parameterization does not capture information about the similarity between environments. For instance, the pair of environments $\{e_1, e_2\}$ could be more similar to each other than the pair $\{e_2, e_3\}$. Second, because the index of the test environment e is unknown to us, we cannot condition the machine as $f(x, e)$. Third, even if we knew the value of e, the test input (x, e) would inhabit a disjoint support with respect to the training environments for any $e \notin \mathcal{E}_{\text{tr}}$.

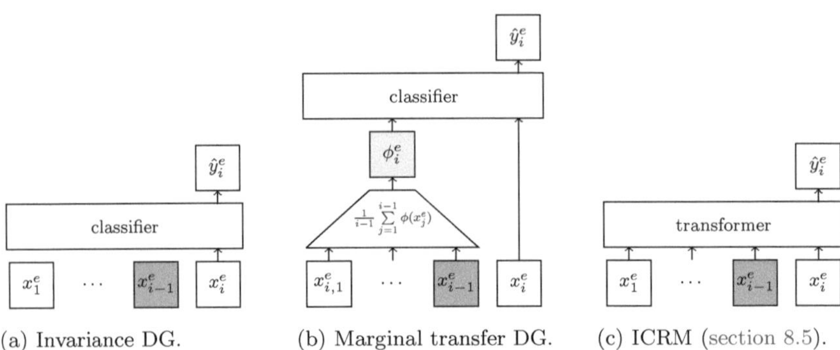

(a) Invariance DG.   (b) Marginal transfer DG.   (c) ICRM (section 8.5).

Figure 8.5: Three frameworks to predict the target y_i^e from the input x_i^e in test environment e. Depicted in dark shading, the last example x_{i-1}^e contains relevant features for the current prediction. (a) Invariance learning discards all the previously observed information from the test environment, removing too much of the predictive signal. (b) Marginal transfer learning summarizes all the previously observed test inputs as a coarse embedding, diluting the predictive signal found at the example level. (b) In-context risk minimization directly observes all the previous test inputs, allowing a search for *needle-in-the-haystack* patterns, including the relevant one in this illustration, x_{i-1}^e.

But one might employ richer, overlapping descriptors to characterize environments. For instance, consider sequential learning problems where each environment provides a sequence of unlabeled data. These unlabeled examples, arriving as *context*, could also serve as *environment* information useful to reveal invariant predictors.

One technique for parameterizing environments using unlabeled data is known as *marginal transfer learning*.[382–385] MTL implements a predictor of the form $f(x, \mu_e)$, where μ_e is a distributional footprint or summary of environment e. Most MTL implementations[382,384] build environment summaries as *mean embeddings* with the form

$$\mu_e = \frac{1}{m} \sum_{i=1}^{m} \psi(x_i^e),$$

where ψ is a nonlinear function and $\{x_i^e\}_{i=1}^m$ is the set of the unlabeled examples observed so far in environment e. By endowing ψ with sufficient capacity, the summary μ_e can encapsulate increasing amounts of information about the environment e, including invariance-inducing patterns. However, the summary μ^e is typically quite coarse, diluting the features of individual unlabeled examples, therefore leading to poor performance in *needle-in-the-haystack* prediction tasks.

Interestingly, the in-context learning ability of LLMs[26,55,370] is an elegant mechanism to adapt to environmental unlabeled test data $\{x_i^e\}_{i=1}^m$. In particular, consider predictions

$$\hat{y}_{m+1}^e = \text{LLM}(\underbrace{x_1^e, \ldots, x_m^e}_{\text{env.} \approx \text{context}}, x_{m+1}^e),$$

where every example (x_i^e, y_i^e) is drawn from the test environment e. This reveals a compelling parallel between the concept of *environment* in domain generalization and the concept of *context* in next-token prediction. Broadly speaking, different environments describe varying contextual circumstances—such as time, location, experiment, and background conditions. By describing environments in terms of rich contextual information, we aim to increase the amount of support overlap and amortized learning across environments. These rich descriptions, when expressed as free-form textual information, provide annotations about invariances shared across domains, including—as Judea Pearl notes—causal knowledge:

> Aside from being impressed, I have had to reconsider my proof that one cannot get any answer to any causal or counterfactual query from observational studies. What I didn't take into account is the possibility that the text in the training database would itself contain causal information. The programs can simply cite information from the text without experiencing any of the underlying data.[386]

In sum, viewing *environments as context* opens the door to using powerful next-token predictors off-the-shelf to address invariance (causal) learning problems, as these predictors are known for their ability to learn in-context. Conversely, describing *context as environment* helps frame LLM research within the framework of domain generalization, motivating the use of invariance learning algorithms across contexts.

8.5   In-Context Risk Minimization

The in-context risk minimization (ICRM) algorithm,[387] illustrated in figure 8.5c, is a practical application of in-context learning to address multiple environment and domain generalization problems. It works as follows.

- Collect a dataset of triplets $\mathcal{D} = \{(x_i, y_i, e_i)\}_{i=1}^n$, where the input-output (x_i, y_i) is drawn from environment e_i. Initialize a next-token predictor $\hat{y} = f(x; c)$, tasked with predicting the label y associated with the input x, as supported by the context c.

- During training, select $e \in \mathcal{E}_{\mathrm{tr}}$ at random. Draw t examples iid from this environment, then construct one input sequence $(x_1^e, \ldots, x_t^e)$ and its associated target sequence $(y_1^e, \ldots, y_t^e)$. Update the next-token predictor to minimize the auto-regressive loss $\sum_{j=1}^{t} \ell(f(x_j^e; c_j^e), y_j^e)$, where the context is $c_j^e = (x_1^e, \ldots, x_{j-1}^e)$, for all $j = 2, \ldots, t$, and $c_1^e = \emptyset$.

- During test time, a sequence of inputs $(x_1^{e'}, \ldots, x_{t'}^{e'})$ arrives for prediction, one by one, all from the test environment $e' \in \mathcal{E}_{\mathrm{te}}$. Predict $\hat{y}_j^{e'} = f(x_j^{e'}, c_j^{e'})$ for $x_j^{e'}$, where the context $c_j^{e'} = (x_1^{e'}, \ldots, x_{j-1}^{e'})$, for all $j = 2, \ldots, t'$, and $c_1^{e'} = \emptyset$.

While the most natural way to construct contexts would be to use the natural order of examples, most existing datasets contain shuffled examples. Therefore, the rest of this chapter considers building contexts by using unordered sets of unlabeled examples x_i^e sharing the same environment index e.

8.5.1 Theoretical Guarantees

The following results concern the joint distribution of

$$((X_1, \cdots X_t), (Y_1, \ldots, Y_t), E),$$

where each X_j, Y_j is drawn iid from the environment joint distribution $P^E(X, Y)$. The context of a given query X_j from environment E is $C_j = (X_1, \cdots, X_{j-1})$, also drawn from environment E. To orient these results, recall three predictors featured in the exposition so far, also summarized in table 8.1. First, the global empirical risk minimizer over the pooled training data estimates $P(Y \mid X)$. Second, the environment risk minimizer estimates $P(Y \mid X, E)$. Third, ICRM estimates the conditional expectation $P(Y \mid X, C)$.

Using the binary cross-entropy loss ℓ, the first result shows that ICRM *zooms-out* to the global ERM in the absence of context.

Proposition 8.1 (Zoom-out). *In the absence of context, ICRM behaves as a global ERM across the support of the training environments.*

A second result shows that ICRM zooms-in to the environment risk minimizer for sufficiently long contexts. Technically,

$$P(Y = 1 \mid X = x, E = e) = f^\star(x, \theta_x^e),$$

where θ_x^e are the environment features relevant to the test input x, for all $e \in \mathcal{E}$. Also, assume that there exists an ideal *amortization function* b taking the test input X and its preceding context C_t—both drawn from environment E—and converging almost surely to θ_X^E.

Paradigm	Training data	Testing data	Estimates
ERM	x, y	$x^{e'}$	$P(Y \mid X)$
IRM	x, y, e	$x^{e'}$	$P(Y \mid \phi^{\mathrm{inv}}(X))$
LLM	z	z_t and context $z_{j<t}$	$P(Z_{t+1} \mid Z_t, \ldots, Z_1)$
ICRM	x, y, e	$x_t^{e'}$ and context $c_t^{e'} = (x_j^{e'})_{j<t}$	$P(Y\mid X, C) \rightsquigarrow P^{e'}(Y \mid X)$

Table 8.1: Different learning paradigms discussed in this work, together with their training data and testing data formats, as well as the estimated predictors. In ICRM, we amortize the current input $x^{e'}$ and its context $c^{e'}$, containing previously experienced unlabeled examples from the same environment e', and *zoom-in* ($\rightsquigarrow$) to the appropriate local risk minimizer.

Theorem 8.1 (Full iid zoom-in). *Given the conditions in the previous paragraph, ICRM zooms-in to the environment risk minimizer in cross-entropy loss as the context length grows. Furthermore, if $I(Y; E \mid X) > 0$, then ICRM achieves lower cross-entropy loss than ERM.*

Theorem 8.1 states that ICRM converges (zooms-in) to the environment empirical risk minimizer given infinitely long contexts. The next result shows that ICRM can partially zoom-in to the environment risk minimizer with short contexts.

Theorem 8.2 (Partial iid zoom-in). *Assume that*

$$((X_1, \cdots X_t), (Y_1, \ldots, Y_t), E)$$

are Markovian with respect to a Bayesian network, where the query X and the environment E are statistically dependent and constitute the Markov blanket of Y. Then, ICRM partially zooms-in to the environment risk minimizer, improving the cross-entropy loss of the global empirical risk minimizer. The improvement is strictly monotonic with respect to context length.

To provide guarantees when the training and test environments differ, place assumptions on the data generation process. Consider the case

$$z \mid y, e \sim \mathcal{N}(\mu_e^y, \Sigma_e^y), \text{ and } x \leftarrow g(z).$$

Then, summarize the environment $e \in \mathcal{E}$ by the parameter vector

$$\gamma_e = \left[(p_e^y, \mu_e^y, \Sigma_e^y)_{y \in \{0,1\}} \right],$$

where p_e^y is the probability of label y in environment e. Unlike ERM algorithms that ignore context, the following result shows the robustness of in-context learners under such distribution shifts.

Theorem 8.3 (Full OOD zoom-in). *Consider the data triplets (x, y, e) generated from $z \sim \mathcal{N}(\mu_e^y, \Sigma_e^y)$ and $x \leftarrow g(z)$, $\forall e \in \mathcal{E}$, where g is a diffeomorphism. Then, there exists an in-context learner that, for infinitely long contexts, produces Bayes optimal predictions for all the test environments in the Voronoi cells[387] of the training environments.*

8.5.2 Empirical Performance

The following experiments assess the empirical performance of ICRM against marginal transfer methods such as adaptive risk minimization (ARM),[384] test-time adaptation proposals such as TENT,[379] and ERM. Following the DomainBed protocol,[301] all methods follow the same hyper-parameter selection criteria and employ the same convolutional neural network backbone to featurizer image inputs. For ICRM, a decoder-only GPT-2 further processes these features.[388] The experiments involve four image classification benchmarks, each offering a unique problem setting. FEMNIST[389] contains MNIST digits and handwritten letters from individual writers as environments. Rotated MNIST concerns varied rotational angles as environments. Tiny ImageNet-C[390] introduces diverse image corruptions to create multiple environments. Lastly, WILDS Camelyon17[391] studies tumor detection and sourcing data from multiple hospitals as distinct environments.

First, let us consider the adaptation of various algorithms to distribution shifts for increasing context lengths. Table 8.2 shows that ICRM outperforms all competing methods, both in terms of worst-group and average test accuracy. Interestingly, as seen for the Camelyon17 and ImageNet-C datasets, ICRM shows the best performance even in the absence of context. This is because ICRM benefits from context as privileged information during training,[392] allowing it to learn distributional features that can later be extracted from the query image alone.

A distinctive feature of ICRM is its ability to simultaneously consider the test input and its context for generating predictions. To visualize this capability, figure 8.6 shows the attention scores between some test inputs (in blue) and each element in their context. In the first row, the model attends to images featuring a digit *2* or two curved arcs (marked in green), while largely ignoring partial circles (marked in red). In the second row, ICRM pays most attention to those examples in the context with long horizontal lines, similar to those found in the test input. In the third row, ICRM attends not only to trains but also to the semantically related category of buses. In the fourth and last row, ICRM focuses on images containing people. Importantly, these attention patterns emerge solely from exposure to unlabeled examples, highlighting the strength of amortizing learning across multiple environments.

Data / method	Average test accuracy					Worst case test accuracy				
FEMNIST	0	25	50	75	100	0	25	50	75	100
ARM	49.5	83.9	84.4	84.7	84.6	23.6	59.5	60.7	57.0	58.8
TENT	78.1	77.9	81.2	82.5	83.3	55.2	57.2	63.3	65.9	67.2
ERM	**79.3**	79.3	79.3	79.3	79.3	59.0	59.0	59.0	59.0	59.0
ICRM	78.7	**87.2**	**87.4**	**87.5**	**87.8**	**59.8**	**69.3**	**70.6**	**70.6**	**70.6**
Rotated MNIST	0	25	50	75	100	0	25	50	75	100
ARM	36.5	94.2	95.1	95.3	95.5	28.2	85.3	87.2	87.9	87.9
TENT	94.1	88.0	91.9	93.8	94.3	80.2	88.5	88.5	80.2	81.3
ERM	**94.2**	94.2	94.2	94.2	94.2	80.8	80.8	80.8	80.8	80.8
ICRM	93.6	**96.1**	**96.2**	**96.2**	**96.2**	**82.5**	**88.5**	**88.5**	**88.8**	**88.8**
WILDS Camelyon17	0	25	50	75	100	0	25	50	75	100
ARM	61.2	59.5	59.7	59.7	59.7					
TENT	67.9	81.8	87.2	89.4	89.4			same as average accuracy		
ERM	68.6	68.6	68.6	68.6	68.6					
ICRM	**92.0**	**90.7**	**90.8**	**90.8**	**90.8**					
Tiny ImageNet-C	0	25	50	75	100	0	25	50	75	100
ARM	30.8	31.0	31.0	31.0	31.0	8.2	8.3	8.2	8.3	8.2
TENT	31.7	1.6	1.7	2.0	2.1	9.4	1.2	1.4	1.6	1.6
ERM	31.8	31.8	31.8	31.8	31.8	9.5	9.5	9.5	9.5	9.5
ICRM	**38.3**	**39.2**	**39.2**	**39.2**	**39.2**	**18.8**	**19.2**	**19.5**	**19.5**	**19.4**

Table 8.2: Average/worst OOD test accuracy for different context lengths, for adaptive risk minimization (ARM), empirical risk minimization (ERM), test entropy minimization (TENT), and ICRM on FEMNIST, Rotated MNIST, WILDS Camelyon17, and Tiny-ImageNet-C.

8.5.3 ICRM and the Invariance Principle

Thus far, this book has championed the Invariance Principle to learn robust predictors from data—that is, to find a feature representation such that the optimal classifier matches across environments. At first glance, ICRM seems to deviate from the Invariance Principle, as the algorithm relies on environment-specific information through context. Yet, as the following example illustrates, ICRM pursues the Invariance Principle on a different plane—namely, by estimating a "zooming-in" mechanism invariant across contexts (environments). To see this, consider a linear least-squares regression problem mapping two dimensional inputs $x = (x^1, x^2)$ onto a target y under environments $e \in \mathcal{E}$ as:

$$y = \alpha \cdot x^1 + \beta \cdot \mu_e^2 + \varepsilon, \tag{8.5}$$

where $\mu_e^i = \mathbb{E}[X^i \mid E = e]$, the pair (α, β) are invariant regression coefficients, and ε is an independent noise term. To ease exposition, let us provide ICRM directly with the relevant extended feature space $(x^1, x^2, \mu_e^1, \mu_e^2)$, rather than

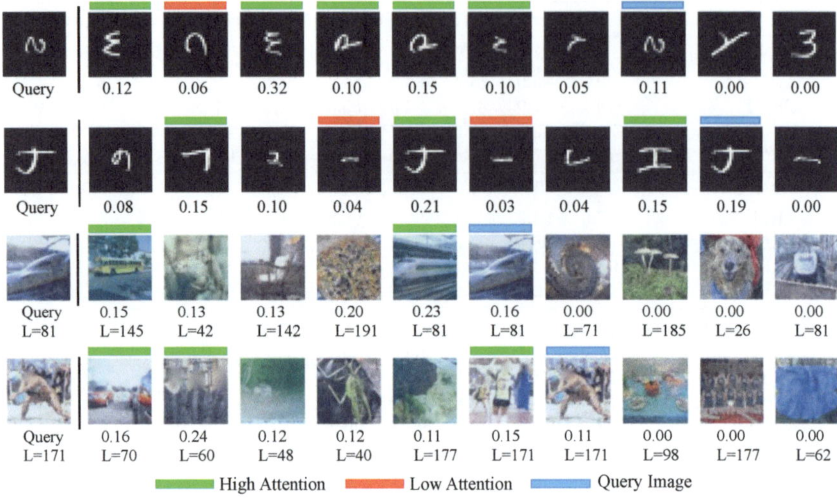

Figure 8.6: ICRM attention scores for test queries and their context, on FEMNIST (top two rows) and Tiny ImageNet-C (bottom two rows).

requiring the algorithm to learn such a representation from context.

In this setup, ICRM learns to predict using $\alpha \cdot x^1 + 0 \cdot x^2 + 0 \cdot \mu_e^1 + \beta \cdot \mu_e^2$. In contrast, ERM learns to predict using $\tilde{\alpha} \cdot x^1 + \tilde{\beta} \cdot x^2$. The key point is this: If $\beta \neq 0$ and $\mathrm{cov}(X^1, X^2) \neq 0$, then $\tilde{\alpha} \neq \alpha$, and the error rate of ERM grows with the variance of x^1 in new environments. By estimating the true invariant coefficient α, the error rate of ICRM remains unaffected by the variance of x^1. In addition, ICRM requires context *only during training* to learn the invariant predictor, ensuring robust zero-shot generalization to novel test environments. This demonstrates ICRM's capability to leverage privileged information[392] available only in training contexts.

The ICRM algorithm—and more generally, in-context learning—offers a fresh perspective on invariance. While classic invariance algorithms discard information in search of robustness, in-context learners include distributional footprints to reveal local invariances that might otherwise go unnoticed. While a zoomed-in environment risk minimizer may not be an invariant predictor across multiple environments, the *overall process of zooming-in* could be itself an invariant mechanism. Consider once again the question: Does smoking cause cancer? Not invariably across all relevant contexts or environments. Yet, smoking may cause cancer invariably across environments when conditioning on the appropriate environment distributional footprints Z, such as those concerning diet and genetic predispositions. Consequently, if I can estimate the distributional footprints Z_{te} via unlabeled examples from the test environment $\mathcal{E}_{\text{te}}$, then conditioning my predictor on Z_{te} is a legitimate route toward invariance and robustness. Of course, the success of this strategy depends on learning a zooming mechanism that focuses on—adjusts for—the right contextual patterns.

Under the ICRM perspective, the general problem of next-token prediction affords out-of-distribution generalization by describing environments as rich, hierarchical, and partially overlapping contexts that appear in natural order. Interestingly, the cognitive science literature describes mechanisms analogous to the zooming processes described in this chapter. For instance, Vervaeke and colleagues propose that such adaptive mechanisms govern the efficiency-resiliency, exploitation-exploration, specialization-generalization, and focusing-diversifying trade-offs fundamental to human intelligence:

> A brain ... will dynamically couple to its world in a way that is always trading off between being an efficient general purpose machine and being a resilient set of special purpose machines. Neither strategy is comprehensively fit, but to continually shift between them is. The brain is not trying to be either type of machine; the type of machine it becomes results from the coupling of its internal processing to both cross contextually invariant patterns, tracked by compression, and more contextually specific patterns which are tracked by particularization.[252]

Our ability to adapt to a given test environment, informed by unsupervised signals, gives rise to the two zooming processes discussed in this chapter. On one hand, unsupervised signals about the test environment allow us to tighten our grip, specialize, and *zoom-in* to spurious environmental correlations.[342] For example, doctors take into account comorbidities to tune their diagnoses, traders factor in noncausal indicators to make decisions, and when seeing green grass, we expect cows rather than camels. On the other hand, in the total absence of information about a test environment, we *zoom-out* and default to a generalist model based only on invariant correlations. Nonetheless, how to adapt the ICRM algorithm to zoom-out to IRM, rather than ERM, remains an open area for research.

8.6   Chain of Thought

The performance of LLMs improves when prompted to verbalize a *chain-of-thought* (CoT)[393]—that is, a series of intermediate steps explaining how to arrive at the solution of a reasoning task. To illustrate, consider the standard single-shot prompt to address arithmetic tasks:

> Q: Roger has 5 tennis balls. He buys 2 more cans of tennis balls.
> Each can has 3 tennis balls. How many tennis balls does he have
> now?
>
> A: The answer is 11.
>
> Q: The cafeteria had 23 apples. If they used 20 to make lunch and
> bought 6 more, how many apples do they have?[393]

Assume that the LLM replies with the wrong answer:

> A: The answer is 27.

Chain-of-thought prompting attempts to elucidate a correct answer by annotating the answer of the single-shot prompt with intermediate computation
steps. Consider the same example once again, where the chain-of-thought is
highlighted in italics:

> Q: Roger has 5 tennis balls. He buys 2 more cans of tennis balls.
> Each can has 3 tennis balls. How many tennis balls does he have
> now?
>
> A: *Roger started with 5 balls. 2 cans of 3 tennis balls each is 6 tennis
> balls. 5 + 6 = 11.* The answer is 11.
>
> Q: The cafeteria had 23 apples. If they used 20 to make lunch and
> bought 6 more, how many apples do they have?[393]

This time, let us assume, the LLM replies outputs a correct answer:

> A: *The cafeteria had 23 apples originally. They used 20 to make
> lunch. So they had 23 - 20 = 3. They bought 6 more apples, so they
> have 3 + 6 = 9.* The answer is 9.[393]

Because the machine was invited to generate a long response, this answer
contains its own chain-of-thought (also highlighted in italics). It is also
possible to prompt LLMs to produce chain-of-thought zero-shot, such as in:

> Q: The cafeteria had 23 apples. If they used 20 to make lunch and
> bought 6 more, how many apples do they have? *Please think step by
> step.*

Recent works have shown how to use reinforcement learning ("do more
of what works") to incentivize LLMs to produce increasingly long chains-
of-thought given the same question,[394] where CoT length often correlates
positively with reasoning performance. Lastly, it has been shown that
supervised fine-tuning on a handful of diverse, high-quality chain-of-thought
examples reveals significant reasoning capabilities hidden in pretrained LLM
models.[395]

Researchers have proposed various theories regarding the effectiveness of chain-of-thought. One theory suggests that longer sequences enable transformer-based language models to perform more extensive computations, thereby improving their likelihood of reaching correct answers. Another theory posits that encouraging chains-of-thought may prompt these models to zoom-in on statistical patterns gleaned from high-quality training data, because these often appear as meticulous step-by-step explanations in sources such as academic textbooks. In contrast, prompting models to deliver a "quick and dirty answer" might lead them to zoom-in on patterns learned from informal conversations, where participants are less cautious about their reasoning.

In my view, high-quality chain-of-thought prompting provides supervision about the invariant mechanism necessary to solve the task at hand. More precisely, chain-of-thought data expands input-output pairs $(x, w(\phi(x))$ into triplets $(x, \phi(x), w(\phi(x)))$ containing annotations about the intermediate computations performed by the invariant mechanism $\phi(x)$. Kartik Ahuja expresses a similar view, whereby "CoT annotations serve as privileged information, helpful in reducing underspecification and in learning a model that generalizes beyond training distribution."[396] Ahuja demonstrates that, for a variety of function classes and sufficiently diverse datasets, minimizing training error with chain-of-thought data aligns the learned function with the target function across relevant environments, thereby ensuring mechanism invariance and achieving out-of-distribution generalization.

Figure 8.7 illustrates these concepts by training two students to emulate the function $f = w \circ \phi$ implemented by a fixed teacher. All the networks involved are multilayer perceptrons with two input neurons, three hidden ReLU neurons, and one output neuron. The first student learns by empirical risk minimization on (x_i, y_i) pairs, where $x_i \sim \mathcal{N}(0, I_2)$ and $y_i = f(x_i)$. The second student has access to chain-of-thought data (x_i, c_i, y_i), where $c_i = \phi(x_i)$ is the three-dimensional vector of hidden activations happening in the teacher network when processing the input x_i. Therefore, the second student $\hat{f} = \hat{w} \circ \hat{\phi}$ trains to minimize both $\ell(\hat{f}(x_i), f(x_i))$ and $\ell(\hat{\phi}(x_i), \phi(x_i))$. The students are evaluated on in-domain data, where $x_i \in \mathcal{N}(0, I_2)$, and on out-domain data, where $x_i \in \mathcal{N}(\mu, \Sigma)$, for randomly chosen mean and covariance parameters. The student without access to CoT data obtains $6.386 \cdot 10^{-5}$ in-domain mean-squared error, 0.012 out-domain mean-squared error, and a parameter distance of 1.074 to the teacher network. In contrast, the student with access to CoT data obtains $5.681 \cdot 10^{-14}$ in-domain error, $1.501 \cdot 10^{-11}$ out-domain error, and a parameter distance of $1.529 \cdot 10^{-12}$. Therefore, CoT supervision enables mechanistic invariance and perfect out-of-distribution generalization.

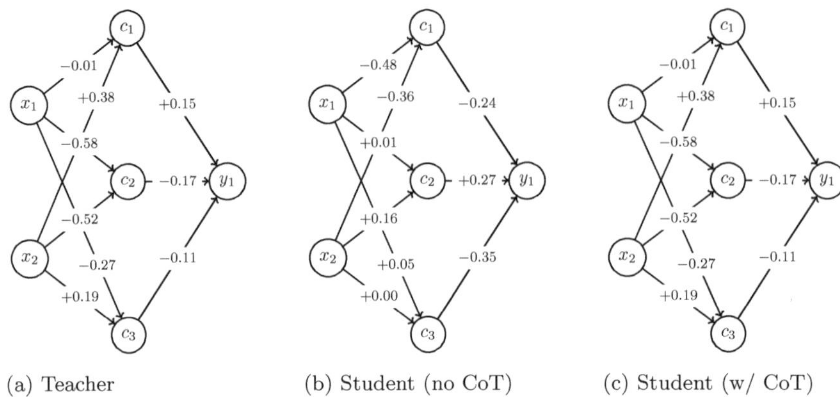

(a) Teacher (b) Student (no CoT) (c) Student (w/ CoT)

Figure 8.7: (a) Experiments using chain-of-thought data, where we train two students to imitate a teacher network. (b) The first student, learning with ERM on non-CoT data (x_i, y_i), converges to a collection of parameters quite different from those of the teacher. (c) The second student, learning with ERM on CoT data (x_i, c_i, y_i), achieves functional invariance with respect to the teacher network.

8.7 Future Prediction

In-context learning (ICL) and chain-of-thought (CoT) are two powerful mechanisms to mitigate underspecification and learn invariant predictors that generalize beyond the training distribution. When compared to next-token prediction (NTP), ICL and CoT enrich the input sequence to yield higher quality next-token predictions:

$$\text{NTP}: \quad P(\text{next-token} \mid \text{query}),$$
$$\text{ICL}: \quad P(\text{next-token} \mid \text{context}, \text{query}),$$
$$\text{CoT}: \quad P(\text{next-token} \mid \text{query}, \text{chain-of-thought}).$$

A second strategy to reduce underspecification is to learn LLMs that predict multiple tokens into the future at once.[371] This multi-token prediction[397] approach involves modeling conditional distributions such as:

$$\text{MTP}: \quad P(\text{next-token}, \text{second-next-token} \mid \text{query}).$$

MTP is effective at reducing underspecification by limiting the learning of spurious correlations due to teacher forcing[371,398] This argument becomes apparent as we increase the number of future tokens predicted at once. In the limit of predicting infinitely many tokens, MTP would be predicting the entire response sequence in one step, circumventing solutions that rely on teacher-forcing spurious correlations.

In practice, multi-token prediction architectures have (1) a common transformer architecture trunk, (2) one main output head in charge of next-token prediction, and (3) one auxiliary output head in charge of predicting the second next-token or a more advanced summary statistic about the future of the sequence. During inference time, the auxiliary head can either be discarded—yielding a regular next-token predictor—or utilized to accelerate token generations by means of speculative decoding.[397] State-of-the-art LLMs such as DeepSeek-V3[394,399] make use of multi-token prediction to improve their performance on reasoning benchmarks and accelerating token generation by a factor of $1.8\times$.

8.8   LLMs: Just Fiction Machines?

We must remember that LLMs, while undeniably impressive, are but sophisticated machines designed to

generate the most likely next word given a sequence of past words.

This function is often mistakenly equated with the far more challenging task of

generate the most verisimilar word given a sequence of past words.

Here, likelihood refers to "the chance that something will happen." Yet, as it turns out, truth is in many cases unexpected, surprising, and unpredictable[400]—in fact, low-probability events happen *all the time*. Confusing truth with likelihood is akin to mistaking the grass for the cow. Strictly speaking, LLMs are not guided by truth, but rather by narrative necessity:[372] With each new word generated, the set of likely continuations narrows and potentially departs from truth.

Before the theory of relativity was invented, as Léon Bottou notes in his talk "The Fiction Machine" to contrast likelihood and verisimilitude, its mathematical description was very far into the tail of likely sequences. The strong extrapolation capabilities necessary to develop new physical theories involve applying transformations learned in training to new, unseen content. For example, long conversations with a chatbot can evolve in ways that extend far beyond the pretraining corpus. In these scenarios, the machine continues to function effectively, Bottou argues, because the transformations that map *valid* sentences into other valid sentences can be learned from the training data and then applied to novel combinations of concepts. However, the structure of *true* sentences is much weaker, as it is broken by many transformations yielding valid sentences: For instance, changing the year in the sentence "America was discovered in 1492" yields an untruthful, yet valid sentence. Once again, truthfulness demands not only predictive power but invariance across a set of relevant predictive environments. Therefore, we must not confuse the awe-inspiring fluency of these models—attainable by mastery of syntax and other statistical patterns—with truthfulness. As discussed in chapter 5, truth requires a deep understanding of the invariances that structure the world, a challenging task that mere empirical risk minimization cannot achieve, no matter how large the dataset. As argued in chapter 3, humans often grasp these invariances by means of story-telling[401]—that is, the use of causal language to describe patterns that remain invariant under counterfactual versions of reality. The voice of Patrick Henry Winston (1943–2019) helps substantiate this argument:

> My belief is the distinguishing characteristic of humanity is this keystone ability to have descriptions with which we construct stories. I think stories are what make us different from chimpanzees and Neanderthals. And if story-understanding is really where it's at, we can't understand our intelligence until we understand that aspect of it.[402]

Nonetheless, following Nozick (section 5.6.5), if truthfulness is predictive power—likelihood—across environments, then the Invariance Principle should play a prominent role in creating grounded and factual LLMs.

Part IV

Related Technologies

Chapter 9

Learning Diverse Features

9.1   Introduction

This chapter examines a well-known[345,403,404] empirical observation: Learning invariant predictors $w \circ \phi$ is easier when we're given diverse features ϕ. In such cases, learning invariances w can reduce to selecting a few coordinates from $\phi(x)$, a task much simpler than modeling nonlinear, invariance-inducing representations directly from raw inputs x. This notion of leaving "breathing room" for multiple explanations, rather than prematurely committing to a single solution, dates back to the ancient Greek philosopher Epicurus (341–270 BCE):

> The wanings of the moon and its subsequent waxings might be due to the revolution of its own body, or equally well to successive conformations of the atmosphere, or again to the interposition of other bodies; they may be accounted for in all the ways in which phenomena on earth invite us to such explanations of these phases; provided only one does not become enamoured of the method of the single cause and groundlessly put the others out of court.[405]

In the context of this book, implementing the Epicurean method of multiple explanations requires avoiding *simplify-and-memorize* biases, preserving instead a diverse collection of features to predict the phenomena of interest from different perspectives. Taking the Waterbirds dataset as an example, a diverse feature method should extract *both* animal and landscape features, differing from empirical risk minimization (which tends to extract only landscape features) and direct invariance (which tends to extract only animal features) learning methods. Diverse features differ from disentangled features, which are often defined as independent factors of variation (section 3.4.4).[406] While disentangled features are diverse, the converse does not necessarily hold, as diverse features may include redundancies.

To learn diverse features, one must prioritize exploration over optimization, mine more information than necessary to attain zero training error, and deploy the procured redundancies as protection against distribution shifts. This tension between committing to the simplest zero training error solution versus affording multiple explanations is known as the *optimization-generalization dilemma*.[403] While learning multiple solutions to a single problem seems to contravene Vapnik's advice—"when solving a problem of interest, do not solve a more general problem as an intermediate step"[78]—the methods described in this chapter have proven valuable when the structure of the test environment (that is, the "problem of interest") is uncertain.

9.2 Diverse Features via a Single Model

This section explores three methods to learn a single machine with a diverse feature space: spectral decoupling, dropout, and self-supervised learning. Broadly speaking, these strategies increase the difficulty of the learning process, in order to prevent the machine from becoming overly confident in its predictions. Mitigating this overconfidence helps avoid a common phenomenon known as "neural collapse,"[407] where over-parameterized models map all examples from the same class to a singular point, significantly reducing feature diversity.

9.2.1 Spectral Decoupling

Pezeshki and colleagues describe the *simplify-and-memorize* bias in terms of *gradient starvation*, a phenomenon where "loss is minimized by capturing only a subset of features relevant for the task, despite the presence of other predictive features that fail to be discovered." Figure 9.1 exemplifies gradient starvation by means of a two-dimensional, linearly separable binary classification problem. On the left, ERM simplifies-and-memorizes to learn a zero training error solution that uses the horizontal feature exclusively. However, the fast and confident learning of this solution suppresses the gradients that are necessary to explore a richer feature space—one that also incorporates the vertical feature—and to estimate a decision boundary capturing the data's underlying nonlinear structure.

To mitigate gradient starvation, Pezeshki and colleagues propose reducing predictive overconfidence by means of the *spectral decoupling* (SD)[105]

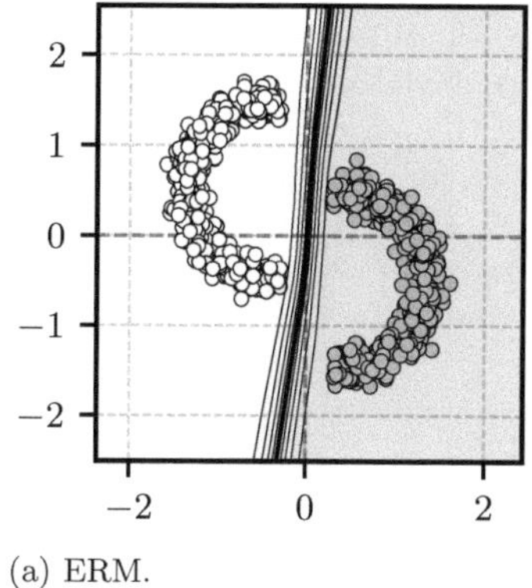

(a) ERM.

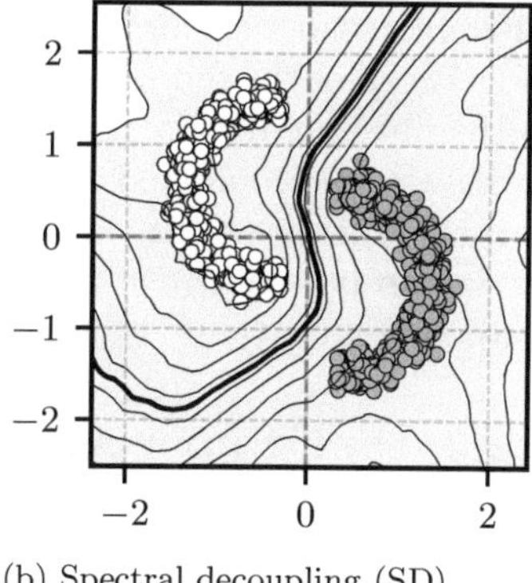

(b) Spectral decoupling (SD).

Figure 9.1: ERM and SD learn a different decision boundary on a two-dimensional, linearly separable binary classification problem. ERM quickly and tightly grips the horizontal feature, the simplest explanation attaining zero training error. In contrast, SD minimizes predictive overconfidence to recruit all available features, capturing the data's nonlinear structure.

regularizer:

$$\frac{1}{n}\sum_{i=1}^{n}\ell(f(x_i), y_i) + \lambda \cdot \|f(x_i)\|^2.$$

To understand the impact of the SD regularizer, recall that neural networks optimize cross-entropy loss by producing large logits, resulting in neural collapse. In contrast, the SD regularizer fights against overconfident predictions by penalizing large logits. Consequently, the machine is compelled to recruit more features: not too tightly to avoid large logits, but not too loosely to ensure low cross-entropy loss. As illustrated in figure 9.1b, SD recruits all available features to implement a decision boundary that captures the data's nonlinear structure. The resulting solution exhibits a larger margin, potentially enhancing robustness in testing scenarios where the two classes approach each other.

9.2.2 Dropout

Dropout[408] is a regularization method for training neural networks; it involves setting to zero a small percentage—typically, around 20%—of neural activations during each forward pass. This mechanism prevents the network from becoming overly dependent on specific neurons, encouraging the learning of diverse features. In essence, dropout implements a slightly different predictor during each forward pass, implemented as a random subnetwork of the full neural architecture. At test time, dropout is disabled, so the final predictor can be interpreted as the average of all the random subnetworks encountered during training, therefore bearing some similarities to a bagging ensemble (section 9.3.1).[409] As we will review in chapter 11, leaving dropout active at test time is one popular technique to estimate the predictive uncertainty of a neural network.

9.2.3 Self-Supervised Learning

The goal of self-supervised learning (SSL) algorithms is to extract *general purpose* features from large amounts of unlabeled data. By sidestepping the constraints of predefined labels, SSL algorithms offer the potential to reduce simplify-and-memorize biases and discover more diverse features. SSL algorithms proceed by defining a *pretext* learning task on a large corpus of unlabeled data. These pretext tasks often involve solving "fill in the blanks" problems, such as reconstructing masked regions in images[410] or predicting the next word in large language modeling (chapter 8).

For example, consider the problem of learning representations of images useful across various downstream tasks. A standard approach in self-supervised learning[411] follows these steps:

1. Produce two randomized data augmentations of the same image x, denoted as x_s and x_t. The specific choice of augmentations determines the invariances encoded in the learned representation; for instance, random rotations induce rotational invariance.

2. Encode x_s by means of a student encoder ϕ_s, and encode x_t by means of a teacher encoder ϕ_t.

3. Update the encoders as to minimize the distance $d(\phi_s(x_s), \phi_t(x_t))$. Common choices for d include the mean-squared error, the cross-entropy loss (after sending both student and teacher representations through a softmax layer), or the InfoNCE loss (described below).

4. While updating the encoders, implement a mechanism to prevent *representational collapse*, whereby the encoders trivially minimize distances by producing constant outputs $\phi_s(x_s) = \phi_t(x_t) = c$. Some popular techniques include:

   - Slow down the teacher's updates by defining them as a running average of the student's updates.[411]

   - When using the cross-entropy loss as the distance function, center the teacher's outputs by means of the Sinkhorn-Knopp algorithm.[9]

- When using the InfoNCE loss, maximize the distance between random data augmentations of *different pairs* of images. This strategy, known as contrastive SSL, requires large mini-batches to find dissimilar random image pairs, and it scales poorly to high-dimensional representations.[412] In addition, contrastive learning struggles with class imbalances, as they decrease the probability of finding dissimilar random image pairs.

- Implement explicit regularizers to maximize the information content of the encoders. For example, the VICReg method[413] uses the mean squared-error distance function, while promoting features with unit variance and pairwise null covariances.

5. Let the resulting student encoder $\phi_s = \phi_{s,p} \circ \phi_{s,b}$, where $\phi_{s,p}$ is known as the projector and $\phi_{s,b}$ is known as the backbone. The final representation function is the backbone $\phi_{s,b}$. Often, the projector $\phi_{s,p}$ consists of the last two or three layers of the student encoder. Discarding the projector alleviates neural collapse,[407] recovers some of the low-level and mid-level features necessary to distinguish individuals within the same class, and yields better downstream performance.

SSL frameworks lend themselves naturally to problems involving prediction under uncertainty. To illustrate, consider Yann LeCun's well-known *falling pen* video prediction task. The examples in this task are short videos in which a pen, initially held upright against a flat surface, is released to fall in an unpredictable direction. When facing this task, classic supervised learning algorithms, shown in figure 9.2a, would learn a machine $w \circ \phi$ by minimizing some pixel reconstruction loss $\ell(w(\phi(x)), y)$. However, since all the videos begin in a similar fashion but diverge in their outcomes, the resulting machine would always predict an average sequence of frames $\hat{y}$, where a blurry pen appears to fall in all directions simultaneously.

Joint embedding predictive architectures (JEPAs),[410] illustrated in figure 9.2b, form a self-supervised learning framework capable of predicting under uncertainty. A JEPA can be implemented in three steps. First, encode the input x as the input embedding $\phi_x(x)$ and encode the target y as the target embedding $\phi_y(y)$. Second, predict the target embedding $\phi_y(y)$ as $w(\phi_x(x), z)$, where $\phi_x(x)$ is the input embedding, z is a latent variable, and w is a predictor function. Third, update the parameters in (ϕ_x, ϕ_y, w) by minimizing the distance between $\phi_y(y)$ and $w(\phi_x(x), z)$. At test-time, JEPA formulates *prediction as optimization*:

$$\hat{y} = \arg\min_y \min_z \ell(w(\phi_x(x), z), \phi_y(y)). \tag{9.1}$$

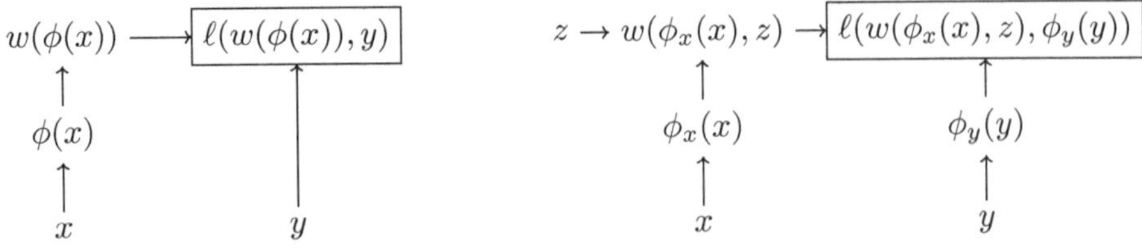

(a) Classic architecture with predictions $\hat{y} = w(\phi(x))$.

(b) JEPA architecture, with predictions $\hat{y} = \arg\min_y \min_z \ell(w(\phi_x(x), z), \phi_y(y))$.

Figure 9.2: Comparison of classic supervised learning architectures with the joint embedding predictive architecture (JEPA).

This optimization searches for both (1) the configuration of the latent variable z, explaining away the unpredictable patterns in data, and (2) the requested prediction $\hat{y}$. To make JEPA computationally efficient, one can solve equation (9.1) by performing gradient descent directly on the continuous space associated with the target embedding $\phi_y(y)$, then use a separate decoding process to produce $\hat{y}$ from the optimized continuous vector. However, the JEPA equation (9.1) relates to energy-based models,[414] where an *energy function* $F(x, y) = \min_z \ell(w(\phi_x(x), z), \phi_y(y))$ is learned to be a surface with low values for coherent (x, y) pairs, and with high values elsewhere. The problem of guaranteeing high values for incoherent pairs $(x, y' \neq y)$ is nontrivial and relates to the aforementioned problem of avoiding representational collapse. Because of this issue, implementing JEPA at scale is an ongoing research direction.

9.3 Diverse Features via Ensembles

A popular strategy to learn diverse features is to combine multiple predictors, also called *members*, into one *ensemble model*. Thomas G. Dietterich lists three reasons why model ensembles can be more accurate than the individual members that constitute them.[415] As illustrated in figure 9.3, these three reasons concern the statistical, computational, and representational aspects of learning. First, the statistical reason argues that combining multiple zero training error solutions reduces the risk of overcommitting to the wrong solution. Second, the computational reason builds on the fact that some learning algorithms, such as gradient descent, require a lot of computation to converge to the bottom of the loss landscape. By combining multiple optimization trajectories that approach the same basin of the loss landscape from different angles, the ensemble model can land closer to the center

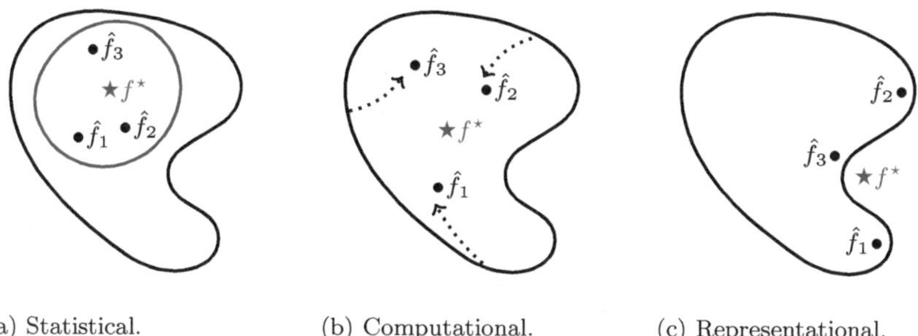

| (a) Statistical. | (b) Computational. | (c) Representational. |

Figure 9.3: Dietterich's three reasons for why ensembling three predictors $(\hat{f}_1, \hat{f}_2, \hat{f}_2)$ can bring us closer to the best possible predictor $f^\star$, namely statistical (reducing overcommitment to a wrong predictor), computational (approaching the same wide minima from different angles), and representational (being able to model functions outside the hypothesis space).

and bottom of the loss basin and enjoy better generalization properties.[336] Third, the representational issue argues that combining multiple predictors enlarges our hypothesis space, allowing us to estimate target functions out of reach for individual predictors.

Because of these reasons, consequential decisions are often made by ensembles: juries, committees, panels of experts, and voters, among others. In "Man Versus Model of Man," Paul E. Meehl compares the performance of human clinicians versus their machine learning distillations, illustrating the power of ensemble methods:

> Linear regression models of clinical judges can be more accurate diagnostic predictors than are the humans who are modeled. ... For the clinician is not a machine. While he possesses his full share of human learning and hypothesis-generating skills, he lacks the machine's reliability. He "has his days:" boredom, fatigue, illness, situational and interpersonal distractions all plague him, with the result that his repeated judgments of the exact same stimulus configuration are not identical. ... The composite [average] judgment of all 29 clinicians, which was more accurate than that of the typical individual judge, was not improved by the modeling procedure.[416]

The rest of this section surveys the three main strategies to build ensembles: combining model predictions, features, and weights.

9.3.1 Combining Model Predictions

Combining member predictions is a common strategy for building an ensemble model. A typical approach involves training K diverse neural networks f_k. To achieve diversity, each neural network can be initialized randomly, use different hyper-parameters, or observe the data in different orders and under various data augmentations.[417] In particular, averaging member predictions results in the *bagging* ensemble:

$$f(x) = \frac{1}{K} \sum_{k=1}^{K} f_k(x).$$

The error of such a bagging ensemble can be decomposed as

$$\underset{x}{\mathbb{E}} \left[\mathrm{Bias}(f \mid x)^2 + \frac{1}{K} \cdot \mathrm{Var}(f \mid x) + \left(1 - \frac{1}{K} \right) \cdot \mathrm{Cov}(f \mid x) \right], \qquad (9.2)$$

where the terms represent the conditional bias, variance, and covariance averaged over the K members.[418] Bagging ensembles are most effective when their members strike a good balance between bias and variance, and when their predictions are uncorrelated. Consequently, bagging ensembles outperform their members in the presence of feature diversity—the key concept in this chapter. Beyond improving performance on iid data, bagging offers advantages in predictive calibration, uncertainty quantification, and generalization to out-of-distribution settings.[417] Unlike bagging, *boosting* ensembles adopt a sequential learning strategy, where each model is trained to address the errors made by the previous ones.[419]

Some recent research has focused on building ensembles with *maximally diverse* members. In the *agree to disagree*[340] model, members are designed to agree on in-distribution labeled data and disagree on out-distribution unlabeled data. To achieve this, the first member h_1 learns using ERM on in-domain data. Then, the second member h_2 also learns using ERM on in-domain data, but uses out-domain data to increase its predictive discrepancy against h_1. This idea is similar to the *Universum*,[420] where predictors learn to have high-confidence (large margin), in-distribution, and low-confidence (small margin) out-distribution. Similarly, *diversify and disambiguate*[339] trains a predictor with multiple output heads that (1) have low error on the in-domain labeled data, (2) produce predictions with low pairwise mutual information on the out-domain unlabeled data, and (3) reproduce the marginal distribution of the in-domain labels across predictions in the out-domain unlabeled data. Finally, the method chooses as a final predictor the output head with the best accuracy on a validation set of labeled out-domain samples.

The Bonsai algorithm[403] implements a discovery phase and a synthesis phase. The discovery phase comprises multiple rounds, where each round trains a robust predictor on the mistakes from previous rounds, forcing the discovery of diverse features. The synthesis phase relies on self-distillation to produce a final predictor that recruits all the previously discovered features. Throughout a variety of experiments, Zhang and colleagues show that the feature representation learned by Bonsai is a good initialization for invariance learning algorithms.

9.3.2 Combining Model Features

A second strategy for constructing an ensemble model is to concatenate the representations ϕ_k of their members f_k, then train a wide linear classifier w on this composite input:

$$f(x) = w(\phi_1(x), \ldots, \phi_K(x)).$$

Zhang and Bottou argue that "although optimization can produce diverse features a single run is unable to collect them all into a diverse representation that performs better when tasks or distributions change."[421] Concatenation ensembles, therefore, enjoy "representations [that] roughly carry equivalent information with respect to the training distribution, but, at the same time, may be very far from carrying equivalent information with respect to a new distribution."[421] Empirically, the concatenation approach yields gains in both out-of-distribution performance and the stability of invariance learning algorithms, suggesting that "premature feature selection is not a smart way to prepare for distribution changes,"[421] and that rich representations are advantageous when learning across multiple environments.

9.3.3 Combining Model Weights

Combining member weights is an increasingly popular strategy to construct ensembles:

$$f(x) = f_{\frac{1}{K} \sum_{k=1}^{K} \theta_k}(x),$$

where $\theta_k = (w_k, \phi_k)$. The main benefit of building ensembles by combining model weights is that, at test time, we only need to store one single parameter vector. However, weight average ensembles require that their members are fine-tunings of the same pretrained model. This is because different fine-tunings of a same pretrained model are *linearly connected* within the same basin of the loss landscape, a counterintuitive result first discussed by Behnam Neyshabur and colleagues:

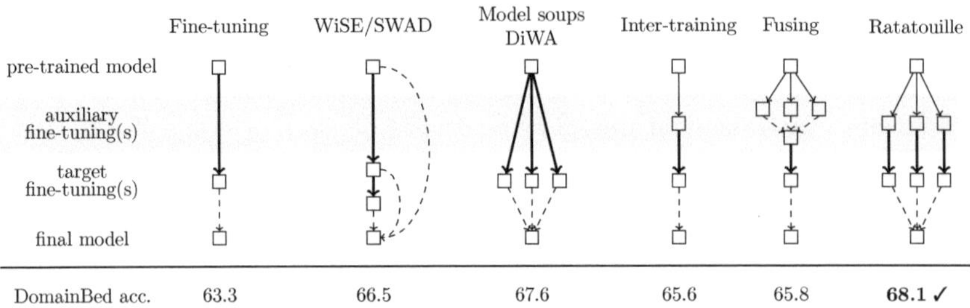

Figure 9.4: Weight combination strategies all start with a pretrained foundation model. Some strategies fine-tune the pretrained model on auxiliary tasks (thin solid arrows): These auxiliary fine-tunings can be performed by different contributors of the community on their own data. Then, all strategies perform fine-tuning on the target task of interest (thick solid arrows). Finally, the weights fine-tuned on the target task are used as is, or are averaged (dashed arrows) into a final model.

> There is no performance barrier between two instances of models trained from pretrained weights, which suggests that the pretrained weights guide the optimization to a flat basin of the loss landscape ... Moreover, interpolating two random solutions from the same basin could generally produce solutions closer to the center of the basin, which potentially have better generalization performance than the endpoints.[422]

In contrast, weight-averaging the members inhabiting different basins of the loss landscape (e.g., different pretrained models) results in ensembles that can no longer address the prediction task.

In recent years, researchers have developed various techniques to combine member weights into high-performing ensembles, illustrated in figure 9.4 and described below. SWAD[336] performs a single fine-tuning of a pretrained model and instantiates one ensemble member every few iterations. Model Soups[423] and DiWA[337] fine-tune the same pretrained model multiple times, using different hyper-parameters and data orderings. The error of the resulting ensembles follows a similar decomposition to equation (9.2), with a fourth term penalizing the distance between each fine-tuning and their common pretraining parameter vector.[337] Model Ratatouille[424] fine-tunes the same pretrained model on different auxiliary datasets, yielding ensembles with very diverse members and state-of-the-art out-of-distribution generalization.

Chapter 10

Learning from Combinations of Examples

10.1 Introduction

This chapter discusses methods to reduce the underspecification in learning problems by imposing equivariance constraints on the predictors. The idea is as follows: Since zero training error solutions make identical predictions on all training examples, good and bad machines must differ in their behavior outside the training data. To further mitigate underspecification (the proliferation of zero training error solutions), our goal is to constrain predictions in the vicinity of training examples. The framework of vicinal risk minimization (VRM),[425] also known as covariant data augmentation, is one tool to achieve this task. In VRM, we train machines that minimize the *vicinal risk*:

$$R_V(f) = \frac{1}{n} \sum_{i=1}^{n} \mathop{\mathbb{E}}_{(\tilde{x}_i, \tilde{y}_i) \sim V(x_i, y_i)} [\ell(f(\tilde{x}_i), \tilde{y}_i)]. \tag{10.1}$$

In contrast to the usual ERM objective (2.3), VRM augments each of the training examples (x_i, y_i) into a collection of virtual examples $(\tilde{x}_i, \tilde{y}_i)$ drawn from the vicinal distribution $V(x_i, y_i)$. In practice, each evaluation of the objective (10.1) replaces the expectation by a fresh draw from the vicinal distribution. Thus, the objective (10.1) guides the model not only in making accurate predictions at each training example (x_i, y_i) but also in how to extrapolate to the surrounding neighborhood described by the vicinal distribution $V(x_i, y_i)$.

VRM relates to well-known learning paradigms. For instance, linear regression under the squared loss and the vicinal distribution $V(x,y) = (N(x,\sigma^2), y)$ results in Tikhonov regularization, leading to the ridge regression reviewed in section 2.3.1:

$$\mathbb{E}\left[y \mid X = x\right] = x(X^\top X + \sigma^2 I)^{-1} X^\top y.$$

As a corner case, VRM falls back to ERM when we let the vicinal distribution be $V(x,y) = \mathrm{Delta}((x,y))$. The original VRM work provides further examples related to Parzen windows estimators, restricted logistic regressors, and support vector machines. This pioneering work also introduces the use of consistency regularization to leverage unlabeled data,[425] discussed here in section 10.5. Within the context of supervised learning $y \approx f(x)$, we will consider two types of vicinal distributions useful to model different mathematical constraints:

- Vicinal distributions $(\tilde{x}, y) \sim V(x,y)$ that transform only inputs allow modeling invariances $f(g \cdot x) = f(x)$, where g stands for a group action on the input space.

- Vicinal distributions $(\tilde{x}, \tilde{y}) \sim V(x,y)$ jointly transforming inputs and outputs allow modeling equivariances $f(g \cdot x) = g' \cdot f(x)$, where g' stands for a group action on the target space.

Choosing the appropriate vicinal distribution for the learning problem at hand requires additional assumptions or domain expertise. If chosen correctly, VRM reduces the underspecification of the learning problem by informing the machine about what constitutes good behavior outside the training examples, and consequently reduces the amount of zero training error solutions. However, a poorly chosen vicinal distribution may enforce the wrong set of invariances unto the learning machine—for instance, one should not enforce rotational invariance when the learning problem consists of predicting rotations.

VRM is a data augmentation technique, the practitioner's tool of choice to enforce invariance as early as possible in the prediction pipeline. Consider a vicinal distribution $V(x,y)$ designed to generate versions of the input x rotated by a random angle, paired with the original label y. This is analogous to a data augmentation protocol performing random rotations on the training inputs, a common method to learn classifiers with rotational invariance. However, in addition, VRM allows the simultaneous transformation of a training input x_i and its associated label y_i, resulting in *covariant* data augmentation protocols. Continuing with the rotation example, VRM allows transforming the target y_i of a digit "6" into the label of a digit "9" when a rotation of 180° is applied to the image x_i.

The following introduces a simple—yet incredibly effective—nonparametric vicinal distribution. Specifically, consider machines that consume k inputs to produce their k associated predictions. Considering $k = 2$ to simplify exposition without loss of generality, we will study vicinal distributions with the form

$$V(x_i, y_i) = \frac{1}{n} \sum_{j=1}^{n} \text{Delta}((h_x(x_i, x_j), h_y(y_i, y_j))), \qquad (10.2)$$

where h_x and h_y are a pair of *mixing functions* that instruct the machine about how to behave in between random pairs of training examples (x_i, y_i) and (x_j, y_j). Therefore, the more data we collect, the more augmentations we can provide about one particular example. While often used for image classification tasks, the data augmentation protocols introduced in this chapter are agnostic and applicable to all types of data.

This ability to compose observations to create new exemplars, abstract categories, and concepts is a hallmark of human intelligence.[426] Particularly, humans have envisioned alternatives to reality by combining known objects for as long as art has existed.[427] The earliest cave art, recently discovered on the Indonesian island of Sulawesi, features half-human, half-animal therianthropes. The oldest statue ever discovered is a 35000-year-old lion-man unearthed in Germany.[162] Ancient Egypt was one of many civilizations with a mythology inhabited by half-human, half-animal deities. The rest of this chapter introduces a simple technique to endow learning machines with a preliminary degree of such compositional imagination.

10.2 The mixup Data-Augmentation Technique

mixup is a simple mixing strategy to construct random convex combinations of random pairs of examples:

$$\lambda \sim \text{Beta}(\alpha, \alpha),$$
$$\tilde{x} = h_x^{\text{mix}}(x_i, x_j) = \lambda \cdot x_i + (1 - \lambda) \cdot x_j,$$
$$\tilde{y} = h_y^{\text{mix}}(y_i, y_j) = \lambda \cdot y_i + (1 - \lambda) \cdot y_j. \qquad (10.3)$$

Here (x_i, y_i) and (x_j, y_j) are a random pair of training examples, described in terms of their features x and one-hot labels y. (To extend mixup to regression problems, a nearest-neighbor approach has been suggested.[428]) The scalar $\lambda \in [0, 1]$ is a mixing coefficient drawn at random from the Beta(α, α) distribution. As illustrated in figure 10.1, the mixup parameter $\alpha > 0$ denotes the strength of mixing, recovering the usual ERM principle as $\alpha \to 0$, the uniform$(0, 1)$ distribution for $\alpha = 1$, and solely producing

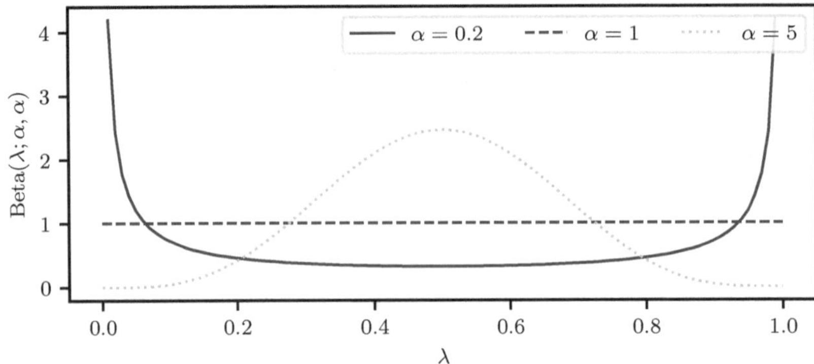

Figure 10.1: Examples of the Beta(α, α) distribution used in *mixup*. Some important cases include (1) the uniform$[0, 1]$ distribution for $\alpha = 1$, (2) the Bernoulli($\frac{1}{2}$) distribution for $\alpha \to 0$, and (3) the Delta($\frac{1}{2}$) distribution for $\alpha \to \infty$. Therefore, mixup reverts to ERM for $\alpha \to 0$.

averages of examples as $\alpha \to \infty$. The Beta(α, β) distribution, thanks to Karl Pearson's work over a century ago, is commonly used to describe probabilities of percentages. Letting $\beta := \alpha$ results in symmetric distributions, assigning the same probability to both λ and $1 - \lambda$, which is appropriate for our purposes. The generalization of the Beta distribution to multiple variables is known as the Dirichlet distribution, but research suggests there is no empirical advantage to mixing more than two examples.[429] The mixup hyperparameter α is chosen by cross-validation. Algorithm 10.1 lists the few lines of PyTorch necessary to implement mixup, which results in minimal computational overhead with respect to ERM. Mathematically, mixup training tries to preserve the equivariance expressed by the formula $f(\lambda x_i + (1 - \lambda)x_j) = \lambda f(x_i) + (1 - \lambda)f(x_j)$.

```
1  def mixup(x, y, alpha=1):
2      l = torch.distributions.Beta(alpha, alpha).sample()
3      p = torch.randperm(len(x))
4      xm = l * x + (1 - l) * x[p]
5      ym = l * y + (1 - l) * y[p]  # y has one-hot-vector rows
6      return xm, ym
```

Algorithm 10.1: PyTorch code to produce a mixup mini-batch.

Figure 10.2: Illustration of *mixup* on the cow-on-the-beach problem. mixup constructs random convex combinations of examples and their one-hot labels. In this example, the random mixing coefficient is $\lambda = 0.3$. When both images have similar backgrounds, the machine must rely on animal features to classify all possible random convex combinations. This results in less reliance on background spurious correlations.

Training a machine on examples (10.3) is known as *mixup*,[429] a process illustrated in figure 10.2. mixup gained popularity by improving the generalization performance,[430–432] predictive calibration,[433,434] uncertainty estimation,[435,436] resilience to noisy labels,[429] and adversarial robustness[437,438] of learning machines in various domains, including computer vision, speech recognition, natural language processing, and generative adversarial networks.[429] At the time of the original publication, mixup ($\alpha = 0.4$) set a new state of the art on the ImageNet dataset, lowering the top-5 error percentage from 22.0% to 20.8%, the top-1 error percentage from 6.1% to 5.4%, and the adversarial error under FSGM attack from 90% to 75%, all for a ResNet-101 trained during 200 epochs. Likewise, it achieved a new state of the art for the CIFAR-10 (lowering classification error from 5.6% to 4.2% on clean labels, and from 36% to 24% on 80% corrupted labels) and CIFAR-100 (from 25.6% to 21.1%) datasets for a ResNet-18. Since its inception, mixup has become a central component in the training of large neural networks[439] and certain language models.[440] While straightforward, the application of mixup in next-token prediction tasks is currently underexplored. For these models, we draw two random mini-batches of size $b \times d \times t$, embed all tokens, mix the two mini-batches with a random coefficient, and train to predict the corresponding mixed one-hot labels.

There are three main data augmentation techniques related to mixup. First, the synthetic minority over-sampling technique (SMOTE) manufactures virtual examples by interpolating inputs of nearby examples from small classes, while leaving the labels unchanged.[441] Second, *cutmix*[442] extends mixup by creating virtual examples:

$$\lambda \sim \mathrm{Beta}(\alpha, \alpha),$$
$$\tilde{x} = h_x^{\mathrm{cut}}(x_i, x_j) = M \odot x_i + (1 - M) \odot x_j,$$
$$\tilde{y} = h_y^{\mathrm{cut}}(y_i, y_j) = \lambda \cdot y_i + (1 - \lambda) \cdot y_j,$$

where M is a binary mask filled with ones, except for a random box filled with zeros and occupying an area of percentage $1 - \lambda$. When dealing with image data, cutmix constructs virtual examples by pasting a random box from x_j into the corresponding location of x_i. Third, the data augmented loss invariant regularization method (DAIR)[443] minimizes the variance in loss between each example and its augmentations:

$$\mathrm{DAIR}(f) = \ell(f(x_i), y_i) + \ell(f(\tilde{x}_i), y_i) + \lambda \cdot \left(\sqrt{\ell(f(x_i), y_i)} - \sqrt{\ell(f(\tilde{x}_i), \tilde{y}_i)} \right)^2.$$

One special feature of mixup, cutmix, and DAIR is their ability to handle *covariant* augmentations, which perturb both input and target jointly to enforce equivariance constraints.

10.2.1 Why Does mixup Work?

It is unclear why training on mixtures of examples, often blurry and unnatural, would improve the performance of learning machines on clean test instances. So why exactly does mixup work? While the full answer is a matter of active research, we can identify three intertwined effects arising from the deceivingly simple mixup rule.

First, mixup promotes machines that behave linearly in between training examples. In particular, mixup forces the learning machine to behave like the linear discriminant, where any point between two points from the same class region also falls in that same class region. Linear behavior counters undesired oscillations that the machine may exhibit in untrained regions of the input space. This inductive bias is similar to that achieved by ensembling, where the averaged members agree on training examples and differ only due to random initialization, thus averaging out random fluctuations and enhancing linearity. mixup enforces this criterion explicitly in the directions spanned by convex combinations of random pairs of training examples. In fact, as shown in figure 10.3, mixup and ensemble decision boundaries are alike, both providing more gradual transitions in between classes than ERM.[436] Moreover, ensembles minimize the mixup loss without ever seeing or optimizing for such a criterion.

Promoting linear behavior in turn promotes smoothness. Because decision boundaries that transition linearly in between classes lead to better

(a) ERM   (b) Ensemble   (c) mixup   (d) mixup loss

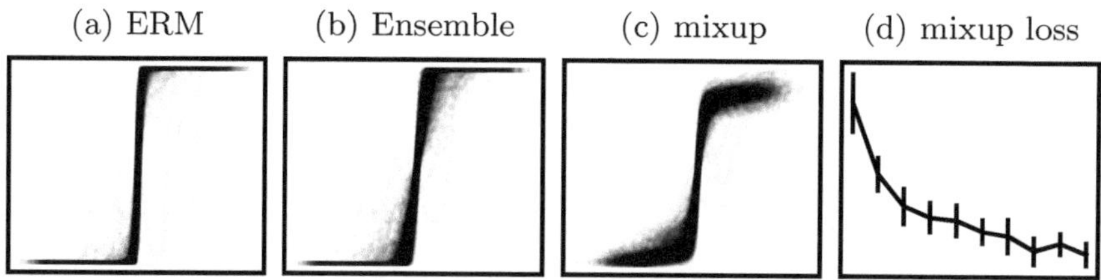

Figure 10.3: Deep ensembles and mixup show smoother decision boundaries than ERM (first three panels). On one hand, ensembles linearize their decision boundaries by averaging zero training error predictors that fluctuate randomly in-between training examples. On the other hand, mixup optimizes for this linear behavior explicitly during training. As we add more members to a deep ensemble, the resulting predictor exhibits a lower mixup loss, though it has never been trained to minimize that statistic (fourth panel).

calibrated predictions,[434] the softmax output $\sigma(f(x))_j$ of mixup machines better estimates the true conditional probability $p(y = j \mid x)$. In contrast, ERM decision boundaries are sharp step functions that transition suddenly from one class to another in a narrow band of input space. The two middle plots in figure 10.4 illustrate this difference in smoothness between ERM and mixup decision boundaries. Formal efforts to understand this inductive bias reveal that mixup has a regularizing effect on the first and second derivatives $(\nabla_x f(x), \nabla_x^2 f(x))$ of the machine under training.[431,444,445] These regularization forces effectively control the Rademacher complexity of the machine and approximately minimize its adversarial loss. The two right-hand plots in figure 10.4 show that the gradient norm $\|\nabla_x f(x)\|$ of the mixup machine is indeed much smaller than the one trained by ERM—in plain words, mixup machines implement smoother classification rules. (In fact, mixup originated as we were brainstorming how to control the gradient norm of a classifier.) The interpretation of mixup as a gradient penalty explains its stabilizing properties when applied to the training of generative adversarial networks since gradient penalties were first proposed for the same purpose.[446] Finally, it has been argued that mixup accelerates learning on very separable distributions, where ERM quickly runs out of gradient signal toward the Bayes separator.[447] As shown in figure 10.4, mixup populates the entire gap between classes, accelerating learning in low-density regions at the expense of predictive certainty.

Second, using mixup leads to label smoothing, a popular regularization technique[448] to aid generalization,[449] calibration,[450] as well as robustness against adversarial perturbations[449] and label noise.[451] Classic label smoothing adjusts hard one-hot label vectors y_i toward the high-uncertainty label

253

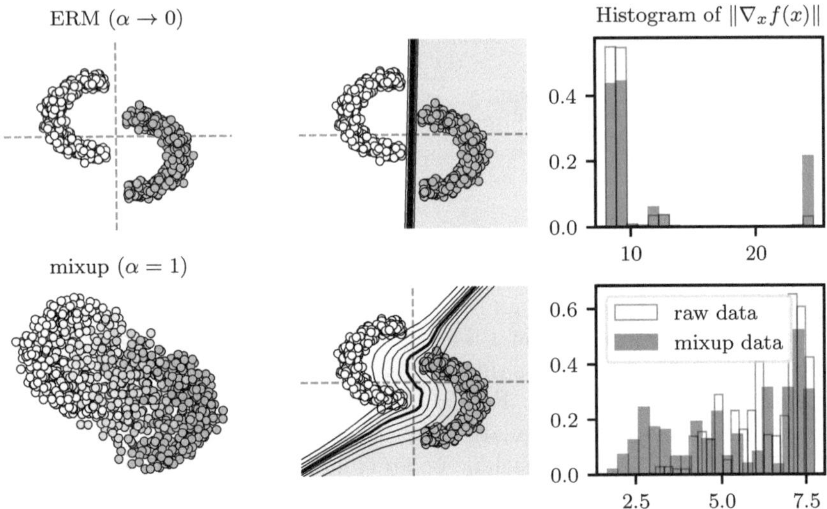

Figure 10.4: Illustration of *mixup* on a separable binary classification problem. mixup leads to smoother classifiers, as measured in terms of the norm of the Jacobian for the resulting machine. Also, mixup machines use more features; while ERM focus solely on the vertical feature, mixup also recruits the horizontal feature to design a decision boundary with larger margin that better reflects the nonlinear structure of the training data.

$u = (\frac{1}{c}, \ldots, \frac{1}{c})$. The resulting smooth labels follow the equation:

$$\tilde{y}_i = (1 - \lambda) \cdot y_i + \lambda \cdot u = (1 - \lambda) \cdot y_i + \frac{\lambda}{c}. \qquad (10.4)$$

For instance, when considering $c = 4$ classes and the smoothing parameter $\lambda = 0.4$, the hard one-hot label $y = (0, 1, 0, 0)$ becomes the soft label $\tilde{y} = (0.1, 0.7, 0.1, 0.1)$. If using the cross-entropy loss ℓ_{CE}, learning with smooth labels is equivalent to learning over the weighted sum

$$
\begin{aligned}
\mathrm{loss}^{\mathrm{LS}(\lambda)}(p_i, y_i) &= (1 - \lambda) \cdot \ell_{\mathrm{CE}}(p_i, y_i) + \lambda \cdot \ell_{\mathrm{CE}}(p_i, u) \\
&= -(1 - \lambda) \sum_{j=1}^{c} y_{ij} \log p_{ij} - \lambda \sum_{j=1}^{c} u_j \log p_{ij},
\end{aligned}
$$

where p_i the softmax probability vector predicted by the learning machine. Therefore, learning about the mixup example (10.3) with cross-entropy loss can be written as $\lambda \cdot \ell_{\mathrm{CE}}(\tilde{x}, y_i) + (1 - \lambda) \cdot \ell_{\mathrm{CE}}(\tilde{x}, y_j)$.

The notations above allow us to better understand the practical implications of learning with smooth labels. Firstly, the loss $\mathrm{loss}^{\mathrm{ERM}}(p_i, y_i)$ reaches zero only as the correct logit tends to infinity. Therefore, the cross-entropy loss compels machines to allocate all probability mass to a single class, inhibiting them from expressing uncertainty. This leads to machines with large weights, saturated softmax vectors, excessive confidence, and poor calibration. On the other hand, minimizing $\mathrm{loss}^{\mathrm{LS}}(p_i, y_i)$ makes for a more uniform distribution of logits across classes. This reduces the difference between the top two logits, resulting in smaller weights, non-saturated softmax vectors, less overconfident predictions, and better calibration. In sum, training with soft labels yields smoother machines.

Figure 10.5 illustrates these points on a one-dimensional classification problem with three classes. First off, training with hard labels induces large logits (top left). This happens because the logits minimizing the cross-entropy loss with hard labels tend to infinity (bottom left, shaded area). An *overshooting problem* ensues, where the machine loses its awareness about uncertainty, including its ability to detect when the test examples lay far away from the training data. By contrast, training with soft labels produces logits with moderate magnitude (top right). These logits are better calibrated—the winning logit achieves and maintains unit magnitude, and the two losing logits achieve and maintain matching values. This happens because the logit interval minimizing the cross-entropy loss with smooth labels is finite and narrow (bottom right, shaded area).

Third, mixup aids generalization similarly to other data augmentation protocols. However, unlike classic data augmentation, mixup circumvents the need for handcrafted augmentations by building virtual examples by means of other training data. The augmentation effects of mixup combat

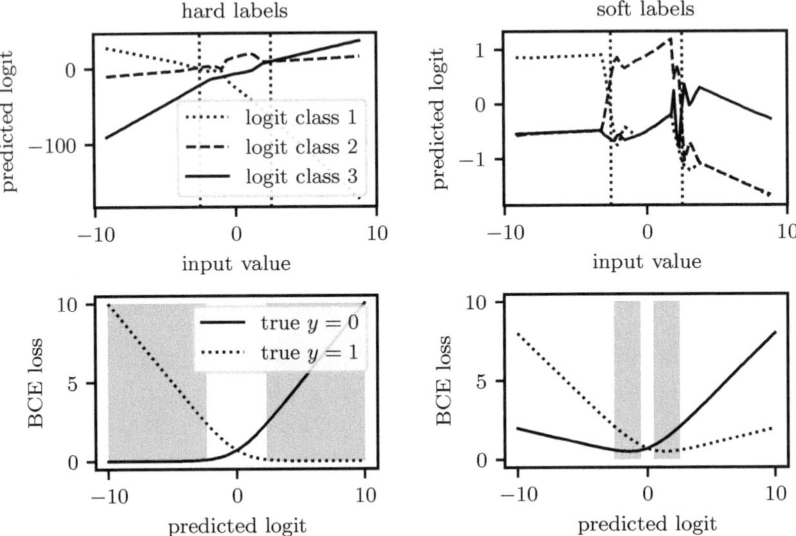

Figure 10.5: On the left, training with hard labels leads to machines that produce extreme logits, are overly confident, and are badly calibrated. This is because the logit values minimizing the cross-entropy loss with hard labels tend to infinity. On the right, training with soft labels leads to machines that produce units winning logits and matching losing logits, leading to machines that are less overconfident and better calibrated. This is because the logit values minimizing the cross-entropy loss with soft labels fall in a narrow range.

simplicity biases by extracting more features from data[452] and increasing the exposure to rare groups.[453] To illustrate this point, figure 10.4 compares the ERM and mixup solutions to a separable binary classification problem. By manufacturing virtual examples in-between the two classes, mixup recruits additional features to better capture the structure of the data, resulting in a decision boundary with maximum margin. mixup also improves robustness against adversarial examples by producing high rank representations.[454]

At the time of its initial publication,[429] mixup set a new state-of-the-art classification error percentage on the CIFAR-10 dataset (4.24%), outperforming ERM (5.18%). While it is possible to improve performance and calibration by adding Gaussian noise to inputs (5.04%), smoothing labels (5.02%), mixing only inputs (either from all classes or just the same classes, and either random pairs or nearby pairs, 5.17), or simultaneously mixing inputs and applying a uniform label smoothing (5.02%), none of these individual solutions match the benefits provided by mixup. Performing mixup on the hidden layers of the neural network (4.44%) or only between random pairs of nearby examples (4.98%) also underperforms vanilla mixup training.

10.2.2   Points of Care

mixup is a heavy regularizer. Therefore, we should expect the most gains when it's applied to large models and proceed with caution in the small model regime.[431] Practitioners should also take care to use mixup in conjunction with other regularizers. For instance, the simultaneous use of mixup and ensembling leads to overregularization and underconfident models.[455] Similarly, when using mixup, it is often necessary to reduce the intensity of weight decay and increase the number of learning iterations.[429]

Two additional points are helpful to bear in mind. First, as a general rule, mixup training requires twice the amount of epochs vs. ERM. Second, mixup introduces a risk commonly known as *manifold intrusion*, where the mixture of two examples from one class resembles an example from another class. To illustrate, considering averaging the two negative examples along the real segment $[-, +, -]$. The produced virtual input coincides with the positive example, albeit with a negative virtual label, providing the machine with contradictory learning signals. Fortunately, the likelihood of manifold intrusion decreases exponentially as the dimensionality of the input grows.

10.3   Mixing on Hidden Layers

Manifold mixup[456] applies mixup to any layer h in a deep neural network $f = g \circ h$. The motivation behind manifold mixup is to flatten the spectrum of hidden representations, increasing the amount of information retained from the input space and minimizing the probability of manifold intrusion. Manifold mixup proceeds by computing the hidden representations of two training inputs, $z_i = h(x_i)$ and $z_j = h(x_j)$, respectively, to construct the mixed-up representation $z_\lambda = \lambda \cdot z_1 + (1-\lambda) \cdot z_0$. This mixed-up representation is used to produce the mixed-up prediction $\hat{y}_\lambda = g(z_\lambda)$. Finally, all the parameters of the deep neural network f are updated to minimize the cross-entropy loss between the mixed-up prediction $\hat{y}_\lambda$ and the mixed-up label $y_\lambda = \lambda \cdot y_i + (1-\lambda) \cdot y_j$. Manifold mixup shows similar performance to vanilla mixup in most applications, but it crucially enables interpolation-based data augmentation across fields that rely on discrete raw inputs, such as natural language processing.[433,457]

Another extension are multi-input multi-output neural networks,[458] which amounts to ERM on examples

$$\tilde{x} = h_x^{\mathrm{MIMO}}(x_i, x_j) = (x_i, x_j),$$
$$\tilde{y} = h_y^{\mathrm{MIMO}}(y_i, y_j) = (y_i, y_j).$$

A MIMO neural network processes k inputs jointly to produce k associated predictions. During training, the MIMO framework samples k random examples from the training set, feeds the k inputs to the network, and requests the corresponding k predictions. The network parameters are updated to minimize the cross-entropies associated with each of the produced softmax vectors and their respective labels. For example, a MIMO network with $k = 3$ for image classification accepts three images concatenated along the channel axis (thus handling images with nine channels) and produces three softmax vectors. During testing, the MIMO network classifies a single test instance x by (1) concatenating the test instance three times, and (2) averaging the three softmax vectors as a final prediction.

Both mixup and MIMO are instances of VRM.[459] In particular, both are machines of the form $f(h(x_1, \ldots, x_k))$, where

$$h^{\mathrm{mixup}}(x, y) = \sum_{i=1}^{k} (\lambda_i \cdot x_i, \lambda_i \cdot y_i), \text{ for } \lambda \sim \mathrm{SymmetricDirichlet}(\alpha),$$
$$h^{\mathrm{MIMO}}(x, y) = ([x_1, \ldots, x_k], [y_1, \ldots, y_k]).$$

During test time, mixup and MIMO apply $f(h(x, x))$ to the test instance x. MIMO, in particular, uses the concatenation operation as its mixing function, extending both the input and output spaces without losing any information about the training data. For a summary of all mixup-based methods described in this section, refer to table 10.1.

Learning setup	Method	Vicinal distribution
supervised learning (§10.2-10.3) $\ell(f(\tilde{x}), \tilde{y})$	ERM	$\tilde{x} \sim \mathrm{Delta}(x),\ \tilde{y} \sim \mathrm{Delta}(y)$
	Aug	$\tilde{x} \sim \mathrm{Aug}(x),\ \tilde{y} \sim \mathrm{Delta}(y)$
	mixup	$\tilde{x} \leftarrow \lambda \cdot x + (1-\lambda) \cdot x_i$ $\tilde{y} \leftarrow \lambda \cdot y + (1-\lambda) \cdot y_i$
	Manifold	$\tilde{\phi} \leftarrow \lambda \cdot \phi(x) + (1-\lambda) \cdot \phi(x_i)$ $\tilde{y} \leftarrow \lambda \cdot y + (1-\lambda) \cdot y_i$
	MIMO	$\tilde{x} \leftarrow \mathrm{Concat}(x, x_i),\ \tilde{y} \leftarrow \mathrm{Concat}(y, y_i)$
domain generalization (§10.4) $\ell(f(\tilde{x}), \tilde{y})$	LISA-S1	$j \sim \mathrm{Index}(\mathcal{D} \mid e_j = e_i, y_j \neq y_i)$ $\tilde{x} \leftarrow \lambda \cdot x_i + (1-\lambda) \cdot x_j$ $\tilde{y} \leftarrow \lambda \cdot y_i + (1-\lambda) \cdot y_j$
	LISA-S2	$j \sim \mathrm{Index}(\mathcal{D} \mid e_j \neq e_i, y_j = y_i)$ $\tilde{x} \leftarrow \lambda \cdot x_i + (1-\lambda) \cdot x_j$ $\tilde{y} \leftarrow \lambda \cdot y_i + (1-\lambda) \cdot y_j$
unsupervised learning (§10.5) $\ell(f(\tilde{x}), \tilde{f}(x))$	ERM	$\tilde{x} \sim \mathrm{Delta}(x),\ \tilde{f} \sim \mathrm{Delta}(f)$
	Aug	$\tilde{x} \sim \mathrm{Aug}(x),\ \tilde{f} \sim \mathrm{Delta}(f)$
	mixup	$\tilde{x} \leftarrow \lambda \cdot x + (1-\lambda) \cdot x_i$ $\tilde{f} \leftarrow \lambda \cdot f + (1-\lambda) \cdot f(x_i)$
test-time augmentation (§10.7) $\frac{1}{k} \sum_{i=1}^{k} \tilde{f}_i(\tilde{x}_i)$	ERM	$\tilde{x}_i \sim \mathrm{Delta}(x),\ \tilde{f}_i \sim \mathrm{Delta}(f)$
	Aug	$\tilde{x}_i \sim \mathrm{Aug}(x),\ \tilde{f}_i \sim \mathrm{Delta}(f)$
	mixup	$\tilde{x} \leftarrow \lambda \cdot x + (1-\lambda) \cdot x_i$ $\tilde{f}_i \leftarrow \lambda^{-1} \cdot (f - (1-\lambda) \cdot f(x_i))$

Table 10.1: Summary of methods to learn from combinations of examples. This table assumes that the learning machine receives a raw example (x, y) from the training dataset $\mathcal{D}$, which is augmented into the example $(\tilde{x}, \tilde{y})$ used for training. When necessary, draw $\lambda \sim \mathrm{Beta}(\alpha, \alpha)$ and $i \sim \mathrm{Index}(\mathcal{D})$. In manifold mixup, one minimizes $\ell(\tilde{\phi} \cdot w, \tilde{y})$.

10.4 Mixing Not at Random

Mixing examples *not* at random can help machines learn invariant patterns and discard spurious correlations. To see this, consider the setup in figure 10.2, where $(x_i, (0, 1))$ is a picture of a cow on the beach, and $(x_j, (1, 0))$ is a picture of a camel on the beach. Mixing these two examples yields the virtual input $\lambda \cdot x_i + (1 - \lambda) \cdot x_j$ and the virtual target $(1 - \lambda, \lambda)$. In this scenario, the machine is encouraged to use animal features to predict the virtual target, as these are the only features correlated to the blending coefficient λ. Similarly, when mixing two images of cows appearing in different backgrounds, the machine will disregard background features, because their correlation with the blending coefficient λ is irrelevant to predict the virtual target $(0, 1)$.

The LISA algorithm[460] implements these ideas by mixing training examples using one of the two following strategies, at random:

(S1) Mix random pairs of examples (x_i, y_i, e_i) and (x_j, y_j, e_j) belonging to the same environment $(e_i = e_j)$ but to different classes $(y_i \neq y_j)$.

(S2) Mix random pairs of examples (x_i, y_i, e_i) and (x_j, y_j, e_j) belonging to different environments $(e_i \neq e_j)$ but of the same class $(y_i = y_j)$.

Returning to the cow-on-the-beach example, strategy (S1) produces examples with the same background, a blend of the two animals, and a label dependent on the blending factor—thus enforcing the learning of foreground animal features. Strategy (S2) produces examples with different backgrounds, only one species of animal, and the corresponding hard and invariant label—once again pushing the machine toward focusing on foreground animal features.

In the absence of environment annotations, two heuristics based on example representation distances are helpful to combine examples not at random. On one hand, combining nearby examples from different classes should recover cows and camels in very similar backgrounds, imitating the strategy (S1) above, pictured in figure 10.2. On the other hand, combining distant examples from the same class should recover cows or camels in different backgrounds, paralleling the strategy (S2) described above. These heuristics are similar to those of the matching methods for causal inference, reviewed in chapter 4.

Let us return to the cow-on-the-beach problem (CoB) to better understand the impact of learning from nonrandom combinations of examples. In this setup, consider training data under $p = 0.9$ and testing data under $1 - p = 0.1$. Assume two environments: $e = [\![Y = C]\!]$ representing animals in their habitat, and $e' = [\![Y \neq C]\!]$ representing animals out of context. To obtain a classifier, consider the following mean-difference decision rule:

$$\hat{w} = \frac{1}{n} \sum_{i=1}^{n} (x_i \cdot (2 \cdot y_i - 1))^{\top}.$$

Then, the risk minimizer has this expression

$$w = \mathbb{E}\left[X(2Y - 1)\right]$$

$$= \frac{1}{2} \cdot \mathbb{E}\left[X \mid Y = 1\right] - \frac{1}{2} \cdot \mathbb{E}\left[X \mid Y = 0\right]$$

$$= \frac{1}{2} \cdot ((1 - p) \cdot \mathbb{E}\left[X \mid Y = 1, C = 0\right] + p \cdot \mathbb{E}\left[X \mid Y = 1, C = 1\right])$$

$$- \frac{1}{2} \cdot ((1 - p) \cdot \mathbb{E}\left[X \mid Y = 0, C = 0\right] + p \cdot \mathbb{E}\left[X \mid Y = 0, C = 1\right])$$

$$= (-0.2, -0.8).$$

In the equation above, we can see that the spurious feature dominates. Consequently, the expected training accuracy is $(100 \times p)\% = 90\%$, while the test accuracy is 10%. Let us continue by analyzing the LISA method on this same problem. For this particular example, doing LISA-S2 ($e_i \neq e_j$ but $y_i = y_j$) will suffice, as LISA-S1 has no effect. Then, the LISA classifier will train on examples built as:

$$\lambda \sim \text{Beta}(\alpha, \alpha),$$
$$X_\lambda = \lambda \cdot X_e + (1 - \lambda) \cdot X_{e'},$$
$$Y_\lambda = \lambda \cdot Y_e + (1 - \lambda) \cdot Y_{e'} = Y.$$

Following a similar derivation to the ERM baseline above, we obtain:

$$w = \mathbb{E}\left[X_\lambda(2Y - 1)\right]$$

$$= \frac{1}{2} \cdot \mathbb{E}\left[X_\lambda \mid Y = 1\right] - \frac{1}{2} \cdot \mathbb{E}\left[X_\lambda \mid Y = 0\right],$$

where

$$\mathbb{E}\left[X_\lambda \mid Y = 1\right] = \mathbb{E}\left[\lambda\right] \cdot \mathbb{E}\left[X_e \mid Y = 1\right] + \mathbb{E}\left[1 - \lambda\right] \cdot \mathbb{E}\left[X_{e'} \mid Y = 1\right]$$

$$= \frac{1}{2} \cdot (-0.2, 1) + \frac{1}{2} \cdot (-0.2, -1) = (-0.2, 0)$$

follows because $\mathbb{E}\left[\lambda\right] = 0$ for all symmetric $\text{Beta}(\alpha, \alpha)$. Similarly, it follows that $\mathbb{E}\left[X_\lambda \mid Y = 0\right] = (-0.2, 0)$. This yields an invariant classifier $w = (-0.2, 0)$ that cancels out the spurious feature and generalizes to all environments.

10.5   Mixing Unlabeled Data

Unlabeled data—collections of inputs x^u with no observed label—are a helpful resource, one that abounds in many applications. Semi-supervised learning algorithms[461] learn from collections of n labeled examples (x_i, y_i) and m unlabeled examples (x_i^u) belonging to the classes of interest. (The related framework of learning with the *Universum*[420] is a variation of semi-supervised learning where unlabeled examples do *not* belong to the classes of interest.) To use VRM for semi-supervised learning, consider the vicinal distributions $(\tilde{x}^u, \tilde{f}) \sim V(x^u, f(x^u))$, where $f(x^u)$ is the current prediction about x^u by the system under training. Then, for the unlabeled datum x^u, semi-supervised learning regularizers follow the general expression:

$$\Omega = \ell(f(\tilde{x}^u), \tilde{f}(x^u)), \text{ for } \tilde{x}^u, \tilde{f} \sim V(x^u, f). \tag{10.5}$$

As in the supervised learning case, we may consider two types of vicinal distributions. Vicinal distributions that only transform the input x^u promote invariances with respect to the input space. In contrast, vicinal distributions that jointly transform the input x^u and the current function estimate $f(x^u)$ enforce equivariances, such as preserving linearity.

Consistency regularization[462] promotes invariance by requesting equal predictions on various augmentations about the same unlabeled datum:

$$\Omega^{\mathrm{aug}} = \|f(\tilde{x}^u)) - f(x^u)\|^2, \text{ where } \tilde{x}^u \sim \mathrm{Aug}(x^u). \tag{10.6}$$

Consistency regularization is effective when applied to unlabeled examples near the decision boundary currently implemented by the machine. At those locations, and if we assume that classes form different clusters separated by low-density valleys, consistency regularization pushes the decision boundary into regions of lower density.

To extend consistency regularization to protocols enforcing equivariances, such as mixup, consider the following objective:[463]

$$\Omega^{\mathrm{mix}} \sim \|f(\lambda \cdot x^u + (1 - \lambda) \cdot x_i^u) - [\lambda \cdot f(x^u) + (1 - \lambda) \cdot f(x_i^u)]\|^2, \tag{10.7}$$

where we have applied (10.5) with $\tilde{x}^u := \lambda \cdot x^u + (1 - \lambda) \cdot x_i^u$, and $\tilde{f} := \lambda f + (1 - \lambda) \cdot f(x_i^u)$. The vicinal distribution arises due to the randomness in $\lambda \sim \mathrm{Beta}(\alpha, \alpha)$ and the random selection of x_i^u from the collection of unlabeled examples.

These regularizers are useful to promote various types of invariances in our predictors. The consistency regularizer (10.6) enforces an *invariance* constraint in f. For instance, if the vicinal distribution $V(x^u)$ in (10.6) produces random rotations of the image x^u, then consistency regularization promotes rotation invariance in f. In contrast, the interpolation regularizer (10.7) enforces an *equivariance* constraint over f, whereby predictions about linear interpolations of unlabeled examples must equal the linear interpolations of their individual predictions.

Consistency and interpolation regularizers work well under the assumption of *low-density class separation*, common in the semi-supervised learning literature. Assuming that x^u is an unlabeled point close to the current decision boundary, it is likely that the second unlabeled point x_i^u belongs to a different class and inhabits a different cluster. If this is the case, it is desirable to push the decision boundary from x^u in the direction of x_i^u, as it is often the case that both unlabeled points are separated by a low-density region. In the case that both x^u and x_i^u lie on the same cluster or belong to the same class, consistency and interpolation regularizers have no effect.

10.6   Mixing by Extrapolation

As illustrated in figure 10.4, both ERM and mixup machines become increasingly confident as we move further from the training data. This overconfidence poses significant risks in safety-critical applications,[464] where it is crucial for the model to indicate low confidence and refrain from making predictions in underrepresented regions of the input space.

Extending mixup to *extrapolate* random pairs of training examples helps alleviate this issue. More specifically, consider

$$(\tilde{x}, \tilde{y}) = \begin{cases} \text{mixup}(x_i, y_i, x_j, y_j, \lambda) & \text{or} \\ \text{mixup}(x_i, y_i, 2x_i - x_j, u, \lambda) & \text{with equal probability.} \end{cases} \tag{10.8}$$

In the previous equation, (x_i, y_i) and (x_j, y_j) are a random pair of training examples, $\lambda \sim \text{Beta}(\alpha, \alpha)$ is a random mixing coefficient, and $u = (1/c, \ldots, 1/c)$ signals the highest uncertainty. The first case in (10.8) is vanilla mixup, where we interpolate between random pairs of instances and their labels. The second case in (10.8) extrapolates beyond x_i from the direction of x_j, interpolating the label y_i with the high-uncertainty label $u = (1/c, \ldots, 1/c)$. This scheme, called *Ex-mixup-v1*, instructs the machine how to become uncertain outside the convex hull described by the training data. Figure 10.4 illustrates how Ex-mixup-v1 results in high predictive uncertainty outside the neighborhood of the training data.

However, choosing the uncertainty label $u = (1/c, \ldots, 1/c)$ can lead to unpredictable behavior far away from the training data. Since the value $u = (1/c, \ldots, 1/c)$ is a non-saturated softmax vector, the network may drift to a saturated softmax vector in distant regions of the feature space. To address this issue, consider instantiating an additional, dedicated $(c + 1)$-th

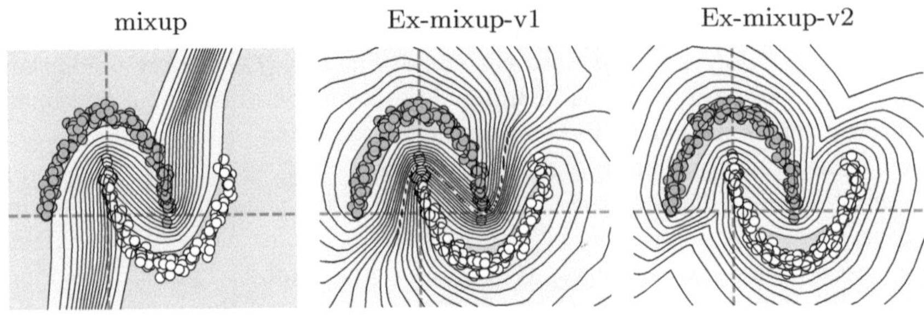

Figure 10.6: Comparison of uncertainty landscapes (darker means more confident) for a binary classification problem as provided by mixup, Ex-mixup-v1, and Ex-mixup-v2. mixup provides limited uncertainty awareness, orthogonal to the 1-dimensional manifold described by the decision boundary. Ex-mixup-v1 is more aware of uncertainty, but the use of the non-saturated uncertainty labels $(\frac{1}{2}, \frac{1}{2})$ results in unpredictable behavior far away from the training data. Ex-mixup-v2 fixes this issue by extending the label space to three classes, where extrapolations are labeled using the saturated uncertain target $(0, 0, 1)$.

uncertainty label. In the resulting method Ex-mixup-v2, the training labels y_i are extended to be $y_i = (y_i, 0) \in \Delta^{c+1}$, the uncertainty label is set to $u = (0, \ldots, 0, 1) \in \Delta^{c+1}$, and we proceed by mixing as in Ex-mixup-v1. Figure 10.6 shows the different behavior of Ex-mixup-v1 and Ex-mixup-v2 in the two moons problem when moving far away from the training data, where Ex-mixup-v2 remains uncertain in all directions.

Lastly, Ex-mixup-v2 allows the separate modeling of aleatoric and epistemic uncertainty, two concepts discussed in detail throughout the next chapter. Specifically, the $(c+1)$-th softmax score signals epistemic uncertainty, while the entropy of the first c logits signals aleatoric uncertainty. When the $(c+1)$-th score equals one, we encounter maximum epistemic uncertainty and zero aleatoric uncertainty. When the $(c+1)$-th score is zero, epistemic uncertainty is absent, and the aleatoric uncertainty is proportional to the entropy of the first c logits.

10.7 Mixing at Test Time

The vicinal risk minimization framework allows multiple predictions about a single test instance through the expression

$$\bar{f}(x) = \frac{1}{k} \sum_{i=1}^{k} \tilde{f}_i(\tilde{x}_i), \tag{10.9}$$

where the values $\tilde{x}_i, \tilde{f}_i$ are sampled from the vicinal distribution $V(x, f)$. This process of averaging predictions over multiple input augmentations is often referred to as *test-time data augmentation*.[465,466] One specific instantiation of test-time data augmentation involves predicting x using

$$\bar{f}^{\text{aug}}(x) = \frac{1}{k} \sum_{i=1}^{k} f(\tilde{x}_i), \text{ where } \tilde{x}_i \sim \text{Aug}(x_i)),$$

where the vicinal distribution transforms the inputs to enforce invariance against the factors varied by the stochastic data augmentation (e.g., rotations).

To use mixup for test-time data augmentation, recall the associated equivariance condition:

$$f(\lambda \cdot x + (1 - \lambda) \cdot x_i) \approx \lambda \cdot f(x) + (1 - \lambda) \cdot f(x_i).$$

Then, the mixup prediction about x around x_i follows the expression:

$$f_i(x) := \frac{f(\lambda \cdot x + (1 - \lambda) \cdot x_i) - (1 - \lambda)f(x_i)}{\lambda}, \tag{10.10}$$

where x_i is a *reference input* and $f(x_i)$ can be replaced by the training label y_i. To remain in the probability simplex, we apply one softmax operation as a last step before returning the prediction. By repeating this process with k reference inputs x_i, we obtain these predictions:

$$\bar{f}^{\text{mix}}(x) = \frac{1}{k} \sum_{i=1}^{k} \frac{f(\lambda \cdot x + (1 - \lambda) \cdot x_i) - (1 - \lambda)f(x_i)}{\lambda},$$

In the equation above, the mixing coefficient λ trades off accuracy as in $\lambda \to 0$ versus prediction diversity as in $\lambda \to 1$. In practical situations, test-time mixup boosts the performance of mixup machines in terms of a variety of metrics, including average accuracy, worst-class accuracy, out-of-distribution detection, negative log-likelihood, and expected calibration error.[436] Test-time mixup is also an effective defense against adversarial examples.[467] To see how, consider first an ERM predictor f, together with an attack δ, such that $f(x + \delta) = f(x) + g(x; \delta)$ for some attack impact $g(x; \delta) = O(\|\delta\|)$. For test-time mixup, consider the virtual input $x_i^\lambda := \lambda \cdot x + (1 - \lambda) \cdot x_i$. Then,

$$f(x_i^\lambda) = f(\lambda \cdot (x + \delta) + (1 - \lambda) \cdot x_i)$$
$$= \lambda \cdot f(x) + (1 - \lambda) \cdot f(x_i) + g(x_i^\lambda; \delta\lambda)$$
$$= f(\lambda \cdot x + (1 - \lambda) \cdot x_i) + g(x_i^\lambda; \delta\lambda).$$

This results in an attack with impact $g(x_i^\lambda; \delta\lambda) = O(\|\delta\lambda\|)$, lower than $O(\|\delta\|)$ for all $\lambda < 1$. In addition, the attack is now more difficult to target due to the randomness involved in constructing the virtual input x_i^λ.

Chapter 11

Uncertainty Estimation

This chapter is based on Kamalika Chaudhuri and David Lopez-Paz. *Unified Uncertainty Calibration*. arXiv, 2023.

11.1   Introduction

I don't think I've ever seen anything quite like this before—HAL 9000 in
2001: A Space Odyssey

What is the capital city of the Republic of Palau? If you know, how confident are you in your answer? If not, how do you recognize your lack of knowledge? (The correct answer, of course, is *Ngerulmud*.) While pondering these questions, you have engaged in *meta-cognition*, "the capacity to reflect on, evaluate, and control mental function."[469] More particularly, you have estimated your *propositional confidence*, defined in psychology as the subjective belief about the validity of one's thoughts or judgments.[469,470]

Our ability to "know that we do not know" has been a subject of debate since the time of the Ancient Greeks. It is best illustrated in Plato's *Apology* where Socrates, discussing with a politician who thought himself very wise, declares:

> Well, although I do not suppose that either of us knows anything really beautiful and good, I am better off than he is—for he knows nothing, and thinks that he knows; I neither know nor think that I know.

This passage, famously paraphrased as "I know that I know nothing," prefaced the first works formally investigating meta-cognition, Aristotle's *On the Soul* and *Parva Naturalia*.

Humans—as well as other animals such as primates, rats, and pigeons—"take into account uncertainty in their behavior, including in experiments on perception, learning, memory, and motor control." However, our ability to assess our own uncertainty is limited:

> Psychological research has revealed that human performance in the face of uncertainty is spotty at best. Humans display suboptimal choice strategies, miscalibrations in assessing probabilities, fallacious statistical inference, and inconsistencies in their preferences for uncertain outcomes. Moreover, both novices and experts are subject to these kinds of inaccuracies and errors.[471]

Much like the machines we've been studying, our meta-cognition is influenced by spurious cues such as stimuli magnitude, as well as internal factors such as pupil dilation and heart rate, often leading to overconfidence.[469] Nobel Laureate Daniel Kahneman considers overconfidence "the most significant of the cognitive biases,"[472] while social psychologist Scott Plous argues that "no problem in judgment and decision-making is more prevalent and more potentially catastrophic than overconfidence."[473] Overconfidence is considered responsible for disasters such as the sinking of the *Titanic*, the Chernobyl nuclear accident, the loss of the space shuttles *Challenger* and *Columbia*, the financial crisis of 2008, the *Deepwater Horizon* oil spill in the Gulf of Mexico, and various wars, strikes, lawsuits, and entrepreneurial failures.[474] Along similar lines, the Dunning-Kruger effect[475] measures how people unskilled at a particular task are most likely to overestimate their abilities. For example, one study documented that 93% of American drivers consider themselves better than the median,[476] while another showed how most bicyclists are unable to draw a correct sketch of a bike.[196] Broadly speaking, uncertainty estimation is important for calibration, and calibration is important for communicating and combining decisions made by one or multiple learning agents.

Facing these challenges, how can we build AI systems able to say "I do not know?" This is the problem of uncertainty estimation, a key to building robust, fair, and safe prediction pipelines.[477] For instance, Edmon Begoli and colleagues, in a perspective for *Nature Machine Intelligence*,[478] note that AI holds extraordinary promise to transform medicine, but they also acknowledge

> the reluctance to delegate decision-making to machine intelligence in cases where patient safety is at stake. To address some of these challenges, medical AI, especially in its modern data-rich deep learning guise, needs to develop a principled and formal uncertainty quantification.

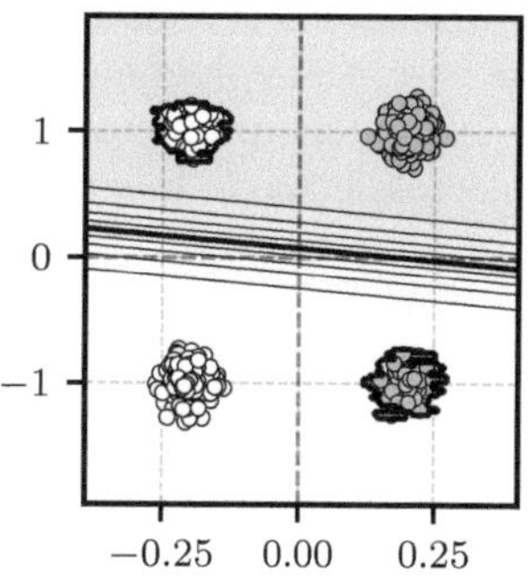
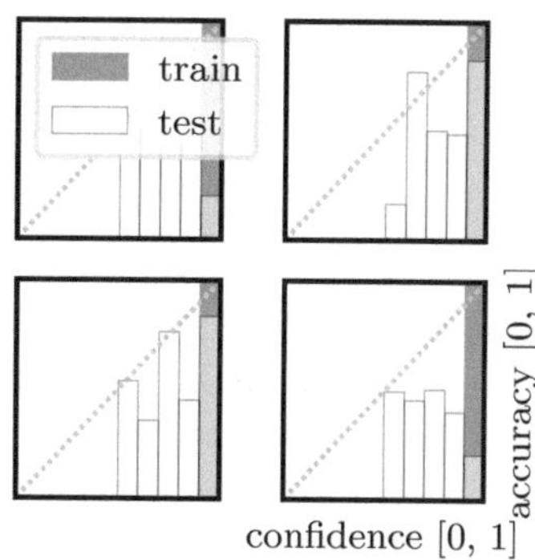

Figure 11.1: On the left, a classifier adopts a simplify-and-memorize strategy to learn the cow-on-the-beach problem. On the right, the classifier is over-confident on every training example and badly calibrated for test data from the minority groups.

More broadly, uncertainty estimation is a crucial and necessary milestone to build transparent and explainable AI systems.[479] Particularly relevant to this book, endowing models with awareness about uncertainty is crucial to determine when they are inside or outside the operational boundaries afforded by their training environments.[480]

Estimating the predictive uncertainty of AI systems is challenging for three reasons. First, training data rarely provides information about out-class data or label confidence. Common one-hot labels obscure rich probability information, such as the percentage of annotators agreeing that a particular input belongs to a certain class. This loss of information increases underspecification: while there might be only one true continuous conditional distribution mapping inputs to targets, a multitude of classifiers could separate a hard labeling of the same data.

Second, the simplify-and-memorize learning strategy decreases uncertainty awareness. In particular, some data features are ignored by the machine on its way to zero training error, eventually becoming *unknown-unknowns*. For example, a digit classifier that focuses exclusively on shape would ignore variations in color. As illustrated in figure 11.1, uncertainty estimates are less precise for minority data groups when spurious correlations are present in the training data.

Third, uncertainty is a local phenomenon, yet most predictors operate nonlocally. As an example, consider a two-dimensional classification problem involving two linearly separable classes, each with a distinctive polygonal shape. While linear classifiers suffice to address this task, their predictions become overly confident as the test inputs move further away from the training data. Estimating uncertainty requires learning about local information irrelevant to the classification task—in this case, the polygonal shapes of the classes. Overconfidence issues persist in modern predictors, such as ReLU deep neural networks trained with the cross-entropy loss function.[481] Some alternatives to tame the confidence of neural networks on extreme examples include spectral decoupling,[105] logit normalization,[482,483] mixup or smooth labels,[429] and replacing ReLUs with radial basis functions.[484] However, since none of these architectural changes fully resolve the problem of uncertainty estimation, it remains an active area of research.[485–489]

The most common approach to prediction under uncertainty is the *reject-or-classify* (RC)[490,491] recipe, coded in algorithm 11.1 and described below. Consider a classifier trained to distinguish $c = 2$ in-class categories, later deployed in a test environment where the examples may also belong to some unseen out-class category $c = 3$. RC requires a softmax vector $\text{sm}(f(x))$ describing the *aleatoric* uncertainty of the two in-class classes, together with a real-valued *epistemic* uncertainty $u(x)$. When the epistemic uncertainty exceeds a threshold $u(x) \geq \theta$, RC considers that the test input x belongs to the unseen out-class category $c = 3$ and abstains from prediction. Otherwise, RC classifies the input into one of the two in-class categories, with probabilities according to the softmax vector $\text{sm}(f(x))$.

While simple, the RC recipe exhibits three issues. First, aleatoric and epistemic uncertainties do not communicate with each other, so we may reject easy-to-classify examples or accept out-class examples for prediction. Second, the RC process results in miscalibrated decisions, since RC abstains or predicts only with absolute (binary) confidence. Third, the recipe does not allow us to correct for any misspecifications in the epistemic uncertainty estimate. The rest of this chapter describes a novel framework to address these issues, which I call unified uncertainty calibration, or U2C.[468]

```
1  def reject_or_classify(f, u, x, theta=10):
2      # softmax vector [0.1, 0.9] describing aleatoric
       uncertainty
3      s_x = sm(f(x))
4      # Does our epistemic uncertainty exceed a threshold?
5      if u(x) >= theta:
6          # yes: abstain with label c + 1 and total confidence
7          return [0, 0, 1]
8      else:
9          # no: predict in-class with total confidence
10         return s_x + [0]
```

Algorithm 11.1: PyTorch code to predict with the option to abstain.

11.2   Learning with Uncertainty

As usual, our goal is to learn a classifier f mapping an input $x_i \in \mathbb{R}^d$ into its label $y_i \in \{1, \ldots c\}$. We consider neural network classifiers of the form $f(x_i) = w(\phi(x_i))$, where $\phi(x_i) \in \mathbb{R}^{d'}$ is the representation of x_i. The classifier outputs logit vectors $f(x_i) \in \mathbb{R}^c$, where $f(x_i)_j$ is a real-valued score proportional to the log-likelihood of x_i belonging to class j, for all $i = 1, \ldots, n$ and $j = 1, \ldots, c$. Let s be the softmax operation normalizing a logit vector $f(x_i)$ into the probability vector $\mathrm{sm}(f(x_i))$, with coordinates

$$\mathrm{sm}(f(x_i))_j = s_f(x_i)_j = \frac{\exp(f(x_i))_j}{\sum_{k=1}^{c} \exp(f(x_i))_k},$$

for all $i = 1, \ldots, n$, and $j = 1, \ldots, c$. Denote by

$$h_f(x_i) = \underset{j \in \{1, \ldots, j\}}{\mathrm{argmax}} \; f(x_i)_j$$

the hard prediction on x_i, where $h_f(x_i) \in \{1, \ldots, c\}$. Analogously, define

$$\pi_f(x_i) = \max_{c \in \{1, \ldots, c\}} \mathrm{sm}(f(x_i))_j$$

as the prediction confidence on x_i, where $\mathrm{sm}(\cdot)$ ensures that $\pi_f(x_i) \in [0, 1]$.

To train our neural network, consider a dataset $\mathcal{D} = \{(x_i, y_i)\}_{i=1}^{n}$ of *in-class* examples (x_i, y_i), drawn iid from the probability distribution $P^{\mathrm{in}}(X, Y)$, where $Y \in \{1, \ldots, c\}$. Using these data, search for the empirical risk minimizer:

$$f = \underset{\tilde{f}}{\mathrm{argmin}} \; \frac{1}{n} \sum_{i=1}^{n} \ell(\tilde{f}(x_i), y_i).$$

Once trained, our classifier faces inputs x' from the *extended test distribution*

$$P^{\star}(X, Y) = \lambda \cdot P^{\mathrm{in}}(X, Y) + (1 - \lambda) \cdot P^{\mathrm{out}}(X, Y), \qquad (11.1)$$

where $P^{\mathrm{out}}(X, Y)$ is a distribution of *out-domain* examples labeled as $Y = c + 1$, and $\lambda \in [0, 1]$ determines the relative quantity of in-class and out-class examples.

To address out-class data, we will extend the classifier f as $f^{\star}$, using one of the uncertainty estimation methods described below. The extended classifier $f^{\star}$ predicts one of $c + 1$ classes by providing hard labels $h_{f^{\star}}(x)$ and predictive confidences $\pi_{f^{\star}}(x)$. Under the test regime described above, we assess the performance of $f^{\star}$ using two metrics. First, we measure the average classification error:

$$\mathrm{err}_P(f^{\star}) = \underset{(x,y) \sim P}{\mathrm{Pr}} \left[h_{f^{\star}}(x) \neq y \right]. \qquad (11.2)$$

Second, to evaluate confidence estimates, we look at the expected calibration error (ece):

$$\text{ece}_P(f^\star) = \mathop{\mathbb{E}}_{(x,y)\sim P}\left[\mathop{\mathbb{E}}_{p\sim U[0,1]}\left[|\Pr\left(h_{f^\star}(x) = y \mid \pi_{f^\star}(x) = p\right) - p|\right]\right]. \quad (11.3)$$

Neural networks with small ece produce calibrated confidence scores $\pi_{f^\star}(x_i) \approx P(Y = y_i \mid X = x_i)$. Said differently, calibrated neural networks satisfy $\mathbb{E}\left[y \mid \pi_{f^\star}(x) = v\right] = v$ for all $v \in [0,1]$, that is, they are right 80% of the time when predicting with 80% confidence. Note that calibration does not imply performance (a coin toss is perfectly calibrated over any balanced binary classification problem), and it is of the greatest importance to be well calibrated on mistakes. As a complementary metric to ece, we also consider the expected negative log-likelihood

$$\text{nll}_P(f^\star) = \mathop{\mathbb{E}}_{(x,y)\sim P}\left[-\log(\pi_{f^\star}(x))_y\right]. \quad (11.4)$$

11.3 Two Types of Uncertainty

Cognitive scientists distinguish between world-centered and self-centered uncertainty:

> We can talk of uncertainty about things in the world, such as sensory uncertainty about the orientation of a line or the frequency of a sound. This is uncertainty in a world-centered reference frame. As we have seen, however, we can also talk of confidence in our own propositions or actions; this is now uncertainty in a self-centered reference frame. ... A key step in forming propositional confidence is shifting between world- and self-centered frames of reference when encoding uncertainty.[469]

In machine learning, a similar distinction is made between aleatoric and epistemic uncertainty.[464,492,493] To see how these two emerge, consider the following factorization of the density value for a training example (x, y) on the in-class distribution

$$p^{\text{in}}(x,y) = \underbrace{p^{\text{in}}(y \mid x)}_{\text{aleatoric}} \cdot \underbrace{p^{\text{in}}(x)}_{\text{epistemic}}. \quad (11.5)$$

On one hand, aleatoric uncertainty concerns the irreducible noise inherent in annotating each input x with its corresponding label y. On the other hand, epistemic uncertainty relates to the atypicality or inverse density of the input x. Aleatoric uncertainty is model-independent (world-centered),

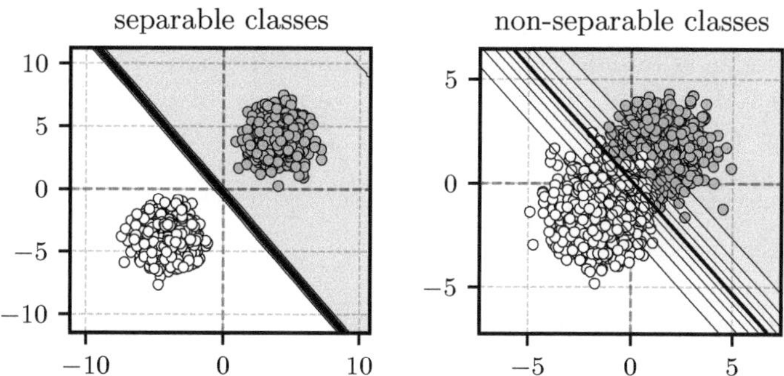

Figure 11.2: Aleatoric uncertainty concerns the irreducible variance of the target variable given the input variable. (Left) In separable classification problems, the decision boundary jumps suddenly, showing zero aleatoric uncertainty everywhere. (Right) In nonseparable problems, the decision boundary transitions smoothly from one class to another, yielding a middle region of high aleatoric uncertainty.

while epistemic uncertainty can be reduced when the agent collects more data at a particular location (self-centered). Next, we will review these two types of uncertainty in more detail, alongside some popular estimators.

11.3.1 Aleatoric Uncertainty

The word *aleatoric* originates from the Latin *āleātōrius*, which pertains to games of chance. In machine learning, aleatoric uncertainty describes irreducible sources of randomness in the data labeling process. Formally, the aleatoric uncertainty of an example (x, y) is a supervised quantity relating to the conditional probability $P(Y = y \mid X = x)$. For instance, if the true data generation process dictates that $P(Y = y \mid X = x) = 0.7$, no additional data can further reduce the aleatoric uncertainty about (x, y). Figure 11.2 shows how aleatoric uncertainty increases in a binary classification problem as the support overlap between classes grows.

Classifiers model aleatoric uncertainty when they are well calibrated.[494-496] Well-calibrated classifiers ensure that $\pi_f(x) \approx P(Y = y \mid X = x)$, allowing us to interpret their maximum softmax score $\pi_f(x)$ as the probability of assigning the right class label to the input x. However, modern machine learning models are not well calibrated by default. Over-parameterized models tend to produce overconfident predictions, whereas those that are heavily regularized often exhibit underconfidence.[495]

One common technique to calibrate deep neural network classifiers is Platt scaling.[497] It consists of minimizing the cross entropy loss over a fresh validation set, with respect to a *temperature* parameter τ scaling the logits. Given τ, we deploy the calibrated neural network $f_\tau(x) = f(x)/\tau$. Platt scaling is an effective tool to minimize the non-differentiable metric of expected calibration error[495] in the absence of distribution shifts.[480] However, no matter how well calibrated, f_τ lacks a mechanism to determine when a test input does not belong to any of the c classes described by the in-class distribution $P^{\text{in}}(X, Y)$. Such mechanisms fall under the purview of epistemic uncertainty.

11.3.2 Epistemic Uncertainty

From the Ancient Greek *epistēmē*, the word *epistemic* relates to the nature and acquisition of knowledge. In machine learning, the epistemic uncertainty $u(x)$ associated with a test input x is inversely related to its in-class input density $p^{\text{in}}(X = x)$. Unlike aleatoric uncertainty, we can reduce our epistemic uncertainty about x by actively collecting new in-class training data around x. Therefore, epistemic uncertainty is not due to irreducible randomness but rather to our lack of knowledge—*What is x like?*—or *episteme*.

As an unsupervised quantity, epistemic uncertainty is more challenging to estimate than its supervised counterpart, aleatoric uncertainty. In practical applications, it is not necessary or feasible to estimate the in-class input density $p^{\text{in}}(X)$, and simpler estimates of support suffice. The literature has produced a wealth of epistemic uncertainty estimates $u(x)$, reviewed in several surveys[485–489] and evaluated across rigorous empirical studies.[480,498,499] In particular, the OpenOOD 1.5 benchmark[499] offers a modern comparison among popular epistemic uncertainty estimates. For completeness, we list some examples below.

- The negative maximum logit[500] estimates epistemic uncertainty as

$$u(x) = -\max_j f(x)_j.$$

  Therefore, test inputs producing large maximum logits are deemed certain, and vice versa.

- The maximum softmax probability, or negative log-likelihood, estimates epistemic uncertainty as $u(x) = -\max_j \text{softmax}(f(x))_j$.

- The entropy method[169] estimates epistemic uncertainty as $u(x) = -\sum_j p_j \log p_j$, where $p_j = \text{softmax}(f(x))_j$.

- Feature pruning methods like ASH[501] construct epistemic uncertainty estimates this way:

$$u(x) = -\max_j w(\phi^p(x))_j,$$

where we build the pruned representation $\phi^p(x)$ from the original representation $\phi(x)$ by (1) zeroing all the representation values below a large percentile p and (2) setting the remaining entries to a constant, ensuring that the pruned representation matches in norm the original representation.

- Methods based on Mahalanobis distances[502–504] estimate one Gaussian distribution $\mathcal{N}(\mu_c, \Sigma_c)$ per class $c = 1, \ldots, C$ in representation space $\phi(x)$. Then, epistemic uncertainty can be defined as the minimum relative Mahalanobis distance:

$$u(x) = \min_c \left\{ (\phi(x) - \mu_c)^\top \Sigma_c^{-1} (\phi(x) - \mu_c) \right.$$
$$\left. - (\phi(x) - \mu_0)^\top \Sigma_0^{-1} (\phi(x) - \mu_0) \right\},$$

where $\mathcal{N}(\mu_0, \Sigma_0)$ is a Gaussian distribution fitted on the entire data without regards to labels. It is possible to fit a number of Gaussians greater than the number of classes by means of clustering algorithms. In the limit, using a number of Gaussians equal to the number of available examples would result in a Gaussian kernel density estimate, related to the nearest neighbor approach, described next.

- k-nearest neighbor approaches[505] estimate epistemic uncertainty as

$$u(x) = \left\| \phi(x) - \phi_{(k)}(x') \right\|,$$

where $\phi(x')_{(k)}$ is the k-nearest neighbor in the representation space among a collection of in-class validation inputs $\{x_i'\}_{i=1}^m$. Some implementations scale representation vectors to unit Euclidean norms; some others return as epistemic uncertainty the average distance to all k-nearest neighbors.

- Distillation methods train a student network, $w_{\text{student}} : \mathbb{R}^d \text{ to} \mathbb{R}^q$ to imitate a fixed teacher network, $w_{\text{teacher}} : \mathbb{R}^d \to \mathbb{R}^q$, by minimizing the distillation objective:

$$\frac{1}{m} \sum_{j=1}^m \left\| w_{\text{student}}(\phi(x_i')) - w_{\text{teacher}}(\phi(x_i')) \right\| + \Omega(w_{\text{student}}).$$

Then, the following epistemic uncertainty estimate is deployed:

$$u(x) = \left\| w_{\text{student}}(x) - w_{\text{teacher}}(x) \right\|.$$

Different methods implement different teacher networks w_{teacher} and student regularizers $\Omega(w_{\text{student}})$:

- The random network distillation or RND method[506] fixes w_{teacher} to be a random network. Intuitively, the student network does not know the shape of the random teacher at novel inputs, resulting in a large prediction error interpreted as high epistemic uncertainty.

- The support vector data description or SVDD method[507] sets $w_{\text{teacher}}(z) = c$ to be a constant function, and sets $\Omega(w_{\text{student}})$ to a weight decay penalty.

- The orthogonal certificates or OC method[508] sets $w_{\text{teacher}}(z) = 0$, and sets $\Omega(w_{\text{student}})$ to an orthonormality penalty, which we may express as $\|WW^{\top} - I_k\|$ for a linear student network $w_{\text{student}}(z) = Wz$. This penalty promotes student networks with diverse and 1-Lipschitz outputs. The intuition behind OC is that, if one finds a way to zero in-class data in diverse and smooth ways, novel out-class inputs should be mapped to nonzero values to signal epistemic uncertainty.

- Loss-prediction methods[509] set $w_{\text{teacher}}(x') = \ell(f(x'), y')$ for every validation example (x', y'), so the task of the student becomes predicting the loss at novel points, assumed to be larger for out-class examples.

- Reconstruction or auto-encoder methods[510] set $w_{\text{teacher}}(\phi(x)) = x$, so the task of the student is to reconstruct its own input, a task assumed to be easier for in-class examples.

- Ensemble methods, such as deep ensembles,[417] multiple-input multiple-output networks,[458] dropout uncertainty,[409] and test-time data augmentation,[511] train or evaluate multiple neural networks on the same test input. Their epistemic uncertainty relates to the variance across predictions. However, none of these methods guarantee increased prediction diversity (increased epistemic uncertainty) as we travel further away from the training data. For more details about ensemble methods, see chapter 9.

Figure 11.3 illustrates some of these epistemic uncertainty estimators. For those requiring their own training data, a fresh set of in-class examples, different from the training data, is required.

Choosing the appropriate epistemic uncertainty estimate $u(x)$ depends on both the learning task and the available computational resources. For example, the logit method incurs no additional computing beyond $f(x)$, but it leads to inappropriately increasing epistemic *certainty* as we move far away from the training data.[512] Conversely, local methods are less likely to overestimate confidence, but they require more computation at

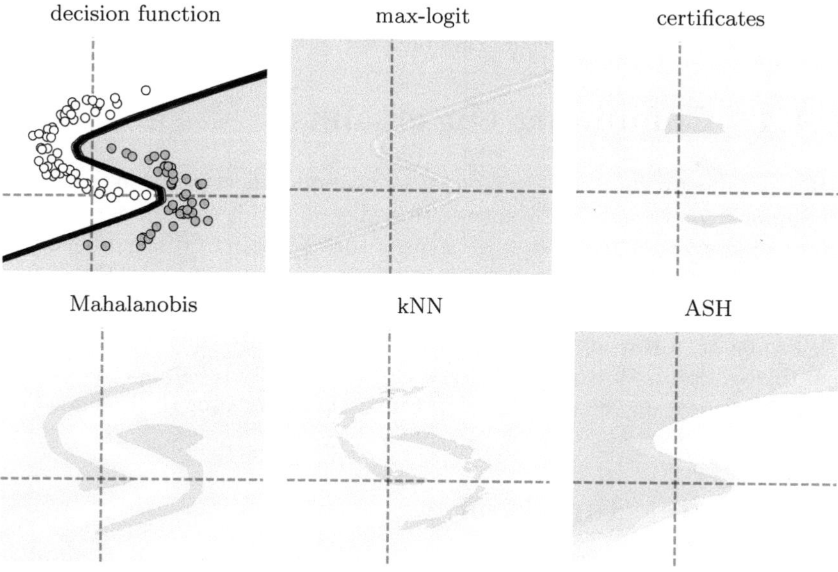

Figure 11.3: Some examples of epistemic uncertainty estimates on a two-dimensional binary classification problem. White denotes high certainty, while darker shades denote high uncertainty. Even in two-dimensional problems, the task of estimating epistemic uncertainty on deep neural networks is a challenging problem.

test time (Mahalanobis methods) or the storage of a validation set in memory (k-NN methods). Finally, constructing the uncertainty estimate $u(x)$ from the ground up[513] can be advantageous over building it on top of the representation space from a trained neural network. This is because neural network representations suffer from the simplify-and-memorize bias, retaining only the input information absolutely essential to address the classification task. However, uncertainty estimation requires additional local information about the input space, such as class boundary shapes. Therefore, estimating uncertainty on top of diverse representations, such as those provided by the the self-supervised learning algorithms described in chapter 9, is a well performing approach in certain applications.

11.4 Combining Uncertainty

How should we combine aleatoric and epistemic uncertainty into a predictive uncertainty score? To answer this question, this section assumes two ingredients as given. First, a neural network f_τ able to discern between c in-class categories with well calibrated aleatoric uncertainty. Second, an epistemic uncertainty estimator u, helpful for detecting out-class examples. When facing a test input x, and by means of these two ingredients, the aim of this section is to construct a $(c+1)$-dimensional probability vector with high classification accuracy and low calibration error over the extended test distribution $P^\star$.

11.4.1 Reject-or-classify

The simplest strategy to combine aleatoric and epistemic uncertainty is to follow a simple *reject-or-classify* (RC)[490,491] recipe. In particular, RC classifies a test input x as follows:

$$\hat{y} = \begin{cases} h_{f_\tau}(x) & \text{if } u(x) < \theta, \\ c+1 & \text{else.} \end{cases} \tag{11.6}$$

Thus, RC classifies as out-class those examples exceeding a threshold θ of epistemic uncertainty and assigns the in-class label $h_{(}f_\tau)$ otherwise. Typically, a fresh validation set $\{(x_i^{\text{va}})\}_{i=1}^m$, from the in-class distribution $P^{\text{in}}(X, Y)$, is used to determine the threshold θ. Most applications set θ to the $\alpha = 0.95$ percentile of $u(x^{\text{va}})$ across the validation inputs. This approach results in abstaining from classification on the 5% most uncertain inputs from the in-class distribution, according to the epistemic measure u.

The RC pipeline produces extended $(c+1)$-dimensional softmax vectors:

$$s_{\text{RC}}^\star(x) = \text{concat}\left(s\left(f_\tau(x)_1, \ldots, f_\tau(x)_c\right) \cdot [u(x) < \theta], 1 \cdot [u(x) \geq \theta]\right). \tag{11.7}$$

This construction has three shortcomings. First, aleatoric and epistemic uncertainties do not communicate with each other. For example, if $u(x)$ is misspecified, we may reject in-class inputs that are easy to classify and fail to reject out-class inputs. Second, the softmax vector (11.7) is not calibrated over the extended problem on $c+1$ classes, as we always accept or reject with total confidence for the out-domain class. Third, the uncertainty estimate $u(x)$ could speak in different units than the in-class logits. For instance, it could happen that $u(x)$ grows too slowly as to dominate the in-class logits on out-class examples.

11.4.2 Unified Uncertainty Calibration

To address the limitations of the RC recipe, *unified uncertainty calibration* (U2C) learns a good combination of aleatoric and epistemic uncertainties into a propositional uncertainty score. The goal is to construct an extended softmax vector—over $c+1$ classes—resulting in low test classification error and high calibration across both in-class and out-class data. To accomplish this, we start by collecting a fresh validation set $\{(x_i^{\mathrm{va}}, y_i^{\mathrm{va}})\}_{i=1}^m$ from the in-class distribution $P^{\mathrm{in}}(X, Y)$. Then, we compute the threshold θ as the $\alpha = 0.95$ percentile of $u(x_i^{\mathrm{va}})$ across all inputs in the validation set, and relabel the 5% of examples over the threshold with $y_i^{\mathrm{va}} = c+1$. (Other strategies are possible for selecting the 5% of in-class examples to be declared as out-class. For instance, it may be advantageous to relabel confident in-class errors as out-class.[514,515]) Next, learn a nonlinear epistemic calibration function $\tau_u : \mathbb{R} \to \mathbb{R}$ by minimizing the cross-entropy on the relabeled validation set:

$$\tau_u = \operatorname*{argmin}_{\tilde{\tau}_u} - \sum_{i=1}^m \log \operatorname{concat}\left(f_\tau(x_i^{\mathrm{va}}), \tilde{\tau}_u(x_i^{\mathrm{va}})\right)_{y_i^{\mathrm{va}}}. \tag{11.8}$$

Finally, the U2C pipeline deploys a machine producing extended $(c+1)$-dimensional softmax vectors following the expression:

$$s_{\mathrm{U2C}}^\star(x) = s\left(f_\tau(x)_1, \ldots f_\tau(x)_c, \tau_u(u(x))\right). \tag{11.9}$$

The U2C construction (11.9) addresses all three shortcomings from the previous RC (11.7). First, because aleatoric and epistemic uncertainties now compete for classification, there is an opportunity to accept easy in-class examples that would otherwise be rejected. Second, U2C can reject examples with different levels of confidence, because calibration happens jointly over the $(c+1)$-dimensional extended softmax vectors. Third, the *nonlinear* epistemic calibration $\tau_u(u(x))$ allows the $c+1$ logits to speak in the same units, so aleatoric and epistemic uncertainty share appropriate rates of growth.

Unified calibration translates the problem of combining aleatoric and epistemic uncertainty over c classes into the problem of optimizing for aleatoric uncertainty (expected calibration error) over $c + 1$ classes. The resulting extended softmax vectors provided by U2C facilitate reasoning akin to the *quadrant of knowledge*[516] described by former Secretary of Defense Donald H. Rumsfeld:

> Reports that say that something hasn't happened are always interesting to me, because as we know, there are known knowns; there are things we know we know. We also know there are known unknowns; that is to say we know there are some things we do not know. But there are also unknown-unknowns—the ones we don't know we don't know. And if one looks throughout the history of our country and other free countries, it is the latter category that tends to be the difficult ones.[517]

To translate the quote above into a machine learning context, consider a binary classification problem with uncertainties jointly calibrated with U2C, resulting in three-dimensional extended softmax vectors that describe the probability of the first class, second class, and out-class class. Then,

- vectors such as $(0.9, 0.1, 0.0)$ are *known-knowns*, things that we are aware of (we can classify) and we understand (we know how to classify), no uncertainty;

- vectors such as $(0.4, 0.6, 0.0)$ are *known-unknowns*, things we are aware of but we do not understand. These are instances with aleatoric uncertainty, but no epistemic uncertainty;

- vectors such as $(0.1, 0.0, 0.9)$ are *unknown-knowns*, things we understand but are not aware of. These are instances with epistemic uncertainty, but no aleatoric uncertainty.

In addition, *unknown-unknowns* refer to patterns ignored by the representation space. For example, if color is irrelevant for shape classification, simplify-and-memorize learning strategies will often discard color information. In that case, should we be uncertain on how to classify known shapes of unseen colors? (For instance, kittens housed from birth in a cage containing only vertical stripes were, later in life, unable to react to horizontal patterns.[518]) Because no representation can capture the inexhaustible amount of detail in the world, unknown-unknowns are a necessary evil when learning from a combinatorially explosive amount of patterns under a limited computational budget.[160]

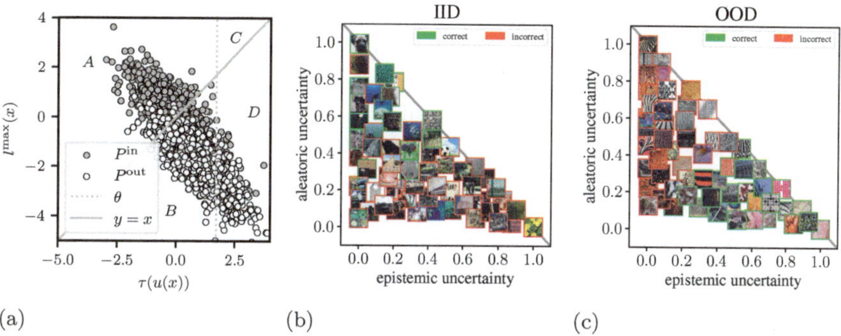

Figure 11.4: Panel (a) shows the acceptance/rejection regions of RC and U2C, serving as a visual support for our theoretical analysis. Panel (b) shows examples of IID images according to their epistemic uncertainty ($u(x)$, horizontal axis), aleatoric uncertainty ($\pi_f(x)$, vertical axis), and correctness of classification (border color). Panel (c) illustrates OOD images similarly. The last two panels illustrate how U2C covers all possible aleatoric-epistemic combinations, in a way that correlates appropriately to (mis)classification, both IID and OOD.

11.4.3   Theoretical Analysis of U2C

To understand the relative performance of RC and U2C, one needs to study where data points from P^{in} and P^{out} lie. Recall that reject-or-classify rejects data when $u(x) \geq \theta$, and unified uncertainty calibration rejects it when $\max_i f_\tau(x)_i \leq \tau(u(x))$. Therefore, it makes sense to center our analysis on the space induced by $\tau(u(x))$ and the max-logit. Figure 11.4a shows that the accept/reject regions break up the space into four parts: A, where both methods predict with the neural network f; B, where U2C rejects but not RC; C, where RC rejects but not U2C; and D, where both reject. A and D are clear in-class and out-class regions, respectively. In region C, the uncertainty is high but max-logits are higher. This is the *Dunning-Kruger* region—little data is seen here during training, yet the network is highly confident. Lastly, B is the region of high in-class aleatoric uncertainty, with low to moderate epistemic uncertainty.

Under certain conditions, U2C outperforms RC. If P^{out} has a lot of mass in B and little in C, then U2C outperforms RC. B is the region of high aleatoric uncertainty and low to moderate epistemic uncertainty, so communication between different kinds of uncertainties helps improve performance. In contrast, if P^{in} has a lot of mass in C but little in B, then RC outperforms U2C in terms of hard predictions. The training loss for τ ensures that at least 95% of the validation data lies in A and at most 5% in D. Therefore, if the underlying neural network has high accuracy, and if τ

generalizes well, then we expect $P^{\text{in}}(B \cup C)$ to be low. A related question is what happens in C, which is the region where U2C predicts with high confidence yet low evidence. Since both the max-logit and the uncertainty are complex functions of x, all possible values of $(\max_i(f_\tau(x))_i, \tau(u(x)))$ are not achievable, and varying x within the instance space induce pairs within an allowable set. Choosing u to limit that allowable set will permit us to bound C. For example, for binary linear classification, if we ensure that the uncertainty estimate u grows faster than the logits, then C will be bounded by design. Finally, the negative log-likelihood of RC will be infinite if P^{in} has some probability mass in $C \cup D$; this is bound to happen since the construction of τ ensures that 5% of in-distribution examples from P^{in} are constrained to be in D. The negative log-likelihood of RC will also be infinite if P^{out} has some probability mass in $A \cup B$, which is also likely to happen. This is a consequence of the highly confident predictions made by RC. Conversely, U2C makes softer predictions that lower negative log-likelihood values.

11.5   Empirical Analysis of U2C

Next, let us compare the empirical performance of the RC and U2C methods for combining aleatoric and epistemic uncertainty. The following experiments implement a full-spectrum out-of-distribution detection analysis[499] on four ImageNet-based uncertainty estimation benchmarks: in-class, covariate shift, near-ood, and far-ood. First, to evaluate in-class we construct two equally sized splits of the original ImageNet validation set,[519] called ImageNet-va and ImageNet-te. The split ImageNet-va is used to find the epistemic uncertainty threshold θ and calibration parameters (τ, τ_u). The split ImageNet-te is our true in-class *test set* used for model evaluation. Second, we evaluate metrics under covariate shift using the in-class datasets ImageNet-C[306] containing image corruptions, ImageNet-R[307] containing artistic renditions, and the ImageNet-v2 validation set.[308] For these first two benchmarks, we expect the predictors to classify examples x into the appropriate in-class label $y \in \{1, \dots, c\}$. Third, we evaluate metrics for the near-ood datasets NINCO[520] and SSB-Hard.[521] Near-ood datasets are difficult out-of-distribution detection benchmarks containing examples from the out-of-distribution class $y = c+1$ that are visually similar to the in-class classes. Finally, we evaluate metrics on the far-ood datasets iNaturalist,[522] Texture,[523] and OpenImage-O.[524] Far-ood datasets contain examples from the out-of-distribution class $y = c+1$, but should be easier to distinguish from those belonging to the in-class classes. Both methods under comparison, RC and U2C, require an epistemic uncertainty estimate $u(x)$. The analysis below compares some of the most popular approaches for this purpose: MaxLogit,[500] ASH,[501] Mahalanobis,[504] and KNN,[505] all described in section 11.3.2 above.

Table 11.1 shows err/ece metrics for RC on various benchmarks for uncertainty estimation. Parentheses show improvements (in black) or deterioration (in gray) brought about by replacing RC by U2C. Error-bars are absent because there is no randomness involved in these experiments—the splits ImageNet-va and ImageNet-te are computed once and set in stone for all runs. In most experiments, U2C brings improvements in both test classification accuracy and calibration error. When U2C deteriorates results, it does so with a small effect. Figure 11.4b and figure 11.4c shows that the U2C-calibrated epistemic-aleatoric uncertainty space covers the entire lower-triangle of values—in contrast, RC could only cover two crowded vertical bars at the two extremes of epistemic uncertainty. The original work proposing U2C shows additional experiments on *linear* U2C (showcasing the importance of calibrating nonlinearly), as well as other neural network architectures, such as visual transformers.

11.6   Uncertainty in Sequential Environments

What does uncertainty estimation look like in sequence-to-sequence models, such as LLMs? Recently, "an urgent common concern about LLMs has [been] the propensity of generating erroneous information without warning."[525] The materials in this chapter are relevant to this problem since "higher predictive uncertainty corresponds to a higher chance of hallucination,"[526] Yijun Xiao et al. argue, whereby "epistemic uncertainty is more indicative of hallucination than aleatoric or total uncertainties."[526]

Before progressing any further, it is useful to set up some notation to explore uncertainty estimation in LLMs. Given a prompt x, sample a response $\hat{y}_i = \hat{y}_{i,1}, \ldots, \hat{y}_{i,t_i}$ from the LLM by executing:

$$\phi_{i,j} = \phi(x, \hat{y}_{i,<j}), \tag{11.10}$$

$$l_{i,j} = w(\phi_{i,j}), \tag{11.11}$$

$$\hat{y}_{i,j} \sim \text{Categorical}(\text{softmax}(l_{i,j}, \tau = 1)), \tag{11.12}$$

for all $i = 1, \ldots, t_i$, where $\phi_{i,j}$ is the last-layer hidden representation to produce the token $\hat{y}_{i,j}$, $l_{i,j}$ is the logit vector to produce the token $\hat{y}_{i,j}$, $\hat{y}_{i,<j} = \hat{y}_{i,1}, \ldots, \hat{y}_{i,j-1}$ are all the tokens produced so far, and we sample a total of k responses $\hat{y}_1, \ldots, \hat{y}_k$.

The notations above suggest four strategies to estimate the predictive uncertainty about a response sequence $\hat{y}_i$ provided by an LLM. One avenue is to reuse the machinery developed earlier in this chapter for classification

		MaxLogit	**ASH**	**Mahalanobis**	**KNN**
ImageNet-va	err	25.1 (+0.2)	25.6 (−0.0)	24.9 (−0.0)	26.7 (−0.2)
	ece	7.0 (−0.7)	7.1 (−0.6)	7.7 (−0.6)	7.2 (−0.9)
ImageNet-te	err	25.2 (+0.2)	25.8 (−0.0)	34.1 (−0.5)	27.4 (−0.3)
	ece	6.2 (−0.6)	6.6 (−0.6)	21.4 (−1.6)	7.3 (−0.8)
ImageNet-v2	err	38.7 (+0.4)	39.0 (+0.2)	49.8 (−0.5)	40.3 (−0.0)
	ece	14.5 (−0.1)	13.5 (−0.2)	35.9 (−1.5)	12.0 (−0.0)
ImageNet-C	err	67.7 (+0.5)	69.7 (+0.2)	77.1 (+0.2)	72.7 (+1.0)
	ece	48.0 (−0.4)	52.2 (−0.2)	67.4 (−0.2)	55.0 (+1.6)
ImageNet-R	err	79.8 (+0.4)	78.7 (+0.3)	87.4 (−0.0)	81.4 (+0.7)
	ece	56.3 (−1.0)	53.1 (−0.0)	74.9 (−0.0)	54.5 (+2.9)
NINCO	err	77.2 (−2.2)	67.6 (−1.4)	30.8 (−0.4)	73.3 (−5.1)
	ece	40.3 (−3.3)	35.4 (−2.4)	18.6 (−1.5)	35.1 (−4.1)
SSB-Hard	err	84.8 (−1.7)	83.2 (−1.1)	47.2 (−0.0)	87.1 (−2.0)
	ece	51.8 (−2.4)	50.3 (−1.6)	33.1 (−0.9)	49.9 (−1.7)
iNaturalist	err	51.8 (−3.5)	15.9 (−0.2)	16.5 (−2.2)	58.5 (−7.4)
	ece	22.6 (−5.3)	8.9 (−1.3)	7.3 (−2.0)	19.6 (−5.0)
Texture	err	52.9 (−2.9)	16.3 (+0.3)	28.0 (−3.1)	10.5 (−1.2)
	ece	29.8 (−4.1)	11.1 (−0.7)	14.6 (−2.7)	6.0 (−1.2)
OpenImage-O	err	58.6 (−3.3)	34.6 (−1.3)	21.5 (−1.9)	55.3 (−5.9)
	ece	28.6 (−5.0)	17.5 (−2.4)	11.1 (−2.0)	21.9 (−4.4)

Table 11.1: Classification errors (err) and expected calibration errors (ece) for reject-or-classify across a variety of benchmarks and uncertainty estimates. In parenthesis, we show the metric improvements (negative numbers) or deterioriation (positive numbers) from using U2C over different types of benchmarks: training distribution (rows 1-2), in-class covariate shift (3-5), near out-of-distribution (rows 6-7), and far out-of-distribution (rows 8-10).

problems. To do so, aggregate the representation and logit vectors associated to the response sequence as

$$\bar{\phi}_i = \text{aggregate}(\phi_{i,1}, \ldots, \phi_{i,t_i}), \tag{11.13}$$

$$\bar{l}_i = \text{aggregate}(l_{i,1}, \ldots, l_{i,t_i}), \tag{11.14}$$

where the function "aggregate" can be the average or the maximum operations. Then, apply the aleatoric and epistemic uncertainty estimates developed in section 11.3.1 and section 11.3.2 on the aggregated representation and logit vectors.

Second, we may operate at the sequence level. To this end, let us assume that the first response $\hat{y}_1$ is sampled with a temperature parameter $\tau = 1$, and that the rest of the responses $\hat{y}_2, \ldots, \hat{y}_k$ employ a temperature parameter $\tau < 1$ to increase their diversity.[525] Then, we can estimate uncertainty as

$$u(x) = 1 - \frac{1}{k-1} \sum_{i=2}^{k} (1 - d(\hat{y}_1, \hat{y}_i)), \tag{11.15}$$

where d is a sentence embedding distance function, often provided by an external language model.

Third, we may prompt the LLM as to verbalize its uncertainty. On multiple-choice questions, LLMs provide estimates about their own uncertainty by prompting them with questions such as "How sure are you?"[527] Therefore, we may estimate the uncertainty of an LLM given a prompt x by (1) adding an uncertainty-eliciting question to the prompt, (2) sampling multiple responses, and (3) averaging the verbalized uncertainty estimates across responses.[528] It is worth noting some subtle differences between predictive and verbalized uncertainties. For instance, when asking an LLM "What's the probability of a fair coin toss landing heads?" the verbalized confidence should say "50%," yet the predictive uncertainty to generate the tokens 5-0-% should be low. That is, the machine is sure that it is unsure how the coin will land. The difference between predictive and verbalized uncertainty is a cue to study the phenomenon of hallucination,[529] whereby LLMs confidently generate nonfactual data.[372]

Fourth, the semantic entropy[530] method computes the uncertainty of a prompt x by (1) sampling K responses $y_1, \ldots, y_K$, (2) clustering these responses into C clusters, and (3) computing the sum of cluster entropies. In the second step, clustering is performed by means of an external LLM capable of estimating entailment. Specifically, we provide this external LLM with the prompt "When evaluating the question x, consider the two possible answers y_i and y_j; do these two answers semantically entail each other?" Then, responses (y_j, y_j) estimated to entail each other are groups into the same cluster. The cluster entropy $P(C_i \mid x) \log P(C_i \mid x)$ is computed using the expression $P(C_i \mid x) = \sum_{y \in C_i} P(y_i \mid x)$, where $P(y_i \mid x)$ follows the auto-regressive probability formula for the response sequence y_i. As a final remark, LLM uncertainty estimates improve with model size and temperature scaling,[531] while they suffer under distribution shifts.[527]

11.7 Uncertainty and Invariance

Awareness of uncertainty is helpful to determine whether we are within the operating conditions of an invariant mechanism. In that sense, the problem of uncertainty estimation can be understood as estimating a support indicator about the relevant environments $\mathcal{E}$ given the training environments $\mathcal{E}_{\text{tr}}$. Woodward makes a similar point when suggesting that a causal theory is supposed to provide both a law and a range of operation:

> First, we have some target relationship or generalization ϕ whose invariance we are assessing. Second, we have a range $\mathcal{E}$ of changes or conditions over which ϕ is claimed to be invariant, where—this is important for reasons described subsequently—this range may be very incompletely or inexactly specified. In this model, ϕ and $\mathcal{E}$ are (or are permitted to be) specified separately or independently: that is, in contrast to the exception-incorporating model, we do not always or automatically build information about $\mathcal{E}$ into ϕ, although in some circumstances it may be appropriate to do this. [notation mine][134]

The specification of rule ϕ and range of operation $\mathcal{E}$, Woodward continues, admits separate specification:

> A very common situation is that although some candidate generalization is invariant over some changes and although we know some of the circumstances under which it is invariant, the information we have about the exact boundaries of its domain of invariance is often vague, incomplete, and perhaps in part mistaken. Because of this, such information is often inappropriate for incorporation into the generalization itself, which, for explanatory and modeling purposes, we generally want to be as clear and precise as possible. The independent specification model allows us represent this imprecise information separately in the domain description, where such imprecision is more tolerable, rather than attempting to incorporate it into our candidate generalizations. We segregate off the vagueness and imprecision by putting it into the specification of the domain and keeping it out of generalization itself.[134]

In conclusion, learning invariant predictors and modeling their operating conditions are two necessary yet distinct ingredients of generalizing across multiple environments.

Chapter 12

Fairness and Alignment

This chapter is based on David Lopez-Paz et al. *Measuring and Signing Fairness as Performance Under Multiple Stakeholder Distributions*. arXiv, 2022.

12.1 Introduction

AI systems are increasingly embedded in critical sectors such as banking,[533] justice,[534] citizen services,[535] government,[536] policing,[537,538] and other public services.[539] Given their impact on billions of lives, it is crucial to monitor and enforce the *fairness* of the automated decisions made by these systems.[540] When do machine learning systems provide impartial treatment to individuals, steering clear of discrimination between social groups, such as those defined by socioeconomic status, skin tone, or gender?[541–543] Taking the field of medicine as an example, caution should abound when relying on automated statistical methods for clinical decisions:

> Black patients, whose lesions may have different characteristics from white patients, may thus be less likely to be accurately diagnosed by automated algorithms. This omission should not be taken lightly, as Black patients have the highest mortality rate for melanoma, with an estimated 5-year survival rate of only 70%, versus 94% for white patients.[544]

Similarly:

> In cardiology, a heart attack is overwhelmingly misdiagnosed in women. Nevertheless, prediction models for cardiovascular disease that claim

to predict heart attacks 5 years before they happen are trained in predominantly male datasets.[544]

Currently, our primary tools to measure fairness in machine learning are *fairness metrics*. These are mathematical one-liners probing specific conditional independence relationships among predictions, targets, and a given sensitive attribute, manually annotated for all training examples.[545] These metrics, however, face three fundamental shortcomings. First, fairness metrics lack *flexibility* and are often mutually incompatible. Simple mathematical expressions are unlikely to capture the complexity and subtlety required to articulate a socially ambiguous and evolving concept like fairness.[540] Second, fairness metrics fail to accommodate for *subjectivity*. In particular, they limit the participation of those stakeholders not directly involved in training data collection or system training. Third, fairness metrics lack *robustness*: They are easy to game, and their optimization can in some circumstances *degrade* the fairness of the system.[546] For instance, deciding court cases through coin tosses would ensure statistical independence between rulings and the defendant's race, yet such a decision-making system would undeniably be unjust.

The present chapter shifts the focus from rule-based to data-driven approaches in evaluating the fairness of machine learning systems. The central idea draws from the Invariance Principle and the domain generalization literature, where fairness metrics emerged independently as regularizers to encourage out-of-distribution performance. In essence, we define the fairness of a machine learning system as

> the ability to generalize across multiple, societally relevant *stress environments* $\mathcal{E}$, as collected by various stakeholders.

By linking the fairness and invariance properties of a system, this definition underscores the societal consequences of learning spurious correlations, as well as the importance of specifying the relevant environments for their measurement. Stress environments do, in addition, address the three main shortcomings of fairness metrics.

First, the framework of stress environments is *flexible*. As with invariance, any claim of fairness should invite the question: fair across which environments? The framework is in accordance with Irene Chen and colleagues, who argue that fairness should be "addressed through data collection, rather than by constraining the model."[547] In the realm of AI safety, Arvind Narayanan and Sayash Kapoor also recommend identifying a collection of relevant environments to establish a comprehensive evaluation protocol:

> AI safety is not a model property. With a few exceptions, AI safety questions cannot be asked and answered at the levels of models alone.

Safety depends to a large extent on the context and the environment in which the AI model or AI system is deployed. We have to specify a particular context before we can even meaningfully ask an AI safety question.[38]

Second, stress environments embrace *subjectivity*, providing a participatory framework in which stakeholders can use their data to measure the fairness of a system according to their own values. "When members of underrepresented groups are actively engaged in science," Natalia Norori and colleagues note, "they can contribute to the identification of bias against their communities, and with solutions to increase their representations in the datasets used to develop AI algorithms."[544]

Third, stress environments are a *robust*, difficult-to-manipulate alternative to measure fairness. Assessing the fairness of machine learning systems by means of challenging examples is an increasingly common practice,[548–557] and the importance of diverse datasets that fairly represent various social groups is widely recognized.[558,559] For instance, Holstein and colleagues[560] highlight "the central importance of careful test set design to detecting potential fairness issues" and consider it "extremely useful" to "support practitioners in collecting and curating high-quality datasets in the first place, with an eye towards fairness in downstream ML models."

This chapter focuses on assessing the fairness of binary classifiers. However, the concepts introduced here can be generalized to more advanced prediction systems, such as LLMs,[561,562] by examining how well they respond to stress prompts with appropriate outputs. A similar framework could also apply to the study of alignment, which concerns evaluating whether a learning machine assists its user in achieving the intended objectives while avoiding unintended consequences.[563,564]

12.2 The Status Quo in Learning Fair Classifiers

Without loss of generality, consider learning fair binary classifiers. To this end, collect a training set of examples, each comprising a triplet (x, a, y). In this chapter, x denotes a vector of input features, a is a sensitive attribute (cf. environment), and $y \in \{-1, +1\}$ is a binary label. As discussed in chapter 2, assume that all training examples originate from some unknown training distribution P^{tr}. Once our training data is available, train the classifier so it produces appropriate prediction scores f_i for each individual i in the training set. In particular, ask the classifier to predict high scores (often logits) when given input features x_i associated with positive labels $y_i = +1$, and low scores otherwise. These scores can be later calibrated (scaled) to represent probabilities by means of the softmax operation (chapter 11).

To settle our notation, consider the controversial COMPAS decision support tool, designed by Northpointe Inc. and employed by US Courts to determine the likelihood of a defendant reoffending.[565] Here, training examples (x, a, y) are a limited description of past defendants. This description includes some input features x (such as past criminal records, drug involvement), a sensitive attribute a (such as race), and a binary target y determining whether the past defendant has reoffended. In the following, let us assume that the training set is an incomplete list of past defendants from Florida's Broward County, which would serve as our training distribution P^{tr}. Using this training data, we train our classifier to predict high scores f_i when given features x_i of reoffenders (labeled with $y_i = +1$), and low scores otherwise.

12.2.1 Evaluating Performance Metrics

Once trained, we assess the performance of our classifier on new, testing examples (x', a', y'). To summarize the discussions in previous chapters, there are two strategies to evaluate a classifier. On one hand, *in-domain* evaluation considers that the training and testing examples are all identically and independently distributed according to the same probability distribution. On the other hand, *out-domain* evaluation considers testing examples drawn from a novel, unknown test distribution.

Back to our running example, we can evaluate the performance of the COMPAS recidivism classifier by collecting two types of new cases for defendants. When these testing cases concern Florida's Broward County, we are evaluating the classifier in-domain ($P^{\text{te}} = P^{\text{tr}}$). On the other hand, when collecting these testing cases from a different state in the US, we are evaluating the classifier out-domain ($P^{\text{te}} \neq P^{\text{tr}}$). The following sections argue that measuring performance out-domain is closely related to the primary focus of this chapter: evaluating fairness.

12.2.2 Evaluating Fairness Metrics

Assessing the fairness of classification systems is often done in reference to some sensitive attribute a, which, in this example (but not in stress environments), is assumed to be available for all training and testing examples. Different values of the sensitive attribute a stratify data into societally important groups, such as gender or household income. The research community has proposed various metrics to evaluate the fairness of machine learning systems.[545] These metrics can be enforced during preprocessing, training, or postprocessing of AI systems.[566] A more informal, yet useful approach to AI fairness is John Rawls's *veil of ignorance*:[567] What AI systems would I like to be subject to, if I were to ignore my race, gender, and position in society?

The three most popular metrics of fairness are the independence, separation, and sufficiency criteria.[540] These metrics, already discussed in the context of invariant learning in section 5.5, are summarized below.

- First, *independence* (also known as parity or equality of outcome) measures fairness as the level of statistical independence between the prediction scores f and the sensitive attribute A. Thus, a classification rule satisfies the independence metric when the distributions of scores are the same across values for the sensitive attribute, that is, $F \perp A$. Simply *hiding* or *omitting* sensitive attributes does not lead to independence, as these attributes may be correlated to other visible features in unforeseen manners. One oft-cited example is redlining, where financial services are withheld from neighborhoods that have significant numbers of racial and ethnic minorities (protected attributes) by means of tracking ZIP codes (correlated visible feature).

- Second, *separation* (or equality of opportunity) measures fairness as the level of the similarity between false negative and false positive errors across values of the sensitive attribute. Mathematically, this amounts to requiring that the prediction score f and the sensitive attribute a are conditionally independent given the label y, that is, $F \perp A \mid Y$.

- Third, *sufficiency* (or equality of treatment) requires calibrated prediction scores (representing probabilities) for every group defined by the sensitive attribute. This is requiring that the label y and the sensitive attribute a are conditionally independent given the predictions score f, that is, $Y \perp A \mid F$. Sufficiency is enforced by the Invariance Principle across sensitive attribute values, highlighting the relationship between *equality of treatment* and the *invariance of the optimal classifier*.

Returning to COMPAS, an influential article in ProPublica[565] claimed that the recidivism classifier was unfair under the separation metric:

> Blacks are almost twice as likely as whites to be labeled a higher risk but not actually reoffend. It makes the opposite mistake among whites: They are much more likely than Blacks to be labeled lower risk but go on to commit other crimes.

In response, the developer of COMPAS issued a technical report to rebut ProPublica's analysis by arguing that the system satisfied other fairness metrics, such as sufficiency.[568] While a *metric fight* unfolded throughout the controversy,[569–571] discussions about the distributions of examples used to compute these metrics were disappointingly thin. Yet this is a critical issue, because a COMPAS classifier passing any fairness metric for Florida's Broward County could fail resoundingly when evaluated on defendants from a different state. Following this line of reasoning, what insights can a thorough investigation into the distribution of out-domain failure cases reveal about the unfairness of a classification system?

12.3   Unfairness in-the-Wild: A Catalog

The previous section hints at a possible relationship between out-domain generalization and fairness. Building on that foundation, this section provides a list of examples of claims about unfairness found in the research literature and popular press. The purpose of this catalog is twofold. To be sure, we would like to build a better intuition about the subjectivity involved in defining fairness in different contexts. But we also want to sharpen our sense of connection between the unfairness of a learning system and its failure to generalize out-domain. To this end, for each entry in the catalog, the reader can find (1) a claim about unfairness concerning some underlying classifier, (2) one or more references to the relevant literature and popular press, and (3) one possible distribution of examples out-domain under which the classifier does not seem to generalize.

- Algorithms to predict recidivism flagging non reoffending Black people twice as often as white people.[565] Out-domain example: Black people.

- Commercial gender classification systems misclassifying Black women forty times more often than white men.[39] Out-domain example: Black women.

- Nikon cameras detecting Asian people as blinking.[572] Out-domain example: Asian people.

- Object classifiers underperforming on images of lower-income households[552] and Asian bridge-rooms.[551] Out-domain example: Low-income households and Asian bridge-rooms.

- Google tagging photos of Black people with nonhuman labels.[573] Out-domain example: Black people.

- Facebook's video-caption matching system propagating a racially sensitive tag from a past user-supplied text caption into a video showing a Black person.[574] Out-domain example: Black people.

- Automatic grading systems assigning lower scores to highly qualified students belonging to minorities[575] or attending schools with a worse track record.[576] Out-domain example: High-performing students from minority groups and lower-performing schools.

- Amazon's recruitment system disregarding highly qualified female candidates.[577,578] Out-domain example: Résumés from high-performing female candidates.

- Apple assigning low credit scores to highly qualified female applicants.[579] Out-domain example: Female applicants with a strong credit record.

- YouTube's captioning system underperforming for female voices.[580] Out-domain example: Audio recordings of female speakers.

- Healthcare systems labeling sick Black patients with similar scores to healthy white patients.[581] Out-domain example: Black patients with urgent healthcare needs.

- Toxicity prediction systems exhibiting a negative bias against minoritized speakers.[582] Out-domain example: Non-toxic tweets of African-American speakers.

- Sentiment prediction systems labeling sentences involving certain gender-race combinations with higher intensity.[583] Out-domain example: Neutral tweets from Black women writers.

- Speech-to-text systems underperforming on certain accents[584] and African-American speakers.[585] Out-domain example: Audio recordings of speakers from minority groups and with foreign accents.

- Language identification systems underperforming on African-American English.[586] Out-domain example: Texts by African-American writers.

- Google Translate showing gender-role stereotypes when translating from gender-neutral languages such as Turkish.[587] Out-domain example: Turkish-English Sentences breaking gender-role stereotypes.

- Word embeddings showing gender-role stereotypes to a disturbing extent.[588] Out-domain example: Texts to translate breaking gender-role stereotypes.

- LinkedIn classifying female names as misspelled male names.[589] Out-domain example: Female names.

Some claims about unfairness, denouncing the disparity of outcome between different groups of people,[540] can also be rephrased as generalization issues. In these cases, we must examine the performance of the classifier for *two or more* datasets:

- Google Search showing ads for arrest records when querying Black-sounding names.[590] Out-domain example: Datasets of white-sounding and Black-sounding names.

- Black people targeted twice as often as whites by predictive policing algorithms.[538] Out-domain example: Datasets of Black and white people.

- White residents being twice as likely as Black residents to qualify for Amazon's free same-day delivery.[591] Out-domain example: Lists of predominantly Black and white neighborhoods.

- Google Image Search shows men when querying for pictures of CEOs.[41] Out-domain example: Datasets of query-image pairs with annotated gender.

Regrettably, the list goes on.[38] Yet the central insight emerging from this catalog is clear: Failures in fairness often arise from the inability to generalize to minority groups. Because of simplify-and-memorize biases, the fairness of a classification system and its ability to generalize out-of-distribution appear to be two sides of the same coin. Next, let us deepen this connection by reframing the Invariance Principle through the lens of fairness.

12.4 From Fairness to Invariance and Back

The previous catalog underscores three central themes. First, fairness is inherently context-specific and influenced by human intentions, making it difficult to encapsulate in a straightforward mathematical formula. Second, allegations of unfairness often reflect harm to the interests of multiple, potentially overlapping groups. Third, meeting formal mathematical definitions of fairness does not guarantee fair classifiers.[546] For example, system developers might suppress concerns about disparate error rates by resorting to random classification or deliberately degrading performance for certain values of the sensitive attribute.[546] Despite these shortcomings, simplistic one-line rules remain a popular method for assessing fairness.

Historical records offer at least two cautionary tales about the dangers of defining complex concepts using simple rules. Building an ever-growing list of fairness metrics brought to halt a similar research effort in the 1970s:

It is during this time that we see the introduction of mathematical criteria for fairness identical to the mathematical criteria of modern day. Unfortunately, this fairness movement largely disappeared by the end of the 1970s, as the different and sometimes competing notions of fairness left little room for clarity on when one notion of fairness may be preferable to another.[592]

Similar testimonies recount the failure of rule-based systems to deliver intelligent behavior in the 1980s, leading AI research into its second *winter*:

Eventually, the Advanced Research Projects Agency (ARPA), the research arm of the U.S. Defense Department (later renamed to DARPA) and the primary funder of AI research and development, cut its funding of AI researchers because they had failed to deliver on most of their promises. At the time, the dominating form of creating software was still rule-based programming, in which developers explicitly specify all rules that define the behavior of a computer program.[593]

Crafting a complete set of rules to describe "what makes a cow a cow" proved dauntingly difficult in the 1980s. Why would it be simpler to define as rules an incredibly nuanced concept such as fairness?

Seeking alternatives, various fields of engineering offer clues about how to assess complex metrics such as fairness. Some examples include measuring *quality* in quality assurance,[594] *security* in penetration testing,[595] *reliability* in reliability engineering,[596] *safety* in systems safety engineering,[597] or *correctness* in software unit testing.[598] In each case, assessing a nuanced property of a complex system relies on a common strategy: Subject the system to a broad spectrum of experimental conditions, observe its outputs, and compare them to expected behaviors.

As we know by now, evaluating the performance and robustness of classification systems in novel environments falls within the scope of *domain generalization* (chapter 5, chapter 6). Interestingly, the research literature in domain generalization has independently developed formulæ akin to fairness metrics (section 12.2.2), utilizing them as regularizers to promote out-of-distribution performance (section 5.5). While choosing the best domain generalization regularizer depends on the invariances governing our data, the gold standard for model evaluation is always the same: measuring out-of-distribution generalization across a collection of relevant test environments. Given that each claim about unfairness in the catalog from section 12.3 signals a failure to generalize out-of-distribution, might it not be reasonable to evaluate fairness as the capacity to generalize across societally relevant test environments? This perspective shifts our focus from refining fairness metrics to thoughtfully curating the examples over which classification performance is measured.

12.5 The Framework of Stress Environments

The framework of *stress environments* measures the fairness of a learning machine as

> the ability to generalize across multiple, societally relevant *stress environments* $\mathcal{E}$, as collected by various stakeholders.

Each stress environment serves as a *unit test* to assess the machine's performance across a collection of examples relevant to one or more stakeholders. The machine passes a stress environment if it matches or exceeds a predefined accuracy, and fails it otherwise. A machine is said to pass a collection of stress environments $\mathcal{E}$ if it successfully passes every individual stress environment $e \in \mathcal{E}$. In that case, the system is *fair with respect to the collection of stress environments* $\mathcal{E}$, a valuable piece of information to feature in the system's specification.[599]

In practice, the framework of stress environments implements the information flow illustrated in figure 12.1. The framework encourages every stakeholder in the learning task to collect examples to illustrate their—possibly competing and even incompatible—interests about fairness, all without the need for explicitly sensitive attribute annotations. These stakeholders might include data collectors, model trainers, ethics teams, activists, journalists, expert witnesses, groups, and individual users. System creators subject the machine to each of the stress environments, and return a *pass* or *fail* signal, depending on whether the system falls short or exceeds a predefined accuracy. Using these outcomes, the different stakeholders discuss how to improve the fairness of the machine learning system. Some avenues include upgrading the training data and stress environments, enhancing the system architecture, limiting the scope of the problem, or even questioning if the task belongs to the realm of machine learning at all.

12.5.1 Flexibility

By shifting from a rule-based to a data-driven paradigm, the stress environment framework enables stakeholders to express fairness criteria in a manner that is flexible, nonparametric, and sensitive to context. Crucially, this focus on the system's input-output behavior under stress examples aligns with the intuitive strategies users have traditionally employed to identify unfairness in systems.

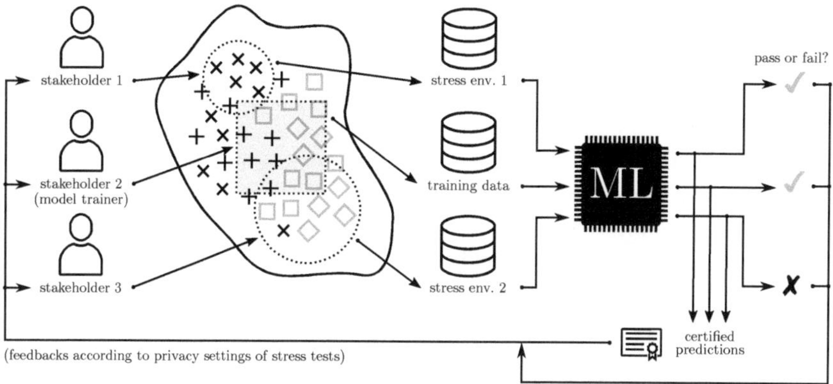

Figure 12.1: The proposed framework of *stress environments*. Stakeholders curate *stress environments* containing examples that illustrate their competing interests. The machine learning system passes or fails each stress environment, informing the relevant stakeholders on how to improve the fairness of the system. This feedback flows according to the privacy settings of each stress environment—set to avoid, for example, their incorporation as training data.

Stress environments can vary in size, and may even contain just one single example. Small stress environments could contain noteworthy cases revealing critical mistakes that would otherwise contribute a negligible percentage to the average error of the system.[600] For instance, mislabeling a single person as nonhuman might seem negligible in terms of average error, yet such a mistake is severe enough to deem the entire learning system unacceptable.

Stress environments capture data groups that transcend simplistic stratification by sensitive attributes. These include variations in environmental factors during data collection, hidden confounders, spurious correlations, or protected groups that overlap or elude explicit definition. In particular, constructing stress environments does not necessitate direct access to or annotation of sensitive attributes; these attributes are inherently shaped by the circumstances under which data is collected for each stakeholder.

12.5.2 Subjectivity

Findings in domains as general as visual perception show substantial differences across societies.[601] By embracing this subjectivity, stress environments invite all stakeholders to articulate their—potentially incompatible—fairness criteria. The resulting framework distributes the power associated with data, arguably the most important asset in AI systems. Mary Gray emphasized a similar point during her invited talk at NeurIPS 2021:

> Because data has become so powerful it is imperative that we make it our professional collective responsibility to transfer the tools of data collection, aggregation, and sharing from engineers and the institutions that underwrite their work, wherever they might be, to the communities and members of society caring about the benefits and risks of what can be built.[602]

Like several frameworks of invariance discussed throughout this book, stress environments echo Karl Popper's critical rationalism.[61] That is, the fairness of learning systems is hereby never demonstrated (although our confidence about it increases proportionally to the amount of passed stress tests), but it remains perpetually falsifiable.

After the various stakeholders articulate their perspectives on fairness, successful generalization across their stress environments requires learning statistical invariances. In essence, the framework of stress environments applies the Invariance Principle to the problem of fairness assessment, where the notion of relevance is closely tied to societal importance. In his commentary about Nozick's *Invariances*,[211] Robert Hopkins explores the interplay between invariance and truth as situated within a social context:

> Generalizing an idea from physics, Nozick suggests that what con-stitutes the objectivity of facts is invariance under certain transfor-mations. What remains constant under certain transformations is, to that extent, more objective than what does not. ... However, as Nozick concedes, the notion of invariance gives us little handle on objectivity unless we know which are the relevant transformations. ... And this is an empirical matter, depending on which transformations turn out to matter, in our best accounts of various aspects of our world and life.[603]

Reinterpreting this quote, each stress environment provides an angle on fairness by stratifying reality according to the perspective of a relevant stakeholder. Consequently, invariance across stress environments relates to fairness in the same manner that invariance across interventions relates to causation or, following Nozick and Hopkins, in the same manner that invariance relates to truth (section 5.6.5).

12.5.3 Robustness

Charles Goodhart famously remarked that "when a metric becomes a target, it ceases to be a good metric."[604] This insight is particularly relevant for learning machines, which are remarkably adept at achieving zero training error in unexpected and often undesirable ways.[5] More precisely, examples abound of undesirable classification systems that satisfy various metrics of fairness.[546] Indeed, there are numerous examples of flawed classification systems that technically satisfy various metrics of fairness.[546] A more promising approach may lie in stress environments, which inherently make it harder for machines to rely on superficial shortcuts: Succeeding across diverse stress conditions demands a deeper alignment between their reasoning and the problem at hand. When considering the fairness of a machine learning system, we must remind ourselves about the ever-present gap between our human understanding of the problem and the contorted shortcuts taken by machines to attain zero training error.

The manipulability of stress environments decreases when placing privacy constraints among stakeholders. For instance, it is important to establish the necessary protocols to avoid the incorporation of stress examples into the training data. This would implement an interface akin to a Kaggle leaderboard[605] and allow the reusability of the same stress data for multiple iterations. Tools from differential privacy[606] can further limit the information flow between stress data and system trainers. (The question of preserving the privacy of benchmarking datasets has garnered significant attention in recent years, as the widespread training of large language models on Internet-scale data has rendered publicly available datasets less effective for evaluation.) When omitted from training, public stress environments remain valuable for evaluation purposes, serving as standard datasets to assess *out-of-domain* generalization and fairness. Results on standardized, public stress environments should be integrated into model cards.

12.5.4 Limitations

Building stress environments is in some circumstances difficult or even impossible. When stress testing a third-party system over the Internet, for example, one may face legal consequences when querying the system indiscriminately.[607] In other situations, querying the system may be impossible for some of the stakeholders involved—for instance, it is not possible to query at will a banking system that assists the granting and denial of loans.

Stress environments should contain only real-world examples, excluding synthetic, adversarial, or mislabeled data.[27] Otherwise, bad actors could craft stress environments containing adversarial examples to manipulate fairness assessments. In the absence of reliable methods for detecting adversarial examples, one possible mitigation against this type of fraud may require oath-taking in court. Fabricated stress environments, in this context, are akin to false testimonies, art forgery, and evidence tampering.

Another important question is how to aggregate multiple stress environments into a single score that reflects the overall fairness of a system. Summarizing the opinions of multiple stakeholders into one number, I contend, takes away the value from analyses where different stress environments surface problems that are difficult to compare. In fact, active discussions between stakeholders are essential to improve the fairness of predictive systems. When conflicts between stakeholders' fairness criteria prove irreconcilable, we must ask whether the prediction problem lies within the scope of machine learning itself.

12.6 Relation to Prior Work

A small body of literature explicitly addresses the link between fairness and out-domain generalization.[608,609] In recent years, it's become common practice to assess the fairness of machine learning systems by testing them on various distributions of examples.[548–557]

Stress environments resemble data-driven audits[540,607] and offer system developers proper accountability guardrails.[610] Recently, startup companies have offered fairness audits of machine learning systems, where their private stress environments play a crucial role. These third-party *red teams* assume an adversarial role, akin to a hacker performing a penetration test. Consequently, their reputation hinges on the audited systems' ability to avoid fairness issues throughout their operational lifetime.

Part V

Closing

Chapter 13

Esoterica

Transcription of a notebook written while on leave in Luang Prabang, Laos.

13.1 Introduction

In a moment of his characteristic wisdom, my friend Cijo once remarked that spirituality is "the search of an invariant foundation supporting a changing Universe." Cijo, originally hailing from Kerala, South India, is admittedly influenced by Eastern traditions such as Buddhism and Hinduism. Scholar Eknath Easwaran (1910–1999), also from Kerala, notes that the sages of these traditions "sought invariants in the contents of consciousness, and discarded everything impermanent as ultimately unreal."[611] This quest for an elemental invariance lies at the heart of the Upanishads, a collection of Sanskrit texts considered the philosophical foundation of Hinduism. Easwaran elaborates:

> In the constantly changing flow of human experience, is there anything that remains the same? In the constantly changing flow of thought, is there an observer who remains the same? Is there any thread of continuity, some level of reality higher than waking, in which these states of mind cohere?[612]

Aldous Huxley (1894–1963) contends that these questions are not exclusive to Eastern thought but permeate spiritual and religions traditions across civilizations. He calls this the *perennial philosophy*, which Easwaran summarized as follows in his introduction to the *Bhagavad Gita*:

> (1) there is an infinite, changeless reality beneath the world of change;
> (2) this same reality lies at the core of every human personality; (3)

the purpose of life is to discover this reality experientially: that is, to realize God while here on earth.[613]

Here God, or the Universe, can be understood as the bedrock invariance with objective meaning beyond subjective perspective, where Vervaeke defines meaning as "to judge and experience oneself as connected appropriately to something that has an important value independent of one's valuing of it."[252] In fact, it is not surprising that our ancient ancestors turned to the night sky as one invariant to anchor their narratives and meaning. Throughout the years I dedicated to writing this book, I developed a deep fascination with the concept of invariance within various spiritual and wisdom traditions. If assuming one of the slogans in this book—"no invariance in, no invariance out"—where does the edifice of patterns and experiences stand?

This final chapter serves as a collection of personal reflections on self-discovery, aiming to illuminate the structure of our subjective experience through the concept of invariance. Investigating our own first-person consciousness is helplessly out of reach for the third-person approach followed by the scientific method. Sam Harris regards consciousness as one of "the deepest mysteries given to us to contemplate," arguing that

> there is nothing about a brain, studied at any scale, that even suggests that it might harbor consciousness—apart from the fact that we experience consciousness directly and have correlated many of its contents, or lack thereof, with processes in our brains. ... Arranging atoms in certain ways appears to bring about an experience of being that very collection of atoms.[614]

These thoughts echo what Francis Crick (1916–2004), the co-discoverer of the helical structure of DNA, called the *Astonishing Hypothesis*:

> "You," your joys and your sorrows, your memories and your ambitions, your sense of personal identity and free will, are in fact no more than the behavior of a vast assembly of nerve cells and their associated molecules. ... You're nothing but a pack of neurons.[615]

To motivate this search, Arthur Schopenhauer (1788–1860), a contemporary of Kant, suggested that inner exploration is the sole endeavor offering a chance to contact the otherwise elusive *thing-in-itself*:

> One will thus remain at the outside of things, and will never be able to penetrate to their inner nature and investigate what they are in themselves, that is, for themselves. So far I agree with Kant. But, as the counterpart of this truth, I have given prominence to this other truth, that we are not merely the *knowing subject*, but, in

> another aspect, we ourselves also belong to the inner nature that is
> to be known, *we ourselves are the thing-in-itself*; that therefore a
> *way from within* stands open for us to that inner nature belonging
> to things themselves, to which we cannot penetrate *from without*,
> as it were a subterranean passage, a secret alliance, which, as if by
> treachery, places us at once within the fortress which it was impossible
> to take by assault from without. The thing-in-itself can, as such, only
> come into consciousness quite directly, in this way, that *it is itself
> conscious of itself*: to wish to know it objectively is to desire something
> contradictory. Everything objective is idea, therefore appearance,
> mere phenomenon of the brain.[616]

That is, as Carl Jung (1935–1961) famously remarked: "Who looks outside,
dreams; who looks inside, awakes."

None of the conclusions in this chapter should be accepted on faith—
instead, test them in the private laboratory of your own mind. Through
this exploration, I aim to offer two insights. First, recognize the value of
invariance not only as a predictive tool for understanding the external world
but also as a guide to our internal mental landscape. Second, consider that
a deeper understanding of our own consciousness—where quintessentially
human phenomena arise and fade—can better equip us to develop AI systems
that behave like humans, for humans. While some may find them premature,
I hope these insights help us think better about topics such as machine
psychology, suffering, and wisdom.[617]

13.2 Buddhist Teachings

No philosophical tradition has delved as profoundly into the contemplation
of invariance—or the lack thereof—as Buddhism. In fact, Shunryū Suzuki,
who established the first Zen Buddhist monastery outside Asia, encapsulated
the teachings of Siddhartha Gautama (the Buddha, 563–483 BCE) with the
aphorism "Everything changes." At the heart of the Buddha's teachings lie
the Four Noble Truths:

1. *Life involves suffering.* Life comprises sickness, poverty, death, and
   ceaseless change—each contributing to psychological suffering.

2. *Suffering is due to attachment.* We suffer because we fail to accept
   reality *as it is*, driven instead by the pursuit of pleasure and the
   avoidance of pain.

3. *The end of attachment results in the end of suffering.* Detachment
   shifts our perspective from scarcity to abundance, where reality *as it
   is* always sums (Nietzsche's *amor fati*).

4. *There are practices to end attachment.* Chief among these is meditation, training our attention away from thought and toward the direct sensory experience of the *here and now*, where our perception of being a separate self dissolves and only *experiencing* remains.

According to the Buddha, phenomena exhibit *three marks of existence*:

- *aniccā*: all phenomena are impermanent;

- *dukkhā*: all phenomena are unsatisfactory;

- *anattā*: all phenomena dependently originated.

Because all phenomena have the nature to arise and subside (*aniccā*), clinging to them is a futile strategy to achieve long-lasting fulfillment and is the root cause of psychological suffering (*dukkhā*). The third mark of existence (*anattā*), also known as the doctrine of dependent origination, is explored next.

13.2.1 The Doctrine of Dependent Origination

In the Saṃyukta Nikāya, the Buddha taught that all phenomena are *dependently originated.* This teaching implies that "any object of experience depends for its existence or occurrence on the necessary and sufficient presence of its cause"[618] and therefore lacks intrinsic essence. For example, a "cow" does not possess essence independent of our cognition, which ascribes identity and meaning to a specific spatiotemporal arrangement of matter.

The Buddha understood different phenomena as "streams of dependently arising processes interacting,"[619] weaving an intricate causal graph where every node has predecessors—a concept sometimes depicted as *Indra's net.* In this network, every object of experience—sensations, thoughts, and emotions—lacks a separate essence because each emerges as the deterministic outcome of a complex network of causes and conditions, stretching back to the beginning of time. Nisargadatta Maharaj (1897–1981) encapsulated this idea:

> Every event is the effect and the expression of the whole and is in fundamental harmony with the whole. ... Each moment contains the whole of the past and creates the whole of the future. ... All I know is that whatever depends, is not real. ... All things depend. And because of that, we cannot be but the totality of existence.[128]

This doctrine of dependent origination—if this exists, that exists—was summarized by Buddhist philosopher Nāgārjuna (c150–250) in a celebrated verse of his *Mūlamadhyamakakārikā*:

Whatever is dependently co-arisen.
That is explained to be emptiness.

In these verses and the paragraph that follows, the term *emptiness* denotes "lacking separate existence or intrinsic essence." This should not be confused with the word *empty* appearing in later sections, which refers to "a perceived sense of spaciousness or lack of content."

As explained by philosopher Jay Garfield,[620] the doctrine of dependent origination also asserts the emptiness of causation:

> To assert the emptiness of causation is to accept the utility of our causal discourse and explanatory practice, but to resist the temptation to see these as grounded in reference to causal powers or as demanding such grounding. Dependent origination simply is the explicability and coherence of the universe. Its emptiness is the fact that there is no more to it than that.[620]

Therefore, Buddhist metaphysics suggests a process ontology that reifies only the invariant mechanism of dependent origination, which governs how the various phenomena—streams of dependently arising processes—arise and subside. (Many others have also focused on processes, such Socrates' *agape*, Simone Weil's attention, Martin Buber's I-thou, George Gurdjieff's self-remembering, Martin Heidegger's *Dasein*, Henri Bergson's *élan vital*, Alfred Whitehead's process philosophy, Nisargadatta Maharaj's sense of "I am," Paul Tillich's courage-to-be, or Ram Dass's loving awareness, to name a few.) Although the mechanism of dependent origination exists independently of its discovery by the Buddha, all phenomena are contingent upon causes and conditions, including the cognitive structures of the observer, as later noted by Kant.

I would like to conclude this subsection by highlighting two parallels. On one hand, the mechanism of dependent origination shares similarities with the Invariance Principle, stated as a theoretical concept satisfied by the laws of nature. On the other hand, variant phenomena are manifestations of this Invariance Principle, each emerging dependently on representations and environments, which themselves depend on further upstream conditions. In essence, "No invariance in, no invariance out," except for the Invariance Principle itself.

13.2.2 The Doctrine of No-Self

The doctrine of dependent origination leads to an unsettling conclusion: Your sense of being a separate self is illusory. David Hume, who likely knew about Buddhism,[621] arrives at a similar realization:

> For my part, when I enter most intimately into what I call myself, I always stumble on some particular perception or other, of heat or cold, light or shade, love or hatred, pain or pleasure. I never can catch myself at any time without a perception, and never can observe any thing but the perception. ... I may venture to affirm of the rest of mankind, that they are nothing but a bundle or collection of different perceptions, which succeed each other with an inconceivable rapidity, and are in a perpetual flux and movement.[60]

Here, the notion of *self* refers to our everyday experience of being a subject separate from the confronted objects, an ego, a thinker of thoughts outside of thoughts, an experiencer of experiences outside of experiences, the passenger inside our own bodies and behind our face.[614] Specifically, as Garfield argues, our illusion is to incur the "fallacy of going from the mere fact of awareness to the existence of a subject of awareness."[622] What is raining? There's just *raining*. Who is thinking? There's just *thinking*. It's all mechanisms.

The Buddha considered the illusion of a separate self as the root of all psychological suffering. When we mistakenly perceive ourselves as isolated fragments distinct from the world, we experience feelings of limitation, alienation, and a persistent threat of disintegration. In truth, we cannot define ourselves independently of the environment, nor can the environment be understood without reference to us. Through process of reciprocal disclosure (cf. section 5.6.4 and the concept of *resonance* below), we contribute to the formation of what we regard as external, and what is external to us shapes our internal experience.[622] We cannot be but interdependent processes within a unified whole—for how else could two truly separate entities interact?

To break the spell of separation, the fundamental insight of some Buddhist teachings—such as those found in the Dzogchen and Mahamudra texts—is the realization that we are none of the transient contents appearing in awareness, but rather the invariant container that is awareness itself. The screen upon which the film plays, the mirror in which reflections effortlessly appear. This space of awareness, ever-present and readily accessible, called the sense of "I am" by Nisargadatta Maharaj (1897–1981), exists prior to and as the backdrop for all phenomena. For example, awareness might contain emotions like sadness at any given time, yet it itself is never sad. As the Dozgchen master Tulku Urgyen Rinpoche explains using Tibetan Buddhist terminology:

> This is what we actually are: empty in essence, cognizant by nature, able to perceive, with no barrier between these two aspects. This empty quality is called dharmakaya. But we are not only empty— unlike space, we possess a knowing quality. This is what is described

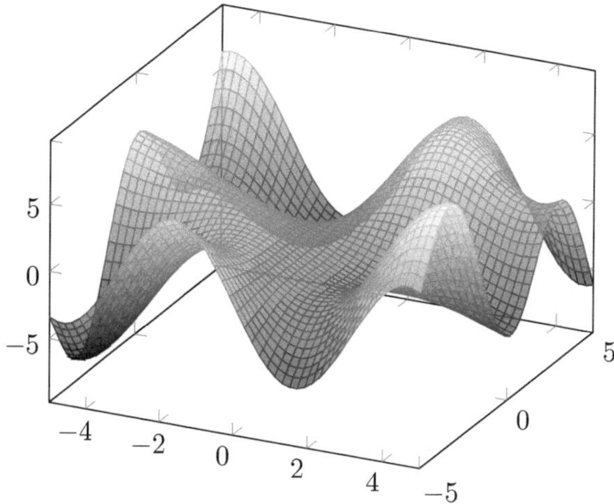

Figure 13.1: In Dzogchen, awareness can be understood as *empty cognizance,* where the *empty* quality is akin to a vector space, and the *cognizance* quality is akin to a function producing outputs in such vector space. These two combine into the invariant mechanism of awareness, which manifests transient phenomena such as sensations, thoughts, emotions, and feelings of *self* as transient vectors in that space.

as cognizant nature, sambhogakaya.[623]

Figure 13.1 explains this insight through simple mathematical concepts.

How does one, in practical terms, realize their own true nature as empty cognizance? By turning attention inward, one can attempt to locate the *self,* the vantage point from which we perceive the world. In that initial moment of turning attention upon itself, it is possible to fail to find the *self* in a way that feels conclusive.[614] (Repeatedly attempting to locate the center of consciousness, and failing to do so, is a practice known as *self-enquiry,* made popular by Ramana Maharshi.) When executed properly, this gesture precipitates a sensation of openness, where the boundary between the self and the world dissolves, leaving in its wake a unified sense of empty cognizance or *raw experiencing.* (The sensation feels similar to being absorbed while watching a film, where the sense of being a separate subject fades away.) To stabilize this insight, one can repeat the gesture in brief intervals throughout the day. With practice, a growing detachment from transient phenomena and thoughts emerges, leading to the rediscovery of one's true nature: the invariant backdrop to all experiences, which is awareness itself.

John Wheeler elucidates this process with remarkable clarity in his now out-of-print book *You Were Never Born.* His section titled "Basic Points" encapsulates our discussion in this subsection succinctly:

> It all comes down to clarifying your identity. You are already present. So there is no need to look for a future state, experience or attainment. What you are seeking to know is not separate or distant, since it is your own self. What you are must be always with you. Anything which appears and disappears cannot, by definition, be what you are. Thoughts, feelings, perceptions, experiences, objects——these all come and go. None of them as such can be the essence of what you are. So set those aside and continue to look into your true nature. What is left to consider? Surprisingly little! ... If the person is discovered as not real, not present, a mere unexamined assumption, then the root of all self-centered, conceptual thoughts, beliefs, habits, and attachments is severed. With this recognition, the interest in the self-centered stories fades naturally and effortlessly because there is no more belief in the reality of the central concept, the person. The thoughts and beliefs unwind and scatter like autumn leaves in the wind. There is no more belief in the fixed reference point of a self or a central character. You simply remain as the open sky of awareness in which all thoughts arise and set—untouched, spacious, clear and always unmodified. ... Everything that appears arises from, exists upon and returns into awareness. Even time, space and seeming external objects are present experiences contained in your knowing presence. There is nothing separate and apart from this—ever. In fact, there is just this—only this inescapable presence-awareness. You are that.[624]

> The presence-awareness that you are continues to shine through all circumstances and outcomes, regardless of what the mind thinks should be happening. If you align yourself with your true center instead of the thoughts and judgments in the mind, you cannot be moved or shaken from your center. Then all is fine as is, whatever happens. You see through to the deep essence supporting all appearances.[624]

To summarize, the project of liberation involves progressively shedding layers of misidentification with transient phenomena, thereby revealing our true nature as the spacious, invariant background condition upon which they appear. This is not a pursuit that "David"—a bundle of concepts and thoughts—can survive! Ram Dass captures the idea beautifully:

> The most exquisite paradox: as soon as you give it all up, you can have it all ... Any way you define yourself is already a prison.

When the sense of separation dissolves, the resulting awareness is all-encompassing, leaving no separate entity outside to act as a subject. Transient phenomena appear in awareness *as* awareness. Awareness is thus understood as being without a second, which is why these teachings are often referred to as *non-dual*.

13.3   The Headless Way

This section presents a series of experiments designed by Douglas Harding (1909–2007)[625] to explore the fundamental insight of no-self or non-duality, described in the previous sections. This beautiful teaching, imparted to me by Harding's student Richard Lang[626] during a retreat, has profoundly changed my understanding of subjective experience and greatly alleviated psychological suffering. As you undertake these exercises, it is vital to adopt a radical first-person perspective and scrutinize your direct experience with renewed curiosity. To do so, you must forget everything that you have been told to be by external observers at a distance, and look at your true center by yourself.

I start by noting a simple fact: I cannot see my head. Where my head is supposed to be, I find the world unfolding in all of its magnificence, with everything arising and subsiding in its own place, all on its own. Ernst Mach (1838–1916) had a similar revelation while painting his self-portrait, resulting in the headless depiction (see figure 13.2) featured in his essay "The Analysis of Sensations." Inspired by Mach's self-portrait, Harding (1909–2007) realized his own headlessness during a hike in the Himalayas:

> What actually happened was something absurdly simple and un-spectacular: just for the moment I stopped thinking. Reason and imagination and all mental chatter died down. For once, words really failed me. I forgot my name, my humanness, my thingness, all that could be called me or mine. Past and future dropped away. It was as if I had been born that instant, brand new, mindless, innocent of all memories. There existed only the Now, that present moment and what was clearly given in it. To look was enough. And what I found was khaki trouser legs terminating downwards in a pair of brown shoes, khaki sleeves terminating sideways in a pair of pink hands, and a khaki shirt iron terminating upwards in—absolutely nothing whatever! Certainly not in a head. It took me no time at all to notice that this nothing, this hole where a head should have been, was no ordinary vacancy, no mere nothing. On the contrary, it was very much occupied. It was a vast emptiness vastly filled, a nothing that found room for everything—room for grass, trees, shadowy distant hills, and far above them snow-peaks like a row of angular clouds riding the blue sky. I had lost a head and gained a world.[625]

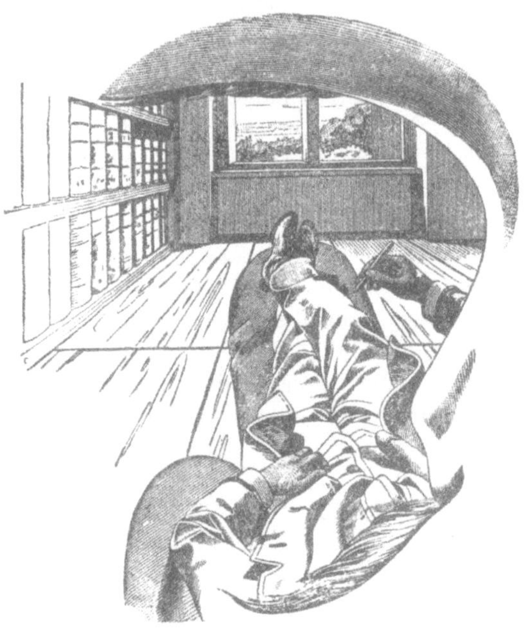

Figure 13.2: Ernst Mach's headless self-portrait.

Isn't your experience just as Harding describes? Take a closer look: Are you looking at the world out of two tiny pupils? Based on present evidence, aren't you experiencing the world through a vast, open window devoid of form, color, and frame? A window serving as the invariant context to all experience.

I realize that at the very center—at zero centimeters—I am empty capacity for the world to happen in. Like a polished mirror, this awake space effortlessly takes what's on offer—it is empty cognizance. I realize that the bird's song, thoughts, the sense of a separate self, and my own acts of attention are all pieces of the view out into the world, occurring at a distance from my untouched, invariant, transparent center. As Nisargadatta stated, "The painter is always in the picture," and to Mach's self-portrait we can refer. I conclude that the only way to have the capacity for everything is to be empty at center (cf. autonomy and independence of causal mechanisms, section 3.4.4).

This realization holds profound implications for my relationships with others. These cease to be symmetric face-to-face confrontations, becoming instead asymmetric face-to-space interactions. When we meet, we trade faces, gifting precious content to each other. I find that we are built bust-open for loving, to serve as capacity for one another.

The *pointing experiment*, shown in figure 13.3, can help you experience this for yourself. Begin by directing your index finger toward a distant object, such as a wall. Observe that it is a distinct entity in the external world, complete with shape, color, texture, and edges. Move on to pointing at your knee; similar observations can be made. Next, point to your chest. Here, the object falls at the periphery of your visual field, its outline neither sharp nor clear. Finally, turn your attention 180 degrees to point to the place from which you perceive the world. What do you see? You perceive "no thing"—a vast window without shape, color, or boundaries. When this turning gesture is executed properly, the sense of being a separate center of consciousness drops and a feeling of openness ensues. Subject and object unify, and only experiencing remains.

You may also consider the following *moving experiment*. Stand up and point with your finger to the place that you are looking out from. Slowly rotate on your feet and ask yourself: Am I moving, or is the world rotating around my still center? Ponder a similar question when traveling in a car: Am I in motion, or is the landscape flowing into my still center? While seated in a train facing against the direction of travel, does it not seem as though the entire world is pouring out of my center?

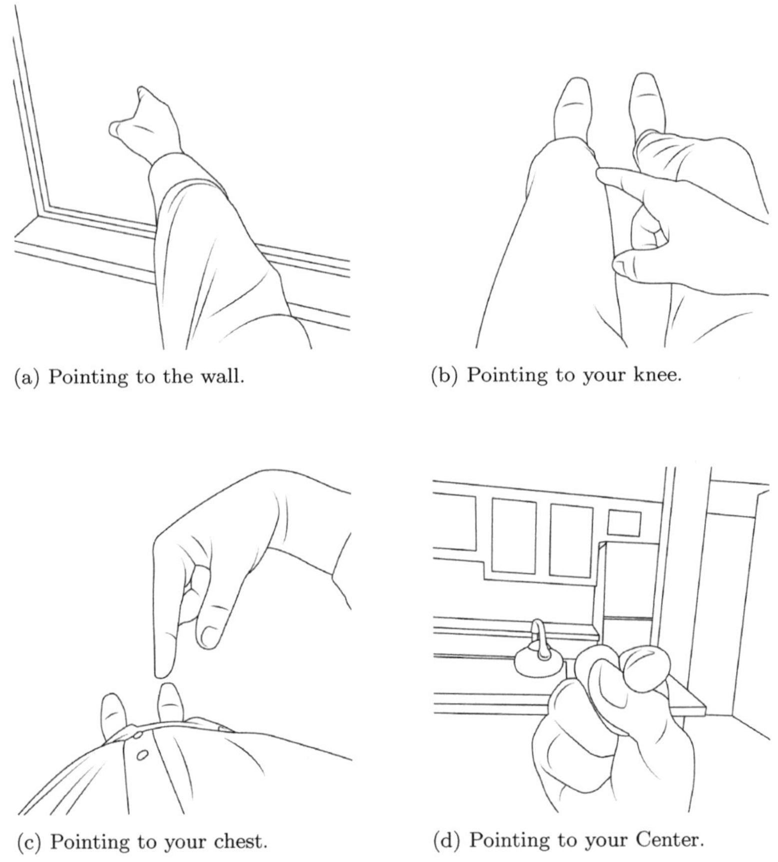

(a) Pointing to the wall.

(b) Pointing to your knee.

(c) Pointing to your chest.

(d) Pointing to your Center.

Figure 13.3: Harding's pointing exercise. Illustrations by Jamie Watters.

13.4   Living by the Invariance Principle

Love says: I am everything.
Wisdom says: I am nothing.
Between the two my life flows—Nisargadatta Maharaj.

According to Fritz Perls (1893–1970), the founder of Gestalt therapy, psychological maturation involves translating environment-support into self-support. This transformation leads to individuals with an increasing ability to respond creatively to the present moment. Much like meditation, the basic exercise in Gestalt therapy is to avoid conceptualization, seize the present moment, attend closely to our bodily sense data, and trust the self-regulation processes that sustain our organism. The goal of such exercise is what is termed *final contact*, described as "a relaxation of conscious considering, the dissolving of boundaries, and a unity of figure and ground in which splits of mind, body and external world are healed; and in the aftermath, growth occurs." According to Antonio Blay,[627] and as illustrated in figure 13.4, attaining this goal involves both horizontal work (realizing that all subjects share the same empty cognizance nature) and vertical work (realizing that all subjects are but expressions of One). Such "merging and returning to the Source" closely parallels the original meaning of *union* in the Buddhist concept of *yoga*.

If we were to formalize this model of psychological maturation, we could consider two strategies to maximize

$$\text{happiness} = \text{cognition(state of affairs)}.$$

On one hand, we could strive to maximize happiness via environment-support, that is, by tampering with the external state of affairs while keeping our cognition mechanism fixed—perhaps by acquiring a sports car. This is John Vervaeke's *having mode*, Martin Buber's *I-It mode*, or Ram Dass' *getting high*, an act of outward expression ($\phi \to E$). On the other hand, we might seek to maximize happiness via self-support, by refining our internal cognition mechanism applied on the fixed external state of affairs—for instance, by engaging in meditative practices. This is John Vervaeke's *being mode*, Martin Buber's *I-Thou mode*, or Ram Dass's *becoming free*, an act of inward impression ($E \to \phi$).

Modern society is heavily inclined toward seeking happiness through environment-support and state-goals. Our society, entrenched in causal language, is captivated with control, exploitation, and endless optimization, where individuals as exploiters confront an exploited world. However, as Hartmut Rosa argues in his book *The Uncontrollability of the World*, the

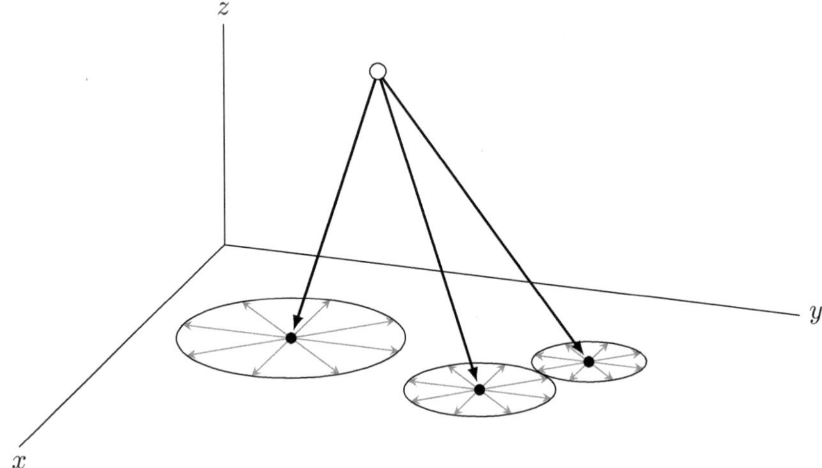

Figure 13.4: Schematic of *transpersonal psychology*, where each conscious subject (small dot) expresses a field of phenomena (small arrows) on the horizontal plane. This suggests that, in the world of phenomena—pleasure, pain, thoughts—we do not meet at our center, but rather at a distance, in the realm of abstractions, concepts, and dualities. Different subjects are different expressions (big arrows) of a common Subject (big dot) along the vertical plane. In transpersonal psychology, horizontal work consists in backtracking the small arrows to realize that all subjects share the same nature of empty cognizance. Vertical work consists in backtracking the big arrows to realize that all subjects are the same, numerically, one in number.

more we try to control external state-of-affairs, the more stagnated our internal cognitive processes become:

> The driving cultural force of that form of life we call "modern" is the idea, the hope and desire, that we can make the world controllable. Yet it is only in encountering the uncontrollable that we really experience the world. Only then do we feel touched, moved, alive. A world that is fully known, in which everything has been planned and mastered, would be a dead world.[400]

According to Rosa, "the basic mode of vibrant human existence consists not in exerting control over things but in resonating with them, making them respond to us—thus experiencing self-efficacy—and responding to them in turn."[400] Rosa denotes this aspect of engaging with the world as *resonance*, a concept akin to reciprocal disclosing, previously discussed in the context of relevance realization in chapter 5.

The end of suffering, I would therefore argue, signifies contentment by self-support and mechanism-goals; as argued by Nisargadatta:

> It is not experience that you need, but the freedom from all experience.
> ... Self-realisation is not an acquisition. It is more of the nature of understanding.[128]

Placing focus on mechanisms, as done throughout this book, it is sensible to explore the role of spurious correlations—often acquired during childhood—as potential sources of psychological distress. In fact, in his book *Painful Intelligence*, Aapo Hyvärinen parallels psychological suffering to prediction error.[617] Consequently, one route to reduce psychological suffering is to replace spurious mechanisms with invariant counterparts, helpful to generalize more effectively across the diverse situations presented by life. In this light, meditative practices can be seen as deepening the understanding that every phenomenon universally coappears with well-being, except for the invariant mechanism of empty cognizance discussed in this chapter. This reiterates a point that has been belabored throughout this book, and shall be mentioned one last time. In a world where the unobserved laws of nature take ontological priority over observed phenomena, truth resides in mechanisms, and true mechanisms are invariant.

Bibliography

1. Shane Legg and Marcus Hutter. *Universal Intelligence: A Definition of Machine Intelligence*. IJCAI, 2005. (p. 4)

2. Edward T. Heyn. *Berlin's Wonderful Horse; He Can Do Almost Everything but Talk; How He Was Taught*. The New York Times, 1904. (pp. 4, 5)

3. Laasya Samhita and Hans J. Gross. *The "Clever Hans Phenomenon" Revisited*. Communicative & Integrative Biology, 2013. (p. 4)

4. Oskar Pfungst. *Clever Hans (The Horse of Mr. von Osten): A Contribution to Experimental Animal and Human Psychology*. Henry Holt and Company, 1911. (p. 5)

5. Robert Geirhos et al. *Shortcut Learning in Deep Neural Networks*. Nature Machine Intelligence, 2020. (pp. 5, 8, 10, 197, 299)

6. Reza Bayat, Mohammad Pezeshki, Elvis Dohmatob, David Lopez-Paz, and Pascal Vincent. *The Pitfalls of Memorization: When Memorization Hinders Generalization*. arXiv, 2024. (pp. 7, 20, 45, 50, 174, 200)

7. Christopher M. Bishop and Hugh Bishop. *Deep Learning: Foundations and Concepts*. Springer, 2023. (pp. 6, 102, 212–214)

8. Alexey Dosovitskiy et al. *An Image Is Worth 16x16 Words: Transformers for Image Recognition at Scale*. arXiv, 2020. (p. 6)

9. Maxime Oquab et al. *DINOv2: Learning Robust Visual Features Without Supervision*. arXiv, 2023. (pp. 6, 19, 240)

10. James Betker et al. *Improving Image Generation with Better Captions*. OpenAI, 2023. (p. 6)

11. Alec Radford et al. *Robust Speech Recognition via Large-Scale Weak Supervision*. ICML, 2023. (p. 6)

12. Jacob Devlin, Ming-Wei Chang, Kenton Lee, and Kristina Toutanova. *BERT: Pretraining of Deep Bidirectional Transformers for Language Understanding*. arXiv, 2018. (p. 6)

13. Marta R. Costa-Jussà et al. *No Language Left Behind: Scaling Human-Centered Machine Translation*. arXiv, 2022. (p. 6)

14. David Silver et al. *Mastering the Game of Go with Deep Neural Networks and Tree Search*. arXiv, 2017. (p. 6)

15. Matej Moravčík et al. *Deepstack: Expert-Level Artificial Intelligence in Heads-up No-Limit Poker*. Science, 2017. (p. 6)

16. Oriol Vinyals et al. *Grandmaster Level in StarCraft II Using Multi-Agent Reinforcement Learning*. Nature, 2019. (p. 6)

17. Anton Bakhtin et al. *Human-Level Play in the Game of Diplomacy by Combining Language Models with Strategic Reasoning*. Science, 2022. (p. 6)

18. Mariusz Bojarski et al. *End to End Learning for Self-Driving Cars*. arXiv, 2016. (p. 6)

19. Tesla. *Autopilot and Full Self-Driving Capability*. Tesla.com, 2023. (p. 6)

20. Fei Jiang et al. *Artificial Intelligence in Healthcare: Past, Present and Future*. Stroke and vascular neurology, 2017. (p. 6)

21. Pranav Rajpurkar et al. *CheXNet: Radiologist-Level Pneumonia Detection on Chest X-Rays with Deep Learning*. arXiv, 2017. (p. 6)

22. Rhodri H. Davies et al. *Precision Measurement of Cardiac Structure and Function in Cardiovascular Magnetic Resonance Using Machine Learning*. Journal of Cardiovascular Magnetic Resonance, 2022. (p. 6)

23. Matthew Gault. *An AI-Generated Artwork Won First Place at a State Fair Fine Arts Competition, and Artists Are Pissed*. Vice Motherboard, 2022. (p. 6)

24. John Jumper et al. *Highly Accurate Protein Structure Prediction with AlphaFold*. Nature, 2021. (p. 8)

25. David Rolnick et al. *Tackling Climate Change with Machine Learning*. ACM Computing Surveys, 2022. (p. 8)

26. OpenAI. *GPT-4 Technical Report*. arXiv, 2023. (pp. 8, 205, 206, 223)

27. Ian J. Goodfellow, Jonathon Shlens, and Christian Szegedy. *Explaining and Harnessing Adversarial Examples*. arXiv, 2014. (pp. 8, 186, 299)

28. Michael A. Alcorn et al. *Strike (with) a Pose: Neural Networks Are Easily Fooled by Strange Poses of Familiar Objects*. CVPR, 2019. (p. 8)

29. Sara Beery, Grant Van Horn, and Pietro Perona. *Recognition in Terra Incognita*. ECCV, 2018. (pp. 8, 10, 46)

30. Jiawei Su, Danilo V. Vargas, and Kouichi Sakurai. *One Pixel Attack for Fooling Deep Neural Networks*. IEEE Transactions on Evolutionary Computation, 2019. (p. 8)

31. Yash Goyal, Tejas Khot, Douglas Summers-Stay, Dhruv Batra, and Devi Parikh. *Making the V in VQA Matter: Elevating the Role of Image Understanding in Visual Question Answering*. CVPR, 2017. (p. 8)

32. Timothy Niven and Hung-Yu Kao. *Probing Neural Network Comprehension of Natural Language Arguments*. ACL, 2019. (p. 8)

33. Tom Murphy VII. *The First Level of Super Mario Bros. Is Easy with Lexicographic Orderings and Time Travel*. SIGBOVIK, 2013. (p. 8)

34. Alex J. DeGrave, Joseph D. Janizek, and Su-In Lee. *AI for Radiographic COVID-19 Detection Selects Shortcuts over Signal*. Nature Machine Intelligence, 2021. (p. 8)

35. Will D. Heaven. *Hundreds of AI Tools Have Been Built to Catch COVID. None of Them Helped*. MIT Technology Review, 2021. (p. 8)

36. Michael Roberts et al. *Common Pitfalls and Recommendations for Using Machine Learning to Detect and Prognosticate for COVID-19 Using Chest Radiographs and CT Scans*. Nature Machine Intelligence, 2021. (p. 8)

37. Liv McMahon. *Glue Pizza and Eat Rocks: Google AI Search Errors Go Viral*. BBC, 2024. (p. 8)

38. Arvind Narayanan and Sayash Kapoor. *AI Snake Oil: What Artificial Intelligence Can Do, What It Can't, and How to Tell the Difference*. Princeton University Press, 2024. (pp. 8, 289, 294)

39. Joy Buolamwini and Timnit Gebru. *Gender Shades: Intersectional Accuracy Disparities in Commercial Gender Classification*. FAccT, 2018. (pp. 9, 292)

40. Julia Angwin, Jeff Larson, Surya Mattu, and Lauren Kirchner. *Machine Bias*. ProPublica, 2016. (p. 9)

41. Andrew Van Dam. *Searching for Images of CEOs or Managers? The Results Almost Always Show Men*. The Washington Post, 2019. (pp. 9, 294)

42. Pierre Stock and Moustapha Cisse. *ConvNets and ImageNet Beyond Accuracy: Understanding Mistakes and Uncovering Biases*. ECCV, 2018. (p. 9)

43. Trisha Thadani, Rachel Lerman, Imogen Piper, Faiz Siddiqui, and Uraizee Irfan. *The Final 11 Seconds of a Fatal Tesla Autopilot Crash*. The Washington Post, 2023. (p. 9)

44. The Dawn Project. *Super Bowl Commercial*. YouTube, 2023. (p. 9)

45. JordanTeslaTech. *Tesla Autopilot Mistakes Moon for Yellow Traffic Light*. X, 2021. (p. 9)

46. DeltyThe73rd. *AI Generations of Salmon Swimming down the River*. X, 2022. (p. 9)

47. Gwern Branwen. *The Neural Net Tank Urban Legend*. Gwern.net, 2023. (p. 9)

48. Antonio Torralba and Alexei A. Efros. *Unbiased Look at Dataset Bias*. CVPR, 2011. (p. 9)

49. Martin Arjovsky, Léon Bottou, Ishaan Gulrajani, and David Lopez-Paz. *Invariant Risk Minimization*. arXiv, 2019. (pp. 10, 12, 13, 147, 151, 152)

50. Sara Santora. *Beaches Forced to Close After Multiple Cow Attacks Leave People Injured*. Newsweek, 2014. (p. 10)

51. Robin L. Plackett. *Studies in the History of Probability and Statistics. XXIX: The Discovery of the Method of Least Squares*. Biometrika, 1972. (p. 19)

52. Marvin Minsky and Seymur Papert. *Perceptrons: An Introduction to Computational Geometry*. MIT Press, 1969. (p. 19)

53. Yann LeCun, Yoshua Bengio, and Geoffrey Hinton. *Deep Learning*. Nature, 2015. (p. 19)

54. Ian Goodfellow, Yoshua Bengio, and Aaron Courville. *Deep Learning*. MIT Press, 2016. (p. 19)

55. Hugo Touvron et al. *Llama 2: Open Foundation and Fine-Tuned Chat Models*. arXiv, 2023. (pp. 19, 205, 223)

56. Tom Mitchell. *Machine Learning*. McGraw Hill, 1997. (p. 22)

57. Eugene P. Wigner. *Symmetries and Reflections*. Ox Bow Press, 1979. (pp. 22, 76, 89, 155, 209)

58. Bertrand Russell. *The Problems of Philosophy*. Oxford University Press, 1912. (p. 22)

59. Francis Bacon. *Novum Organum*, 1620. (p. 23)

60. David Hume. *A Treatise of Human Nature*, 1739. (pp. 25, 62, 63, 308)

61. Karl Popper. *The Logic of Scientific Discovery*. Julius Springer, 1959. (pp. 25, 27, 28, 36, 298)

62. David Hume. *An Enquiry Concerning Human Understanding*, 1748. (pp. 25, 62, 63, 80)

63. Helen Beebee, Christopher Hitchcock, and Peter Menzies. *The Oxford Handbook of Causation*. Oxford University Press, 2009. (pp. 26, 58, 59, 68, 79, 83, 86, 89–91, 96, 109, 162)

64. Charlie D. Broad. *Ethics and the History of Philosophy: Selected Essays*. Taylor and Francis, 1952. (p. 26)

65. Leah Henderson. *The Problem of Induction*. The Stanford Encyclopedia of Philosophy, 2020. (p. 26)

66. Karl Popper. *Conjectures and Refutations, the Growth of Scientific Knowledge*. Routledge, 1962. (p. 26)

67. Wesley C. Salmon. *Rational Prediction*. The British Journal for the Philosophy of Science, 1981. (p. 27)

68. Paul E. Meehl. *Philosophical Psychology*. University of Minnesota, 1989. (p. 28)

69. Paul E. Meehl. *Theoretical Risks and Tabular Asterisks: Sir Karl, Sir Ronald, and the Slow Progress of Soft Psychology*. Journal of Consulting and Clinical Psychology, 1992. (p. 28)

70. Moritz Hardt and Benjamin Recht. *Patterns, Predictions, and Actions: Foundations of Machine Learning*. Princeton University Press, 2022. (p. 29)

71. Like Hui and Mikhail Belkin. *Evaluation of Neural Architectures Trained with Square Loss Versus Cross-Entropy in Classification Tasks*. arXiv, 2020. (p. 33)

72. Francis Bach. *Learning Theory from First Principles*. MIT Press, 2023. (p. 33)

73. Mehryar Mohri, Afshin Rostamizadeh, and Ameet Talwalkar. *Foundations of Machine Learning*. MIT Press, 2018. (pp. 34, 37)

74. Vladimir Vapnik and Alexei Chervonenkis. *The Uniform Convergence of Frequencies of the Appearance of Events to Their Probabilities*. Doklady Akademii Nauk SSSR, 1968. (p. 34)

75. Vladimir Vapnik and Alexei Chervonenkis. *Uniform Convergence of Frequencies of Occurrence of Events to Their Probabilities*. Soviet Mathematics Doklady, 1968. (p. 34)

76. Bernhard Schölkopf, Zhiyuan Luo, and Vladimir Vovk. *Empirical Inference: Festschrift in Honor of Vladimir N Vapnik*. Springer, 2013. (pp. 34, 35)

77. Vladimir Vapnik and Alexei Chervonenkis. *On the Uniform Convergence of Relative Frequencies of Events to Their Probabilities*. Theory of Probability and Its Applications, 1968. (p. 34)

78. Vladimir Vapnik. *Statistical Learning Theory*. Wiley, 1998. (pp. 34, 238)

79. Vladimir Vovk, Harris Papadopoulos, and Alexander Gammerman. *Measures of Complexity: Festschrift in Honor of Alexey Y Chervonenkis*. Springer, 2015. (p. 35)

80. Steve Hanneke. *Refined Error Bounds for Several Learning Algorithms*. JMLR, 2016. (p. 35)

81. David Corfield, Bernhard Schölkopf, and Vladimir Vapnik. *Falsificationism and Statistical Learning Theory: Comparing the Popper and Vapnik-Chervonenkis Dimensions*. Journal for General Philosophy of Science, 2009. (p. 36)

82. Kamalika Chaudhuri and Sanjoy Dasgupta. *Rates of Convergence for Nearest Neighbor Classification*. NeurIPS, 2014. (p. 37)

83. David H. Wolpert and William G. Macready. *No Free Lunch Theorems for Optimization*. IEEE Transactions on Evolutionary Computation, 1997. (p. 37)

84. Vladimir Koltchinskii and Dmitriy Panchenko. *Rademacher Processes and Bounding the Risk of Function Learning*. arXiv, 2000. (p. 37)

85. Peter L. Bartlett, Andrea Montanari, and Alexander Rakhlin. *Deep Learning: A Statistical Viewpoint*. Acta numerica, 2021. (pp. 38, 45, 201)

86. Chiyuan Zhang, Samy Bengio, Moritz Hardt, Benjamin Recht, and Oriol Vinyals. *Understanding Deep Learning Requires Rethinking Generalization*. ICLR, 2016. (pp. 38, 40, 199)

87. Vaishnavh Nagarajan. *Explaining Generalization in Deep Learning: Progress and Fundamental Limits*. arXiv, 2021. (p. 38)

88. Vaishnavh Nagarajan and Zico Kolter. *Generalization in Deep Networks: The Role of Distance from Initialization*. arXiv, 2019. (pp. 39, 40)

89. Moritz Hardt, Ben Recht, and Yoram Singer. *Train Faster, Generalize Better: Stability of Stochastic Gradient Descent*. ICML, 2016. (p. 39)

90. Vaishnavh Nagarajan and Zico Kolter. *Uniform Convergence May Be Unable to Explain Generalization in Deep Learning*. arXiv, 2019. (p. 40)

91. Yiding Jiang, Behnam Neyshabur, Hossein Mobahi, Dilip Krishnan, and Samy Bengio. *Fantastic Generalization Measures and Where to Find Them*. arXiv, 2019. (p. 40)

92. Mikhail Belkin, Daniel Hsu, Siyuan Ma, and Soumik Mandal. *Reconciling Modern Machine-Learning Practice and the Classical Bias-Variance Trade-Off*. PNAS, 2019. (p. 40)

93. Yehuda Dar, Vidya Muthukumar, and Richard G. Baraniuk. *A Farewell to the Bias-Variance Tradeoff? An Overview of the Theory of Over-Parameterized Machine Learning*. arXiv, 2021. (p. 40)

94. Ali Rahimi and Benjamin Recht. *Random Features for Large-Scale Kernel Machines*. NeurIPS, 2007. (p. 41)

95. Trevor Hastie, Robert Tibshirani, Jerome H. Friedman, and Jerome H. Friedman. *The Elements of Statistical Learning: Data Mining, Inference, and Prediction*. Springer, 2009. (p. 41)

96. Leo Breiman. *Reflections After Refereeing Papers for NIPS*. The Mathematics of Generalization, 1995. (p. 41)

97. Robert E. Schapire, Yoav Freund, Peter Bartlett, and Wee S. Lee. *Boosting the Margin: A New Explanation for the Effectiveness of Voting Methods*. The Annals of Statistics, 1998. (p. 43)

98. Alethea Power, Yuri Burda, Harri Edwards, Igor Babuschkin, and Vedant Misra. *Grokking: Generalization Beyond Overfitting on Small Algorithmic Datasets*. arXiv, 2022. (p. 44)

99. Mikhail Belkin. *Fit Without Fear: Remarkable Mathematical Phenomena of Deep Learning Through the Prism of Interpolation*. Acta Numerica, 2021. (p. 44)

100. Roman Novak, Yasaman Bahri, Daniel A. Abolafia, Jeffrey Pennington, and Jascha Sohl-Dickstein. *Sensitivity and Generalization in Neural Networks: An Empirical Study*. arXiv, 2018. (p. 45)

101. Benoit Dherin, Michael Munn, Mihaela Rosca, and David Barrett. *Why Neural Networks Find Simple Solutions: The Many Regularizers of Geometric Complexity*. NeurIPS, 2022. (p. 45)

102. Andrew G. Wilson. *Deep Learning Is Not so Mysterious or Different*. arXiv, 2025. (p. 45)

103. Harshay Shah, Kaustav Tamuly, Aditi Raghunathan, Prateek Jain, and Praneeth Netrapalli. *The Pitfalls of Simplicity Bias in Neural Networks*. NeurIPS, 2020. (pp. 45, 197)

104. Devansh Arpit et al. *A Closer Look at Memorization in Deep Networks*. ICML, 2017. (p. 45)

105. Mohammad Pezeshki et al. *Gradient Starvation: A Learning Proclivity in Neural Networks*. NeurIPS, 2021. (pp. 45, 197, 238, 270)

106. Yoav Wald, Amir Feder, Daniel Greenfeld, and Uri Shalit. *On Calibration and Out-of-Domain Generalization*. NeurIPS, 2021. (pp. 45, 143)

107. Samuel J. Bell and Levent Sagun. *Simplicity Bias Leads to Amplified Performance Disparities*. FAccT, 2023. (pp. 46, 175, 186)

108. Robert Geirhos et al. *Shortcut Learning in Deep Neural Networks*. Nature Machine Intelligence, 2020. (p. 46)

109. Daniel Soudry, Elad Hoffer, Mor S. Nacson, Suriya Gunasekar, and Nathan Srebro. *The Implicit Bias of Gradient Descent on Separable Data*. JMLR, 2018. (p. 48)

110. Kartik Ahuja et al. *Invariance Principle Meets Information Bottleneck for Out-of-Distribution Generalization*. arXiv, 2021. (pp. 50, 51, 143, 150, 180)

111. Alexander D'Amour et al. *Underspecification Presents Challenges for Credibility in Modern Machine Learning*. arXiv, 2020. (p. 51)

112. Patrik Reizinger et al. *Understanding LLMs Requires More than Statistical Generalization*. arXiv, 2024. (p. 51)

113. Nancy Cartwright. *How the Laws of Physics Lie*. Oxford University Press, 1983. (pp. 51, 85, 95–97, 111, 152)

114. Judea Pearl. *The Limitations of Opaque Learning Machines*. Possible minds, 2019. (p. 55)

115. Jonathan Richens and Tom Everitt. *Robust Agents Learn Causal World Models*. arXiv, 2024. (p. 56)

116. John Aldrich. *Correlations Genuine and Spurious in Pearson and Yule*. Statistical science, 1995. (p. 56)

117. Elliott Sober. *Venetian Sea Levels, British Bread Prices, and the Principle of the Common Cause*. British Journal for the Philosophy of Science, 2001. (p. 56)

118. Graham E. Quinn, Chai H. Shin, Maureen G. Maguire, and Richard A. Stone. *Myopia and Ambient Lighting at Night*. Nature, 1999. (p. 56)

119. Bertrand Russell. *On the Notion of Cause*. Proceedings of the Aristotelian Society, 1912. (p. 58)

120. E. Mach and T. J. McCormack. *The Science of Mechanics: A Critical and Historical Exposition of Its Principles*. Open Court Publishing Company, 1893. (p. 58)

121. Peter Menzies and Helen Beebee. *Counterfactual Theories of Causation*. Stanford Encyclopedia of Philosophy, 2021. (pp. 58, 83, 84)

122. Rani L. Anjum and Stephen Mumford. *Causation in Science and the Methods of Scientific Discovery*. Oxford University Press, 2018. (pp. 59, 84)

123. Mathias Frisch. *Causation in Physics*. Stanford Encyclopedia of Philosophy, 2022. (p. 59)

124. Phyllis Illari and Federica Russo. *Causality: Philosophical Theory Meets Scientific Practice*. Oxford University Press, 2014. (pp. 59, 67, 81)

125. Nancy Cartwright. *Nature's Capacities and Their Measurement*. Oxford University Press, 1994. (pp. 59, 76, 97, 153)

126. Menno Hulswit. *From Cause to Causation: A Peircean Perspective*. Springer Science & Business Media, 2002. (pp. 60, 61, 77, 78)

127. Ludwig Wittgenstein. *Tractatus Logico-Philosophicus*. Annalen der Naturphilosophie, 1922. (p. 62)

128. Nisargadatta Maharaj. *I Am That*. Chetana Publishing, 1973. (pp. 63, 306, 317)

129. Immanuel Kant. *Prolegomena to Any Future Metaphysics*, 1783. (pp. 63, 64)

130. Immanuel Kant. *Critique of Pure Reason*, 1781. (pp. 63, 65, 66)

131. Alex Broadbent. *Causation*. Internet Encyclopedia of Philosophy, 2023. (p. 65)

132. Donald Hoffman. *The Case Against Reality: Why Evolution Hid the Truth from Our Eyes*. WW Norton, 2019. (pp. 66, 163)

133. David Lewis. *Philosophical Papers Volume I*. Oxford University Press, 1983. (p. 67)

134. James Woodward. *Causation with a Human Face: Normative Theory and Descriptive Psychology*. Oxford University Press, 2021. (pp. 67, 84, 85, 89, 90, 95, 286)

135. J. L. Mackie. *The Cement of the Universe: A Study of Causation*. Oxford University Press, 1974. (p. 67)

136. Hans Reichenbach. *The Direction of Time*. University of California Press, 1956. (p. 68)

137. Jonas Peters, Dominik Janzing, and Bernhard Schölkopf. *Elements of Causal Inference: Foundations and Learning Algorithms*. MIT Press, 2017. (pp. 68, 77, 107, 114)

138. Tyler Vigen. *Spurious Correlations*. Hachette Books, 2015. (p. 69)

139. Curt J. Ducasse. *On the Nature and the Observability of the Causal Relation*. The Journal of Philosophy, 1926. (pp. 70, 74)

140. James Woodward. *Making Things Happen: A Theory of Causal Explanation*. Oxford University Press, 2005. (pp. 70, 71, 73–75, 89, 95, 132, 133)

141. Paul W. Holland. *Statistics and Causal Inference*. Journal of the American Statistical Association, 1986. (pp. 71, 112)

142. Donald T. Campbell and Thomas D. Cook. *Quasi-Experimentation: Design & Analysis Issues for Field Settings*. Rand Mc-Nally, 1979. (p. 71)

143. Kevin Hoover. *The New Classical Macroeconomics*. Blackwell Group, 1988. (p. 71)

144. Michael Redhead. *Incompleteness, Nonlocality, and Realism: A Prolegomenon to the Philosophy of Quantum Mechanics*. Clarendon Press, 1987. (pp. 71, 76)

145. Ellery Eells. *Probabilistic Causal Levels*. Causation, Chance and Credence, 1988. (p. 74)

146. Ragnar Frisch. *Autonomy of Economic Relations: Statistical Versus Theoretical Relations in Economic Macrodynamics*. The Foundations of Econometric Analysis, 1938. (p. 75)

147. Trygve Haavelmo. *The Probability Approach in Econometrics*. Econometrica: Journal of the Econometric Society, 1944. (p. 75)

148. Brian Skyrms. *Resiliency, Propensities, and Causal Necessity*. The Journal of Philosophy, 1977. (p. 76)

149. John Aldrich. *Autonomy*. Oxford Economic Papers, 1989. (p. 76)

150. Sandra D. Mitchell. *Pragmatic Laws*. Philosophy of science, 1997. (p. 76)

151. David F. Hendry. *Econometrics: Alchemy or Science?* Oxford University Press, 2000. (pp. 76, 134)

152. Judea Pearl. *Causality*. Cambridge University Press, 2009. (pp. 76, 96, 97, 102)

153. Bernhard Schoelkopf et al. *On Causal and Anticausal Learning*. arXiv, 2012. (pp. 76, 87, 88)

154. Bernhard Schölkopf and Julius von Kügelgen. *From Statistical to Causal Learning*. arXiv, 2022. (pp. 76, 104)

155. Robin G. Collingwood. *On the So-Called Idea of Causation*. Proceedings of the Aristotelian Society, 1938. (p. 77)

156. Peter Menzies and Huw Price. *Causation as a Secondary Quality*. The British Journal for the Philosophy of Science, 1993. (p. 78)

157. David Lewis. *Counterfactuals*. John Wiley & Sons, 1986. (pp. 79, 80)

158. David Lewis. *Causation*. The Journal of Philosophy, 1973. (p. 81)

159. Nelson Goodman. *Seven Strictures on Similarity*. Problems and projects, 1972. (pp. 82, 186)

160. John Vervaeke, Timothy P. Lillicrap, and Blake A. Richards. *Relevance Realization and the Emerging Framework in Cognitive Science*. Journal of Logic and Computation, 2012. (pp. 82, 159, 161, 162, 280)

161. Christopher Hitchcock and Joshua Knobe. *Cause and Norm*. The Journal of Philosophy, 2009. (p. 82)

162. Judea Pearl and Dana Mackenzie. *The Book of Why: The New Science of Cause and Effect*. Basic Books, 2018. (pp. 82, 97, 98, 107, 108, 116, 249)

163. Ned Hall. *Two Concepts of Causation*. Causation and Counterfactuals, 2004. (pp. 83, 84)

164. John S. Mill. *A System of Logic*. Harper, 1843. (pp. 83, 96)

165. Carl G. Hempel. *The Function of General Laws in History*. The Journal of Philosophy, 1942. (p. 85)

166. Marc Lange. *Because Without Cause: Non-Casual Explanations in Science and Mathematics*. Oxford University Press, 2016. (p. 86)

167. Moritz Schlick. *Naturphilosophische Betrachtungen über das Kausalprinzip*. The Science of Nature, 1920. (p. 86)

168. Clive W. J. Granger. *Investigating Causal Relations by Econometric Models and Cross-Spectral Methods*. Econometrica: Journal of the Econometric Society, 1969. (p. 86)

169. Claude E. Shannon. *Coding Theorems for a Discrete Source with a Fidelity Criterion*. IRE Nat. Conv. Rec, 1959. (pp. 87, 274)

170. Yoshua Bengio et al. *A Meta-Transfer Objective for Learning to Disentangle Causal Mechanisms*. arXiv, 2019. (pp. 88, 178)

171. Bernhard Schölkopf et al. *Towards Causal Representation Learning*. arXiv, 2021. (pp. 88, 97)

172. Albert Michotte. *The Perception of Causality*. Routledge, 1945. (p. 88)

173. Albert Michotte. *Phänomenale Kausalität nach Michotte*. TIB AV-Portal, 1998. (p. 88)

174. Fritz Heider and Marianne Simmel. *An Experimental Study of Apparent Behavior*. The American Journal of Psychology, 1944. (p. 89)

175. Anthony Dickinson and David Shanks. *Instrumental Action and Causal Representation*. Causal cognition: A multidisciplinary debate, 1995. (p. 89)

176. Alison Gopnik. *Scientific Thinking in Young Children: Theoretical Advances, Empirical Research, and Policy Implications*. Science, 2012. (p. 90)

177. Patricia W. Cheng and Hongjing Lu. *Causal Invariance as an Essential Constraint for Creating Representation of the World: Generalizing the Invariance of Causal Power*. The Oxford handbook of causal reasoning, 2017. (p. 90)

178. A. Miguel, Robins Hernán, and M. James. *Causal Inference: What If*. CRC Press, 2023. (pp. 94, 112, 114, 116, 117)

179. Patrick Suppes. *A Probabilistic Theory of Causality*. North-Holland, 1968. (p. 95)

180. Arthur S. Goldberger. *Reverse Regression and Salary Discrimination*. Journal of Human Resources, 1984. (p. 95)

181. Krzysztof Chalupka. *Automated Macro-Scale Causal Hypothesis Formation Based on Micro-Scale Observation*. California Institute of Technology, 2017. (p. 95)

182. Paul K. Rubenstein et al. *Causal Consistency of Structural Equation Models*. arXiv, 2017. (p. 95)

183. Taco Cohen. *Towards a Grounded Theory of Causation for Embodied AI*. arXiv, 2022. (p. 95)

184. Alan Watts. *The Book on the Taboo Against Knowing Who You Are*. Vintage, 1966. (p. 97)

185. David Lopez-Paz, Robert Nishihara, Soumith Chintala, Bernhard Scholkopf, and Léon Bottou. *Discovering Causal Signals in Images*. CVPR, 2017. (p. 97)

186. Sewall Wright. *Correlation and Causation*. Journal of Agricultural Research, 1921. (p. 97)

187. Eugene P. Wigner. *Invariance in Physical Theory*. Proceedings of the American Philosophical Society, 1949. (pp. 98, 156)

188. Madelyn Glymour, Judea Pearl, and Nicholas P. Jewell. *Causal Inference in Statistics: A Primer*. John Wiley & Sons, 2016. (pp. 99, 111)

189. David Freedman. *From Association to Causation: Some Remarks on the History of Statistics*. Journal de la Société Française de Statistique, 1999. (p. 103)

190. Austin B. Hill. *The Environment and Disease: Association or Causation?* Sage Publications, 1965. (p. 109)

191. Patrik Hoyer, Dominik Janzing, Joris M. Mooij, Jonas Peters, and Bernhard Schölkopf. *Nonlinear Causal Discovery with Additive Noise Models*. NeurIPS, 2008. (p. 109)

192. David Lopez-Paz and Maxime Oquab. *Revisiting Classifier Two-Sample Tests*. arXiv, 2018. (p. 109)

193. Povilas Daniusis et al. *Inferring Deterministic Causal Relations*. arXiv, 2012. (p. 110)

194. George A. Miller. *The Magical Number Seven, Plus or Minus Two: Some Limits on Our Capacity for Processing Information*. Psychological Review, 1956. (p. 111)

195. Leonid Rozenblit and Frank Keil. *The Misunderstood Limits of Folk Science: An Illusion of Explanatory Depth*. Cognitive science, 2002. (p. 111)

196. Rebecca Lawson. *The Science of Cycology: Failures to Understand How Everyday Objects Work*. Memory & Cognition, 2006. (pp. 111, 268)

197. Arthur S. Reber. *Implicit Learning of Artificial Grammars*. Journal of Verbal Learning and Verbal Behavior, 1967. (p. 111)

198. Jerzy Neyman. *Sur Les Applications De La Theorie Des Probabilites Aux Experiences Agricoles: Essai Des Principes*. Roczniki Nauk Rolniczych, 1923. (p. 111)

199. Donald B. Rubin. *Estimating Causal Effects of Treatments in Randomized and Nonrandomized Studies*. Journal of Educational Psychology, 1974. (p. 111)

200. Joshua D. Angrist and Jörn-Steffen Pischke. *Mostly Harmless Econometrics: An Empiricist's Companion*. Princeton University Press, 2009. (pp. 112, 113, 116, 118)

201. Uri Shalit, Fredrik D. Johansson, and David Sontag. *Estimating Individual Treatment Effect: Generalization Bounds and Algorithms*. ICML, 2017. (p. 117)

202. Paul R. Rosenbaum and Donald B. Rubin. *The Central Role of the Propensity Score in Observational Studies for Causal Effects.* Biometrika, 1983. (p. 117)

203. Jin Tian and Judea Pearl. *Probabilities of Causation: Bounds and Identification.* Annals of Mathematics and Artificial Intelligence, 2000. (p. 118)

204. Angus Deaton and Nancy Cartwright. *Understanding and Misunderstanding Randomized Controlled Trials.* Social Science & Medicine, 2018. (pp. 119, 122)

205. Alexander Krauss. *Why All Randomised Controlled Trials Produce Biased Results.* Annals of Medicine, 2018. (p. 119)

206. Kjell Benson and Arthur J. Hartz. *A Comparison of Observational Studies and Randomized, Controlled Trials.* New England Journal of Medicine, 2000. (p. 119)

207. John Concato, Nirav Shah, and Ralph I. Horwitz. *Randomized, Controlled Trials, Observational Studies, and the Hierarchy of Research Designs.* New England Journal of Medicine, 2000. (p. 119)

208. John C. Crabbe, Douglas Wahlsten, and Bruce C. Dudek. *Genetics of Mouse Behavior: Interactions with Laboratory Environment.* Science, 1999. (p. 122)

209. Frederick S. Perls. *Gestalt Therapy Verbatim.* The Gestalt Journal Press, 1969. (p. 123)

210. Giambattista Parascandolo, Alexander Neitz, Antonio Orvieto, Luigi Gresele, and Bernhard Schölkopf. *Learning Explanations that Are Hard to Vary.* arXiv, 2020. (pp. 128, 129, 179)

211. Robert Nozick. *Invariances: The Structure of the Objective World.* Harvard University Press, 2001. (pp. 129, 163, 298)

212. Mateo Rojas-Carulla, Bernhard Schölkopf, Richard Turner, and Jonas Peters. *Invariant Models for Causal Transfer Learning.* JMLR, 2018. (pp. 130, 166)

213. Kartik Ahuja, Jun Wang, Amit Dhurandhar, Karthikeyan Shanmugam, and Kush R. Varshney. *Empirical or Invariant Risk Minimization? A Sample Complexity Perspective.* arXiv, 2020. (p. 130)

214. Leo Breiman. *Statistical Modeling: The Two Cultures.* Statistical Science, 2001. (p. 131)

215. Federica Russo. *What Invariance Is and How to Test for It.* International Studies in the Philosophy of Science, 2014. (pp. 132, 133)

216. Nancy Cartwright. *Causality, Invariance, and Policy*. The Oxford Handbook of Philosophy of Economics, 2009. (p. 134)

217. Olivier Bousquet and André Elisseeff. *Stability and Generalization*. JMLR, 2002. (p. 136)

218. Ronald A. Fisher. *Statistical Methods for Research Workers*. Oliver & Boyd, 1925. (p. 137)

219. John W. Tukey. *Causation, Regression and Path Analysis*. Statistics and Mathematics in Biology, 1954. (p. 137)

220. Chelsea Finn, Pieter Abbeel, and Sergey Levine. *Model-Agnostic Meta-Learning for Fast Adaptation of Deep Networks*. ICML, 2017. (pp. 140, 178, 218)

221. Jun-Hyun Bae, Inchul Choi, and Minho Lee. *Meta-Learned Invariant Risk Minimization*. arXiv, 2021. (pp. 140, 178)

222. Ursula Hébert-Johnson, Michael Kim, Omer Reingold, and Guy Rothblum. *Multicalibration: Calibration for the (Computationally-Identifiable) Masses*. ICML, 2018. (pp. 143, 203)

223. Nisha Muktewar and Chris Wallace. *Causality for Machine Learning*. Cloudera Fast Forward Labs Research, 2020. (p. 145)

224. Robert Adragna, Elliot Creager, David Madras, and Richard Zemel. *Fairness and Robustness in Invariant Learning: A Case Study in Toxicity Classification*. arXiv, 2020. (p. 145)

225. Shiyu Chang, Yang Zhang, Mo Yu, and Tommi Jaakkola. *Invariant Rationalization*. ICML, 2020. (pp. 145, 168)

226. Maxime Peyrard et al. *Invariant Language Modeling*. arXiv, 2021. (p. 145)

227. James Casaletto et al. *Analyzing the Relationship Between Gene Expression and Phenotype in Space-Flown Mice Using a Causal Inference Machine Learning Ensemble*. Nature Scientific Reports, 2023. (p. 145)

228. Elliot Creager, Jörn-Henrik Jacobsen, and Richard Zemel. *Environment Inference for Invariant Learning*. arXiv, 2020. (pp. 145, 186, 193)

229. Yoav Wald, Amir Feder, Daniel Greenfeld, and Uri Shalit. *On Calibration and Out-of-Domain Generalization*. NeurIPS, 2021. (p. 145)

230. Elan Rosenfeld, Pradeep Ravikumar, and Andrej Risteski. *The Risks of Invariant Risk Minimization*. arXiv, 2020. (p. 148)

231. Kartik Ahuja, Jun Wang, Amit Dhurandhar, Karthikeyan Shanmugam, and Kush R. Varshney. *Empirical or Invariant Risk Minimization? A Sample Complexity Perspective.* arXiv, 2020. (p. 148)

232. Advait U. Parulekar, Karthikeyan Shanmugam, and Sanjay Shakkottai. *PAC Generalization via Invariant Representations.* ICML, 2023. (p. 148)

233. Pritish Kamath, Akilesh Tangella, Danica Sutherland, and Nathan Srebro. *Does Invariant Risk Minimization Capture Invariance?* AISTATS, 2021. (p. 148)

234. Divyat Mahajan et al. *Compositional Risk Minimization.* arXiv, 2024. (p. 148)

235. Nevin L. Zhang et al. *A Causal Framework to Unify Common Domain Generalization Approaches.* arXiv, 2023. (p. 148)

236. Marco Federici, Ryota Tomioka, and Patrick Forré. *An Information-Theoretic Approach to Distribution Shifts.* arXiv, 2021. (p. 149)

237. Vaishnavh Nagarajan, Anders Andreassen, and Behnam Neyshabur. *Understanding the Failure Modes of Out-of-Distribution Generalization.* arXiv, 2021. (p. 150)

238. Henry Hazlitt. *Economics in One Lesson.* Harper and Brothers, 1946. (p. 153)

239. Michael M. Bronstein, Joan Bruna, Taco Cohen, and Petar Veličković. *Geometric Deep Learning: Grids, Groups, Graphs, Geodesics, and Gauges.* arXiv, 2021. (p. 153)

240. Philip W. Anderson. *More Is Different: Broken Symmetry and the Nature of the Hierarchical Structure of Science.* Science, 1972. (p. 154)

241. Caspar Jacobs. *Invariance or Equivalence: A Tale of Two Principles.* Synthese, 2021. (p. 154)

242. Paul A. M. Dirac. *The Principles of Quantum Mechanics.* Oxford University Press, 1930. (p. 154)

243. Hermann Weyl. *Symmetry.* Princeton University Press, 1952. (p. 154)

244. Steven Weinberg. *Dreams of a Final Theory: The Scientist's Search for the Ultimate Laws of Nature.* Vintage, 1993. (p. 154)

245. Simon Saunders. *Physics and Leibniz's Principles.* Symmetries in physics: Philosophical reflections, 2003. (p. 154)

246. David J. Baker. *Symmetry and the Metaphysics of Physics.* Philosophy Compass, 2010. (p. 154)

247. E. Noether. *Invariante Variationsprobleme*. Nachrichten von der Gesellschaft der Wissenschaften zu Göttingen, Mathematisch Physikalische Klasse, 1918. (p. 155)

248. Eugene P. Wigner. *Events, Laws of Nature, and Invariance Principles*. Nobel Lecture, 1963. (pp. 155, 156)

249. Max Born. *Physical Reality*. Philosophical Quarterly, 1953. (p. 156)

250. Shamik Dasgupta. *Symmetry and Superfluous Structure: A Metaphysical Overview*. Routledge, 2021. (pp. 157, 158)

251. Katherine Brading, Elena Castellani, and Nicholas Teh. *Symmetry and Symmetry Breaking*. The Stanford Encyclopedia of Philosophy, 2023. (pp. 158, 163)

252. John Vervaeke and Leonardo Ferraro. *Relevance, Meaning and the Cognitive Science of Wisdom*. The Scientific Study of Personal Wisdom, 2013. (pp. 159, 160, 162, 163, 229, 304)

253. Brett P. Andersen, Mark Miller, and John Vervaeke. *Predictive Processing and Relevance Realization: Exploring Convergent Solutions to the Frame Problem*. Phenomenology and the Cognitive Sciences, 2022. (pp. 160, 162)

254. John Vervaeke and Tim Ferriss. *How to Build a Life of Wisdom, Flow, and Contemplation*. The Tim Ferriss Show, 2023. (p. 160)

255. Brian C. Smith. *Inference in a Nonconceptual World*. Understanding the nature of inference colloquium series, Yale university. YouTube video, 2022. (p. 161)

256. Damian G. Stephen, James A. Dixon, and Robert W. Isenhower. *Dynamics of Representational Change: Entropy, Action, and Cognition*. Journal of Experimental Psychology: Human Perception and Performance, 2009. (p. 162)

257. Craig A. Kaplan and Herbert A. Simon. *In Search of Insight*. Cognitive Psychology, 1990. (p. 162)

258. Paul M. Churchland. *Scientific Realism and the Plasticity of Mind*. Dialectica, 1979. (p. 163)

259. John Worrall. *Structural Realism: The Best of Both Worlds?* Dialectica, 1989. (p. 164)

260. James Ladyman and Don Ross. *Every Thing Must Go: Metaphysics Naturalized*. Oxford University Press, 2009. (p. 164)

261. Charles S. Peirce. *How to Make Our Ideas Clear*. Popular Science Monthly, 1878. (p. 164)

262. Jean Kaddour, Aengus Lynch, Qi Liu, Matt J. Kusner, and Ricardo Silva. *Causal Machine Learning: A Survey and Open Problems*. arXiv, 2022. (p. 165)

263. Jonas Peters, Peter Bühlmann, and Nicolai Meinshausen. *Causal Inference by Using Invariant Prediction: Identification and Confidence Intervals*. Journal of the Royal Statistical Society Series B: Statistical Methodology, 2016. (p. 166)

264. Nicolai Meinshausen. *Causality from a Distributional Robustness Point of View*. IEEE Data Science Workshop, 2018. (p. 167)

265. Peter Bühlmann. *Invariance, Causality and Robustness*. Neyman Lecture, 2018. (p. 167)

266. David Krueger et al. *Out-of-Distribution Generalization via Risk Extrapolation*. ICML, 2020. (pp. 167, 178)

267. Alexander Henzi, Xinwei Shen, Michael Law, and Peter Bühlmann. *Invariant Probabilistic Prediction*. arXiv, 2023. (p. 167)

268. Kartik Ahuja, Karthikeyan Shanmugam, Kush Varshney, and Amit Dhurandhar. *Invariant Risk Minimization Games*. ICML, 2020. (pp. 168, 169)

269. Olawale Salaudeen and Oluwasanmi Koyejo. *Target Conditioned Representation Independence (TCRI). From Domain-Invariant to Domain-General Representations*. arXiv, 2022. (p. 169)

270. Wale Salaudeen and Sanmi Koyejo. *On Learning Domain General Predictors*. ICML Workshop on spurious correlations, invariance and stability, 2023. (p. 169)

271. Abhin Shah, Karthikeyan Shanmugam, and Kartik Ahuja. *Finding Valid Adjustments Under Non-Ignorability with Minimal DAG Knowledge*. AISTATS, 2022. (p. 170)

272. Abhin Shah et al. *Treatment Effect Estimation Using Invariant Risk Minimization*. ICASSP, 2021. (p. 170)

273. Claudia Shi, Victor Veitch, and David M. Blei. *Invariant Representation Learning for Treatment Effect Estimation*. UAI, 2021. (p. 170)

274. Tyler J. VanderWeele and Peng Ding. *Sensitivity Analysis in Observational Research: Introducing the E-Value*. Annals of internal medicine, 2017. (p. 171)

275. J. A. Bagnell. *Robust Supervised Learning*. AAAI, 2005. (p. 171)

276. Aharon Ben-Tal, Laurent El Ghaoui, and Arkadi Nemirovski. *Robust Optimization*. Princeton University Press, 2009. (p. 171)

277. Hamed Rahimian and Sanjay Mehrotra. *Distributionally Robust Optimization: A Review*. arXiv, 2019. (p. 171)

278. Weihua Hu, Gang Niu, Issei Sato, and Masashi Sugiyama. *Does Distributionally Robust Supervised Learning Give Robust Classifiers?* ICML, 2018. (p. 171)

279. Aman Sinha, Hongseok Namkoong, Riccardo Volpi, and John Duchi. *Certifying Some Distributional Robustness with Principled Adversarial Training*. arXiv, 2017. (p. 171)

280. Badr Y. Idrissi, Martin Arjovsky, Mohammad Pezeshki, and David Lopez-Paz. *Simple Data Balancing Achieves Competitive Worst-Group-Accuracy*. CLeaR, 2022. (p. 172)

281. Niladri S. Chatterji, Saminul Haque, and Tatsunori Hashimoto. *Undersampling Is a Minimax Optimal Robustness Intervention in Nonparametric Classification*. arXiv, 2022. (p. 172)

282. Kamalika Chaudhuri, Kartik Ahuja, Martin Arjovsky, and David Lopez-Paz. *Why Does Throwing Away Data Improve Worst-Group Error?* arXiv, 2022. (p. 173)

283. Shiori Sagawa, Pang W. Koh, Tatsunori B. Hashimoto, and Percy Liang. *Distributionally Robust Neural Networks for Group Shifts: On the Importance of Regularization for Worst-Case Generalization*. arXiv, 2019. (p. 173)

284. Aditya K. Menon et al. *Long-Tail Learning via Logit Adjustment*. arXiv, 2020. (p. 174)

285. Sheng Liu et al. *Avoiding Spurious Correlations via Logit Correction*. arXiv, 2022. (p. 174)

286. Christos Tsirigotis, Joao Monteiro, Pau Rodriguez, David Vazquez, and Aaron Courville. *Group Robust Classification Without Any Group Information*. NeurIPS, 2024. (p. 174)

287. Yuhui Li, Zejia Wu, Chao Zhang, and Hongyang Zhang. *Direct-Effect Risk Minimization for Domain Generalization*. arXiv, 2022. (p. 175)

288. Baochen Sun and Kate Saenko. *Deep CORAL: Correlation Alignment for Deep Domain Adaptation*. ECCV Workshops, 2016. (pp. 175, 193)

289. Yaroslav Ganin et al. *Domain-Adversarial Training of Neural Networks*. JMLR, 2016. (p. 175)

290. Ya Li, Mingming Gong, Xinmei Tian, Tongliang Liu, and Dacheng Tao. *Domain Generalization via Conditional Invariant Representations*. AAAI, 2018. (p. 176)

291. Victor Veitch, Alexander D'Amour, Steve Yadlowsky, and Jacob Eisenstein. *Counterfactual Invariance to Spurious Correlations: Why and How to Pass Stress Tests.* arXiv, 2021. (p. 176)

292. Christina Heinze-Deml and Nicolai Meinshausen. *Conditional Variance Penalties and Domain Shift Robustness.* arXiv, 2017. (pp. 176, 202)

293. Yong Lin et al. *Continuous Invariance Learning.* arXiv, 2023. (p. 177)

294. Niklas Pfister, Peter Bühlmann, and Jonas Peters. *Invariant Causal Prediction for Sequential Data.* Journal of the American Statistical Association, 2018. (p. 177)

295. Margherita Lazzaretto, Jonas Peters, and Niklas Pfister. *Invariant Subspace Decomposition.* arXiv, 2024. (p. 177)

296. Rémi Le Priol, Reza Babanezhad, Yoshua Bengio, and Simon Lacoste-Julien. *An Analysis of the Adaptation Speed of Causal Models.* AISTATS, 2021. (p. 178)

297. Yuge Shi et al. *Gradient Matching for Domain Generalization.* arXiv, 2021. (p. 178)

298. Alexandre Ramé, Corentin Dancette, and Matthieu Cord. *Fishr: Invariant Gradient Variances for Out-of-Distribution Generalization.* ICML, 2022. (p. 178)

299. Alex Nichol, Joshua Achiam, and John Schulman. *On First-Order Meta-Learning Algorithms.* arXiv, 2018. (p. 178)

300. David Lopez-Paz and Marc'Aurelio Ranzato. *Gradient Episodic Memory for Continual Learning.* NeurIPS, 2017. (p. 179)

301. Ishaan Gulrajani and David Lopez-Paz. *In Search of Lost Domain Generalization.* arXiv, 2020. (pp. 180, 191, 193, 195, 226)

302. Pang W. Koh et al. *WILDS: A Benchmark of In-the-Wild Distribution Shifts.* arXiv, 2021. (p. 180)

303. Yuzhe Yang, Haoran Zhang, Dina Katabi, and Marzyeh Ghassemi. *Change Is Hard: A Closer Look at Subpopulation Shift.* arXiv, 2023. (pp. 180, 192)

304. Olga Russakovsky et al. *ImageNet Large Scale Visual Recognition Challenge.* IJCV, 2015. (p. 180)

305. Dan Hendrycks, Kevin Zhao, Steven Basart, Jacob Steinhardt, and Dawn Song. *Natural Adversarial Examples.* CVPR, 2021. (p. 180)

306. Dan Hendrycks and Thomas Dietterich. *Benchmarking Neural Network Robustness to Common Corruptions and Perturbations.* arXiv, 2019. (pp. 180, 282)

307. Dan Hendrycks et al. *The Many Faces of Robustness: A Critical Analysis of Out-of-Distribution Generalization*. ICCV, 2021. (pp. 180, 282)

308. Benjamin Recht, Rebecca Roelofs, Ludwig Schmidt, and Vaishaal Shankar. *Do ImageNet Classifiers Generalize to ImageNet?* ICML, 2019. (pp. 180, 282)

309. Badr Y. Idrissi et al. *ImageNet-X: Understanding Model Mistakes with Factor of Variation Annotations*. arXiv, 2022. (p. 180)

310. Mohammad Pezeshki et al. *Discovering Environments with XRM*. arXiv, 2023. (pp. 181, 182, 187, 195)

311. Léon Bottou. *Learning Representation with Causal Invariance*. ICLR Keynote, 2019. (p. 181)

312. Luke Oakden-Rayner, Jared Dunnmon, Gustavo Carneiro, and Christopher Ré. *Hidden Stratification Causes Clinically Meaningful Failures in Machine Learning for Medical Imaging*. arXiv, 2019. (p. 181)

313. Frederick M. Howard et al. *The Impact of Site-Specific Digital Histology Signatures on Deep Learning Model Accuracy and Bias*. Nature Communications, 2021. (p. 181)

314. Endel Tulving and Donald M. Thomson. *Encoding Specificity and Retrieval Processes in Episodic Memory*. Psychological review, 1973. (p. 183)

315. Steven M. Smith and Edward Vela. *Environmental Context-Dependent Memory: A Review and Meta-Analysis*. Psychonomic Bulletin & Review, 2001. (pp. 183, 184)

316. Harry M. Grant et al. *Context-Dependent Memory for Meaningful Material: Information for Students*. Applied Cognitive Psychology: The Official Journal of the Society for Applied Research in Memory and Cognition, 1998. (p. 183)

317. Duncan R. Godden and Alan D. Baddeley. *Context-Dependent Memory in Two Natural Environments: On Land and Underwater*. British Journal of Psychology, 1975. (p. 183)

318. Steven M. Smith. *A Comparison of Two Techniques for Reducing Context-Dependent Forgetting*. Memory & Cognition, 1984. (pp. 183, 184)

319. Amanda Parker and Angus Gellatly. *Moveable Cues: A Practical Method for Reducing Context-Dependent Forgetting*. Applied Cognitive Psychology: The Official Journal of the Society for Applied Research in Memory and Cognition, 1997. (p. 183)

320. Gabriel A. Radvansky and David E. Copeland. *Walking Through Doorways Causes Forgetting: Situation Models and Experienced Space.* Memory & cognition, 2006. (p. 184)

321. John Elliotson. *Human Physiology.* Longman, Rees, Orme, Brown, Green, and Longman, 1835. (p. 184)

322. Donald W. Goodwin, Barbara Powell, David Bremer, Haskel Hoine, and John Stern. *Alcohol and Recall: State-Dependent Effects in Man.* Science, 1969. (p. 184)

323. Penelope A. Lewis and Hugo D. Critchley. *Mood-Dependent Memory.* Trends in cognitive sciences, 2003. (p. 184)

324. Shiori Sagawa, Tatsunori B. Koh Pang W. wand Hashimoto, and Percy Liang. *Distributionally Robust Neural Networks for Group Shifts: On the Importance of Regularization for Worst-Case Generalization.* arXiv, 2019. (p. 185)

325. Nikolay Dagaev et al. *A Too-Good-to-Be-True Prior to Reduce Shortcut Reliance.* arXiv, 2021. (p. 186)

326. Michael Zhang, Nimit S. Sohoni, Hongyang R. Zhang, Chelsea Finn, and Christopher Ré. *Correct-n-Contrast: A Contrastive Approach for Improving Robustness to Spurious Correlations.* arXiv, 2022. (pp. 186, 193)

327. Evan Z. Liu et al. *Just Train Twice: Improving Group Robustness Without Training Group Information.* arXiv, 2021. (pp. 186, 193)

328. Junhyun Nam, Hyuntak Cha, Sungsoo Ahn, Jaeho Lee, and Jinwoo Shin. *Learning from Failure: Training Debiased Classifier from Biased Classifier.* arXiv, 2020. (pp. 186, 191, 193)

329. Yujia Bao and Regina Barzilay. *Learning to Split for Automatic Bias Detection.* arXiv, 2022. (pp. 186, 193)

330. Preethi Lahoti et al. *Fairness Without Demographics Through Adversarially Reweighted Learning.* arXiv, 2020. (p. 186)

331. Gaotang Li, Jiarui Liu, and Wei Hu. *Bias Amplification Enhances Minority Group Performance.* arXiv, 2023. (p. 186)

332. Nimit Sohoni, Jared Dunnmon, Geoffrey Angus, Albert Gu, and Christopher Ré. *No Subclass Left Behind: Fine-Grained Robustness in Coarse-Grained Classification Problems.* NeurIPS, 2020. (p. 186)

333. Pavel Izmailov, Polina Kirichenko, Nate Gruver, and Andrew G. Wilson. *On Feature Learning in the Presence of Spurious Correlations.* NeurIPS, 2022. (p. 187)

334. Vitaly Feldman and Chiyuan Zhang. *What Neural Networks Memorize and Why: Discovering the Long Tail via Influence Estimation.* NeurIPS, 2020. (p. 190)

335. Jihye Kim, Aristide Baratin, Yan Zhang, and Simon Lacoste-Julien. *CrossSplit: Mitigating Label Noise Memorization Through Data Splitting.* ICML, 2023. (pp. 190, 191, 201)

336. Junbum Cha et al. *SWAD: Domain Generalization by Seeking Flat Minima.* NeurIPS, 2021. (pp. 191, 243, 246)

337. Alexandre Ramé et al. *Diverse Weight Averaging for Out of Distribution Generalization.* NeurIPS, 2022. (pp. 191, 246)

338. Mitchell Wortsman et al. *Model Soups: Averaging Weights of Multiple Fine-Tuned Models Improves Accuracy Without Increasing Inference Time.* ICML, 2022. (p. 191)

339. Yoonho Lee, Huaxiu Yao, and Chelsea Finn. *Diversify and Disambiguate: Learning from Underspecified Data.* ICLR, 2023. (pp. 191, 244)

340. Matteo Pagliardini, Martin Jaggi, François Fleuret, and Sai Praneeth Karimireddy. *Agree to Disagree: Diversity Through Disagreement for Better Transferability.* ICLR, 2023. (pp. 191, 244)

341. Yong Lin et al. *Spurious Feature Diversification Improves Out-of-Distribution Generalization.* arXiv, 2023. (p. 191)

342. Cian Eastwood et al. *Spuriosity Didn't Kill the Classifier: Using Invariant Predictions to Harness Spurious Features.* arXiv, 2023. (pp. 191, 229)

343. Faisal Kamiran and Toon Calders. *Classifying Without Discriminating.* International Conference on Computer, Control and Communication, 2009. (p. 191)

344. Binh T. Luong, Salvatore Ruggieri, and Franco Turini. *K-NN as an Implementation of Situation Testing for Discrimination Discovery and Prevention.* KDD, 2011. (p. 191)

345. Polina Kirichenko, Pavel Izmailov, and Andrew G. Wilson. *Last Layer Re-Training Is Sufficient for Robustness to Spurious Correlations.* arXiv, 2022. (pp. 192, 237)

346. Catherine Wah, Steve Branson, Peter Welinder, Pietro Perona, and Serge Belongie. *The Caltech-UCSD Birds-200-2011 Dataset.* California Institute of Technology, 2011. (p. 192)

347. Ziwei Liu, Ping Luo, Xiaogang Wang, and Xiaoou Tang. *Deep Learning Face Attributes in the Wild.* ICCV, 2015. (p. 192)

348. Weixin Liang and James Zou. *Metashift: A Dataset of Datasets for Evaluating Contextual Distribution Shifts and Training Conflicts.* arXiv, 2022. (p. 192)

349. Kai Xiao, Logan Engstrom, Andrew Ilyas, and Aleksander Madry. *Noise or Signal: The Role of Image Backgrounds in Object Recognition.* arXiv, 2020. (p. 192)

350. Adina Williams, Nikita Nangia, and Samuel R. Bowman. *A Broad-Coverage Challenge Corpus for Sentence Understanding Through Inference.* ACL, 2017. (p. 192)

351. Daniel Borkan, Lucas Dixon, Jeffrey Sorensen, Nithum Thain, and Lucy Vasserman. *Nuanced Metrics for Measuring Unintended Bias with Real Data for Text Classification.* WWW, 2019. (p. 192)

352. Shikai Qiu, Andres Potapczynski, Pavel Izmailov, and Andrew G. Wilson. *Simple and Fast Group Robustness by Automatic Feature Reweighting.* arXiv, 2023. (p. 193)

353. Alex Krizhevsky, Vinod Nair, and Geoffrey Hinton. *CIFAR-10*, 2009. (p. 195)

354. Yong Lin, Shengyu Zhu, Lu Tan, and Peng Cui. *ZIN: When and How to Learn Invariance Without Environment Partition?* NeurIPS, 2022. (pp. 195, 197)

355. Xiaoyu Tan et al. *Provably Invariant Learning Without Domain Information.* ICML, 2023. (p. 195)

356. Yongqiang Chen et al. *Rethinking Invariant Graph Representation Learning Without Environment Partitions.* ICLR DG Workshop, 2023. (p. 195)

357. Vitaly Feldman and Chiyuan Zhang. *What Neural Networks Memorize and Why: Discovering the Long Tail via Influence Estimation.* NeurIPS, 2020. (pp. 197, 199)

358. Yoav Wald, Gal Yona, Uri Shalit, and Yair Carmon. *Malign Overfitting: Interpolation Can Provably Preclude Invariance.* arXiv, 2022. (p. 199)

359. Hwanjun Song, Minseok Kim, Dongmin Park, Yooju Shin, and Jae-Gil Lee. *Learning from Noisy Labels with Deep Neural Networks: A Survey.* IEEE Transactions on Neural Networks and Learning Systems, 2022. (pp. 200, 201)

360. Eran Malach and Shai Shalev-Shwartz. *Decoupling when to Update from How to Update.* NeurIPS, 2017. (p. 201)

361. Bo Han et al. *Co-Teaching: Robust Training of Deep Neural Networks with Extremely Noisy Labels*. NeurIPS, 2018. (p. 201)

362. Xingrui Yu et al. *How Does Disagreement Help Generalization Against Label Corruption?* ICML, 2019. (p. 201)

363. Hongxin Wei, Lei Feng, Xiangyu Chen, and Bo An. *Combating Noisy Labels by Agreement: A Joint Training Method with Co-Regularization*. CVPR, 2020. (p. 201)

364. Junnan Li, Richard Socher, and Steven C. H. Hoi. *DivideMix: Learning with Noisy Labels as Semi-Supervised Learning*. arXiv, 2020. (p. 201)

365. Nazmul Karim, Mamshad Nayeem Rizve, Nazanin Rahnavard, Ajmal Mian, and Mubarak Shah. *UNICON: Combating Label Noise Through Uniform Selection and Contrastive Learning*. CVPR, 2022. (p. 201)

366. Jovana Mitrovic, Brian McWilliams, Jacob Walker, Lars Buesing, and Charles Blundell. *Representation Learning via Invariant Causal Mechanisms*. arXiv, 2020. (p. 202)

367. Polina Kirichenko et al. *Understanding the Detrimental Class-Level Effects of Data Augmentation*. arXiv, 2023. (p. 202)

368. Wayne X. Zhao et al. *A Survey of Large Language Models*. arXiv, 2023. (p. 205)

369. Shervin Minaee et al. *Large Language Models: A Survey*. arXiv, 2024. (p. 205)

370. Ashish Vaswani et al. *Attention Is All You Need*. NeurIPS, 2017. (pp. 205, 209, 214, 223)

371. Gregor Bachmann and Vaishnavh Nagarajan. *The Pitfalls of Next-Token Prediction*. arXiv, 2024. (pp. 207, 232)

372. Léon Bottou and Bernhard Schölkopf. *Borges and AI*. arXiv, 2023. (pp. 207, 233, 285)

373. Andrej Karpathy. *Deep Dive into LLMs like ChatGPT*. YouTube, 2025. (p. 208)

374. Andrej Karpathy. *Let's Build the GPT Tokenizer*. YouTube, 2024. (p. 211)

375. Tong Xiao and Jingbo Zhu. *Foundations of Large Language Models*. arXiv, 2025. (pp. 212, 213)

376. Tom Brown et al. *Language Models Are Few-Shot Learners*. NeurIPS, 2020. (p. 216)

377. Catherine Olsson et al. *In-Context Learning and Induction Heads*. arXiv, 2022. (pp. 216, 219)

378. Jürgen Schmidhuber. *Evolutionary Principles in Self-Referential Learning, or on Learning How to Learn: The Meta-Meta-... Hook*. Technical University of Munich, 1987. (p. 218)

379. Dequan Wang, Evan Shelhamer, Shaoteng Liu, Bruno Olshausen, and Trevor Darrell. *Tent: Fully Test-Time Adaptation by Entropy Minimization*. arXiv, 2020. (pp. 218, 226)

380. Gaurav R. Ghosal, Amrith Setlur, Daniel S. Brown, Anca Dragan, and Aditi Raghunathan. *Contextual Reliability: When Different Features Matter in Different Contexts*. arXiv, 2023. (p. 218)

381. Alberto Bietti, Vivien Cabannes, Diane Bouchacourt, Herve Jegou, and Leon Bottou. *Birth of a Transformer: A Memory Viewpoint*. arXiv, 2023. (p. 219)

382. Gilles Blanchard, Aniket A. Deshmukh, Ürun Dogan, Gyemin Lee, and Clayton Scott. *Domain Generalization by Marginal Transfer Learning*. JMLR, 2011. (p. 222)

383. Yanghao Li, Naiyan Wang, Jianping Shi, Jiaying Liu, and Xiaodi Hou. *Revisiting Batch Normalization for Practical Domain Adaptation*. arXiv, 2016. (p. 222)

384. Marvin Zhang et al. *Adaptive Risk Minimization: Learning to Adapt to Domain Shift*. NeurIPS, 2020. (pp. 222, 226)

385. Yujia Bao and Theofanis Karaletsos. *Contextual Vision Transformers for Robust Representation Learning*. arXiv, 2023. (p. 222)

386. Dana McKenzie. *Judea Pearl, AI, and Causality: What Role Do Statisticians Play?* Amstat News, 2023. (p. 223)

387. Sharut Gupta, Stefanie Jegelka, David Lopez-Paz, and Kartik Ahuja. *Context Is Environment*. arXiv, 2023. (pp. 223, 226)

388. Alec Radford et al. *Language Models Are Unsupervised Multitask Learners*. OpenAI blog, 2019. (p. 226)

389. Gregory Cohen, Saeed Afshar, Jonathan Tapson, and Andre Van Schaik. *EMNIST: Extending MNIST to Handwritten Letters*. IJCNN, 2017. (p. 226)

390. Dan Hendrycks and Thomas Dietterich. *Benchmarking Neural Network Robustness to Common Corruptions and Perturbations*. arXiv, 2019. (p. 226)

391. Pang W. Koh et al. *WILDS: A Benchmark of In-the-Wild Distribution Shifts*. ICML, 2021. (p. 226)

392. David Lopez-Paz, Léon Bottou, Bernhard Schölkopf, and Vladimir Vapnik. *Unifying Distillation and Privileged Information*. arXiv, 2016. (pp. 226, 228)

393. Jason Wei et al. *Chain-of-Thought Prompting Elicits Reasoning in Large Language Models*. NeurIPS, 2022. (pp. 229, 230)

394. Daya Guo et al. *DeepSeek-R1: Incentivizing Reasoning Capability in LLMs via Reinforcement Learning*. arXiv, 2025. (pp. 230, 233)

395. Yixin Ye et al. *LIMO: Less Is More for Reasoning*. arXiv, 2025. (p. 230)

396. Kartik Ahuja. *The Influence of Chain-of-Thought on Out of Distribution Generalization*. arXiv, 2025. (p. 231)

397. Fabian Gloeckle, Badr Y. Idrissi, Baptiste Rozière, David Lopez-Paz, and Gabriel Synnaeve. *Better & Faster Large Language Models via Multi-Token Prediction*. arXiv, 2024. (pp. 232, 233)

398. Vaishnavh Nagarajan, Chen H. Wu, Charles Ding, and Aditi Raghunathan. *Multi-Token Prediction Boosts Creativity in Algorithmic Tasks*. ICLR SCSL Workshop, 2025. (p. 232)

399. DeepSeek Team. *DeepSeek-V3 Technical Report*. arXiv, 2024. (p. 233)

400. Hartmut Rosa. *The Uncontrollability of the World*. John Wiley & Sons, 2020. (pp. 233, 317)

401. Léon Bottou. *The Fiction Machine*. SIAM Conference on Mathematics of Data Science, 2024. (p. 234)

402. M. R. O'Connor. *The Storytelling Computer*. Nautilus, 2019. (p. 234)

403. Jianyu Zhang, David Lopez-Paz, and Léon Bottou. *Rich Feature Construction for the Optimization-Generalization Dilemma*. ICML, 2022. (pp. 237, 238, 245)

404. Elan Rosenfeld, Pradeep Ravikumar, and Andrej Risteski. *Domain-Adjusted Regression Or: ERM May Already Learn Features Sufficient for Out-of-Distribution Generalization*. arXiv, 2022. (p. 237)

405. Voula Tsouna. *The Method of Multiple Explanations in Epicureanism*. British School at Athens, 2021. (p. 237)

406. Xin Wang, Hong Chen, Si'ao Tang, Zihao Wu, and Wenwu Zhu. *Disentangled Representation Learning*. arXiv, 2022. (p. 238)

407. Vardan Papyan, X. Y. Han, and David L. Donoho. *Prevalence of Neural Collapse During the Terminal Phase of Deep Learning Training*. PNAS, 2020. (pp. 238, 241)

408. Nitish Srivastava, Geoffrey Hinton, Alex Krizhevsky, Ilya Sutskever, and Ruslan Salakhutdinov. *Dropout: A Simple Way to Prevent Neural Networks from Overfitting*. JMLR, 2014. (p. 239)

409. Yarin Gal and Zoubin Ghahramani. *Dropout as a Bayesian Approximation: Representing Model Uncertainty in Deep Learning*. ICML, 2016. (pp. 240, 276)

410. Yann LeCun. *A Path Towards Autonomous Machine Intelligence*. OpenReview, 2022. (pp. 240, 241)

411. Randall Balestriero et al. *A Cookbook of Self-Supervised Learning*. arXiv, 2023. (p. 240)

412. Ting Chen, Simon Kornblith, Mohammad Norouzi, and Geoffrey Hinton. *A Simple Framework for Contrastive Learning of Visual Representations*. ICML, 2020. (p. 241)

413. Adrien Bardes, Jean Ponce, and Yann LeCun. *VICReg: Variance-Invariance-Covariance Regularization for Self-Supervised Learning*. arXiv, 2021. (p. 241)

414. Yann LeCun, Sumit Chopra, Raia Hadsell, M. Ranzato, and Fujie Huang. *A Tutorial on Energy-Based Learning*. Predicting structured data, 2006. (p. 242)

415. Thomas G. Dietterich. *Ensemble Methods in Machine Learning*. International Workshop on Multiple Classifier Systems, 2000. (p. 242)

416. Lewis R. Goldberg. *Man Versus Model of Man: A Rationale, Plus Some Evidence, for a Method of Improving on Clinical Inferences*. Psychological Bulletin, 1970. (p. 243)

417. Balaji Lakshminarayanan, Alexander Pritzel, and Charles Blundell. *Simple and Scalable Predictive Uncertainty Estimation Using Deep Ensembles*. NeurIPS, 2017. (pp. 244, 276)

418. Naonori Ueda and Ryohei Nakano. *Generalization Error of Ensemble Estimators*. ICNN, 1996. (p. 244)

419. Peter Bartlett, Yoav Freund, Wee S. Lee, and Robert E. Schapire. *Boosting the Margin: A New Explanation for the Effectiveness of Voting Methods*. The Annals of Statistics, 1998. (p. 244)

420. Jason Weston, Ronan Collobert, Fabian Sinz, Léon Bottou, and Vladimir Vapnik. *Inference with the Universum*. ICML, 2006. (pp. 244, 262)

421. Jianyu Zhang and Léon Bottou. *Learning Useful Representations for Shifting Tasks and Distributions*. ICML, 2023. (p. 245)

422. Behnam Neyshabur, Hanie Sedghi, and Chiyuan Zhang. *What Is Being Transferred in Transfer Learning?* NeurIPS, 2020. (p. 246)

423. Mitchell Wortsman et al. *Model Soups: Averaging Weights of Multiple Fine-Tuned Models Improves Accuracy Without Increasing Inference Time*. ICML, 2022. (p. 246)

424. Alexandre Ramé et al. *Model Ratatouille: Recycling Diverse Models for Out-of-Distribution Generalization*. arXiv, 2022. (p. 246)

425. Olivier Chapelle, Jason Weston, Léon Bottou, and Vladimir Vapnik. *Vicinal Risk Minimization*. NeurIPS, 2000. (pp. 247, 248)

426. Brenden M. Lake, Ruslan Salakhutdinov, and Joshua B. Tenenbaum. *Human-Level Concept Learning Through Probabilistic Program Induction*. Science, 2015. (p. 249)

427. Ruth M. J. Byrne. *The Rational Imagination: How People Create Alternatives to Reality*. MIT Press, 2007. (p. 249)

428. Huaxiu Yao, Yiping Wang, Linjun Zhang, James Y. Zou, and Chelsea Finn. *C-mixup: Improving Generalization in Regression*. NeurIPS, 2022. (p. 249)

429. Hongyi Zhang, Moustapha Cisse, Yann N. Dauphin, and David Lopez-Paz. *mixup: Beyond Empirical Risk Minimization*. ICLR, 2018. (pp. 250, 251, 257, 270)

430. Sanghyuk Chun et al. *An Empirical Evaluation on Robustness and Uncertainty of Regularization Methods*. arXiv, 2020. (p. 251)

431. Linjun Zhang, Zhun Deng, Kenji Kawaguchi, Amirata Ghorbani, and James Zou. *How Does mixup Help with Robustness and Generalization?* arXiv, 2021. (pp. 251, 253, 257)

432. Parth Natekar and Manik Sharma. *Representation Based Complexity Measures for Predicting Generalization in Deep Learning*. arXiv, 2020. (p. 251)

433. Sunil Thulasidasan, Gopinath Chennupati, Jeff Bilmes, Tanmoy Bhattacharya, and Sarah Michalak. *On mixup Training: Improved Calibration and Predictive Uncertainty for Deep Neural Networks*. arXiv, 2020. (pp. 251, 258)

434. Linjun Zhang, Zhun Deng, Kenji Kawaguchi, and James Zou. *When and How mixup Improves Calibration*. arXiv, 2021. (pp. 251, 253)

435. Hansang Lee, Haeil Lee, Helen Hong, and Junmo Kim. *Test-Time mixup Augmentation for Uncertainty Estimation in Skin Lesion Diagnosis*. MIDL, 2021. (p. 251)

436. David Lopez-Paz, Diane Bouchacourt, and Elvis Dohmatob. *An Ensemble View on mixup*. arXiv, 2022. (pp. 251, 252, 265)

437. Tianyu Pang, Kun Xu, and Jun Zhu. *mixup Inference: Better Exploiting mixup to Defend Adversarial Attacks*. arXiv, 2020. (p. 251)

438. Guillaume P. Archambault, Yongyi Mao, Hongyu Guo, and Richong Zhang. *mixup as Directional Adversarial Training*. arXiv, 2019. (p. 251)

439. Vasilis Vryniotis. *How to Train State-of-the-Art Models Using Torchvision's Latest Primitives*. PyTorch blog, 2021. (p. 251)

440. Hugo Touvron et al. *Training Data-Efficient Image Transformers & Distillation Through Attention*. ICML, 2021. (p. 251)

441. Nitesh V. Chawla, Kevin W. Bowyer, Lawrence O. Hall, and W. Philip Kegelmeyer. *SMOTE: Synthetic Minority Over-Sampling Technique*. JAIR, 2002. (p. 251)

442. Sangdoo Yun et al. *CutMix: Regularization Strategy to Train Strong Classifiers with Localizable Features*. CVPR, 2019. (p. 251)

443. Tianjian Huang et al. *Robustness Through Data Augmentation Loss Consistency*. TMLR, 2022. (p. 252)

444. Luigi Carratino, Moustapha Cissé, Rodolphe Jenatton, and Jean-Philippe Vert. *On mixup Regularization*. JMLR, 2022. (p. 253)

445. Chanwoo Park, Sangdoo Yun, and Sanghyuk Chun. *A Unified Analysis of Mixed Sample Data Augmentation: A Loss Function Perspective*. arXiv, 2022. (p. 253)

446. Ishaan Gulrajani, Faruk Ahmed, Martin Arjovsky, Vincent Dumoulin, and Aaron Courville. *Improved Training of WGANs*. NeurIPS, 2017. (p. 253)

447. Junsoo Oh and Chulhee Yun. *Provable Benefit of mixup for Finding Optimal Decision Boundaries*. ICML, 2023. (p. 253)

448. Christian Szegedy, Vincent Vanhoucke, Sergey Ioffe, Jon Shlens, and Zbigniew Wojna. *Rethinking the Inception Architecture for Computer Vision*. CVPR, 2016. (p. 253)

449. Gabriel Pereyra, George Tucker, Jan Chorowski, Łukasz Kaiser, and Geoffrey Hinton. *Regularizing Neural Networks by Penalizing Confident Output Distributions*. arXiv, 2017. (p. 253)

450. Rafael Müller, Simon Kornblith, and Geoffrey E. Hinton. *When Does Label Smoothing Help?* NeurIPS, 2019. (p. 253)

451. Michal Lukasik, Srinadh Bhojanapalli, Aditya Menon, and Sanjiv Kumar. *Does Label Smoothing Mitigate Label Noise?* ICML, 2020. (p. 253)

452. Muthu Chidambaram, Xiang Wang, Yuzheng Hu, Chenwei Wu, and Rong Ge. *Towards Understanding the Data Dependency of mixup-Style Training*. arXiv, 2021. (p. 257)

453. Difan Zou, Yuan Cao, Yuanzhi Li, and Quanquan Gu. *The Benefits of mixup for Feature Learning*. arXiv, 2023. (p. 257)

454. Kevin Roth, Yannic Kilcher, and Thomas Hofmann. *Adversarial Training Is a Form of Data-Dependent Operator Norm Regularization*. NeurIPS, 2020. (p. 257)

455. Yeming Wen et al. *Combining Ensembles and Data Augmentation Can Harm Your Calibration*. arXiv, 2020. (p. 257)

456. Vikas Verma et al. *Manifold mixup: Better Representations by Interpolating Hidden States*. ICML, 2019. (p. 257)

457. Hongyu Guo, Yongyi Mao, and Richong Zhang. *Augmenting Data with mixup for Sentence Classification: An Empirical Study*. arXiv, 2019. (p. 258)

458. Marton Havasi et al. *Training Independent Subnetworks for Robust Prediction*. arXiv, 2021. (pp. 258, 276)

459. Alexandre Ramé, Rémy Sun, and Matthieu Cord. *MixMo: Mixing Multiple Inputs for Multiple Outputs via Deep Subnetworks*. ICCV, 2021. (p. 258)

460. Huaxiu Yao et al. *Improving Out-of-Distribution Robustness via Selective Augmentation*. arXiv, 2022. (p. 260)

461. Avital Oliver, Augustus Odena, Colin A. Raffel, Ekin D. Cubuk, and Ian Goodfellow. *Realistic Evaluation of Deep Semi-Supervised Learning Algorithms*. NeurIPS, 2018. (p. 262)

462. Samuli Laine and Timo Aila. *Temporal Ensembling for Semi-Supervised Learning*. arXiv, 2016. (p. 262)

463. Vikas Verma et al. *Interpolation Consistency Training for Semi-Supervised Learning*. arXiv, 2020. (p. 262)

464. Alex Kendall and Yarin Gal. *What Uncertainties Do We Need in Bayesian Deep Learning for Computer Vision?* NeurIPS, 2017. (pp. 263, 272)

465. Alex Krizhevsky, Ilya Sutskever, and Geoffrey E. Hinton. *ImageNet Classification with Deep Convolutional Neural Networks*. NeurIPS, 2012. (p. 265)

466. Connor Shorten and Taghi M. Khoshgoftaar. *A Survey on Image Data Augmentation for Deep Learning*. Journal of Big Data, 2019. (p. 265)

467. Tianyu Pang, Kun Xu, and Jun Zhu. *mixup Inference: Better Exploiting mixup to Defend Adversarial Attacks*. arXiv, 2019. (p. 265)

468. Kamalika Chaudhuri and David Lopez-Paz. *Unified Uncertainty Calibration*. arXiv, 2023. (pp. 267, 270)

469. Stephen M. Fleming. *Metacognition and Confidence: A Review and Synthesis*. Annual Review of Psychology, 2023. (pp. 267, 268, 272)

470. Piercesare Grimaldi, Hakwan Lau, and Michele A. Basso. *There Are Things that We Know that We Know, and There Are Things that We Do Not Know We Do Not Know: Confidence in Decision-Making*. Neuroscience & Biobehavioral Reviews, 2015. (p. 267)

471. Robert F. Hink and David L. Woods. *How Humans Process Uncertain Knowledge: An Introduction*. AI magazine, 1987. (p. 268)

472. Kahneman Daniel. *Thinking, Fast and Slow*. Penguin, 2011. (p. 268)

473. Scott Plous. *The Psychology of Judgment and Decision Making*. Mcgraw-Hill Book Company, 1993. (p. 268)

474. Don A. Moore. *Overconfidence: The Mother of All Biases*. Psychology Today, 2018. (p. 268)

475. Justin Kruger and David Dunning. *Unskilled and Unaware of It: How Difficulties in Recognizing One's Own Incompetence Lead to Inflated Self-Assessments*. Journal of Personality and Social Psychology, 1999. (p. 268)

476. Ola Svenson. *Are We All Less Risky and More Skillful than Our Fellow Drivers?* Acta Psychologica, 1981. (p. 268)

477. Dario Amodei et al. *Concrete Problems in AI Safety*. arXiv, 2016. (p. 268)

478. Edmon Begoli, Tanmoy Bhattacharya, and Dimitri Kusnezov. *The Need for Uncertainty Quantification in Machine-Assisted Medical Decision Making*. Nature Machine Intelligence, 2019. (p. 268)

479. Umang Bhatt et al. *Uncertainty as a Form of Transparency: Measuring, Communicating, and Using Uncertainty*. AAAI/ACM Conference on AI, Ethics, and Society, 2021. (p. 269)

480. Yaniv Ovadia et al. *Can You Trust Your Model's Uncertainty? Evaluating Predictive Uncertainty Under Dataset Shift*. NeurIPS, 2019. (pp. 269, 274)

481. Dennis Ulmer and Giovanni Cinà. *Know Your Limits: Uncertainty Estimation with ReLU Classifiers Fails at Reliable OOD Detection*. Uncertainty in Artificial Intelligence, 2021. (p. 270)

482. Hongxin Wei et al. *Mitigating Neural Network Overconfidence with Logit Normalization*. ICML, 2022. (p. 270)

483. Piotr Bojanowski and Armand Joulin. *Unsupervised Learning by Predicting Noise*. ICML, 2017. (p. 270)

484. Pourya Habib Zadeh, Reshad Hosseini, and Suvrit Sra. *Deep-RBF Networks Revisited: Robust Classification with Rejection*. arXiv, 2018. (p. 270)

485. Jakob Gawlikowski et al. *A Survey of Uncertainty in Deep Neural Networks*. Artificial Intelligence Review, 2023. (pp. 270, 274)

486. Moloud Abdar et al. *A Review of Uncertainty Quantification in Deep Learning: Techniques, Applications and Challenges*. Information fusion, 2021. (pp. 270, 274)

487. Lukas Ruff et al. *A Unifying Review of Deep and Shallow Anomaly Detection*. IEEE, 2021. (pp. 270, 274)

488. Jingkang Yang, Kaiyang Zhou, Yixuan Li, and Ziwei Liu. *Generalized Out-of-Distribution Detection: A Survey*. arXiv, 2021. (pp. 270, 274)

489. Mohammadreza Salehi et al. *A Unified Survey on Anomaly, Novelty, Open-Set, and Out-of-Distribution Detection: Solutions and Future Challenges*. arXiv, 2021. (pp. 270, 274)

490. Chi-Keung Chow. *An Optimum Character Recognition System Using Decision Functions*. IRE Transactions on Electronic Computers, 1957. (pp. 270, 278)

491. Chi-Keung Chow. *On Optimum Recognition Error and Reject Trade-off*. IEEE Transactions on Information Theory, 1970. (pp. 270, 278)

492. Armen D. Kiureghian and Ove Ditlevsen. *Aleatory or Epistemic? Does It Matter?* Structural Safety, 2009. (p. 272)

493. Eyke Hüllermeier and Willem Waegeman. *Aleatoric and Epistemic Uncertainty in Machine Learning: An Introduction to Concepts and Methods*. Machine Learning, 2021. (p. 272)

494. Sarah Lichtenstein, Baruch Fischhoff, and Lawrence D. Phillips. *Calibration of Probabilities: The State of the Art*. Decision Making and Change in Human Affairs, 1975. (p. 273)

495. Chuan Guo, Geoff Pleiss, Yu Sun, and Kilian Q. Weinberger. *On Calibration of Modern Neural Networks*. ICML, 2017. (pp. 273, 274)

496. Deng-Bao Wang, Lei Feng, and Min-Ling Zhang. *Rethinking Calibration of Deep Neural Networks: Do Not Be Afraid of Overconfidence*. NeurIPS, 2021. (p. 273)

497. John Platt. *Probabilistic Outputs for Support Vector Machines and Comparisons to Regularized Likelihood Methods*. Advances in large margin classifiers, 1999. (p. 273)

498. Zachary Nado et al. *Uncertainty Baselines: Benchmarks for Uncertainty & Robustness in Deep Learning*. arXiv, 2021. (p. 274)

499. Jingyang Zhang et al. *OpenOOD V1.5: Enhanced Benchmark for Out-of-Distribution Detection*. arXiv, 2023. (pp. 274, 282)

500. Dan Hendrycks et al. *Scaling Out-of-Distribution Detection for Real-World Settings*. arXiv, 2019. (pp. 274, 283)

501. Andrija Djurisic, Nebojsa Bozanic, Arjun Ashok, and Rosanne Liu. *Extremely Simple Activation Shaping for Out-of-Distribution Detection*. arXiv, 2022. (pp. 274, 283)

502. Kimin Lee, Kibok Lee, Honglak Lee, and Jinwoo Shin. *A Simple Unified Framework for Detecting Out-of-Distribution Samples and Adversarial Attacks*. NeurIPS, 2018. (p. 275)

503. Joost Van Amersfoort, Lewis Smith, Yee W. Teh, and Yarin Gal. *Uncertainty Estimation Using a Single Deep Deterministic Neural Network*. ICML, 2020. (p. 275)

504. Jie Ren et al. *A Simple Fix to Mahalanobis Distance for Improving Near-OOD Detection*. arXiv, 2021. (pp. 275, 283)

505. Yiyou Sun, Yifei Ming, Xiaojin Zhu, and Yixuan Li. *Out-of-Distribution Detection with Deep Nearest Neighbors*. ICML, 2022. (pp. 275, 283)

506. Yuri Burda, Harrison Edwards, Amos Storkey, and Oleg Klimov. *Exploration by Random Network Distillation*. arXiv, 2018. (p. 276)

507. Lukas Ruff et al. *Deep One-Class Classification*. ICML, 2018. (p. 276)

508. Natasa Tagasovska and David Lopez-Paz. *Single-Model Uncertainties for Deep Learning*. arXiv, 2019. (p. 276)

509. Salem Lahlou et al. *DEUP: Direct Epistemic Uncertainty Prediction*. arXiv, 2021. (p. 276)

510. Simon Hawkins, Hongxing He, Graham Williams, and Rohan Baxter. *Outlier Detection Using Replicator Neural Networks*. International Conference on Data Warehousing and Knowledge Discovery, 2002. (p. 276)

511. Arsenii Ashukha, Alexander Lyzhov, Dmitry Molchanov, and Dmitry Vetrov. *Pitfalls of In-Domain Uncertainty Estimation and Ensembling in Deep Learning*. arXiv, 2020. (p. 276)

512. Matthias Hein, Maksym Andriushchenko, and Julian Bitterwolf. *Why ReLU Networks Yield High-Confidence Predictions Far Away from the Training Data and How to Mitigate the Problem.* CVPR, 2019. (p. 276)

513. Dan Hendrycks, Mantas Mazeika, Saurav Kadavath, and Dawn Song. *Using Self-Supervised Learning Can Improve Model Robustness and Uncertainty.* NeurIPS, 2019. (p. 278)

514. Guoxuan Xia and Christos-Savvas Bouganis. *Augmenting Softmax Information for Selective Classification with Out-of-Distribution Data.* ACCV, 2022. (p. 279)

515. Harikrishna Narasimhan, Aditya K. Menon, Wittawat Jitkrittum, and Sanjiv Kumar. *Plugin Estimators for Selective Classification with Out-of-Distribution Detection.* arXiv, 2023. (p. 279)

516. Robert Monarch. *Knowledge Quadrant for Machine Learning.* Medium, 2019. (p. 280)

517. Donald Rumsfeld and Richard Myers. *Defense.gov News Transcript: DoD News Briefing.* United States Department of Defense, 2002. (p. 280)

518. Colin Blakemore and Grahame F. Cooper. *Development of the Brain Depends on the Visual Environment.* Nature, 1970. (p. 280)

519. Jia Deng et al. *ImageNet: A Large-Scale Hierarchical Image Database.* CVPR, 2009. (p. 282)

520. Julian Bitterwolf, Maximilian Müller, and Matthias Hein. *In or Out? Fixing ImageNet Out-of-Distribution Detection Evaluation.* arXiv, 2023. (p. 282)

521. Sagar Vaze, Kai Han, Andrea Vedaldi, and Andrew Zisserman. *Open-Set Recognition: A Good Closed-Set Classifier Is All You Need?* arXiv, 2021. (p. 282)

522. Rui Huang and Yixuan Li. *MOS: Towards Scaling Out-of-Distribution Detection for Large Semantic Space.* CVPR, 2021. (p. 282)

523. Mircea Cimpoi, Subhransu Maji, Iasonas Kokkinos, Sammy Mohamed, and Andrea Vedaldi. *Describing Textures in the Wild.* CVPR, 2014. (p. 282)

524. Haoqi Wang, Zhizhong Li, Litong Feng, and Wayne Zhang. *ViM: Out-of-Distribution with Virtual-Logit Matching.* CVPR, 2022. (p. 282)

525. Yuheng Huang, Jiayang Song, Zhijie Wang, Huaming Chen, and Lei Ma. *Look Before You Leap: An Exploratory Study of Uncertainty Measurement for Large Language Models.* arXiv, 2023. (pp. 283, 285)

526. Yijun Xiao and William Yang Wang. *On Hallucination and Predictive Uncertainty in Conditional Language Generation*. arXiv, 2021. (p. 283)

527. Saurav Kadavath et al. *Language Models (Mostly) Know What They Know*. arXiv, 2022. (p. 285)

528. Miao Xiong et al. *Can LLMs Express Their Uncertainty? An Empirical Evaluation of Confidence Elicitation in LLMs*. arXiv, 2023. (p. 285)

529. Kamalika Chaudhuri. *Uncertainty-Based Abstention in LLMs Improves Safety and Reduces Hallucinations*. arXiv, 2024. (p. 285)

530. Sebastian Farquhar, Jannik Kossen, Lorenz Kuhn, and Yarin Gal. *Detecting Hallucinations in Large Language Models Using Semantic Entropy*. Nature, 2024. (p. 285)

531. Yuxin Xiao et al. *Uncertainty Quantification with Pretrained Language Models: A Large-Scale Empirical Analysis*. arXiv, 2022. (p. 285)

532. David Lopez-Paz, Diane Bouchacourt, Levent Sagun, and Nicolas Usunier. *Measuring and Signing Fairness as Performance Under Multiple Stakeholder Distributions*. arXiv, 2022. (p. 287)

533. David J. Hand and William E. Henley. *Statistical Classification Methods in Consumer Credit Scoring: A Review*. Journal of the Royal Statistical Society: Series A (Statistics in Society), 1997. (p. 287)

534. Julia Dressel and Hany Farid. *The Accuracy, Fairness, and Limits of Predicting Recidivism*. Science advances, 2018. (p. 287)

535. Ninareh Mehrabi, Fred Morstatter, Nripsuta Saxena, Kristina Lerman, and Aram Galstyan. *A Survey on Bias and Fairness in Machine Learning*. ACM Computing Surveys (CSUR), 2021. (p. 287)

536. David F. Engstrom, Daniel E. Ho, Catherine M. Sharkey, and Mariano-Florentino Cuéllar. *Government by Algorithm: Artificial Intelligence in Federal Administrative Agencies*. NYU School of Law, Public Law Research Paper, 2020. (p. 287)

537. Walter L. Perry, Brian McInnis, Carter C. Price, Susan C. Smith, and John S. Hollywood. *Predictive Policing: The Role of Crime Forecasting in Law Enforcement Operations*. Rand Corporation, 2013. (p. 287)

538. Kristian Lum and William Isaac. *To Predict and Serve?* Significance, 2016. (pp. 287, 294)

539. Jamie Berryhill, Kévin Kok Heang, Rob Clogher, and Keegan McBride. *Hello, World: Artificial Intelligence and Its Use in the Public Sector*. OECD Working Papers on Public Governance, 2019. (p. 287)

540. Solon Barocas, Moritz Hardt, and Arvind Narayanan. *Fairness and Machine Learning: Limitations and Opportunities*. MIT Press, 2019. (pp. 287, 288, 291, 294, 300)

541. Brent D. Mittelstadt, Patrick Allo, Mariarosaria Taddeo, Sandra Wachter, and Luciano Floridi. *The Ethics of Algorithms: Mapping the Debate*. Big Data & Society, 2016. (p. 287)

542. Agostina J. Larrazabal, Nicolás Nieto, Victoria Peterson, Diego H. Milone, and Enzo Ferrante. *Gender Imbalance in Medical Imaging Datasets Produces Biased Classifiers for Computer-Aided Diagnosis*. PNAS, 2020. (p. 287)

543. Andreas Tsamados et al. *The Ethics of Algorithms: Key Problems and Solutions*. AI & SOCIETY, 2021. (p. 287)

544. Natalia Norori, Qiyang Hu, Florence M. Aellen, Francesca D. Faraci, and Athina Tzovara. *Addressing Bias in Big Data and AI for Health Care: A Call for Open Science*. Patterns, 2021. (pp. 287–289)

545. Sahil Verma and Julia Rubin. *Fairness Definitions Explained*. IEEE/ACM International Workshop on Software Fairness, 2018. (pp. 288, 290)

546. Sam Corbett-Davies and Sharad Goel. *The Measure and Mismeasure of Fairness: A Critical Review of Fair Machine Learning*. arXiv, 2018. (pp. 288, 294, 299)

547. Irene Chen, Fredrik D. Johansson, and David Sontag. *Why Is My Classifier Discriminatory?* NeurIPS, 2018. (p. 288)

548. Brendan F. Klare et al. *Pushing the Frontiers of Unconstrained Face Detection and Recognition: IARPA Janus Benchmark A**. CVPR, 2015. (pp. 289, 300)

549. Gil Levi and Tal Hassner. *Age and Gender Classification Using Convolutional Neural Networks*. CVPR, 2015. (pp. 289, 300)

550. Nick Statt. *See How an AI System Classifies You Based on Your Selfie*. The Verge, 2019. (pp. 289, 300)

551. Shreya Shankar et al. *No Classification Without Representation: Assessing Geodiversity Issues in Open Data Sets for the Developing World*. NeurIPS 2017 Workshop: Machine Learning for the Developing World, 2017. (pp. 289, 292, 300)

552. Terrance de Vries, Ishan Misra, Changhan Wang, and Laurens van der Maaten. *Does Object Recognition Work for Everyone?* CVPR, 2019. (pp. 289, 292, 300)

553. Kimmo Kärkkäinen and Jungseock Joo. *Fairface: Face Attribute Dataset for Balanced Race, Gender, and Age*. arXiv, 2019. (pp. 289, 300)

554. Caner Hazirbas et al. *Towards Measuring Fairness in AI: The Casual Conversations Dataset*. IEEE Transactions on Biometrics, Behavior, and Identity Science, 2021. (pp. 289, 300)

555. Alec Radford et al. *Learning Transferable Visual Models from Natural Language Supervision*. arXiv, 2021. (pp. 289, 300)

556. Candice Schumann, Susanna Ricco, Utsav Prabhu, Vittorio Ferrari, and Caroline Pantofaru. *A Step Toward More Inclusive People Annotations for Fairness*. arXiv, 2021. (pp. 289, 300)

557. *The Dollar Street Dataset*, 2021. (pp. 289, 300)

558. Marina Drosou, H. V. Jagadish, Evaggelia Pitoura, and Julia Stoyanovich. *Diversity in Big Data: A Review*. Big data, 2017. (p. 289)

559. Kyla Chasalow and Karen Levy. *Representativeness in Statistics, Politics, and Machine Learning*. FAccT, 2021. (p. 289)

560. Kenneth Holstein, Jennifer Wortman Vaughan, Hal Daumé III, Miro Dudik, and Hanna Wallach. *Improving Fairness in Machine Learning Systems: What Do Industry Practitioners Need?* Proceedings of the 2019 CHI Conference on Human Factors in Computing Systems, 2019. (p. 289)

561. Isabel O. Gallegos et al. *Bias and Fairness in Large Language Models: A Survey*. Computational Linguistics, 2024. (p. 289)

562. Percy Liang et al. *Holistic Evaluation of Language Models*. arXiv, 2022. (p. 289)

563. Jiaming Ji et al. *AI Alignment: A Comprehensive Survey*. arXiv, 2023. (p. 289)

564. Tianhao Shen et al. *Large Language Model Alignment: A Survey*. arXiv, 2023. (p. 289)

565. Julia Angwin, Jeff Larson, Surya Mattu, and Lauren Kirchner. *Machine Bias*. ProPublica, 2016. (pp. 290–292)

566. Simon Caton and Christian Haas. *Fairness in Machine Learning: A Survey*. ACM Computing Surveys, 2020. (p. 291)

567. John Rawls. *Justice as Fairness: A Restatement*. Harvard University Press, 1985. (p. 291)

568. William Dieterich, Christina Mendoza, and Tim Brennan. *COMPAS Risk Scales: Demonstrating Accuracy Equity and Predictive Parity*. Northpointe, 2016. (p. 292)

569. Jeff Larson and Julia Angwin. *Machine Bias: Technical Response to Northpointe*. ProPublica, 2016. (p. 292)

570. Anthony W. Flores, Kristin Bechtel, and Christopher T. Lowenkamp. *False Positives, False Negatives, and False Analyses: A Rejoinder to Machine Bias: There's Software Used Across the Country to Predict Future Criminals. And It's Biased Against Blacks*. Fed. Probation, 2016. (p. 292)

571. Sam Corbett-Davies, Emma Pierson, Avi Feller, Sharad Goel, and Aziz Huq. *Algorithmic Decision Making and the Cost of Fairness*. SIGKDD, 2017. (p. 292)

572. Jocelyn Wang. *Racist Camera! No, I Did Not Blink... I'm Just Asian!* JozJozJoz, 2009. (p. 292)

573. Tom Simonite. *When It Comes to Gorillas, Google Photos Remains Blind*. Wired, 2018. (p. 292)

574. Ryan Mac. *Facebook Apologizes After AI Puts "primates" Label on Video of Black Men*. The New York Times, 2021. (p. 292)

575. Chaitanya Ramineni and David Williamson. *Understanding Mean Score Differences Between the E-Rater Automated Scoring Engine and Humans for Demographically Based Groups in the GRE General Test*. ETS Research Report Series, 2018. (p. 293)

576. Greg Satell and Yassmin Abdel-Magied. *AI Fairness Isn't Just an Ethical Issue*. Harvard Business Review, 2020. (p. 293)

577. James Vincent. *Amazon Reportedly Scraps Internal AI Recruiting Tool that Was Biased Against Women*. The Verge, 2018. (p. 293)

578. Jeffrey Dastin. *Amazon Scraps Secret AI Recruiting Tool that Showed Bias Against Women*. Reuters, 2018. (p. 293)

579. Subrat Patnaik. *Apple Co-Founder Says Apple Card Algorithm Gave Wife Lower Credit Limit*. Reuters, 2019. (p. 293)

580. Rachael Tatman. *Google's Speech Recognition Has a Gender Bias*. Making noise and hearing things, 2016. (p. 293)

581. Ziad Obermeyer, Brian Powers, Christine Vogeli, and Sendhil Mullainathan. *Dissecting Racial Bias in an Algorithm Used to Manage the Health of Populations*. Science, 2019. (p. 293)

582. Maarten Sap, Dallas Card, Saadia Gabriel, Yejin Choi, and Noah A. Smith. *The Risk of Racial Bias in Hate Speech Detection*. ACL, 2019. (p. 293)

583. Svetlana Kiritchenko and Saif M. Mohammad. *Examining Gender and Race Bias in Two Hundred Sentiment Analysis Systems*. arXiv, 2018. (p. 293)

584. Rachael Tatman. *Gender and Dialect Bias in YouTube's Automatic Captions*. ACL Workshop on Ethics in Natural Language Processing, 2017. (p. 293)

585. Allison Koenecke et al. *Racial Disparities in Automated Speech Recognition*. PNAS, 2020. (p. 293)

586. Su L. Blodgett and Brendan O'Connor. *Racial Disparity in Natural Language Processing: A Case Study of Social Media African-American English*. arXiv, 2017. (p. 293)

587. Nikhil Sonnad. *Google Translate's Gender Bias Pairs "He" with "Hardworking" and "She" with "Lazy," and Other Examples*. Quartz, 2017. (p. 293)

588. Tolga Bolukbasi, Kai-Wei Chang, James Y. Zou, Venkatesh Saligrama, and Adam T. Kalai. *Man Is to Computer Programmer as Woman Is to Homemaker? Debiasing Word Embeddings*. NeurIPS, 2016. (p. 293)

589. Matt Day. *How LinkedIn's Search Engine May Reflect a Gender Bias*. Seattle Times, 2016. (p. 293)

590. Latanya Sweeney. *Discrimination in Online Ad Delivery*. Communications of the ACM, 2013. (p. 294)

591. David Ingold and Spencer Soper. *Amazon Doesn't Consider the Race of Its Customers. Should It?* Bloomberg, 2016. (p. 294)

592. Ben Hutchinson and Margaret Mitchell. *50 Years of Test (un)fairness: Lessons for Machine Learning*. FaCCT, 2019. (p. 295)

593. Ben Dickson. *What Is the AI Winter?* TechTalks, 2018. (p. 295)

594. Central Secretary. *ISO 9001:2015; Quality Management Systems*. ISO, 2016. (p. 295)

595. Brad Arkin, Scott Stender, and Gary McGraw. *Software Penetration Testing*. IEEE Security & Privacy, 2005. (p. 295)

596. Patrick O'Connor and Andre Kleyner. *Practical Reliability Engineering*. John Wiley & Sons, 2012. (p. 295)

597. Nancy G. Leveson. *Engineering a Safer World: Systems Thinking Applied to Safety*. MIT Press, 2016. (p. 295)

598. Vladimir Khorikov. *Unit Testing Principles, Practices, and Patterns*. Simon and Schuster, 2020. (p. 295)

599. Margaret Mitchell et al. *Model Cards for Model Reporting*. FAccT, 2019. (p. 296)

600. Negar Rostamzadeh, Ben Hutchinson, and Vinod Prabhakaran. *Thinking Beyond Distributions in Testing Machine Learned Models*. NeurIPS Workshop on Distribution Shifts: Connecting Methods and Applications, 2021. (p. 297)

601. Samuel J. Bell and Skyler Wang. *The Multiple Dimensions of Spuriousness in Machine Learning*. arXiv, 2024. (p. 297)

602. Mary Gray. *The Banality of Scale: A Theory on the Limits of Modeling Bias and Fairness Frameworks for Social Justice (and Other Lessons from the Pandemic)*. NeurIPS 2021 (Invited talk), 2021. (p. 298)

603. Robert Hopkins. *Invariances: The Structure of the Objective World (Review)*. Mind, 2003. (p. 298)

604. Marilyn Strathern. *Improving Ratings: Audit in the British University System*. European Review, 1997. (p. 298)

605. Avrim Blum and Moritz Hardt. *The Ladder: A Reliable Leaderboard for Machine Learning Competitions*. arXiv, 2015. (p. 299)

606. Cynthia Dwork et al. *The Reusable Holdout: Preserving Validity in Adaptive Data Analysis*. Science, 2015. (p. 299)

607. Christian Sandvig, Kevin Hamilton, Karrie Karahalios, and Cedric Langbort. *Auditing Algorithms: Research Methods for Detecting Discrimination on Internet Platforms*. Data and discrimination: Converting critical concerns into productive inquiry, 2014. (pp. 299, 300)

608. Marco Federici, Ryota Tomioka, and Patrick Forré. *An Information-Theoretic Approach to Distribution Shifts*. arXiv, 2021. (p. 300)

609. Elliot Creager, Jörn-Henrik Jacobsen, and Richard Zemel. *Environment Inference for Invariant Learning*. ICML, 2021. (p. 300)

610. Inioluwa Deborah Raji et al. *Closing the AI Accountability Gap: Defining an End-to-End Framework for Internal Algorithmic Auditing*. FAccT, 2020. (p. 300)

611. Eknath Easwaran. *The Dhammapada*. Nilgiri Press, 2007. (p. 303)

612. Eknath Easwaran. *The Upanishads*. Nilgiri Press, 2007. (p. 303)

613. Eknath Easwaran. *The Bhagavad Gita*. Nilgiri Press, 2007. (p. 304)

614. Sam Harris. *Waking Up: A Guide to Spirituality Without Religion*. Simon and Schuster, 2014. (pp. 304, 308, 309)

615. Francis Crick and J. Clark. *The Astonishing Hypothesis*. Simon and Schuster, 1994. (p. 304)

616. Arthur Schopenhauer. *The World as Will and Representation*, 1818. (p. 305)

617. Aapo Hyvärinen. *Painful Intelligence: What AI Can Tell Us About Human Suffering*. arXiv, 2022. (pp. 305, 317)

618. Govind C. Pande. *Causality in Buddhist Philosophy*. A Companion to World Philosophies, 2017. (p. 306)

619. Leigh Brasington. *Dependent Origination and Emptiness: Streams of Dependently Arising Processes Interacting*. Published by the author, 2021. (p. 306)

620. Jay L. Garfield et al. *The Fundamental Wisdom of the Middle Way: Nagarjuna's Mūlamadhyamakakārikā*. Oxford University Press, 1995. (p. 307)

621. Alison Gopnik. *Could David Hume Have Known About Buddhism? Charles François Dolu, the Royal College of La Flèche, and the Global Jesuit Intellectual Network*. Hume Studies, 2009. (p. 307)

622. Jay L. Garfield. *Losing Ourselves: Learning to Live Without a Self*. Princeton University Press, 2022. (p. 308)

623. Tulku Urgyen Rinpoche. *As It Is: Volume I*. Rangjung Yeshe Publications, 1999. (p. 309)

624. John Wheeler. *You Were Never Born*. Non-Duality Press, 2007. (p. 310)

625. Douglas Harding. *On Having No Head: Zen and the Rediscovery of the Obvious*. The Shollond Trust, 1961. (p. 311)

626. Richard Lang. *Seeing Who You Really Are*. The Shollond Trust, 2003. (p. 311)

627. Antonio Blay-Fontcuberta. *Ser. Curso De Psicología De La Autorrealización*. Sincronía Editorial, 2016. (p. 315)

Index

These are minutes of your life.

Publisher contact:
The MIT Press
Massachusetts Institute of Technology
77 Massachusetts Avenue, Cambridge, MA 02139
mitpress.mit.edu

EU Authorised Representative:
Easy Access System Europe, Mustamäe tee 50,
10621 Tallinn, Estonia
gpsr.requests@easproject.com

Printed by Integrated Books International,
United States of America